STAR WARS®

OMNIBUS

A LONG TIME AGO. . . .

VOLUME 4

A LONG TIME AGO. . . .

VOLUME 4

DARK HORSE BOOKS®

cover illustration Gene Day
president and publisher Mike Richardson
series editors Jo Duffy, Michael Higgins, Louise Jones, Ann Nocenti
collection editor Randy Stradley
assistant editor Freddye Lins
collection designer Kat Larson

special thanks to Jann Moorhead, David Anderman, Troy Alders, Leland Chee, Sue Rostoni, and Carol Roeder at Lucas Licensing

Star Wars® Omnibus: A Long Time Ago. . . . Volume Four

This volume collects Marvel *Star Wars* issues #68–#85, *Star Wars King Size Annual* #3 and *Star Wars: Return of the Jedi* #1–#4.

Published by Dark Horse Books
A division of Dark Horse Comics, Inc.
10956 SE Main Street
Milwaukie, OR 97222

DarkHorse.com | StarWars.com

To find a comics shop in your area, call the Comic Shop Locator Service toll-free at 1-888-266-4226

Library of Congress Cataloging-in-Publication Data

Star Wars omnibus. A long time ago / writers, Archie Goodwin ... [et al.] ; artists, Howard Chaykin ... [et al.] ; colorists, Janice Cohen ... [et al.]. -- 1st ed.
v. cm.
ISBN 978-1-59582-486-8 (v. 1)
1. Comic books, strips, etc. I. Goodwin, Archie. II. Dark Horse Comics. III. Title: Long time ago.
PN6728.S73S7336 2010
741.5'973--dc22
2010000142

Printed by 1010 Printing International, Ltd., Guangdong Province, China.

First edition: August 2011
ISBN 978-1-59582-640-4

10 9 8 7 6 5 4 3 2 1

CONTENTS

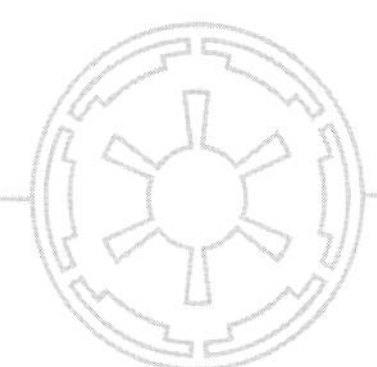

60¢

68
FEB
02817

APPROVED BY THE COMICS CODE AUTHORITY

TM

STAR WARS™

GENE DAY

STAR WARS
DAVID MICHELINIE SCRIPT
GENE DAY LAYOUTS
TOM PALMER FINISHES
JOE ROSEN LETTERS
LOUISE JONES EDITOR
GLYNIS WEIN COLORS
JIM SHOOTER CORELLIAN CHIEF
THE SEARCH BEGINS

FOR SOME MONTHS NOW, THE CAVERNS THAT RUN BENEATH THE PLANET ARBRA HAVE SERVED AS HOME BASE FOR THE OUT-LAWED REBEL ALLIANCE.
BUT EVEN THOUGH THOSE TUNNELS HAVE BEEN FILLED WITH BUSTLE AND ACTIVITY, THEY'VE NEVERTHELESS SEEMED HOLLOW, AS IF EMPTIED BY A CONSPICUOUS ABSENCE...

...AN ABSENCE THAT MAY SOON BE FILLED!
THEN WE'RE AGREED: IT'S ONE FOR ALL, AND ALL--
--FOR HAN SOLO!

GOOD LUCK, CHEWIE, LANDO, LEIA.
MAY THE FORCE BE WITH YOU.
AND WITH YOU, LUKE.

IF WE'RE GOING TO TAKE HAN BACK FROM BOBA FETT, WE'LL NEED ALL THE LUCK--*AND* FORCE--WE CAN GET!
LEFTENANT! IS MY Y-WING READY YET?

JUST ABOUT, PRINCESS. WE'VE FINISHED THE FUELING PROCESS AND THE MAINTENANCE CREW IS RUNNING ITS PRE-FLIGHT CHECK.
YOUR FIGHTER SHOULD BE READY TO GO IN A COUPLE OF MINUTES.
THANKS.
MORE WAITING. I *HATE* WAITING...

AND PRINCESS LEIA ORGANA HAS REASON TO HOLD WAITING IN DISDAIN. FOR IN THE BEGINNING THINGS HAD HAPPENED FAST.
PERHAPS... TOO FAST.
HER INITIAL RELATIONSHIP WITH THE DASHING, SELF-IMPORTANT HAN SOLO-- A RELATIONSHIP THAT HAD BORDERED ON CONTEMPT DURING THE INFAMOUS BATTLE OF THE DEATH STAR--
--HAD QUICKLY TURNED TO ATTRACTION, AND TO A DEEP, ABIDING LOVE THAT EVEN NOW THE PRINCESS DOESN'T FULLY UNDERSTAND.
BUT THAT LOVE HAD BEEN CUT SHORT BY THE CINDER-HEARTED SITH LORD, DARTH VADER, WHO HAD FROZEN THE CAPTIVE SOLO IN AN IMPENETRABLE BLOCK OF CARBONITE--
--AND HAD TURNED HIM OVER TO THE BOUNTY HUNTER, BOBA FETT, WHO HAD THEN MADE GOOD HIS ESCAPE, LEAVING LEIA WITH NOTHING BUT AN EMPTY HEART... AND EMPTY DAYS...
...AND WAITING.

ALL THIS TIME, HAN, I HAVEN'T ALLOWED MYSELF TO THINK OF YOU, TO THINK OF WHAT YOU MEAN TO ME. I'VE BEEN AFRAID THAT SUCH THOUGHTS WOULD DISTRACT ME, AFFECT MY JUDGEMENT AS A LEADER OF THE REBELLION.
BUT NOW... NOW THAT THERE'S HOPE...

DO YOU *REALLY* THINK WE'LL FIND CAPTAIN SOLO, PRINCESS?
WHAT--
--OH, LET'S JUST SAY THERE'S A CHANCE, THREEPIO. WE KNOW THAT BOBA FETT IS HOLED UP SOMEWHERE, WAITING FOR HIS RENDEZVOUS WITH THE MAN WHO PUT A PRICE ON HAN'S HEAD--
--*JABBA THE HUT.*

AND WE'VE RECENTLY LEARNED THAT ONE OF THREE OTHER BOUNTY HUNTERS WAS IN LEAGUE WITH FETT, BUT GOT CUT OUT OF THE DEAL WHEN FETT TOOK HIS PRIZE.
WE'RE HOPING THAT EX-PARTNER WILL BE BITTER ENOUGH TO TELL US WHERE FETT'S HIDEOUT IS.

OF THE THREE BOUNTYMEN IN QUESTION, OUR QUARRY IS A CYBORG NAMED *DENGAR.*
I MUST SAY, HE LOOKS LIKE A THOROUGHLY *NASTY* FELLOW.

HE IS.
AT LAST, FUEL TANKS ARE FULL; FINAL CHECKS HAVE BEEN RUN; THE GREEN LIGHT IS GIVEN...

...AND THREE UNIQUE VEHICLES ROCKET INTO THE VOID--
--EACH CARRYING PASSENGERS WHOSE PASTS ARE AS DIVERSE AS THEIR FUTURE IS COMMON. FOR THEY NOW SHARE A SINGLE, IMMUTABLE GOAL:
THE SALVATION OF A FRIEND!

THE SPACECRAFT DIVERGE, EACH JUMPING INTO A DIFFERENT SECTOR OF HYPERSPACE ON A JOURNEY WHICH, SOME WHILE LATER, TAKES PRINCESS LEIA'S SHIP TO...
MANDALORE! ACCORDING TO INTELLIGENCE REPORTS, DENGAR'S LATEST HUNT BROUGHT HIM HERE.
I'LL SET DOWN NEAR THAT LARGE FOREST AND WE CAN MAKE OUR WAY TO THE CAPITAL CITY, KEDALBE, ON FOOT.
WE'LL BE LESS CONSPICUOUS THAT WAY.
AND SOON...
OH, DEAR! THIS HUMIDITY WILL SIMPLY PLAY HAVOC WITH MY RUST-PREVENTION CIRCUITS!

E YOU CERTAIN
U DON'T WANT
TO STAY AND
ARD THE SHIP,
UR HIGHNESS?
NO, THREEPIO. MOST MANDALORIANS SPEAK GALAXY STANDARD--
BUT I
GHT NEED
OU TO TRANS-
LATE IF--
--WAIT A MINUTE! OVER THERE! A BAND OF HUMANOIDS FOLLOWING A TRAIL! IT MUST BE A CARAVAN!
COME ON!
BUT I THOUGHT OUR OBJECT WAS TO *AVOID* CONTACT!
IT *WAS!* BUT IF WE CAN JOIN THAT CARAVAN, WE CAN ENTER THE CITY WITH THEM!
AND WE WON'T HAVE TO WORRY ABOUT HOW TO SNEAK--
OH, NO! THOSE AREN'T MERCHANTS! THEY'RE--
--SLAVERS!
"TALK ABOUT OUT OF THE FRYING PAN--! NEXT TO FALLEN JEDIS, SLAVERS ARE THE MOST FEARED DENIZENS OF THE GALAXY--AND THEY'RE ALSO SOME OF ITS LOWEST SCUM!
"THEY NAB ANYONE HAPLESS ENOUGH TO FALL INTO THEIR CLUTCHES, THEN SELL THEM TO THE HIGHEST BIDDER! THOSE ENERGY LINKS AROUND THE SLAVES' WRISTS AREN'T JUST TRAPPING THEIR HANDS--
"--THEY'RE HOLDING THE POOR DEVILS' *SOULS* AS WELL!"

AND TO MAKE THINGS WORSE, IT LOOKS LIKE THE SLAVERS ARE UNDER *IMPERIAL* PROTECTION!
I THINK WE'D BEST SLIP AWAY, THREEPIO.
AND AS QUIETLY AS--
"--HUH?!"
SHHUNK
AGGGH!
POOOM
"THE SLAVERS ARE BEING ATTACKED! BY ANOTHER BAND OF WARRIORS!"
BUT PRINCESS LEIA'S CONFUSION GROWS EVEN STRONGER AS THE LEADER OF THE ATTACKING HORDE SWOOPS ONTO THE SCENE--
--FLYING LOW, DEFTLY AVOIDING IMPERIAL LASERS, AND LOOKING FOR ALL THE WORLD LIKE--

--BOBA FETT!
THAT'S IT, LADS!
FRRRIP
WE'LL TEACH THOSE SLAVIN' SLUGS WHAT IT MEANS TO TANGLE WITH MANDALORIANS!
ZATCH
FRRIPIP
AH! THERE'S THE GRUBBER WHAT'S GOT THE CONTROLS TO THEM CURSED ENERGY LINKS!
CONTROLS I WAGER HE'LL NOT BE WORKIN'--
--FER LONG!
FRRIPASH
NOW TO MAKE SURE NO ONE CAN REPAIR THIS UNIT 'FORE WE GET THEM SLAVES TO SAFETY! I'LL JUST--
DIE, YOU OUTLAW SON OF A--
WHA--?!
ZHRRAK

I DON'T BELIEVE IT! I ACTUALLY SAVED THE LIFE OF THE MAN WHO CAPTURED HAN!

IT MUST HAVE BEEN INSTINCT, PURE AND SIMPLE! I JUST COULDN'T WATCH *ANYONE* DIE BY A SLAVER'S HAND!

BUT WHATEVER THE REASON, I'M IN THE FIGHT NOW, AND I'VE CHOSEN A SIDE--

--WHETHER I *WANT* IT OR NOT!

WHILE NEARBY...
Y-YOU WOULDN'T CONSIDER NEGOTI-ATING THIS MATTER, W-WOULD YOU?
SHUT UP, 'BOT!

AN' QUIT QUIVERIN' LIKE THAT! STAND STILL, I SAY! OR YOU'LL MAKE ME--
--MISS!

FTUDD
OOMPH
WELL, I CERTAINLY HOPE *THAT* WILL TEACH YOU NOT TO ACCOST A PROTOCOL DROID!
RUFFIAN!

LOOKS LIKE THE FIGHT'S ABOUT OVER! MOST OF THE SLAVERS ARE DOWN OR RUNNING OFF!
AND MAYBE *I'D* BETTER DO THE SAME BEFORE--

:ULMF!:
BLAST! THERE'S ALWAYS ONE...!
EYAAA!
I JUST HOPE THIS LITTLE MANEUVER DIDN'T DELAY ME TOO LONG! I'VE GOT TO RETRIEVE MY WEAPON AND--
YOU LOOKIN' FER THIS, MISSY?
NOT ANY MORE.
BUT I DON'T NEED IT. ALL I NEED ARE MY BARE HANDS TO KILL YOU--
--BOBA FETT!
"BOBA"--? AH! THEN THAT EXPLAINS YER CHARMIN' HOSTILITY!
HA HA HA HA! PERHAPS IT'S TIME I SHOULD INTRODUCE M'SELF, MISSY.
ME GIVEN NAME IS--
--FENN. FENN SHYSA. I'M THE LEADER O' THIS HARDY CREW. AN' YOU, IF'N ME MEMORY O' LIKENESSES CAN BE TRUSTED, ARE THAT PRINCESS LADY FROM THE REBEL ALLIANCE.
WOULD YA BE JOININ' US FER A LITTLE VICT'RY FEAST NOW?
DO I HAVE A CHOICE?
NOT A'TALL.
I'D BE DELIGHTED.
QUICKLY, EFFICIENTLY, THE ARMED COMPANY MOVES OUT, CARRYING THEIR WOUNDED AND CAPTURED, LEAVING THEIR DEAD TO THE FOREST, AND TO PRAYERS SOFTLY WHISPERED...

WHILE SOME TIME LATER, SOME DISTANCE AWAY, THEY MOVE WITH EQUAL EFFICIENCY INTO AN ENCAMPMENT THAT'S BEEN CARVED, BUILT AND GROWN INTO THE THICKEST PART OF THE DENSE MANDALORIAN WOOD...

WELL, UH, ACTUALLY...
...NO.

I THOUGHT NOT. WE'VE A LOT IN COMMON, YOU AN' I, FIGHTIN' FER WHAT'S RIGHT AGIN WHAT'S WRONG.
AN' SUCH AS THAT DON'T LEAVE MUCH CALL FER LUXURIES.

YO, PARMA! HOW'S THE LEG?
WORKIN' LIKE NEW, FENN! YA SET IT JUST PERFECT!

SO THIS IS HOME, HUH? VERY QUAINT.

QUAINT, IS IT? AN' I SUPPOSE YOU LIVE IN A GRAND PALACE THESE DAYS, ALL MADE OUT O' PINK MARBLE AN' FINERY?

"--LONG YEARS AGO, WHEN I WAS PART OF A GROUP O' SUPERCOMMANDOS CHARGED WITH THE ULTIMATE PROTECTION O' MANDALORE. IT WAS A JOB I WAS PROUD OF. BUT WHEN *PALPATINE* MADE HIS MOVE TO SET UP A GALACTIC EMPIRE, THE GOVERNMENT O' MANDALORE SENT US INTA THE CLONE WARS ON THE EMPEROR'S SIDE.
AN' IT WAS DURIN' BRIEFIN' SESSIONS ON ENEMIES O' THE EMPIRE, PRINCESS, THAT I FIRST BECAME ACQUAINTED WITH YER COMELY FEATURES.
"AT ANY RATE, THE WAR WAS FINALLY WON--BUT AT A TERRIBLE COST. OF TWO HUNDRED AN' TWELVE MANDALORIAN PROTECTORS WHAT WENT INTA BATTLE, ONLY *THREE* SURVIVED.

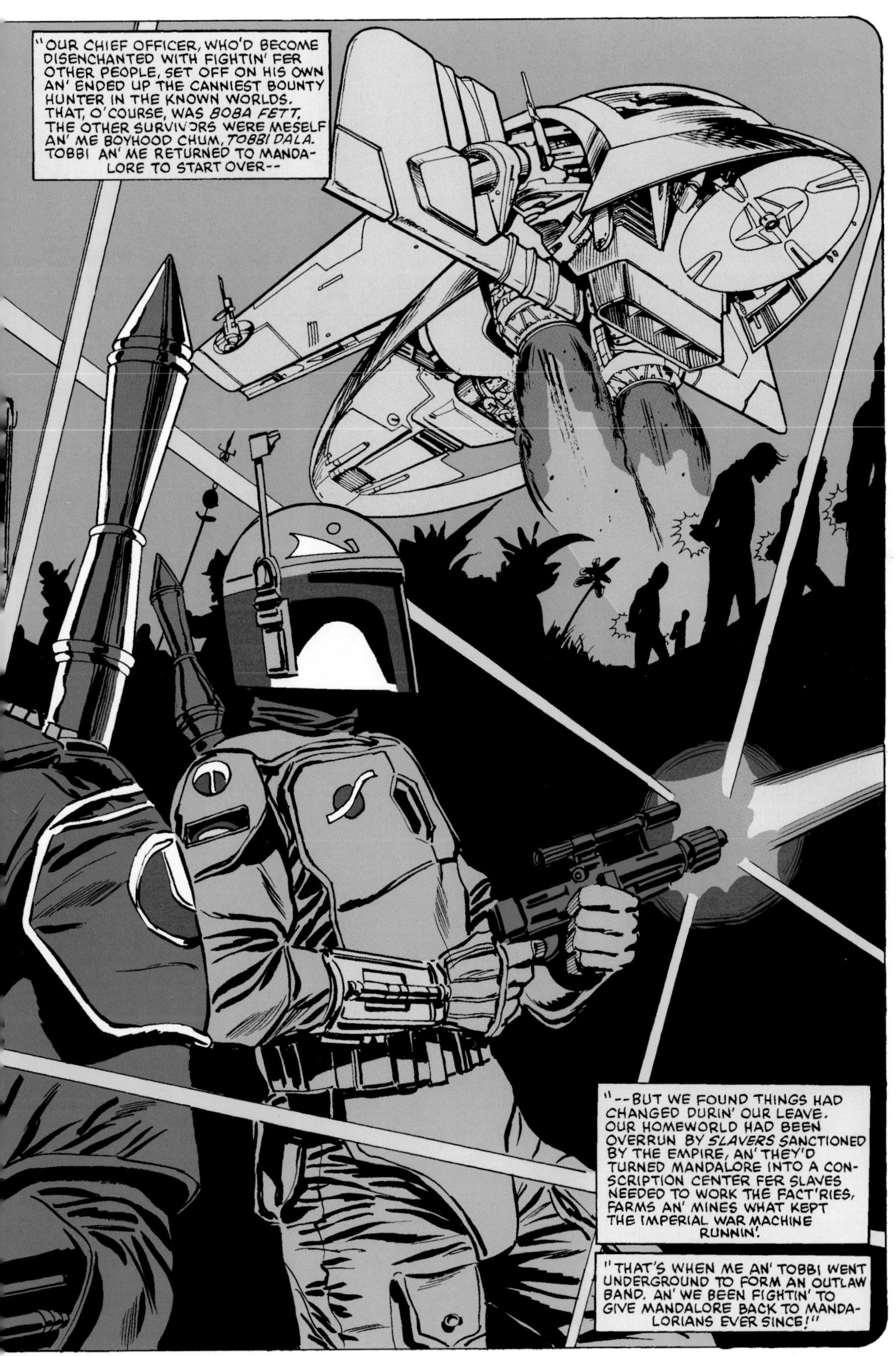
"OUR CHIEF OFFICER, WHO'D BECOME DISENCHANTED WITH FIGHTIN' FER OTHER PEOPLE, SET OFF ON HIS OWN AN' ENDED UP THE CANNIEST BOUNTY HUNTER IN THE KNOWN WORLDS. THAT, O'COURSE, WAS *BOBA FETT*. THE OTHER SURVIVORS WERE MESELF AN' ME BOYHOOD CHUM, *TOBBI DALA*. TOBBI AN' ME RETURNED TO MANDALORE TO START OVER--
"--BUT WE FOUND THINGS HAD CHANGED DURIN' OUR LEAVE. OUR HOMEWORLD HAD BEEN OVERRUN BY *SLAVERS* SANCTIONED BY THE EMPIRE, AN' THEY'D TURNED MANDALORE INTO A CONSCRIPTION CENTER FER SLAVES NEEDED TO WORK THE FACT'RIES, FARMS AN' MINES WHAT KEPT THE IMPERIAL WAR MACHINE RUNNIN'.
"THAT'S WHEN ME AN' TOBBI WENT UNDERGROUND TO FORM AN OUTLAW BAND. AN' WE BEEN FIGHTIN' TO GIVE MANDALORE BACK TO MANDALORIANS EVER SINCE!"

BUT NOW THAT I'VE TOLD YA MY STORY, MISSY, WHAT BRINGS YOU TO THIS --IF YA'LL PARDON THE TERM--NECK O' THE WOODS?
I'M LOOKING FOR INFORMATION, FENN-- AND FOR A MAN.

A MAN IN THE SAME LINE OF WORK AS YOUR EX-COMMANDER, FETT-- A CYBORG MANHUNTER SAID TO BE IN THIS AREA.
CYBORG, EH? I DON'T SUPPOSE YA COULD BE MEANIN'--

--HIM?
WHA-- DENGAR!
AYE, THE SAME.

SEEMS I'VE BECOME SUCH A THORN IN THE EMPIRE'S SIDE THAT THEY'VE PUT A RICH PRICE ON ME CARCASS!
THAT'S WONDERFUL! I- I MEAN, NOT ABOUT YOUR BEING HUNTED, OF COURSE! BUT WITH DENGAR BEHIND BARS, QUESTIONING HIM WILL BE SO MUCH SIMPLER!
I DUNNO, MISSY, DENGAR'S A 'BORG --AN' THEY DON'T TALK EASY.
THEN I'LL JUST TAKE HIM BACK TO OUR BASE AND MAKE HIM TALK!
I'M AFRAID, PRINCESS, THAT I CAN'T ALLOW THAT.
YA REMEMBER THAT BUDDY O' MINE I WAS TALKIN' ABOUT-- TOBBI DALA? WELL IT SEEMS THE POOR LAD WENT AN' GOT HISSELF CAPTURED JUST A FEW DAYS 'EFORE WE CAUGHT HOLD O' THIS DENGAR FELLA. AN' THE SLAVERS HAVE AGREED TO EXCHANGE PRISONERS T'MORROW MORNIN'.
BUT DENGAR MIGHT HAVE INFORMATION THAT COULD AID THE ENTIRE REBELLION!
THAT MAY BE, MISSY, BUT I DON'T CARE FER CAUSES NO MORE. THESE DAYS, I FIGHT ONLY FER ME PLANET, ME PEOPLE... AN' ME FRIENDS.
BUT ENOUGH O' THIS SOBER TALK! THE BANQUET'S A-WAITIN'--AN' I THINK WE COULD BOTH USE A TALL MUG O' THE FOAM!
OF ALL THE--
PSSST!
TELL YA WHAT, SWEETIE, YOU DEAL ME A BREAK, BUST ME OUTTA THIS STINKIN' CAGE--
--AN' I'LL TELL YA ANYTHING YA WANNA KNOW! WHADYA SAY?
AW, C'MON, CUTIE, DON'T LOOK SO GLUM! I'M JUST ASKIN' YA TO THINK ABOUT IT!
BUT THE ERSTWHILE SENATOR FROM ALDERAAN HAS THOUGHT ABOUT IT.
WHICH IS PRECISELY WHY SHE LOOKS SO GLUM...

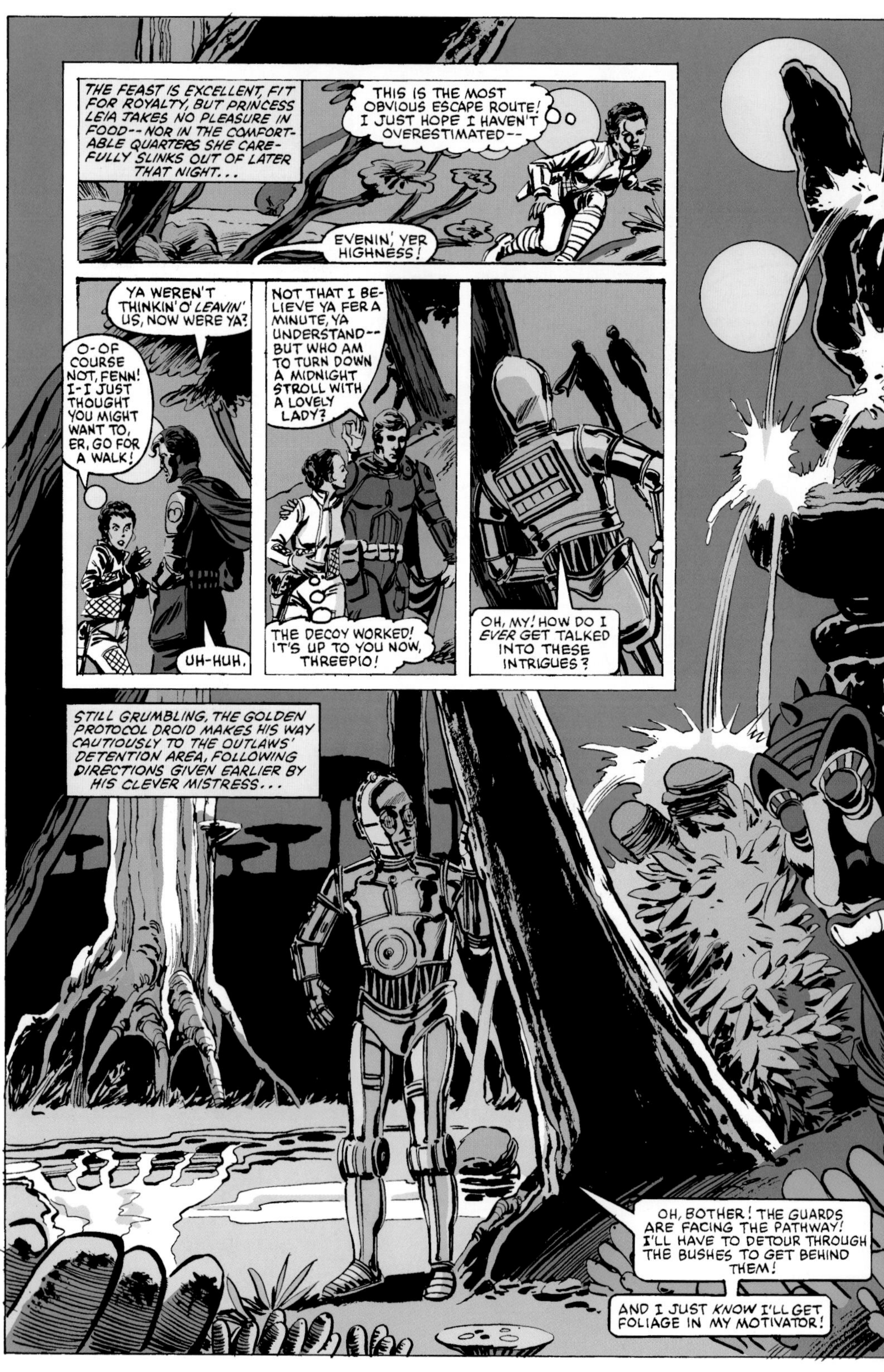
THE FEAST IS EXCELLENT, FIT FOR ROYALTY, BUT PRINCESS LEIA TAKES NO PLEASURE IN FOOD-- NOR IN THE COMFORTABLE QUARTERS SHE CAREFULLY SLINKS OUT OF LATER THAT NIGHT...
THIS IS THE MOST OBVIOUS ESCAPE ROUTE! I JUST HOPE I HAVEN'T OVERESTIMATED--
EVENIN', YER HIGHNESS!
YA WEREN'T THINKIN' O' LEAVIN' US, NOW WERE YA?
O-OF COURSE NOT, FENN! I-I JUST THOUGHT YOU MIGHT WANT TO, ER, GO FOR A WALK!
UH-HUH.
NOT THAT I BELIEVE YA FER A MINUTE, YA UNDERSTAND-- BUT WHO AM I TO TURN DOWN A MIDNIGHT STROLL WITH A LOVELY LADY?
THE DECOY WORKED! IT'S UP TO YOU NOW, THREEPIO!
OH, MY! HOW DO I EVER GET TALKED INTO THESE INTRIGUES?
STILL GRUMBLING, THE GOLDEN PROTOCOL DROID MAKES HIS WAY CAUTIOUSLY TO THE OUTLAWS' DETENTION AREA, FOLLOWING DIRECTIONS GIVEN EARLIER BY HIS CLEVER MISTRESS...
OH, BOTHER! THE GUARDS ARE FACING THE PATHWAY! I'LL HAVE TO DETOUR THROUGH THE BUSHES TO GET BEHIND THEM!
AND I JUST KNOW I'LL GET FOLIAGE IN MY MOTIVATOR!

NEVERTHELESS, MOMENTS LATER...
SNAP
HEY, TEM-- YA HEAR SOMETHIN'?
NAW, MUST BE YER IMAGINATION.

BLAST! I'LL HAVE TO USE A LARGER TWIG!

SNAP
THAT WERE NO IMAGINATION!

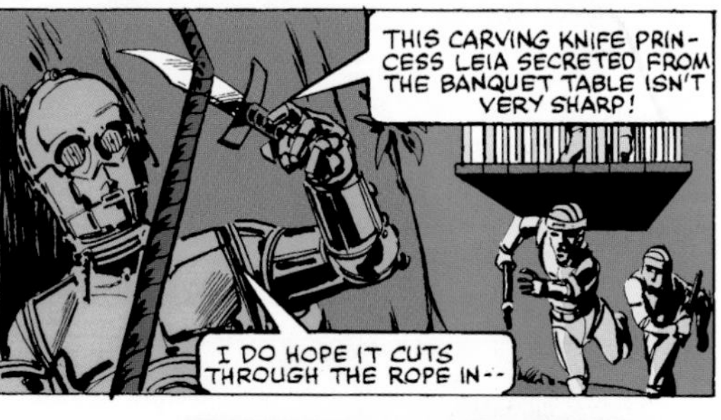
THIS CARVING KNIFE PRINCESS LEIA SECRETED FROM THE BANQUET TABLE ISN'T VERY SHARP!
I DO HOPE IT CUTS THROUGH THE ROPE IN--

"--TIME!"
CHK
KERBLUM
WHRFFF!

WHILE ELSEWHERE...
THAT SHOULD BE ENOUGH TIME FOR THREEPIO-- NOW IT'S MY TURN.
FENN... KISS ME?
UH, ARE YA SURE THIS IS THE TIME AN' PLACE FER--

LEADING A REBELLION IS A LONELY TASK, FENN. YOU TAKE YOUR PLEASURE WHEN YOU CAN.
PLEASE...?

WELL, I SUPPOSE IF YA INSIST...
OH, I DO. ESPECIALLY WHEN IT PUTS ME IN A POSITION TO PULL--

KRAK
--THIS!
HNGG!

I'M SORRY, FENN. I REALLY AM.
BUT I HONESTLY THINK THAT IF OUR ROLES WERE REVERSED ...YOU'D DO EXACTLY THE SAME!

THROUGH PATHS PATTERNED WITH MOON-LIGHT SHADOWS, PRINCESS LEIA TRAVELS SWIFTLY THROUGH THE ALIEN FOREST--
--SPRINTING SILENTLY, HER THOUGHTS TURNED INWARD, HATING THE WAR...HATING HERSELF...
...AND HATING MORE WHAT HAPPENS WHEN THE TWO BECOME ONE.

AS EVENTUALLY...

GOOD WORK, THREEPIO! BUT WE'D BETTER GET DENGAR AWAY FROM HERE FAST!

WHEN FENN COMES TO, HE'LL HAVE THE WHOLE CAMP AFTER US!

I'M AFRAID THERE'S A SLIGHT PROBLEM, PRINCESS. NEITHER OF THE GUARDS SEEM TO HAVE THE KEY!

THEN WE'LL MAKE OUR *OWN* KEY!
ZHRRAK
LET'S GO, BOUNTYMAN!

I'D LOVE TO, SWEETS, BUT MY SLEEVE'S CAUGHT BETWEEN A COUPLA BROKEN BOARDS!
THEN PULL IT LOOSE, BLAST IT!

RIGHT YA ARE. JUST GIMME A SECOND HERE AND I'LL--

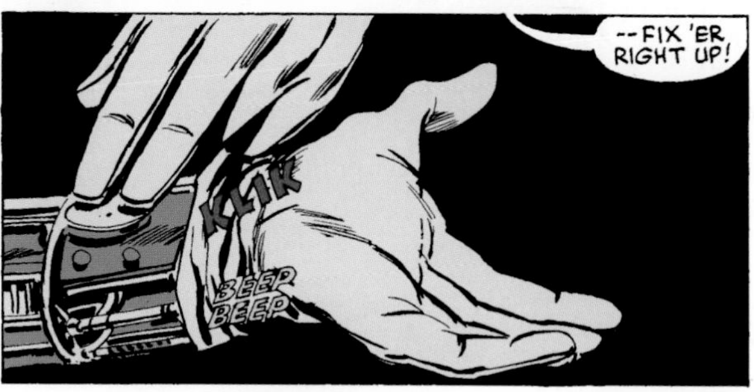

--FIX 'ER RIGHT UP!
KL1K
BEEP BEEP

AH, IT'S GOOD TO BE FREE AGAIN!
JUST DON'T TRY FOR TOO *MUCH* FREEDOM, DENGAR. REMEMBER, YOU CAN STILL TELL ME WHAT I WANT TO KNOW WITH YOUR ARMS BLOWN OFF! NOW MOVE IT!

AND MOVE THEY DO, TRAIPSING THROUGH THE LUSH FOREST TRAILS AS DARKNESS GRADUALLY LIGHTENS INTO DAWN. THEN...
ALL RIGHT, DENGAR, WE'RE SAFE ENOUGH NOW. I THINK IT'S TIME YOU TOLD ME WHAT YOU KNOW ABOUT BOBA FETT.
AND I, CUTIE, THINK *NOT*!
DON'T PUSH ME, BOUNTYMAN! WE HAVE A BARGAIN--!

Y'MEAN WE *HAD* A BARGAIN! WHEN I RECOGNIZED YA, KIDDO, I DECIDED TO *ALTER* OUR AGREEMENT A BIT! AFTER ALL, WHY SETTLE FOR THE REWARD ON A MERE OUTLAW--
--WHEN I CAN TURN IN THE BIG CHIEF OF THE REBEL ALLIANCE!

SEE THIS? IT'S A *HOMING SIGNAL* LINKED TO THE STORMTROOPER GARRISON AT KEDALBE! I *WAS* GONNA ACTIVATE IT AT SHYSA'S CAMP TO BRING THE TROOPERS THERE. BUT WHEN I SAW *YOU*...

WHA--YOUR HIGHNESS! S-SOMETHING'S CRASHING THROUGH THE UNDERBRUSH! MOVING THIS WAY!
HURRY, THREEPIO! MAKE A RUN FOR--
STAND FAST! OR BE BLASTED TO ATOMS!

WE'RE DOOMED. OH, YES. WE'RE MOST DEFINITELY DOOMED.

Y'KNOW, THREEPIO, FOR ONCE... YOU MAY BE *RIGHT*!

NEXT DEATH-BATTLE IN THE CITY OF BONES!

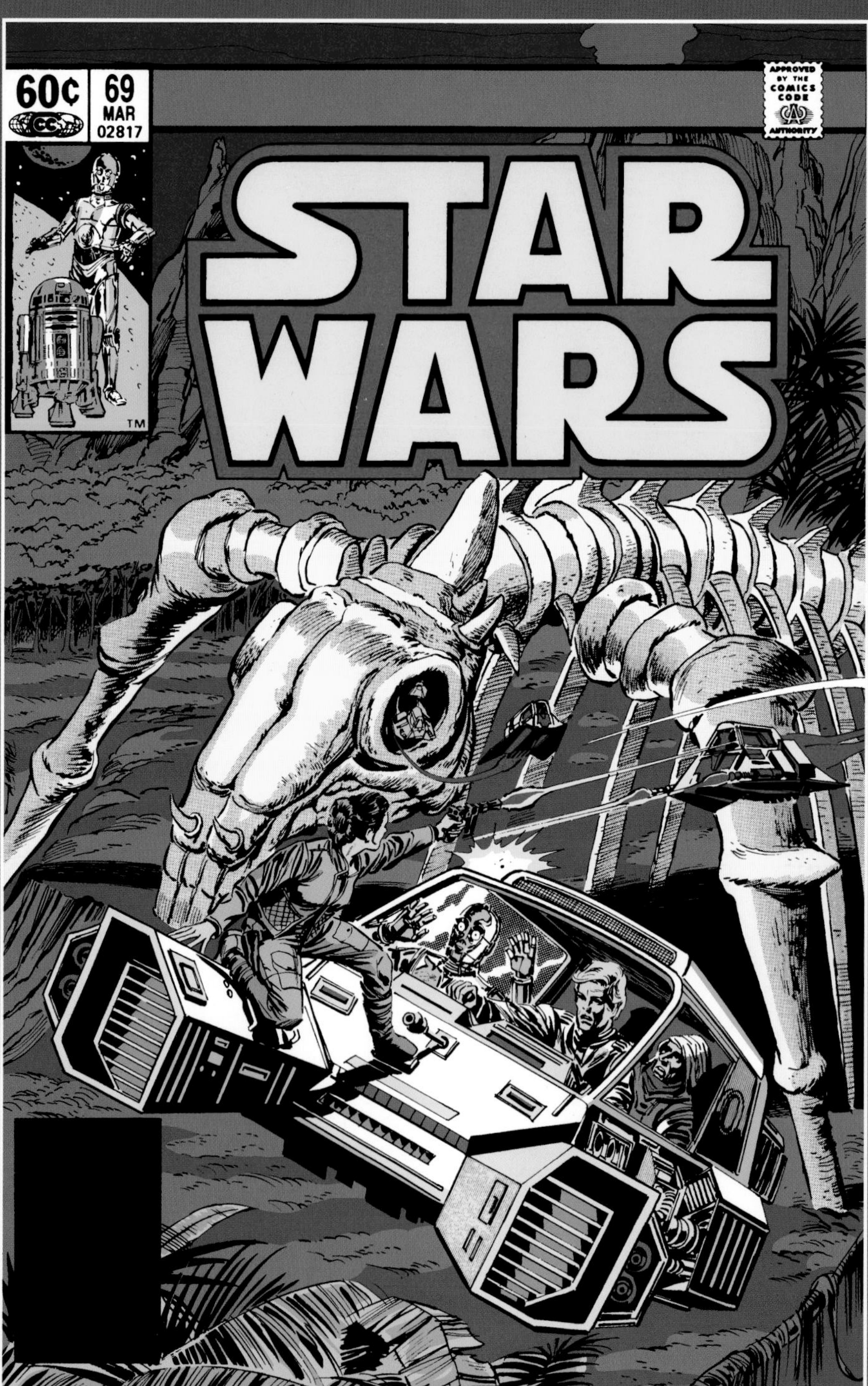

60¢
69
MAR
02817
APPROVED BY THE COMICS CODE AUTHORITY
STAR WARS
TM

DAVID MICHELINIE SCRIPT
GENE DAY PENCILS
TOM PALMER INKS
JOE ROSEN LETTERS
GLYNIS WEIN COLORS
LOUISE JONES EDITOR
JIM SHOOTER MANDALORIAN PROTECTOR
ON HER HOMEWORLD OF ALDERAAN, LEIA ORGANA HAD BEEN A PRINCESS, A SENATOR, AND AS SUCH HAD COMMANDED BOTH THE RESPECT AND THE POWER DUE HER STATION.
BUT NOW, ON THE PLANET MANDALORE, SHE FINDS POWER AND RESPECT IN SHORT SUPPLY. FOR SHE IS HERE NOT AS A DIPLOMAT, BUT RATHER AS A LEADER OF THE REBEL ALLIANCE. SHE IS HERE ON A MISSION TO SAVE THE MAN SHE LOVES. AND, DUE TO AN UNEXPECTED AND DANGEROUS TWIST OF FATE, SHE IS HERE QUITE POSSIBLY--
--FOREVER!
THE ENERGY LINKS ARE SECURE, SIR. THIS REBEL SCUM'LL NEVER GET LOOSE--NOT UNLESS SHE RIPS HER HANDS OFF FIRST!
DEATH IN THE CITY OF BONE!

NOW SEE HERE! YOU JUST WATCH YOUR LANGUAGE! YOU'RE ADDRESSING A MEMBER OF *ROYALTY*, YOU KNOW!
HE KNOWS, THREEPIO. THEY *ALL* KNOW.
THANKS TO *DENGAR*.
RIGHT YA ARE, CUTIE!

AN' THANKS TO THIS *HOMIN' SIGNAL* WHAT BROUGHT THEM STORMTROOPERS RUNNIN', THE WHOLE *GALAXY'S* GONNA KNOW I'VE COPPED THE BOUNTY ON ONE O' THE HOTTEST REBELS AROUND!
WE READY TO GO YET, CAP'N?

JUST ABOUT. THOSE TROOPERS NEXT TO THE TRANSPORT BARGE ARE THE LAST OF OUR PERIMETER SCOUTS TO RETURN. WE SHOULD BE SET TO LIFT OFF ANY TIME NOW.

AND MOMENTS LATER, THEY DO LIFT OFF--
--AS BOTH TRANSPORT AND ESCORT FIGHTERS RISE INTO A SILVERY SKY--

--SKIMMING LOW OVER THE LUSHLY-FORESTED SURFACE OF MANDALORE.
THOUGH, APPARENTLY, NOT LOW ENOUGH *FOR SOME!*
CAREFUL THERE! NOT SO *FAST!* WE'RE ALL GOING TO FALL OUT!
OH, DEAR...

...IF THE MAKER HAD MEANT US TO FLY, HE'D HAVE MANUFACTURED US WITH *ROCKETS!*
BUT PRINCESS LEIA GIVES LITTLE THOUGHT TO THE ERRATIC LISTING OF THE TRANSPORT CRAFT, FOR HER MIND IS FIXED ON OTHER THINGS... ON ENDINGS... AND ON JOYOUS, DECEPTIVELY HOPEFUL--

--BEGINNINGS: THE GENESIS OF A SEARCH FOR A BOUNTY HUNTER PARTNERED WITH BOBA FETT--A PARTNER WHO MIGHT KNOW WHERE FETT HOLDS HIS LATEST PRIZE, REBEL HERO HAN SOLO!
THAT QUEST HAD BROUGHT LEIA TO MANDALORE, LAST KNOWN HUNTING GROUND OF DENGAR--
--A CYBORG BOUNTYMAN THOUGHT TO HOLD A CLUE TO FETT'S WHERABOUTS.
BUT WHAT SHE HAD DISCOVERED INSTEAD APPEARED TO BE FETT HIMSELF!
ONLY LATER HAD SHE FOUND THAT THE WARRIOR IN QUESTION WAS ONE OF THE TWO OTHER MANDALORIAN SUPERCOMMANDOS WHO, LIKE BOBA FETT, HAD SURVIVED THE LEGENDARY CLONE WARS.
THE WARRIOR'S NAME WAS FENN SHYSA, AND HE WAS LEADER OF AN OUTLAW BAND FIGHTING THE IMPERIALLY SANCTIONED SLAVERS NOW RULING HIS PLANET.
AND, AS CHANCE WOULD HAVE IT, HE HAD ALREADY CAPTURED DENGAR, BUT HAD AGREED TO EXCHANGE THE 'BORG FOR A SLAVER PRISONER--HIS CLOSE FRIEND, AND FELLOW COMMANDO, TOBBI DALA.
MAKING A CHOICE THAT WAS AS PAINFUL AS IT WAS NECESSARY, THE PRINCESS HAD RELEASED DENGAR, OFFERING HIM FREEDOM IN RETURN FOR INFORMATION. BUT INSTEAD OF ANSWERS, SHE HAD RECEIVED--
--BETRAYAL!

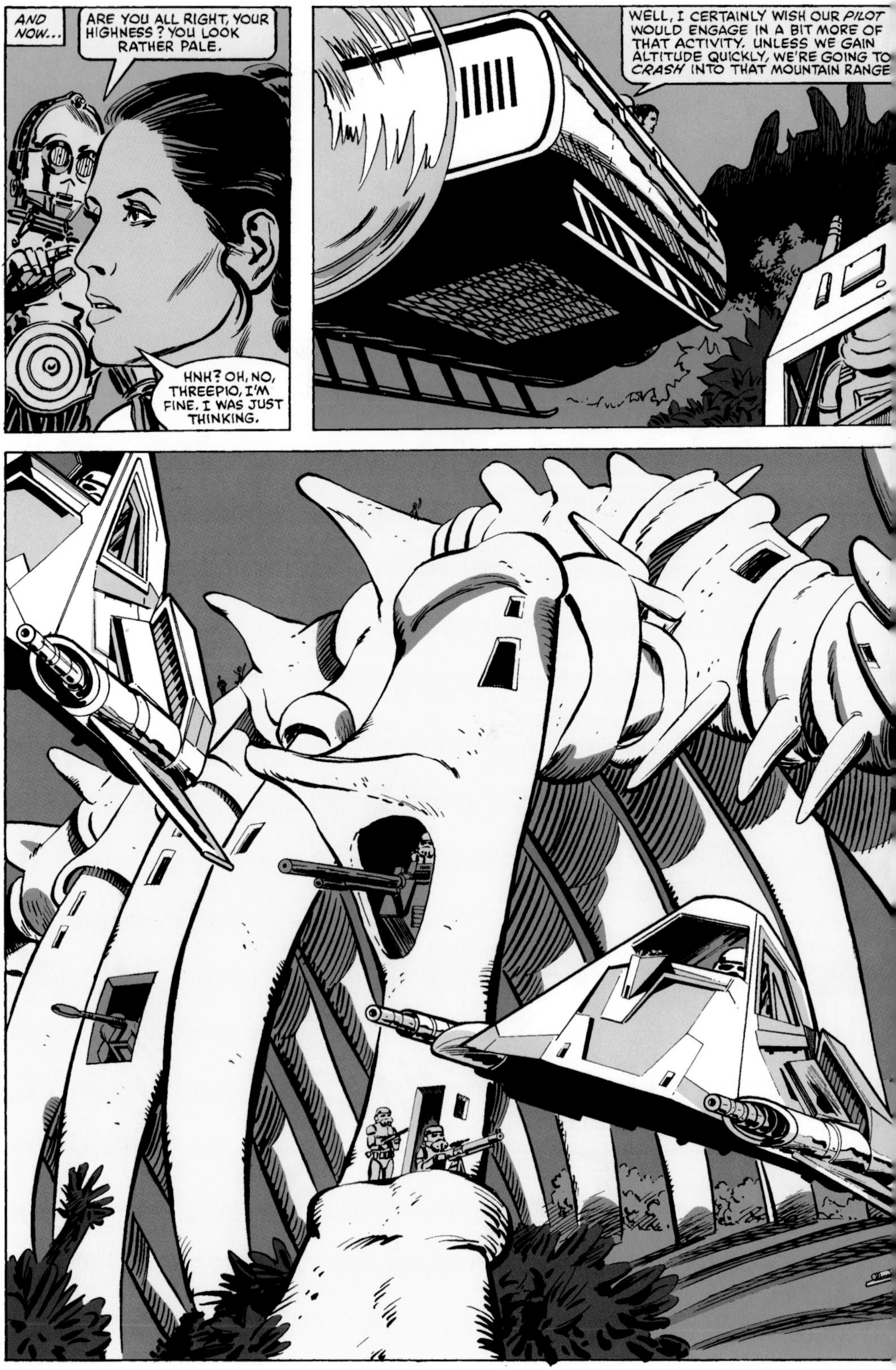

AND NOW...
ARE YOU ALL RIGHT, YOUR HIGHNESS? YOU LOOK RATHER PALE.
HNH? OH, NO, THREEPIO, I'M FINE. I WAS JUST THINKING.

WELL, I CERTAINLY WISH OUR PILOT WOULD ENGAGE IN A BIT MORE OF THAT ACTIVITY. UNLESS WE GAIN ALTITUDE QUICKLY, WE'RE GOING TO CRASH INTO THAT MOUNTAIN RANGE

I WOULDN'T WORRY, THREEPIO. WE'RE MUCH TOO VALUABLE A CATCH TO RISK BY-- WAIT A MINUTE!
THOSE AREN'T *MOUNTAINS!* THEY'RE--

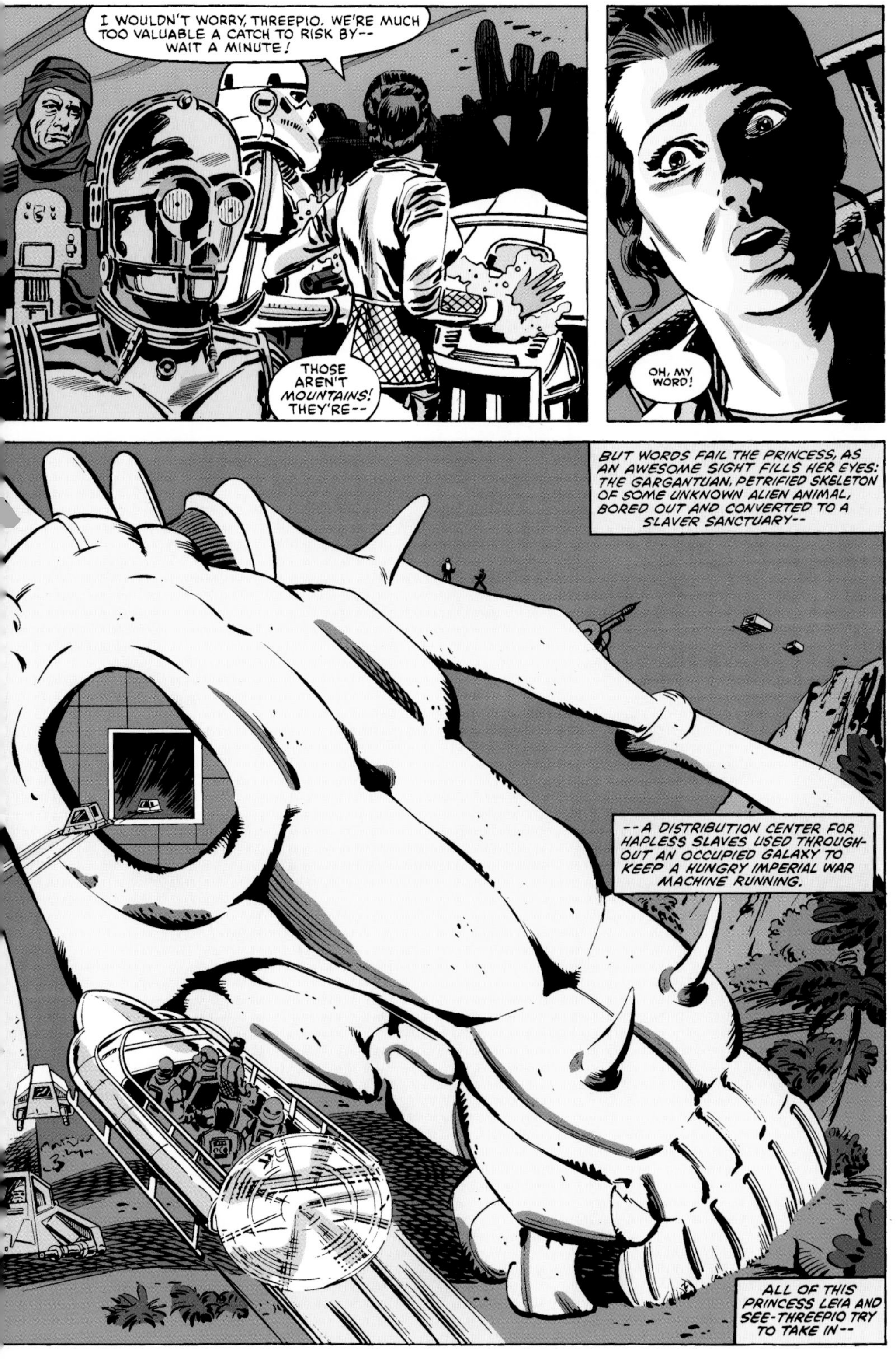

OH, MY WORD!

BUT WORDS FAIL THE PRINCESS, AS AN AWESOME SIGHT FILLS HER EYES: THE GARGANTUAN, PETRIFIED SKELETON OF SOME UNKNOWN ALIEN ANIMAL, BORED OUT AND CONVERTED TO A SLAVER SANCTUARY--

--A DISTRIBUTION CENTER FOR HAPLESS SLAVES USED THROUGHOUT AN OCCUPIED GALAXY TO KEEP A HUNGRY IMPERIAL WAR MACHINE RUNNING.

ALL OF THIS PRINCESS LEIA AND SEE-THREEPIO TRY TO TAKE IN--

--BEFORE THEY THEMSELVES ARE TAKEN INSIDE!
THIS IS INCREDIBLE! THERE'S AN ENTIRE CITY BUILT INTO THE SKULL!

SLAVE CELLS HAVE BEEN CARVED INTO THE VERY BONE OF THE WALLS!
AND THE BASE AREA'S BEEN TURNED INTO ONE BIG PROCESSING CENTER, LIKE A GIANT PEN FOR HERDING--

--ANIMALS?
GLMPH! I-I CAN'T EAT THIS! IT'S STILL ALIVE!
AH, YA JUST GOTTA GET USED TO IT. HERE--

--LEMME HELP!
ALPH! WHY SO TENSE? I MEAN SURE, FUN IS FUN--

--BUT YOU KNOW HOW DEAD SLAVES PUSH UP OUR OVER-HEAD.
HMM, YEAH. I DIDN'T THINK O' THAT.
C'MON, GRUBBER, YOU'VE HAD ENOUGH. FOOD'S EXPENSIVE, Y'KNOW!

THE NEARBY LIFT CONTINUES ITS JOURNEY, RISING SLOWLY TO A PASSAGEWAY HEWN INTO THE MASSIVE SKULL'S SINGLE HORN...
...AS ALL THE WHILE, PRINCESS LEIA SWEARS TO REMEMBER THE CRUELTY SHE'S JUST WITNESSED.

THOUGH WHAT GOOD THAT WILL DO ESCAPES HER FOR THE MOMENT...!
WE CAN GO ON IN-- THE SUPREMA'S EXPECTING US.
TERRIFIC.
WHAT'S A "SUPREMA"?

ONLY THE TOP AUTHORITY ON MANDALORE, LADY. AN OFFICIAL CHOSEN BY THE EMPEROR HIMSELF! HE'S GONNA BE YOUR JUDGE.
AYE, AN' LIKELY YOUR EXECUTIONER!

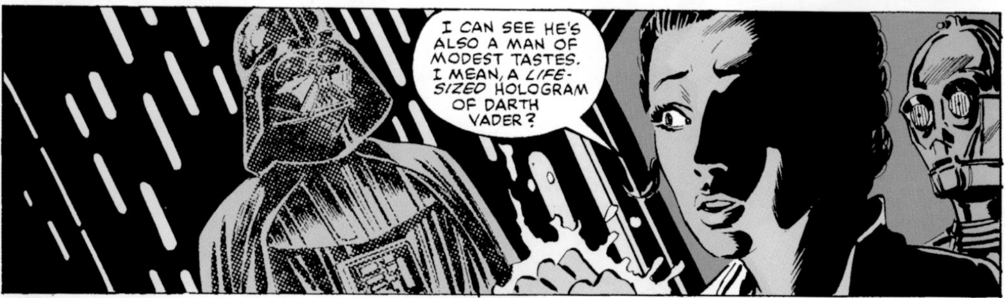
I CAN SEE HE'S ALSO A MAN OF MODEST TASTES. I MEAN, A LIFE-SIZED HOLOGRAM OF DARTH VADER?

MOST IMPERIAL LACKEYS SETTLE FOR A SIMPLE WALL PAINTING.
PERHAPS, MY DEAR. BUT I AM FAR FROM YOUR AVERAGE LACKEY. I AM THE SUPREMA, CHIEFTAIN OF THE ENTIRE MANDALORIAN SLAVE COLONY. BUT YOU, FAIR PRINCESS--

--MAY CALL ME MASTER!
WOULD YOU LIKE A CHAIR?
I'VE A BETTER IDEA, SUPREMA--WHY DON'T YOU SIT ON IT?

AHHH, FIRE. I LIKE FIRE IN A HUMAN.
IT SIZZLES SO NICELY WHEN SQUELCHED...!

TELL ME, SUPREMA, DOES THE EMPIRE GIVE SPECIAL TRAINING IN ARROGANCE--OR ARE YOU ONE OF THE LUCKY ONES WITH NATURAL TALENT?
CHARMING...
SUPREMA? THIS HERE'S DENGAR.

IF THE "GOODS" I DELIVERED ARE AWRIGHT, I THINK I'LL HEAD ON OUT AFTER SHYSA.
EXCELLENT, MY BOY! MAY FORTUNE SMILE UPON YOU!
YOU'RE GOING TO NEED MORE THAN FORTUNE, SLAVER!

ONCE FENN GETS WORD OF WHAT'S HAPPENED, HE'LL HAVE US OUT OF HERE SO FAST IT'LL MAKE YOUR SCALES FLAP!
DEAR PRINCESS, DON'T BE NAIVE. DO YOU REALLY THINK I'D BE ENTRUSTED WITH AN OPERATION OF THESE PROPORTIONS IF I WERE SO INCOMPETENT?

IT'S TRUE THAT TOBBI DALA AND FENN SHYSA ARE GREAT WARRIORS--
--BUT YOU CAN SEE THAT DALA'S ARMOR NOW HANGS IN MY TROPHY CASE. AND SOON, I ASSURE YOU--
--SHYSA'S HEAD WILL JOIN IT!

TAKE THEM TO THE SPECIAL DETENTION CELLS!
YES, SIR!

THE REBELS RETURN TO THE SKULL'S BASE LEVEL--
--AS TWO TROOPERS FROM THE IMPERIAL RAIDING PARTY ACCOMPANY THEIR CHARGES DOWN UNEVEN, ISOLATED HALLWAYS.

UNTIL...
SAY, PAL, DIDJA KNOW YER SHOE-LACES WAS UNTIED?
GOSH, NO. THANKS. I GUESS THEY MUST'VE--
--HEY, WAITA-MINIT! STORM-TROOPER BOOTS DON'T HAVE LACES!

I KNOW...
KZZATCH
THWOK

AN' NOW, MISSY... FER YOU!

NO! I-I WON'T LET YOU HARM THE PRINCESS! YOU'LL HAVE TO GO THROUGH ME FIRST!
ER, I-IF YOU INSIST--!
IT'S A NOBLE CONTRAPTION YA ARE, LADDY, BUT YA GOT NOTHIN' TO FEAR FROM--

--FENN SHYSA!
I HOPE YA'LL FORGIVE MY THROWIN' A BIT O' THE SCARE INTO YA, LEIA, BUT AFTER THAT CLOP ON THE NOGGIN YA GAVE ME,* I COULDN'T RESIST!
B-BUT, HOW--?!
THAT'S QUITE A TALE, DARLIN', AN' I'LL BE HAPPY TO TELL IT--ON OUR WAY TO TOBBI'S CELL!
*LAST ISSUE.

AND SOON, AFTER THE MANDALORIAN OUTLAW HAS REMOVED LEIA'S ENERGY LINKS...
THAT'S RIGHT, MISSY, ME AN' MY LADS WERE FOLLOWIN' YER TRAIL WHEN WE CAME ACROSS YER RUN-IN WITH THEM IMPERIAL WAR DOGS, SO I WHIPPED UP A QUICK PLAN, SLUGGED ONE O' THE PERIMETER SCOUTS AN' TOOK 'IS PLACE!
WHICH BRINGS US TO THE PRESENT SITUATION--AN' A BARGAIN I'M PROPOSIN': YOU HELP ME RESCUE TOBBI, PRINCESS, AN' I'LL SEE THAT DENGAR'S YOURS!
FENN, YOU'VE GOT A DEAL!
OH, WONDERFUL! THEN WE'RE PRACTICALLY HOME!

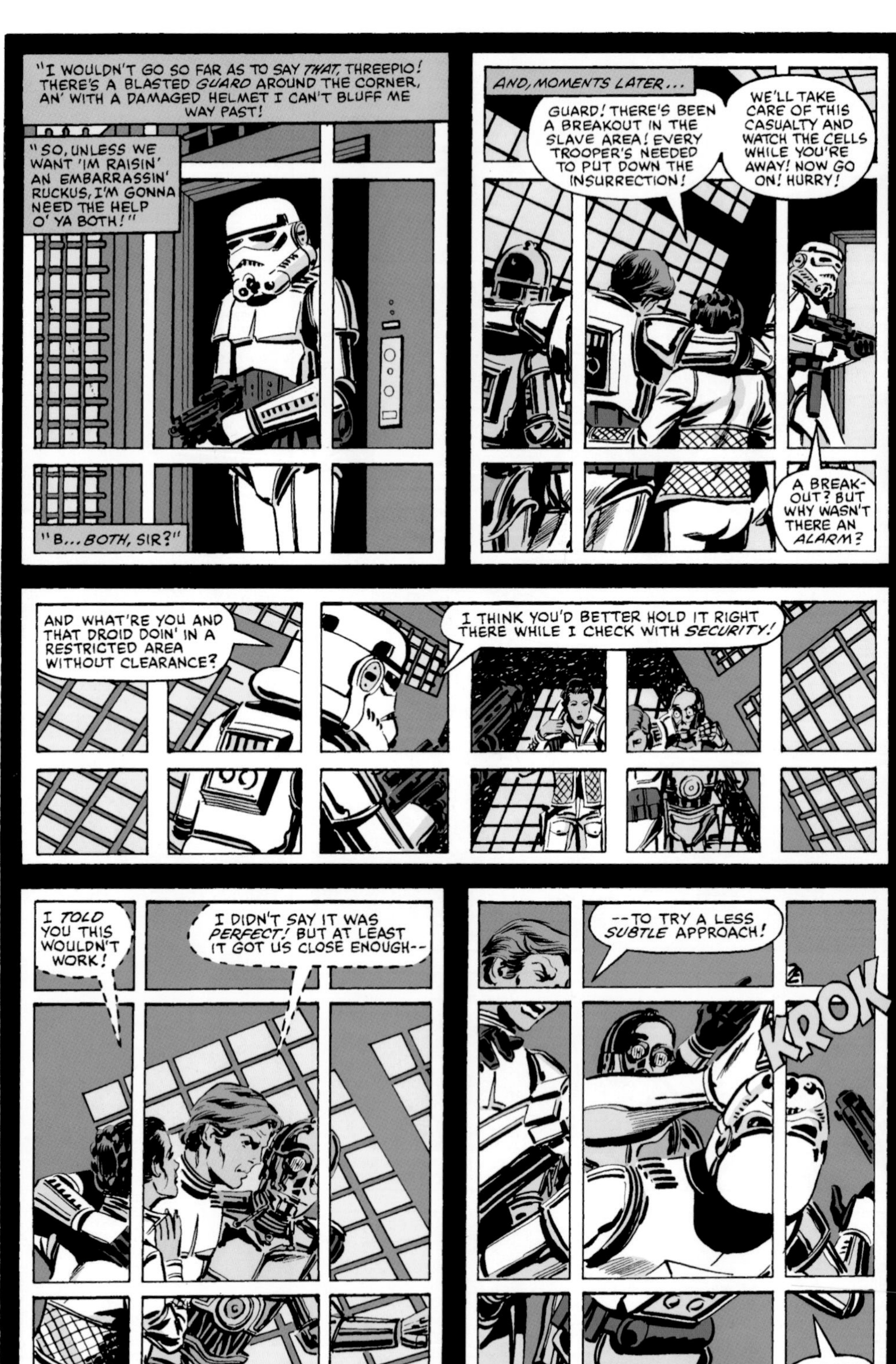

"I WOULDN'T GO SO FAR AS TO SAY *THAT*, THREEPIO! THERE'S A BLASTED *GUARD* AROUND THE CORNER, AN' WITH A DAMAGED HELMET I CAN'T BLUFF ME WAY PAST!
"SO, UNLESS WE WANT 'IM RAISIN' AN EMBARRASSIN' RUCKUS, I'M GONNA NEED THE HELP O' YA BOTH!"
"B... *BOTH*, SIR?"
AND, MOMENTS LATER...
GUARD! THERE'S BEEN A BREAKOUT IN THE SLAVE AREA! EVERY TROOPER'S NEEDED TO PUT DOWN THE INSURRECTION!
WE'LL TAKE CARE OF THIS CASUALTY AND WATCH THE CELLS WHILE YOU'RE AWAY! NOW GO ON! HURRY!
A BREAK-OUT? BUT WHY WASN'T THERE AN *ALARM*?
AND WHAT'RE YOU AND THAT DROID DOIN' IN A RESTRICTED AREA WITHOUT CLEARANCE?
I THINK YOU'D BETTER HOLD IT RIGHT THERE WHILE I CHECK WITH *SECURITY*!
I *TOLD* YOU THIS WOULDN'T WORK!
I DIDN'T SAY IT WAS *PERFECT*! BUT AT LEAST IT GOT US CLOSE ENOUGH--
--TO TRY A LESS *SUBTLE* APPROACH!
KROK
UNF

THAT TOBBI'S CELL?
AYE, ACCORDIN' TO THE GUARD'S REGISTER IT IS! AN' WITH THIS KEY CARD TO OPEN THE DOOR, WE SHOULD--
--EH? THERE'S NO ONE HERE! BUT WHAT'S A GUARD DOIN' KEEPIN' WATCH OVER AN EMPTY--
DIE, YOU SLUG-EATIN' SONOVA--
TOBBI--!
FENN ?!? BUT WHAT'RE YA DOIN' IN THAT SLIMETROOPER GET-UP? I BEEN PLANNIN' THAT LEAP FROM THE CEILIN' FIXTURE FER DAYS--AN' I COULDA TOOK YER HEAD OFF!
IT'S A GOOD THING YOU DIDN'T, TOBBI.
THERE'S A CERTAIN SUPREMA WHO'D BE AWFULLY ANGRY AT HAVING HIS THUNDER STOLEN!
WELL NOW, FENN M'BOY, IT SEEMS YA BEEN RECRUITIN' SOME RIGHT PRETTY OUTLAWS IN ME ABSENCE!
SIR, I'LL ASK YOU TO ADDRESS PRINCESS LEIA WITH THE RESPECT SHE DESERVES!
AN' WHO MIGHT THIS BE, LADY--YER MOM?
BUT SEE-THREEPIO'S SPUTTERING RETORT IS CUT OFF--
--AS HURRIED EXPLANATIONS ARE OFFERED--
--AND A QUICK AND STEALTHY RUN IS MADE TO--

--AN ALMOST DESERTED HANGAR AREA!
THERE'S DENGAR! BUT HOW ARE WE GOING TO GET HIM OUT?
THAT'S THE SECOND PART O'ME PLAN, MISSY!
IT CALLS FER A DIVERSION--

--WITH WHAT YA MIGHT CALL A FLARE FER THE DRAMATIC!
CHUFF

THERE'S FENN'S SIGNAL!
WHUMP
TO THE ATTACK, LADS! HIT 'EM HARD!

AND, TAKING ADVANTAGE OF THE CHAOS THAT FOLLOWS...
YOU--?!
JUST TRY SOMETHIN', BOUNTYMAN!
PLEASE!

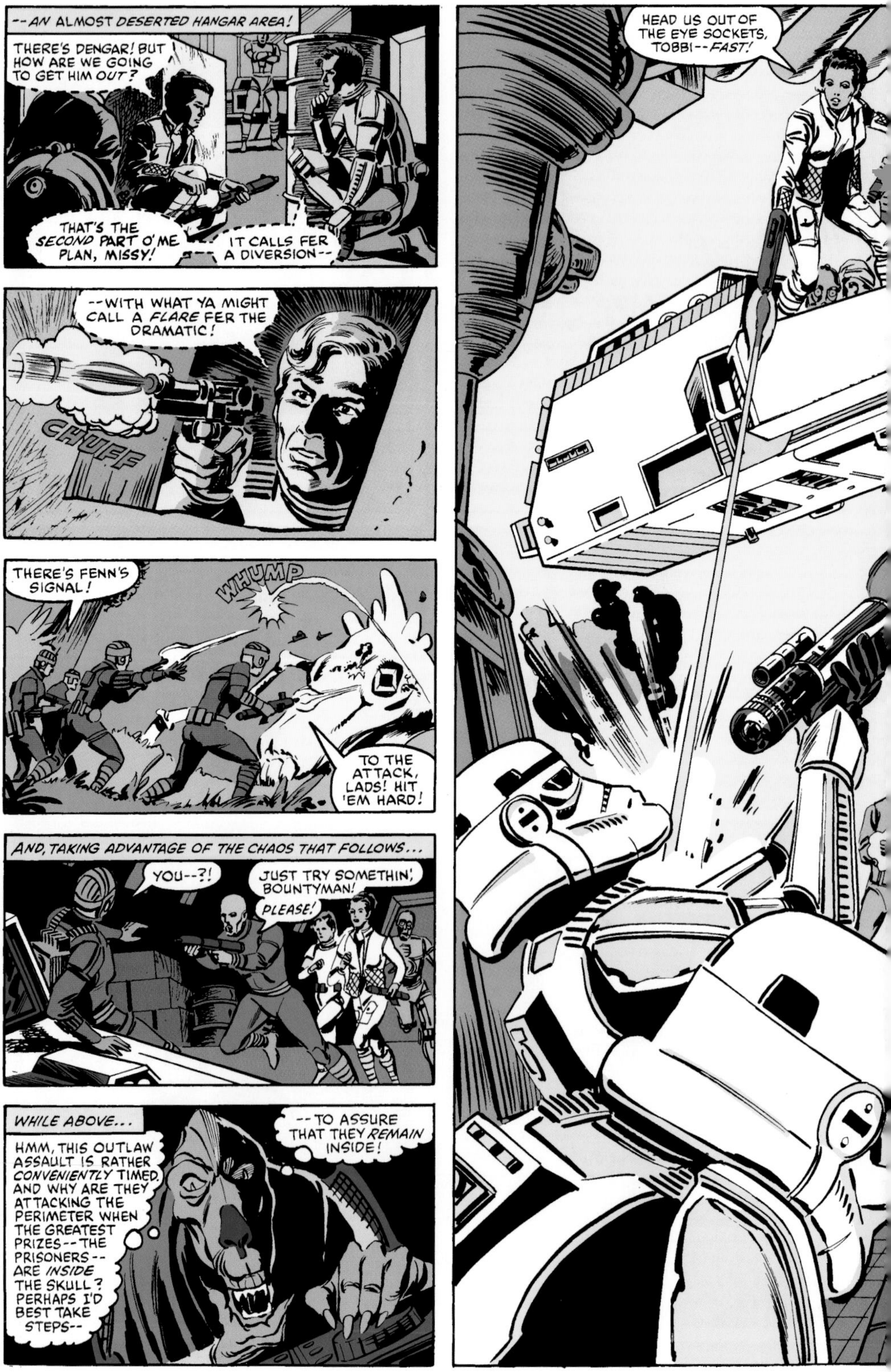

WHILE ABOVE...
HMM, THIS OUTLAW ASSAULT IS RATHER CONVENIENTLY TIMED. AND WHY ARE THEY ATTACKING THE PERIMETER WHEN THE GREATEST PRIZES--THE PRISONERS--ARE INSIDE THE SKULL? PERHAPS I'D BEST TAKE STEPS--
--TO ASSURE THAT THEY REMAIN INSIDE!

HEAD US OUT OF THE EYE SOCKETS, TOBBI--FAST!

I WISH I COULD, PRINCESS-- BUT THE *BLAST DOORS*'RE SLIDIN' SHUT!
THAT SNAKE-TONGUED *SUPREMA* MUST BE ONTO US!

THEN WE'LL JUST HAVE TO IMPROVISE! THAT LOOKS LIKE A MASTER CONTROL --WHAT DOES IT DO?
I *THINK* IT POWERS THE ENERGY LINKS HOLDIN' THE SLAVES, BUT--

MEN OF MANDALORE! YOUR CHAINS ARE GONE AND FREEDOM IS YOURS-- *IF* YOU'RE WILLING TO *TAKE* IT!
TOBBI! GET US TO THE SUPREMA'S OFFICE!

WHILE YOU, SLAVER, SHOULD LOOK OUT FOR YOUR *OVERHEAD!*
THROK
SPLUSH

AND SOON...
YA SURE THEM *ROPES*'LL HOLD DENGAR?
THEY'RE NOT AS STRONG AS ENERGY LINKS, MAYHAPS, BUT THEY'LL DO!

BUT THEN...
OH, FINE! THE BLOODY DOOR'S LOCKED--AN' WE AIN'T GOT A KEY CARD! WHAT NOW?
LIKE I SAID, FENN--

SHAKOW
--WE IMPROVISE!

AH, PRINCESS, PLUCKY TO THE LAST. HOW FESTIVE.
PERHAPS, MY DEAR, I SHALL KEEP YOU FOR MYSELF...

YA'LL BE KEEPIN' NO ONE, SUPREMA! YA'LL BE OPENIN' THEM BLAST DOORS!
AN' YA'LL BE QUICK ABOUT IT, TOO!
YOU ARE A MAN OF DELUSIONS, DALA. POTENTIALLY--

--DEADLY DELUSIONS!
SPAK

F... FENN! G-GRAB 'IM...!
MY WEAPON--! I CAN'T LOWER IT! CAN'T GET A BEAD ON THE OTHERS!
LET GO--!

YOU DUNG-EATIN', RAT-SMELLIN', COLD-LIVERED SONOVA DOG!

I'LL *KILL* YA, I WILL! I'LL--
NO, FENN! DON'T! WE MIGHT NEED HIM! PLEASE--!

AYE, I... I GUESS YER RIGHT. ANYWAY, WE CAN ALWAYS KILL 'IM LATER.
AN' RIGHT NOW TOBBI NEEDS--

--HELP?
I... I'M BEYOND THAT ⋟KOFF⋞ FENN. AN' YA KNOW IT. G-GO ON...
...I'LL SEE TO THINGS ⋟K-KOFF⋞ HERE.

NO! I'LL NOT BE LEAVIN' YA! NOT ALONE!
Y-YA GOT... NO CHOICE. G'WAN...
HE'S RIGHT, FENN! IT'S THE ONLY WAY *ANY* OF US ARE GOING TO MAKE IT! LISTEN TO HIM!

AWRIGHT, BLAST IT! I'LL GO! BUT I'LL BE COMIN' BACK FER YA, BUDDY. JUST AS SOON AS... AS...
I LOVE YA, TOBBI.
G-GIVE 'EM HELL ⋟KOFF⋞ FENN SHYSA...!

THE SHORT SPRINT TO THE WAITING HOVERCRAFT IS MADE SILENTLY, GRIMLY--
--IN A MOOD OF SORROW AND COILING ANGER THAT REMAINS UNBROKEN--

--EVEN AS...
WE'RE UNDER ATTACK! THE SUPREMA MUST'VE GOTTEN A CALL IN TO HIS GUARDS BEFORE WE BROKE INTO THE OFFICE! FENN--
--GET THIS THING *MOVING!*

YOU GUYS GAVE US OUR FREEDOM! AN' WHILE MOST OF OUR LOT'S ESCAPED, *WE* STAYED BEHIND TO RETURN THE FAVOR!

SO JUST ARC YER SHIP DOWN THIS WAY, AN' FLY 'ER AS LOW AS YA CAN! WE'LL TAKE CARE O' THE REST!

DO YOU THINK WE CAN TRUST THEM?

DO WE HAVE A CHOICE?

SHHHWOOMP
GOOD POINT.

AWRIGHT, LADS. THEY'RE PAST! AN' HERE COME THE BLOODHOUNDS!
READY... STEADY...

...NOW!
WHAT THE-- A GRUEL TROUGH?!? B-BUT HOW THE BLAZES DID--

SPLONTSSH
--AIGGH! I- I CAN'T SEE WHERE I'M GOIN'! GOTTA SWITCH TO AUTOPILOT BE-FORE--

KRABAROOUM!

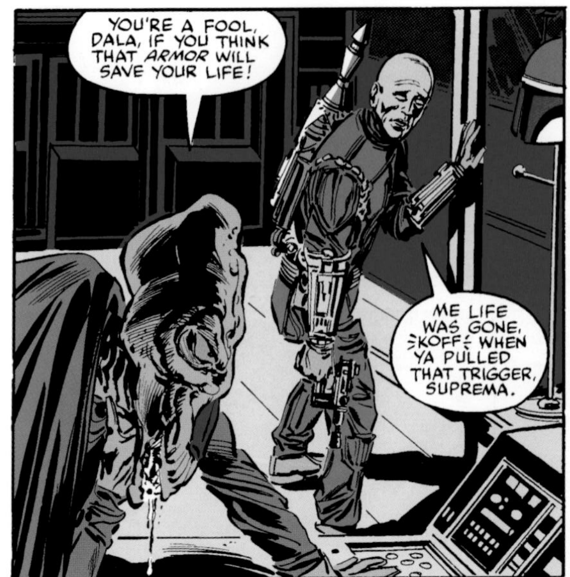
YOU'RE A FOOL, DALA, IF YOU THINK THAT *ARMOR* WILL SAVE YOUR LIFE!
ME LIFE WAS GONE, ⫶KOFF⫶ WHEN YA PULLED THAT TRIGGER, SUPREMA.

BUT THIS HERE UNIFORM... WELL... IT MARKS ME FER A *MANDALORIAN PROTECTOR.* A-AN' I THINK IT'S ONLY FITTIN' ⫶K-KOFF⫶ THAT I WEAR IT...

...WHILE *PROTECTIN'!*
TIK

FENN! LOOK! THE BLAST DOORS ARE OPENING!
TOBBI'S BOUGHT US A CHANCE, PRINCESS!

LET'S *USE* IT!
SHHROOM

AN' NOW ⫘KOFF⫘ AS THEY SAY... FER THE KICKER!
Y-YOU'RE GOING TO CLOSE THE BLAST DOORS?!

BUT THAT'S INSANE! MY MEN ARE FOLLOWING RIGHT BEHIND THE ESCAPEES! THEY'LL NEVER BE ABLE TO STOP IN TIME!
THEY'LL TURN THIS WHOLE INSTALLATION TO CINDERS!

WILL THEY NOW?
⫘KOFF⫘ WHAT A PITY...
TAK

WHA--THE DOORS! THEY'RE CLOSING!
SHRIKE SQUADRON! ABORT MISSION AND PEEL OFF IMMEDIATELY! REPEAT: IMMEDI--

--AAAGGH!
KRAPOOM
VRUPOWWM
SPAKASH
VEER OFF! VEER--
LOOK OUT--!
IN PANIC, THE STARTLED PILOTS PLOW THEIR LURCHING CRAFT INTO WALLS, EACH OTHER... STARTING A CHAIN REACTION OF FUEL AND AMMUNITION THAT BUILDS ON ITSELF, FEEDING HUNGRILY...

WOOM
POOOM
P-P-P
POOOOM
POOOM
...UNTIL, AT LAST, THE PETRIFIED CITADEL LIES SILENT, IMPOTENT, A ONCE-MIGHTY BASTION, NOW A LITTER OF RUBBLE, OF BONE, AND OF DARK, SLAVER BLOOD.

LATER, AFTER A RETURN TO THE OUTLAWS' HIDDEN CAMP...
THE ATTACK FORCE GOT AWAY WITH LIGHT CASUALTIES, FENN--
--AN' MOST O' THE SLAVES HAVE AGREED TO JOIN US!
GOOD.
THEN THAT ONLY LEAVES ONE BIT O' BUSINESS UNFINISHED.
PRINCESS LEIA CAME HERE FER INFORMATION, DENGAR, AN' YER GONNA GIVE IT TO 'ER--
--OR THIS HERE ROTOR'S GONNA TURN YA INTO A PILE O' SCRAPS!
TALK!
B-BUT I AIN'T GOT NOTHIN' TO TALK ABOUT! I WASN'T BOBA FETT'S PARTNER!
SURE, I OVERHEARD FETT TELLIN' SOMEONE ABOUT A HIDEOUT NEAR THE ANGA SYSTEM--
--BUT I DON'T EVEN KNOW WHO HE WAS TALKIN' TO! H-H-HONEST!
AWRIGHT, TAKE 'IM AWAY. NO ONE COULD BE THAT SCARED AN' LIE.
HMPH. IT'S IRONIC, AIN'T IT...?
ME BEST FRIEND'S GONE, THE BLOW WE DEALT THE SLAVERS WAS CRIPPLIN' BUT NOT FINAL--
--AN' WE STILL DIDN'T GET NO HELP FER YER BOYFRIEND.
I'M SORRY, LEIA.
DON'T BE, FENN. IT'S A TOUGH REALITY TO FACE, BUT SOMETIMES...
...THE BAD GUYS WIN.
AYE, WHICH MEANS WE'LL JUST HAFTA HAVE EVEN MORE COURAGE AN' CONVICTION IN THE FUTURE, EH, MISSY?
THAT WE WILL, MY FRIEND. THAT WE WILL...

EPILOGUE: IN A SPARSELY-POPULATED STAR SYSTEM FAR REMOVED FROM MANDALORE, THERE FLOATS A UNIQUE SPACE STATION KNOWN AS THE WHEEL. THIS IS THE HUB OF THE GALAXY'S GAMING TRADE, AND AS SUCH HAS BEEN VISITED BY VETERAN GAMBLER LANDO CALRISSIAN MANY TIMES.
BUT THIS TIME THE MILLENNIUM FALCON HAS BROUGHT LANDO AND HIS WOOKIEE COPILOT, CHEWBACCA, ON A MISSION QUITE DIFFERENT FROM THE USUAL TUMBLING OF DICE AND TURNING OF CARDS...
...THOUGH ITS STAKES ARE EQUALLY AS HIGH!
IF I WERE YOU, VOROL, I'D TELL CHEWIE WHERE THAT BOUNTY HUNTER, BOSSK, WAS HANGIN' OUT.
BUT THEN, I'VE ALWAYS HAD THIS SILLY FONDNESS FOR KEEPING MY HEAD CONNECTED TO MY BODY...
GLREE-SOHN! NACHATA!
I THOUGHT YOU'D SEE THE LIGHT. NOW, WHERE IS HE?
KROTAT! VREECHEE NEK!
AW, NO. NO! NOT... THERE!
NEXT ISSUE...THE SEARCH FOR HAN SOLO CONTINUES IN...
THE STENAX SHUFFLE

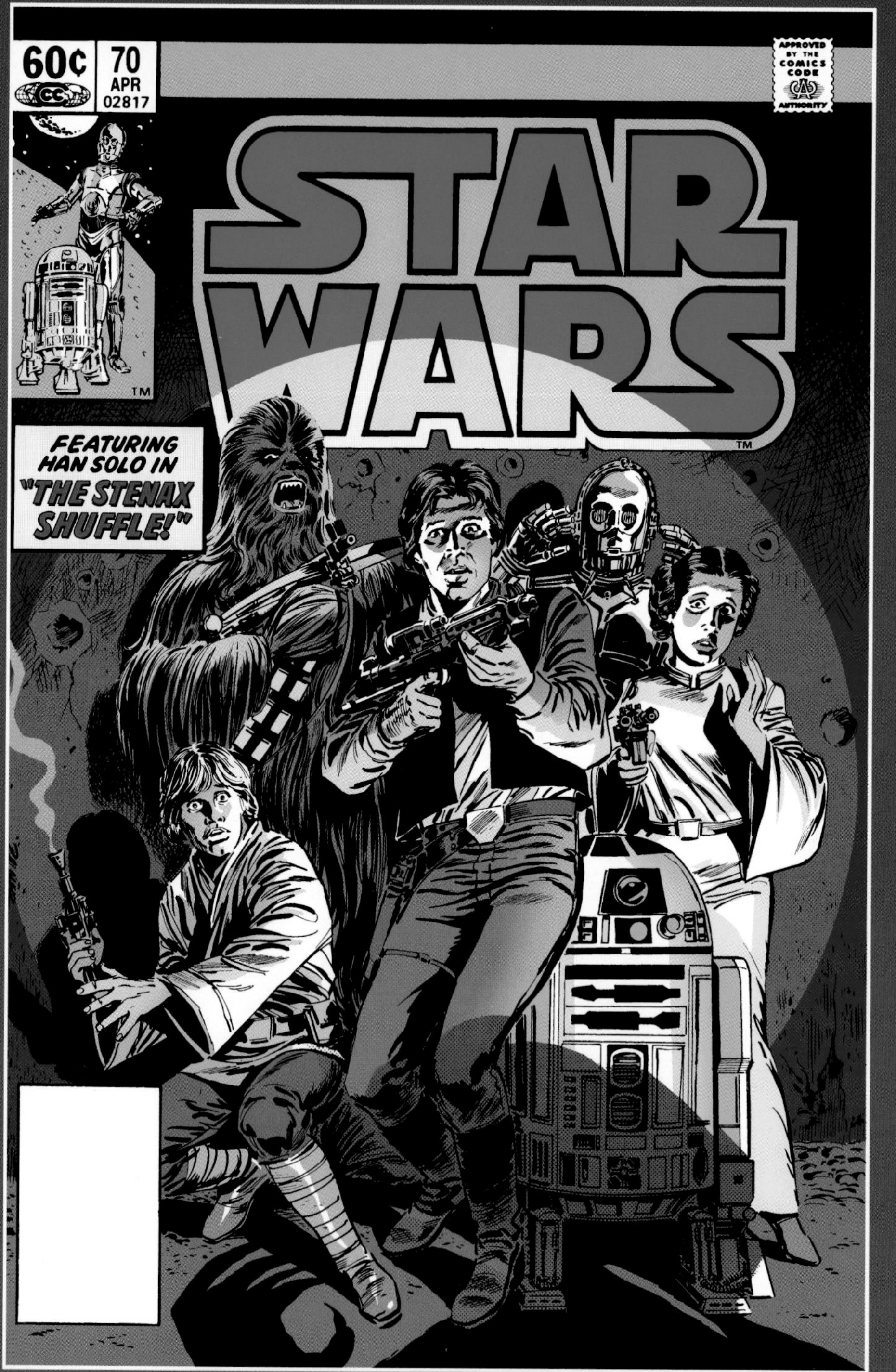

60¢

70
APR
02817

APPROVED BY THE COMICS CODE AUTHORITY

STAR WARS™

TM

FEATURING HAN SOLO IN "THE STENAX SHUFFLE!"

Long ago in a galaxy far, far away. . .there exists a state of cosmic *civil war*. A brave alliance of *underground freedom fighters* has challenged the tyranny and oppression of the awesome *Galactic Empire*. This is their story!

Lucasfilm PRESENTS: **STAR WARS**™ *THE GREATEST* **SPACE FANTASY** OF ALL!

MARY JO DUFFY *PLOT / SCRIPT* — KERRY GAMMILL *PENCILS (PAGES 1, 5-16, 18-21)* — TOM PALMER *PENCILS (PAGES 2-4, 17, 22)*

TOM PALMER *INKS* — JOE ROSEN *LETTERS* — GLYNIS WEIN *COLORS* — LOUISE JONES *EDITOR* — JIM SHOOTER *CHIEF*

THAT'S JUST THE TROUBLE. MAYBE THEY'VE WORKED OUT A LITTLE TOO WELL.
HOW?
WELL, LOOK AT IT LOGICALLY...
"WE'RE HERE TO HELP HAN SOLO, RIGHT? HE'S YOUR FRIEND, HE'S MY FRIEND, HE'S CAPTAIN OF THIS SHIP WE'RE FLYING, AND INCIDENTALLY, HE'S A VALUABLE MEMBER OF THE REBEL ALLIANCE AGAINST THE GALACTIC EMPIRE.
"BUT IN HIS PIRATING DAYS HAN MADE A FEW ENEMIES. AND ONE OF THEM--JABBA THE HUTT--HIRED SOME BOUNTY HUNTERS WHO CAUGHT HAN AND ENCASED HIM IN A BLOCK OF CARBONITE STEEL. THEY'LL BE DELIVERING HIM TO JABBA ANY TIME NOW.

"NOW, WE ALL KNOW THAT THE BOUNTY HUNTER WHO ACTUALLY CAPTURED HAN WAS BOBA FETT, BUT HE WAS ONLY ONE OF MANY WHO TRIED.
"AND RECENT INTELLIGENCE SUGGESTS THAT FETT HAD A PARTNER, ANOTHER BOUNTY HUNTER HE WORKED WITH AND THEN CUT OUT OF THE DEAL. WE'VE NARROWED IT DOWN TO EITHER BOSSK, OR IG-88..."

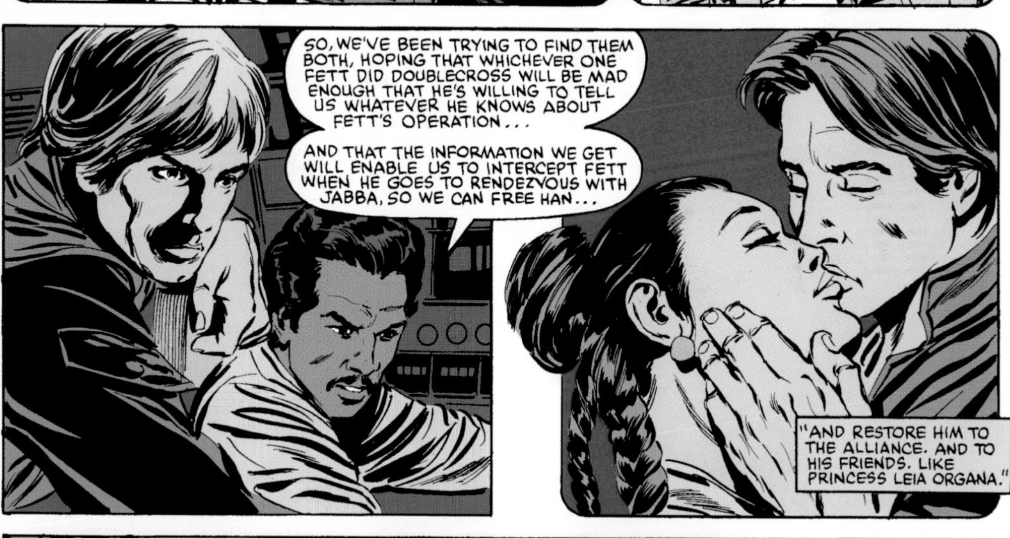
SO, WE'VE BEEN TRYING TO FIND THEM BOTH, HOPING THAT WHICHEVER ONE FETT DID DOUBLECROSS WILL BE MAD ENOUGH THAT HE'S WILLING TO TELL US WHATEVER HE KNOWS ABOUT FETT'S OPERATION...
AND THAT THE INFORMATION WE GET WILL ENABLE US TO INTERCEPT FETT WHEN HE GOES TO RENDEZVOUS WITH JABBA, SO WE CAN FREE HAN...
"AND RESTORE HIM TO THE ALLIANCE. AND TO HIS FRIENDS. LIKE PRINCESS LEIA ORGANA."

GRRROWR!
IT'S ALL RIGHT, CHEWBACCA. WE KNOW NO ONE WANTS HAN BACK MORE THAN YOU DO.
EXCEPT MAYBE ME. I CAN'T GET IT OUT OF MY MIND THAT FETT ONLY CAUGHT HAN BECAUSE I DOUBLE-CROSSED HIM.

THE EMPIRE DIDN'T LEAVE YOU ANY CHOICE. YOU'D ALREADY BEEN BETRAYED BY IMPERIAL AGENTS.
PUH-WHEETT!
YEAH...

AND THEY KEPT RIGHT ON DOUBLE-CROSSING ME, AND MAKING THE DEAL WORSE AND WORSE, UNTIL THERE WAS NO WAY OUT FOR HAN.

BUT, YOU SEE, LUKE, THAT'S WHAT MAKES MEN LIKE HAN AND ME VALUABLE TO THE REBELLION. WE UNDERSTAND DOUBLECROSSES AND DE-CEIT AND ALL THE OTHER THINGS THAT THE EMPIRE EXCELS AT.
AND THAT'S JUST WHAT I DON'T LIKE ABOUT THIS.

YOU AND ARTOO-DEETOO THERE SET OUT IN SEARCH OF IG-88, AND CHEWIE AND I WENT AFTER BOSSK.
BA-DEET!
WE FOLLOWED DIFFERENT LEADS, AND WENT IN DIFFERENT DIRECTIONS, AND YET, WITHIN DAYS, BOTH TRAILS LED US HERE, TO THE PLANET STENOS.
IT'S ALL JUST TOO CONVENIENT.

WELL... IT MAKES A CERTAIN AMOUNT OF SENSE FOR HAN'S FATE TO SOMEHOW BE TIED UP WITH WHAT HAPPENS HERE ON STENOS... AND FOR STENOS TO BE THE SCENE OF SOME TREACHERY...
WE WERE ALL HERE ONCE BE-FORE, RIGHT AFTER HAN AND I JOINED THE REBELLION...

SO THIS IS STENOS?

WELL, I MUST SAY, IT'S ABSOLUTELY CHARMING. THOSE FALLING DOWN BUILDINGS ARE A REAL NICE TOUCH.
WHAT ARE WE DOING HERE, ANYWAY?
I TOLD YOU BEFORE, HAN. THERE WAS A REBEL BASE HERE. THEY WERE SUPPOSED TO CHECK IN FIVE DAYS AGO AND THEY HAVEN'T YET!
WE'RE HERE TO FIND OUT WHAT'S HAPPENED TO THEM.

HHHSSS!
GGGRRR!
WHAT A DUMP!
THE STENAXES SEEM LIKE MOST UNPLEASANT CREATURES. I DON'T CARE FOR THEIR LOOKS AT ALL.
YOU'D BETTER KEEP YOUR VOICE DOWN, SEE-THREEPIO. I DON'T THINK THEY CARE FOR YOUR OPINION AT ALL!

AND I DON'T CARE FOR WHAT I'M SEEIN'.
HEADS UP, GUYS. STORM TROOPERS.

THAT...THAT MAN OVER THERE! IT'S QUORL MATRIN. HE'S AN IMPERIAL GOVERNOR.
WE SERVED IN THE SENATE TO-GETHER. HE'S BOUND TO RECOGNIZE ME!
NOT TO WORRY, YOUR HIGH-NESS.

JUST STICK WITH US. NOTHING OUT OF THE ORDINARY ABOUT OUR GROUP.
NOPE. NO, SIR. JUST ORDINARY TOURISTS. NO REBEL LEADERS HERE...
OH, DEAR...
SHHH.

SOON...
GREAT, YOUR HIGHNESS... JUST GREAT! YOU PICKED THE TALLEST PINNACLE ON THIS ENTIRE ROCKPILE FOR US TO CLIMB...

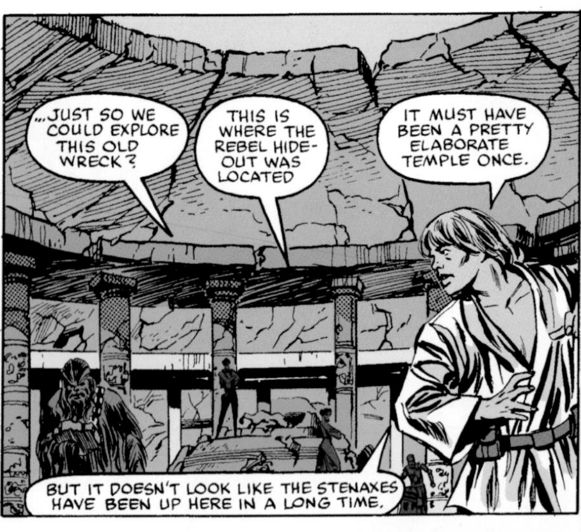
...JUST SO WE COULD EXPLORE THIS OLD WRECK?
THIS IS WHERE THE REBEL HIDE-OUT WAS LOCATED
IT MUST HAVE BEEN A PRETTY ELABORATE TEMPLE ONCE.
BUT IT DOESN'T LOOK LIKE THE STENAXES HAVE BEEN UP HERE IN A LONG TIME.

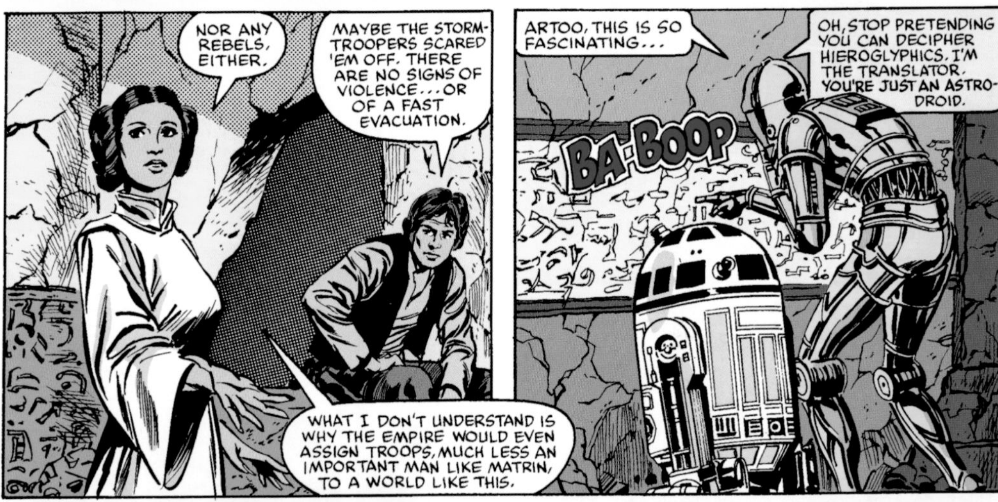
NOR ANY REBELS, EITHER.
MAYBE THE STORM-TROOPERS SCARED 'EM OFF. THERE ARE NO SIGNS OF VIOLENCE...OR OF A FAST EVACUATION.
WHAT I DON'T UNDERSTAND IS WHY THE EMPIRE WOULD EVEN ASSIGN TROOPS, MUCH LESS AN IMPORTANT MAN LIKE MATRIN, TO A WORLD LIKE THIS.
ARTOO, THIS IS SO FASCINATING...
BA-BOOP
OH, STOP PRETENDING YOU CAN DECIPHER HIEROGLYPHICS. I'M THE TRANSLATOR. YOU'RE JUST AN ASTRO-DROID.

WELL, WHAT-EVER MATRIN'S DOING HERE, WE CAN GUESS WHAT HAPPENED TO THE REBELS. THEY MUSTA CLEARED OUT. WE'LL HEAR FROM 'EM ONCE THEY FIND A NEW HIDEOUT. NOW, LET'S HOP INTO THE *FALCON* AND...

NOT SO FAST!
GGGRRROWR
WHO--?

GREETINGS.
HIYA, SOLO.
LONG TIME NO SEE.

RIK DUEL, WITH DANI AND CHIHDO!
AS FAR AS I'M CONCERNED, IT HASN'T BEEN LONG ENOUGH.
DON'T BE UNPLEASANT SOLO.
YOU'LL ONLY REGRET IT LATER.

AND YOU'RE GOING TO REGRET IT...
VORP
IF YOU TRY ANYTHING.

A WOOKIEE, A CLASSY LADY, TWO DROIDS... AND A KID WITH A LIGHTSABER.
A CUTE KID WITH A LIGHT-SABER.
HAN, YOU GOT YOURSELF SOME PRETTY IMPRESSIVE ALLIES, THE DAY YOU JOINED THE REBELLION.

JOINED? WHAT JOINED? WHO JOINED?
WHAT KIND OF A PIRATE DO YOU THINK I AM?
I'M IN THIS GAME 'CAUSE IT PAYS WELL.

DON'T TRY TO CON A FELLOW CON MAN. YOU DON'T HAVE TO APOLOGIZE TO ME. WE'VE JOINED THE REBELLION, TOO.
DON'T MAKE ME LAUGH.
IT'S TRUE, ON MY HONOR. COLONEL KINDAR ASKED US TO STAY BEHIND WHEN THE IMPERIAL TROOPS FORCED THE REST OF OUR GROUP TO LEAVE.

KINDAR...? HE'S THE MAN WE WERE TO CONTACT IF WE FOUND THE REBELS.
RIGHT. HE WANTED US TO FIND SOMETHING THAT'S HIDDEN IN THIS TEMPLE. SOMETHING THAT COULD BE VITAL TO THE REBELLION...
AND THANKS TO YOUR GENEROSITY AND FORESIGHTEDNESS, WE'VE NOW GOT THE ONE THING WE NEEDED TO FIND IT.
AND JUST WHAT ONE THING IS THAT?

YOUR TRANSLATOR DROID.
SEE-THREEPIO!
YEAH, GOOD OLD THREEPIO. DON'T KNOW WHERE WE'D BE WITHOUT 'IM.
ME? REALLY? BUT, I'M SO TOUCHED. I DON'T KNOW WHAT TO SAY...

PPPPLLLL
OH, SHUT UP, ARTOO. NO ONE ASKED YOU.

THIS TEMPLE'S REALLY TOO MUCH OF A RUIN FOR ALL OF US TO LIVE IN. WE NEED THE COMFORTS A STARSHIP CAN OFFER.
WHY DON'T YOU GO GET THE *MILLENNIUM FALCON*?
WHAT'S WRONG WITH YOUR SHIP?

I'D LIKE A CHANCE TO TAKE ANOTHER LOOK AT THE *MOONSHADOW*. AS I RECALL SHE'S A CRAFT WITH REALLY NICE LINES...
NEEDS SOME REPAIRS... SAY, SPEAKING OF NICE LINES...

WHY HASN'T ANYONE INTRODUCED ME TO THIS LITTLE BEAUTY?
DID I HEAR HAN CALL YOU "YOUR HIGHNESS"?
A NICKNAME. IT'S CAPTAIN SOLO'S IDEA OF A JOKE.
MY FRIENDS CALL ME LEIA.

HI, I'M DANI. WHAT DO YOUR FRIENDS CALL YOU?
AH... AH... LUKE.
NICE NAME. I LIKE MEN NAMED LUKE. YOUNG BLONDE MEN NAMED LUKE...
DON'T TAKE IT PERSONALLY, LUKE. SHE'S A ZELTRON. THEY GET LIKE THAT.

HRONK!
YEAH, SURE, LOVER-BOY AND I'LL GO GET THE *FALCON*, CHEWIE.
YOU STAY HERE AN' KEEP AN EYE ON... ON LEIA. AND THINGS.

AH, HAN... I'M SORRY TO HAVE TO SAY THIS ABOUT A FRIEND OF YOURS... BUT I'M NOT SO SURE I TRUST THIS RIK.
KID, YOU GOTTA LEARN TO HAVE MORE FAITH... LIKE ME.
I'VE GOT FAITH THAT CHEWIE'LL PULL THAT CLOWN'S ARMS OFF IF HE TRIES ANYTHING FUNNY.
OH.

LATER, AFTER THE FALCON IS SAFELY STOWED IN THE TEMPLE...
EVER SINCE WE GOT HERE WE'VE DONE NOTHING BUT CLEAR THIS RUBBLE AWAY. I'M BEAT.
BUT IT'S GOOD FOR YOU... IT HELPS BUILD MUSCLES.
I LIKE A MAN WITH A LOT OF MUSCLES. MAYBE WE CAN CARRY THE NEXT BIG ROCK TOGETHER.
STAY WITH IT, OL' PAL. WISH I COULD HELP YOU, BUT I GOTTA ADJUST THE FALCON'S UH...UH...WELL, I'M REALLY BUSY HERE.
OF COURSE YOU ARE, SOLO.

OH YES, ARTOO. VERY GOOD, ARTOO. THAT'S NO END OF HELP!

COME ON, CHEWBACCA. PUT YOUR BACK INTO IT. WE'RE COUNTING ON YOU. I THOUGHT YOU WOOKIEES WERE SUPPOSED TO BE STRONG!

BEFORE YOU WEAR YOUR TONGUE OUT GIVING US ANY MORE ORDERS, WOULD YOU MIND TELLING ME WHAT WE'RE LOOKING FOR?
AN ARTIFACT, VERY ANCIENT AND VALUABLE ...IT WAS LOST HERE SOMETIME SEVERAL CENTURIES AGO...

WHEN ALL OF STENOS WAS SHAKEN BY EARTHQUAKES AND VOLCANIC DISTURBANCES.
HERE, LET ME SKETCH IT OUT FOR YOU... SUPPOSED TO LOOK SOMETHING LIKE THIS...ABOUT A FOOT TALL, CARVED OF RED STONE...

...VOL, GOD OF THE STENAXES.

A STATUE? YOU'VE HAD US WORKING ALL DAY TO HELP YOU FIND AN ORDINARY STATUE?
WHAT VALUE DOES IT HAVE, TO ANYONE BUT AN ART COLLECTOR?

IT'S NOT JUST A STATUE. THE STENAXES BELIEVE THAT THAT HUNK OF CARVED ROCK *IS* VOL-- AN AVATAR OF HIS FORM ON STENOS.
THIS PLACE WAS HIS TEMPLE... AND HIS PEOPLE HAVE BEEN IN DEEP DISGRACE WITH HIM, EVER SINCE THEY LET HIM GET BURIED.
THEY'D DO ALMOST ANYTHING TO GET HIM BACK AND REGAIN HIS FAVOR.
WELL, THEN WHY AREN'T THEY UP HERE *LOOKING*--?

LOOK AT WHAT MASTER LUKE HAS UNCOVERED, ARTOO! THIS PANEL OF STONE HAS THE MOST RECENT CARVINGS WE'VE SEEN SO FAR!
THAT'S IT! THAT'S WHAT THE OTHER REBELS WERE LOOKING FOR!
IT'S THE KEY TO FINDING VOL! IT'LL TELL US WHERE THE STATUE WAS LOCATED BEFORE THE EARTHQUAKE!

BUT WHAT GOOD WILL THAT BE FOR THE REBELLION?
OH, WELL... *KINDAR* FELT THAT THEY...

--HEY, DANI, BREAK IT UP! GET BACK TO WORK! I'M NOT PAYING YOU TO ROMANCE THE KID!
BUT YOU'VE NEVER PAID ME.
AND I NEVER WILL UNLESS YOU START BEHAVING YOURSELF!

MASTER LUKE, I'VE DONE IT! I'VE TRANSLATED THE PANEL.
GREAT! WHERE'S VOL?
IT DOESN'T SAY, SIR. NOT PRECISELY. BUT THERE IS A DESCRIPTION OF WHERE THE ALTAR WAS PLACED.

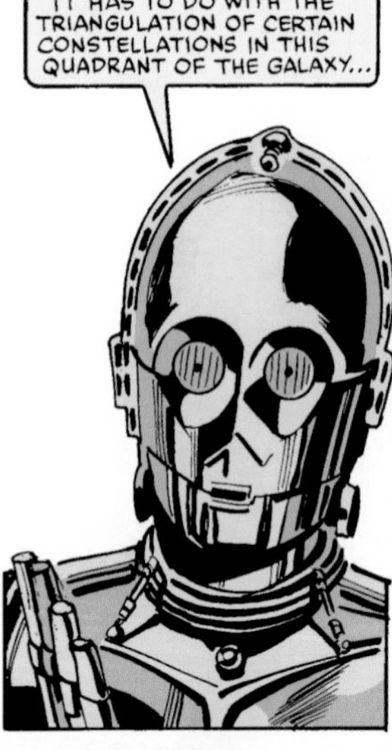
IT HAS TO DO WITH THE TRIANGULATION OF CERTAIN CONSTELLATIONS IN THIS QUADRANT OF THE GALAXY...

REALLY, SIR, IT'S MOST FORTUNATE THAT WE ARRIVED WHEN WE DID! EVEN IF YOU'D TRANSLATED THE PANEL, YOU'D HAVE NEEDED AN ASTRODROID--LIKE ARTOO-DETOO--TO MAKE THE FINAL CALCULATIONS!
BREEP-BLIP-BOOP!

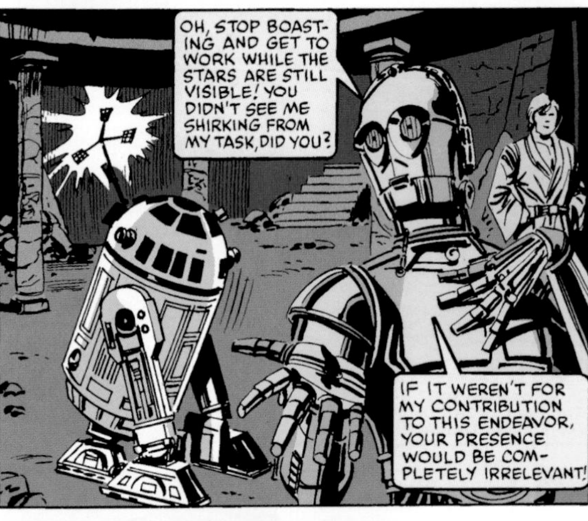
OH, STOP BOASTING AND GET TO WORK WHILE THE STARS ARE STILL VISIBLE! YOU DIDN'T SEE ME SHIRKING FROM MY TASK, DID YOU?
IF IT WEREN'T FOR MY CONTRIBUTION TO THIS ENDEAVOR, YOUR PRESENCE WOULD BE COMPLETELY IRRELEVANT!

PING

ZZZIK

NICE GOING, GUYS. THAT HUNK OF RUBBLE IS EVEN BIGGER THAN THE FIRST ONE WE DUG UP!
YOU'RE RIGHT. THERE'S NO POINT IN TACKLING THAT MESS UNLESS WE GET SOME TOOLS.
THERE'S A SHOP IN THE VILLAGE THAT CARRIES PRIMITIVE IMPLEMENTS. TAKE CHIHDO, SEE IF YOU CAN FIND ANYTHING USEFUL.

I'LL STAY HERE AND KEEP AN EYE ON...ON LEIA.
AND THINGS.
I'D STILL LIKE TO KNOW WHAT ALL THE IMPERIAL BRASS AN' HARDWARE IS DOING IN THIS DESERT.
KEEP YOUR VOICE DOWN, UNLESS YOU'D LIKE THEM TO EXPLAIN IT TO YOU.

HEY, LEVEL WITH ME. WHAT'S IN IT FOR THE REBEL ALLIANCE IF WE DO FIND VOL?
THE GRATITUDE OF ALL OF STENOS FOR THE RESTORATION OF THEIR DEITY.
YOU SEE, ACCORDING TO THE TERMS OF VOL'S CURSE, HIS PEOPLE ARE BOUND TO THE LAND, FORBIDDEN TO FLY, UNTIL THEIR GOD IS FOUND.

THE HIGH PLACES-- THE TOWERS AND PLATEAUS THEIR ANCESTORS BUILT AND LIVED IN-- ARE TABOO TO THEM UNTIL THEN.
PAY THE MAN, WILL YOU? I DON'T HAVE ANY LOCAL CURRENCY.

OUR LEADERS HOPE, ONCE THE STENAXES ARE FAVORABLY DISPOSED TOWARDS US, TO CONVINCE THEM TO THROW OFF THE IMPERIAL YOKE AND BECOME OUR ALLIES.
WHY? WHAT GOOD WOULD THEY BE TO US?

COLONEL KINDAR VALUED THEM, AND I NEVER QUESTION THE JUDGEMENT OF MY BETTERS... BUT I WILL SAY, I'D HATE TO HAVE A STENAX AS AN ENEMY!
I TAKE YOUR POINT!

HEY! YOU, THERE!
GOVERNOR MATRIN!
ULP

I ALMOST TRIPPED OVER THIS! DID YOU DROP IT?
UH... YES, SIR. SORRY, SIR.
I'LL COME BACK AND GET IT, SIR.
IN THE FUTURE, BE MORE CAREFUL.
OH, YES, SIR. I INTEND TO, SIR!

IT'S NICE OF YOU TO FINALLY PITCH IN, RIK. YOU MUST REALLY BE EXCITED ABOUT BEING SO CLOSE TO VOL.
KNOCK IT OFF, SOLO.

GEE, LEIA, YOU DON'T HAVE TO HELP. WHY DON'T YOU REST?
WHY? I NOTICE YOU DON'T MIND DANI'S HELP.
WE'VE DONE OUR PART, ARTOO. WE'D BETTER CONSERVE OUR STRENGTH, IN CASE THEY NEED MORE TRANSLATIONS OR CALCULATIONS.

TWO DAYS OF THIS! I'VE HAD ABOUT ENOU--!
HEY! I THINK I'VE FOUND SOMETHING!
WHAT? WHERE? BE CAREFUL!

I THOUGHT I SAW SOMETHING RED... UNDER THE DIRT HERE...

VOL!
WE DID IT!
THAT'S DONE IT!
THAT'S RIGHT.

COME ON, KID. I'VE GOT YOU COVERED. NOW HAND ME THE IDOL, NICE AND SLOW.
OR WHAT?!

OR DANI WILL BLOW YOUR HEAD OFF.
IT WOULD BREAK MY HEART...
BUT AFTER ALL, ZELTRONS HAVE TO EAT, TOO.

YOU'VE ALL BEEN WONDERFUL, CHILDREN. WITHOUT SUCH HELPFUL, GULLIBLE INNOCENTS ON OUR SIDE, WE MIGHT NEVER HAVE FOUND OLD VOL.
AND GOVERNOR MATRIN HAS BEEN SO ANXIOUS TO ADD TO HIS PRIVATE COLLECTION OF ESOTERIC ARTIFACTS.
THANK YOU, LUKE. FOR EVERYTHING.

LOOK ME UP SOMETIME, IF YOU MAKE IT OFF THIS PLANET ALIVE.

BUT DON'T COUNT ON THAT!

NO ONE DOES THAT TO ME AND GETS AWAY WITH IT! LET'S GET AFTER THEM!
WHAT FOR? WE LEARNED WHAT WE CAME HERE FOR DAYS AGO! LET'S GET OUT OF HERE BEFORE SOMETHING ELSE HAPPENS!

THERE THEY ARE, JUST AS I TOLD YOU, GOVERNOR... NOTORIOUS CRIMINALS! THEY'VE BEEN CONSPIRING AGAINST IMPERIAL INTERESTS!
OH, NO!

OH, YEAH! GOOD OLD RIK HAS REALLY FIXED US!

WE'RE COMPLETELY OUTNUMBERED, AND CLOSED IN ON ALL SIDES!

GREAT!
LUKE, CAN YOU MAKE IT TO THE HATCH OF THE SHIP?

I CAN TRY...

LUKE!

BAD MOVE, JUNIOR!
THEY'D HAVE CUT YOU DOWN BEFORE YOU GOT HALFWAY THERE!

WE HAVE TO DO SOMETHING BEFORE THEY CUT US ALL DOWN!

I THINK I HEAR SOMETHING... ALMOST LIKE A GREAT WIND!
LISTEN, GOLDENROD, IT'S GONNA TAKE MORE THAN A CHANGE IN THE WEATHER TO--!

LOOK UP THERE!

I DON'T BELIEVE IT!
THEY'RE *FLYING!*
I GUESS THEY KNOW THE TABOO'S BEEN LIFTED! CHIHDO MUSTA TALKED TO SOMEONE WHILE HE WAS BUSY SELLIN' US OUT.

COME ON! WE CAN'T LET THEM DO ALL OUR FIGHTING FOR US!
GROONK

RETREAT!
WE CAN'T SURVIVE THESE ODDS!

NICE GOING, PAL. I DON'T KNOW WHY YOU DID IT, BUT THANKS FOR THE TIMELY RESCUE!

HHHISSSS

THEY DON'T SEEM MUCH FRIENDLIER TOWARDS US THAN THEY WERE TOWARDS THE STORMTROOPERS!
I DON'T GET IT! THEN WHY'D THEY HELP US?
HAN...I...I THINK MAYBE THEY WANT VOL.

OH, WELL... IF IT'S VOL YOU WANT...

THIS HAS BEEN A REALLY SWEET CAPER! THERE'S NOTHING LIKE DUMB ALLIES TO BOOST THE PROFITS AND MINIMIZE THE LABOR!
AND SPEAKING OF PROFITS... IT'S OCCURRED TO ME THAT THERE MUST BE OTHER ART COLLECTORS, EVEN RICHER THAN OL' MATRIN.

WHY DON'T WE JUST GET INTO THE *MOONSHADOW* AND...

HELLO, RIK.

I'M GLAD I'VE BEEN HAVING YOU WATCHED! AMONG OTHER THINGS, IT GAVE ME THE OPPORTUNITY TO OVERHEAR YOUR INTERESTING REMARKS JUST NOW!
I ESPECIALLY LIKED YOUR OBSERVATIONS ABOUT "DUMB ALLIES."

MATRIN! NICE OF YOU TO COME AND MEET US.
HERE IT IS! I GOT VOL FOR YOU, JUST LIKE I PROMISED!
NOW, AS TO OUR PAYMENT...

I'M SUR-PRISED YOU WEREN'T MURDERED YEARS AGO!

BUT, TIME ENOUGH FOR THAT NOW!

TAKE IT LIKE A MAN, DUEL. YOU'VE GOT IT CO--

--EH?

HHSSS
HHHIIISSS

SOLO!

I KNOW YOU'RE TO BLAME FOR THIS SOMEHOW, SOLO!
AND SOME DAY, SOMEWHERE, I'M GONNA GET YOU FOR IT!!

NEXT ISSUE: Return to STENOS

TERRY
AUSTIN
1980

60¢ 71 MAY 02817

APPROVED BY THE COMICS CODE AUTHORITY

THE QUEST FOR HAN SOLO...

Long ago in a galaxy far, far away. . .there exists a state of cosmic *civil war*. A brave alliance of *underground freedom fighters* has challenged the tyranny and oppression of the awesome *Galactic Empire*. This is their story!

Lucasfilm PRESENTS: STAR WARS™ THE GREATEST SPACE FANTASY OF ALL!

JO DUFFY SCRIPT AND PLOT · RON FRENZ BREAKDOWNS · TOM PALMER FINISHES · JOE ROSEN LETTERS · CHRISTIE SCHEELE COLORS · LOUISE JONES EDITOR · JIM SHOOTER EDITOR-IN-CHIEF

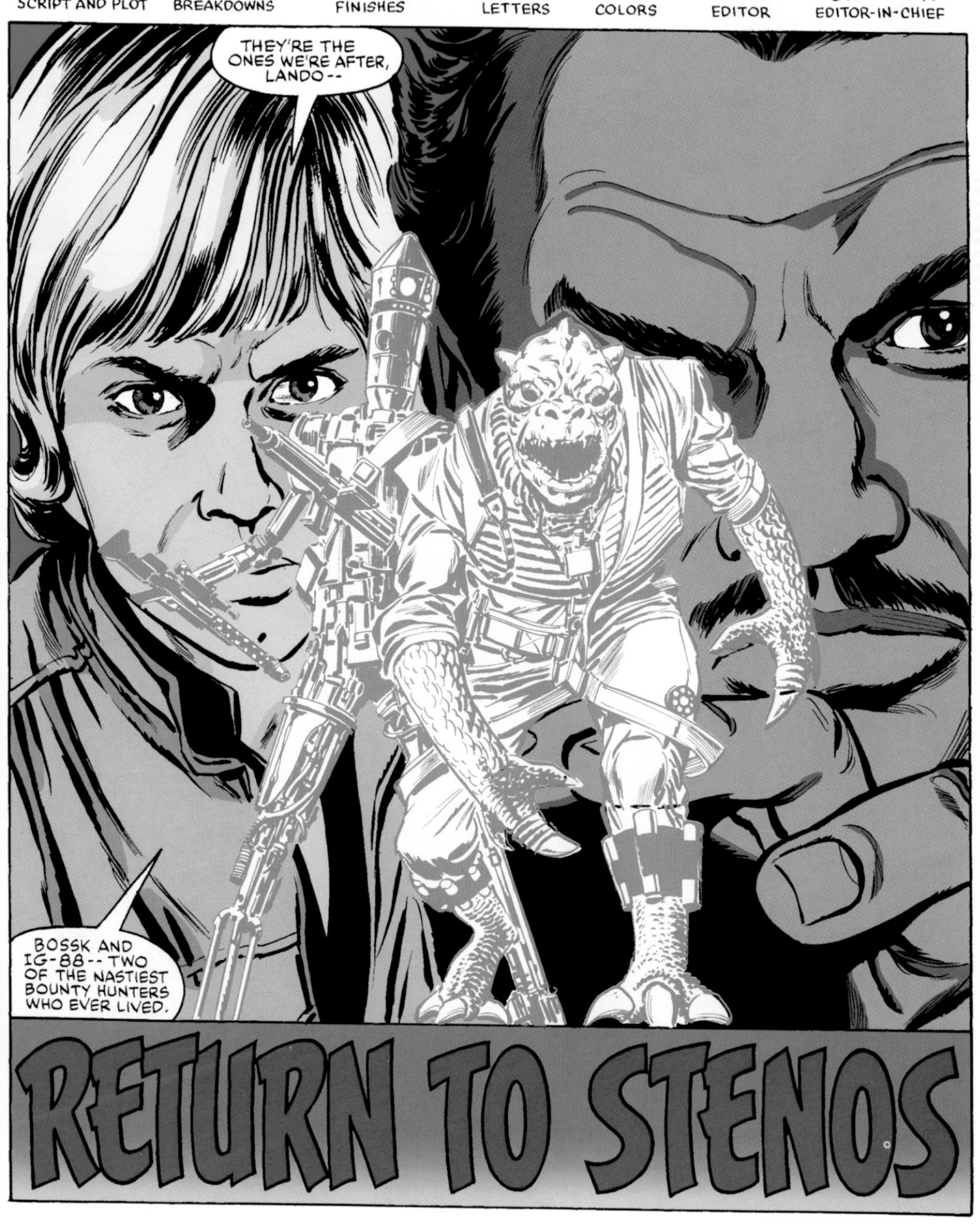

THEY'RE THE ONES WE'RE AFTER, LANDO--
BOSSK AND IG-88-- TWO OF THE NASTIEST BOUNTY HUNTERS WHO EVER LIVED.

RETURN TO STENOS

THINK YOU'LL RECOGNIZE THEM IF YOU EVER SEE THEM?
OF COURSE I WILL, LUKE, WITH WHAT'S AT STAKE HERE.
THEY USED TO BE TEAMED UP WITH BOBA FETT-- THE BOUNTY HUNTER WHO CAUGHT OUR FRIEND HAN SOLO.
RIGHT NOW, IT LOOKS LIKE THE ONLY HOPE WE HAVE OF EVER FINDING AND RESCUING HAN IS THAT ONE OF THESE GUYS KNOWS WHERE FETT WAS PLANNING TO TAKE HIM...
...AND DELIVER HIM TO THE MAN WHO BOUGHT HIM...
JABBA THE HUTT.
OKAY, THANKS, ARTOO-DEETOO. YOU CAN TURN OFF THE HOLOGRAM PROJECTION UNIT.
WE KNOW WHAT THEY LOOK LIKE.
AND AS THE IMAGE FADES...
NOW, ALL WE HAVE TO DO IS FIND ONE --OR BOTH-- OF THEM, AND CONVINCE HIM TO CONFIDE IN US. AND THAT'S A PLEASANT LITTLE JOB--
--I'M LOOKING FORWARD TO.
I STILL CAN'T BELIEVE OUR LUCK-- THAT WE FOLLOWED SEPARATE TRAILS TO THESE GUYS, AND THEY BOTH EVENTUALLY LED US HERE TO STENOS.
IF IT WAS LUCK... I'M NOT WORRIED ABOUT FINDING BOSSK AND IG-88, OR ABOUT MAKING THEM TALK. I'M WORRIED ABOUT WHAT THEY MAY TELL US.
HOW DO WE KNOW HAN'S EVEN STILL ALIVE?
LUKE, HAN WILL BE ALL RIGHT.
I HOPE SO.
I'M SURE OF IT.

GRUMPH
BEEP
YOUR WEAPONS CHECK OUT OKAY?
YEAH.
THEN, LET'S GO.
NOT YOU, CHEWBACCA.
?
BUMP
PUH-WHEET
GRROOWR
H-HEY...DON'T GET MAD ...NOTHING PERSONAL... I WASN'T GOING TO LET ARTOO COME EITHER...HONEST.
LANDO'S RIGHT, CHEWIE. REMEMBER WHAT IT WAS LIKE THE LAST TIME WE WERE HERE, WITH HAN? HUMANOIDS ARE COMMON.
DROIDS AND WOOKIEES AREN'T.
IF THE NATIVES SEE YOU WITH ME, THEY MAY REMEMBER US ALL, AND THAT WOULD JEOPARDIZE EVERYTHING.
BESIDES, YOU AND THE STENAXES DIDN'T LIKE EACH OTHER ANYWAY.
WAIT HERE. WE'LL CALL YOU WHEN WE FIND HAN.
HRONK

SO THAT'S THE CAPITAL OF STENOS? IT SEEMS A LITTLE SMALL.
YOU SHOULD HAVE SEEN HOW IT LOOKED WHEN I WAS HERE THE LAST TIME WITH HAN AND THE PRINCESS.
THE STENAXES WERE UNDER A CURSE, PLACED ON THEM BY THEIR GOD, AND THE WHOLE CITY WAS IN A STATE OF DECAY.
WE, UH... LIFTED THE CURSE FOR THEM, BEFORE WE LEFT...

AND THEY ALMOST KILLED YOU FOR IT.
WELL, YEAH, BUT...
AND THEY ALMOST CERTAINLY KILLED A FEW PEOPLE WHO DOUBLECROSSED YOU.
UH... MAYBE.
COME ON.

IF IT WEREN'T FOR THE TERRAIN, AND THE FACT THAT I KNOW IT'S THE SAME PLACE, I'D NEVER RECOGNIZE THIS CITY.
I SEE A LOT OF HUMANS, A FEW IMPERIAL STORM TROOPERS, ALL SORTS OF OTHER ALIENS... I GIVE UP. WHERE ARE THE NATIVES?

THAT'S SOME OF THEM UP THERE HOLDING THOSE LANTERNS.
CHARMING.
WHEN THEIR GOD FORBADE THEM TO FLY, THE STENAXES LIVED DOWN HERE ON THE GROUND WITH US OFF-WORLDERS. I GUESS THEY'VE NOW GONE BACK TO LIVING IN THE PINNACLES.

NICE PLANET YOU HAVE HERE.
HHHSSSS!
I TOLD YOU--THEY DON'T LIKE ALIENS... OR ANYONE ELSE.
BUT AS LONG AS NO ONE INTERFERES WITH THEM, THEY DON'T SEEM TO CARE WHO VISITS THEIR WORLD, OR WHAT GOES ON HERE.
IT WASN'T THIS CROWDED BEFORE... UH, HOW ARE WE GOING TO FIND TWO BOUNTY HUNTERS IN AN OFF-WORLD POPULATION THIS SIZE?
JUST LEAVE THAT TO ME.
BOUNTY HUNTERS ARE LIKE PIRATES, SMUGGLERS... ANY OTHER SERIOUS BUSINESSMEN.
ANY PLACE THEY VISIT, YOU CAN BET SOONER OR LATER THEY'RE ALL GOING TO END UP...
...IN THE NEAREST BAR.

NOW WHAT?
NOW, WE ORDER.
BARKEEP! MY FRIEND AND I WOULD EACH LIKE A GLASS OF WHATEVER THAT FELLOW WHO'S PASSED OUT HAS BEEN DRINKING.
HRRRR...
WHAT WILL THAT ACCOMPLISH?

LUKE, YOU'VE GOT TO LEAVE THIS TO A MAN WITH SOME STYLE, A MAN OF SUBTLETY, A MAN WHO KNOWS HIS WAY AROUND CITIES.
YOU GO BLUNDERING AROUND WITH THAT DIRECT APPROACH YOU USUALLY FAVOR, AND SOME-ONE MIGHT REMEMBER THAT THEY'VE SEEN YOU HERE BEFORE.
AT LEAST WE KNOW I WON'T BE RECOGNIZED.

STOP THAT MAN! HE'S LANDO CALRISSIAN!!
HUNH?
OH, NO!

I TELL YOU THAT MAN IS A CHEAT! HE ROBBED ME!!
TEN THOUSAND CREDITS TO THE ONE WHO CAPTURES HIM FOR ME!!!

DREBBLE! WITH ALL THE WATERING HOLES ON ALL THE WORLDS... WHY DID I HAVE TO RUN INTO HIM HERE?
WHAT DO WE DO NOW?
NOTHING. WHO'S GOING TO LISTEN TO A BAG OF WIND LIKE HIM?

KLACK
KLIK
UH... EVERYONE?
KLICH
DID SOMEONE MENTION MONEY?
TEN THOUSAND CREDITS.
KLAK
I SAW THEM FIRST!
SNIK

DUCK!!

DID YOU REALLY CHEAT HIM?
LUKE, AMONG MEN OF BUSINESS, CHEAT IS A SUBJECTIVE, RELATIVE TERM.
IT'S OPEN TO SOME VERY BROAD INTERPRETATIONS.
GREAT.

GET THEM! GET THEM! GET THEM!
I'LL GIVE YOU A REWARD FOR THE LITTLE ONE, TOO!

TZING
AND I'LL JUST STEP OUTSIDE AND STAY OUT OF EVERY-ONE'S WAY UNTIL YOU'RE FINISHED.

"LEAVE IT TO ME," HE SAID... "STYLE AND SUBTLETY," HE SAID...
STOP GRUMBLING... I HAVEN'T COMPLETELY BLOWN IT, YOU KNOW.

TRUE. YOU WERE RIGHT ABOUT KNOWING HOW AND WHERE TO FIND BOUNTY HUNTERS.

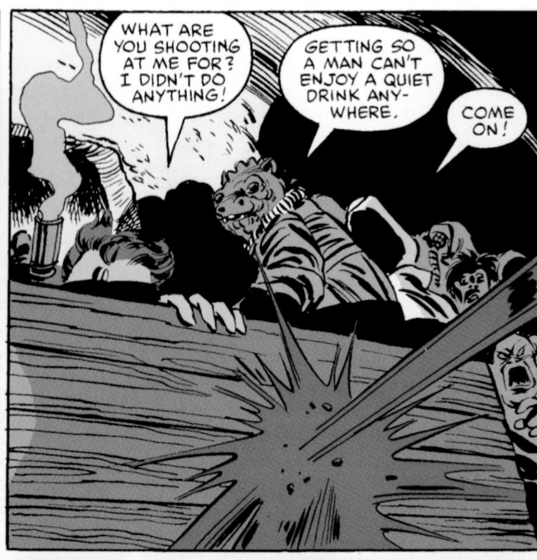
WHAT ARE YOU SHOOTING AT ME FOR? I DIDN'T DO ANYTHING!
GETTING SO A MAN CAN'T ENJOY A QUIET DRINK ANY-WHERE.
COME ON!

LANDO, THERE HE IS-- LEAVING WITH THAT JAWA!
IT'S BOSSK!

WONDERFUL. DO YOU WANT TO GO AFTER HIM, OR ASK HIM TO WAIT FOR US OUT-SIDE?
NEITHER, BUT I DON'T INTEND TO LOSE HIM.

WHAT ARE YOU PLANNING TO DO WITH THAT LIGHTSABER?
YOU'LL SEE. JUST COVER ME WITH YOUR BLASTER.

HE'S GOT A LIGHTSABER!
HEY! IF HE SHEARS THROUGH THAT SUPPORT PILLAR, WE'RE ALL GOING TO--!
LOOK OUT-- WHAT'S HE DOING?
HOW SHOULD I KNOW?
CRASH!!
GOOD WORK! NONE OF THEM WILL BE ABLE TO GET TO US FOR A MINUTE!
WHAT ARE YOU GOING TO DO NOW?
MAKE AN EXIT.
AN EXIT? BUT WE'RE ON THE FIFTH FLOOR!
COME ON!

BLAST.
GO AFTER THEM!!
YOU FIRST.

GO AFTER THEM!
GET ME LANDO CALRISSIAN AND THAT BOY!
I OFFERED YOU GOOD MONEY, AND I'M ORDERING YOU TO--!

BAMM

YOU... YOU HIT ME!
DREBBLE, WHATEVER THAT GUY DID TO YOU, I BET YOU HAD IT COMING.

YOU HIT ME RIGHT IN THE MOST EXPENSIVE TEETH CREDITS CAN BUY!
I WANT THOSE TWO... BARBARIANS CAUGHT AND PUNISHED FOR THIS... I'LL DOUBLE THE REWARD FOR THE PAIR OF THEM!

THEY'RE GOING TO PAY, AND PAY DEARLY!

ARE YOU OKAY, LANDO?
I'LL LET YOU KNOW AS SOON AS I LOSE THIS RINGING IN MY HEAD.
AND MY ARMS. AND MY LEGS.
AND MY STOMACH.

WHO TAUGHT YOU THAT BONEHEADED STUNT, ANYWAY?
COME ON, WE'D BETTER BE GONE BEFORE ANY OF OUR FRIENDS FROM UP-STAIRS DECIDE TO JOIN US DOWN HERE.

I HEAR SOMEONE!

LANDO, LOOK!
BOSSK! WE DIDN'T LOSE HIM AFTER ALL!

WELL, HE'S NOT GOING TO GET AWAY FROM US NOW!
I'M RIGHT BEHIND YOU!

HE'S DUCKED INTO THAT CROWD! DON'T LET HIM GET AWAY!
I'M TRYING NOT TO!

NOW WHERE'D HE GO?

MAYBE DOWN THIS ALLEY?
I THINK WE TOOK A WRONG TURN.
IF YOU ASK ME, THIS ENTIRE PLANET IS A WRONG TURN!

THERE HE IS! LET'S GRAB HIM!

GOT YOU!
EH?
WHAT DO YOU WANT?

UH... UH... SORRY. MISTAKEN IDENTITY. WE THOUGHT YOU WERE SOMEONE ELSE.
YEAH... PARDON US. IT WON'T HAPPEN AGAIN...
...MA'AM.

I WONDER WHAT HAPPENED TO BOSSK...
THERE!
WHERE?
LANDO...

WE'VE CIRCLED BACK TO THE BAR!
GET THEM! GET THEM! GET THEM!
OH, NO!

LET'S GET OUT OF HERE BEFORE THINGS GET WORSE.
I DON'T SEE HOW THINGS COULD GET ANY WORSE!

YOU WOULD... IF THE STENAXES EVER GOT INTERESTED ENOUGH TO HELP THE MOB... OR JUST POINT OUT WHICH WAY WE'VE RUN.
QUICK! WE CAN DUCK INTO THAT NEXT DOORWAY!

RIGHT! FOLLOW ME!

I THINK WE LOST THEM, LANDO.

LANDO?
IS THAT YOU?

ALL RIGHT, WHOEVER YOU ARE--
-- JUST STEP OUT HERE WHERE I CAN SEE YOU!

PRETTY HANDY WITH THAT SABER, AREN'T YOU?
TAKE IT EASY, KID. IT'S ONLY ME.

RICK DUEL!
IN THE FLESH! AND I'LL BET YOU THOUGHT YOU'D NEVER SEE ME AGAIN.

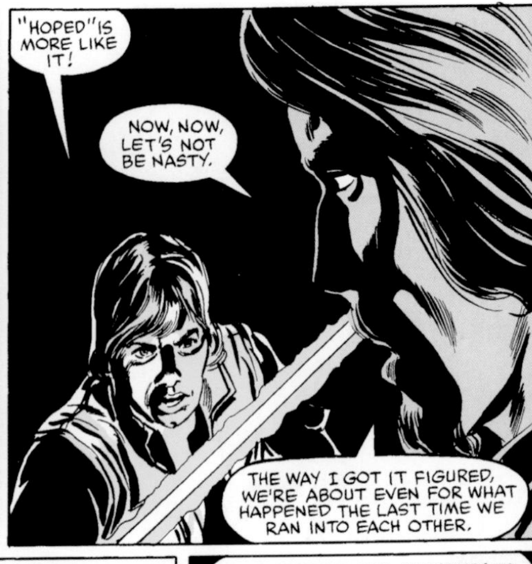
"HOPED" IS MORE LIKE IT!
NOW, NOW, LET'S NOT BE NASTY.
THE WAY I GOT IT FIGURED, WE'RE ABOUT EVEN FOR WHAT HAPPENED THE LAST TIME WE RAN INTO EACH OTHER.

I BETRAYED YOU TO THE STORM TROOPERS. YOU BETRAYED ME TO THE STENAXES.

BESIDES, JUDGING FROM THE SOUND OF THAT LYNCH MOB OUT THERE, RIGHT NOW YOU COULD USE A FEW FRIENDS.

WE EXPECTED THE STENAXES TO KILL YOU FOR TRYING TO SELL THEIR GOD, VOL. WHAT HAPPENED?

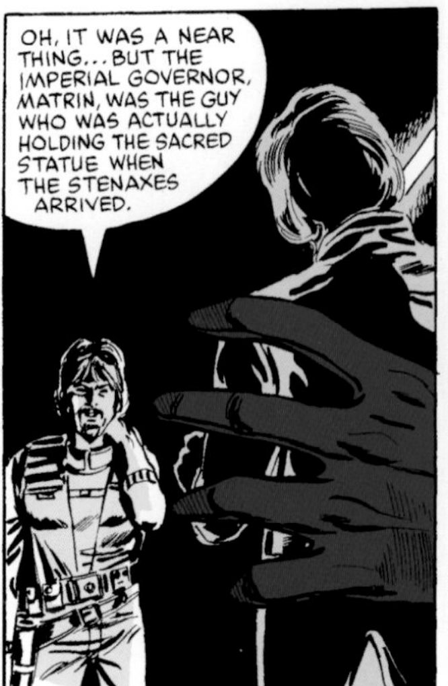
OH, IT WAS A NEAR THING... BUT THE IMPERIAL GOVERNOR, MATRIN, WAS THE GUY WHO WAS ACTUALLY HOLDING THE SACRED STATUE WHEN THE STENAXES ARRIVED.

SO, I JUST YELLED, "HE'S PROFANING VOL! GET HIM!!" END OF STORY.
ALSO, THE END OF MATRIN.

WHAT ABOUT YOUR OTHER FRIENDS -- DANI, AND THAT LITTLE GREEN GUY WITH THE SNOUT AND THE ANTENNAE?
CHIHDO?
THEY'RE AROUND HERE SOMEWHERE.

HUNH?
GOT YOU!!

DANI... HEY, WATCH OUT FOR MY SABER... IF YOU TOUCH THE BLADE, IT'LL...
OH, LUKE, I'M SO GLAD TO SEE YOU! I WAITED AND WAITED FOR YOU TO COME BACK...

DON'T WORRY, LOVER-BOY. I'LL LIGHT A LANTERN SO YOU CAN TURN THE BLADE OFF.
I SEE DANI HASN'T CHANGED MUCH.

ZELTRONS NEVER DO. NOT ONCE YOU'VE AROUSED THEIR... INTEREST.
I'VE BEEN SO LONELY SINCE YOU LEFT... ALONE HERE, WITH ALL THOSE STENAXES, AND ALIENS...
AND ME.
AND RIK...
PRACTICALLY ALONE...

SO WHERE'S CHIHDO?
WHO CARES?
HE WAS HERE A FEW HOURS AGO...

I HAVE A NASTY HUNCH ABOUT WHERE HE MIGHT BE... BUT I'M HOPING I'M WRONG.
DANI AND I COULD USE A LITTLE HELP...
WOULD YOU LET BYGONES BE BYGONES AND JOIN US?
I- I GUESS SO...
AREN'T YOU AFRAID THE STENAXES MIGHT TAKE SIDES IN THIS?
NAH... THEY SHOW A BIG DISINTEREST IN THEIR OWN CIVIC AFFAIRS.
NO ONE'S EVER FIGURED OUT HOW TO MOTIVATE 'EM, EXCEPT BY MESSING WITH VOL...
AND AFTER WHAT HAPPENED TO OL' MATRIN, NO ONE WOULD DARE.
STAY CLOSE.
VERY CLOSE!
BY THE WAY, IS HAN WITH YOU, OR ARE YOU HERE ALONE?
UH... THAT'S KIND OF DIFFICULT TO EXPLAIN...

LUKE! OVER HERE!

WHAT HAPPENED TO YOU?
THAT'S KIND OF DIFFICULT TO EXPLAIN.

THEN FORGET IT.
LUKE, I'VE DONE IT! I'VE FOUND HIM!
BOSSK?

FORGET BOSSK! I'VE FOUND *HAN!*
WHERE? HOW?!

COME ON. I'LL SHOW YOU.

OKAY, NOW KEEP YOUR VOICE DOWN. HE'S RIGHT AROUND THIS CORNER...

THERE.
WHAT IS THAT?!

IT'S A METAL STORAGE BLOCK.
YOU KNOW THAT WHEN THEY CAUGHT HAN, THEY HAD HIM FROZEN IN CARBONITE

YOU TOLD ME... BUT I DIDN'T REALLY SEE IT... I DIDN'T KNOW... JUST HOW...
HAN'S THE BEST FRIEND ANY MAN COULD HAVE...
THE BEST PARTNER ANY WOOKIEE COULD HAVE...
AND WHEN THEY CAUGHT HIM... THEY FROZE HIM... TOOK HIM AWAY...
FROM CHEWBACCA ...AND PRINCESS LEIA...
HOW COULD ANYONE DO A THING LIKE THAT TO ANYONE?

LUKE, IT WILL BE ALL RIGHT.
WE'LL GET HAN BACK, AND FIND A WAY OF THAWING HIM OUT.

YOU BET WE WILL!
COME ON.

I'M GONNA USE THE COM-LINK TO CONTACT THE SHIP.

ARTOO-DETOO, CHEWBACCA, DO YOU READ ME? IT'S LUKE. LANDO AND I HAVE FOUND HAN!
HROWL
WE'LL CALL YOU BACK AS SOON AS WE'VE FREED HIM!

GGRRAH
BUH-WHEET
VOOP

THEY'RE TAKING HIM INTO THAT BIG BUILDING OVER THERE.

MUST BE FOR THE USE OF ALIENS ONLY --THERE'S JUST ONE STORY.

HOW ARE WE GOING TO GET PAST THOSE GUARDS AT THE DOOR?

LEAVE THAT TO ME. THIS SITUATION CALLS FOR STRATEGY . . . FOR SUBTLETY.
OH, NO!

HI, THERE! IS THIS WHERE ALL THE BEST BOUNTY HUNTERS CONGREGATE?
WHAT'S IT TO YOU, WISE GUY?
WELL, YOU SEE, I'M LANDO CALRISSIAN.

THERE'S QUITE A HANDSOME PRICE ON MY HEAD THIS EVENING, AND MY FRIEND AND I ARE A LITTLE SHORT OF CASH.
SO, WE TALKED IT OVER, AND WE'VE DECIDED TO TURN OURSELVES IN AND COLLECT.

FRIEND? WHAT FRIEND?

ME.

NICE WORK.
LET'S GO.

IN HERE.

LET'S MAKE SURE HAN'S ALL RIGHT AND THEN GET BACK TO THE SHIP, BEFORE...

OH, NO... NO...
IT'S HORRIBLE!

THAT'S NOT HAN!
IT'S CHIHDO!
AND YOU'RE SURROUNDED.
NEXT: FOOL'S BOUNTY

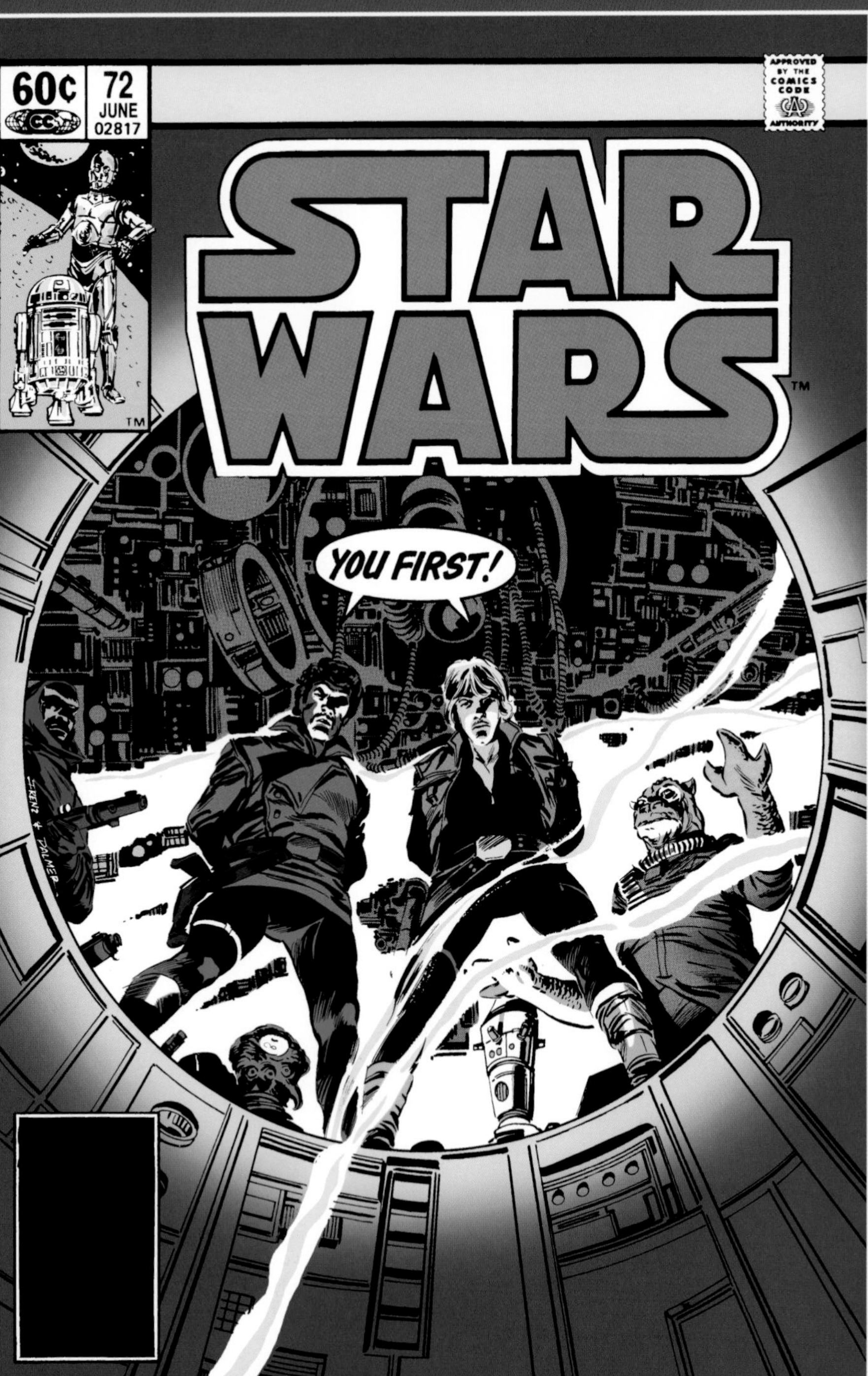
60¢
72
JUNE
02817
APPROVED BY THE COMICS CODE AUTHORITY
STAR WARS
YOU FIRST!

Long ago in a galaxy far, far away. . .there exists a state of cosmic *civil war*. A brave alliance of *underground freedom fighters* has challenged the tyranny and oppression of the awesome *Galactic Empire*. This is their story!

Lucasfilm PRESENTS: STAR WARS™ THE GREATEST SPACE FANTASY OF ALL!

JO DUFFY *SCRIPT AND PLOT* RON FRENZ *BREAKDOWNS* TOM PALMER *FINISHES* JOE ROSEN *LETTERS* STAN G. *COLORS* LOUISE JONES *EDITOR* JIM SHOOTER *EDITOR-IN-CHIEF*

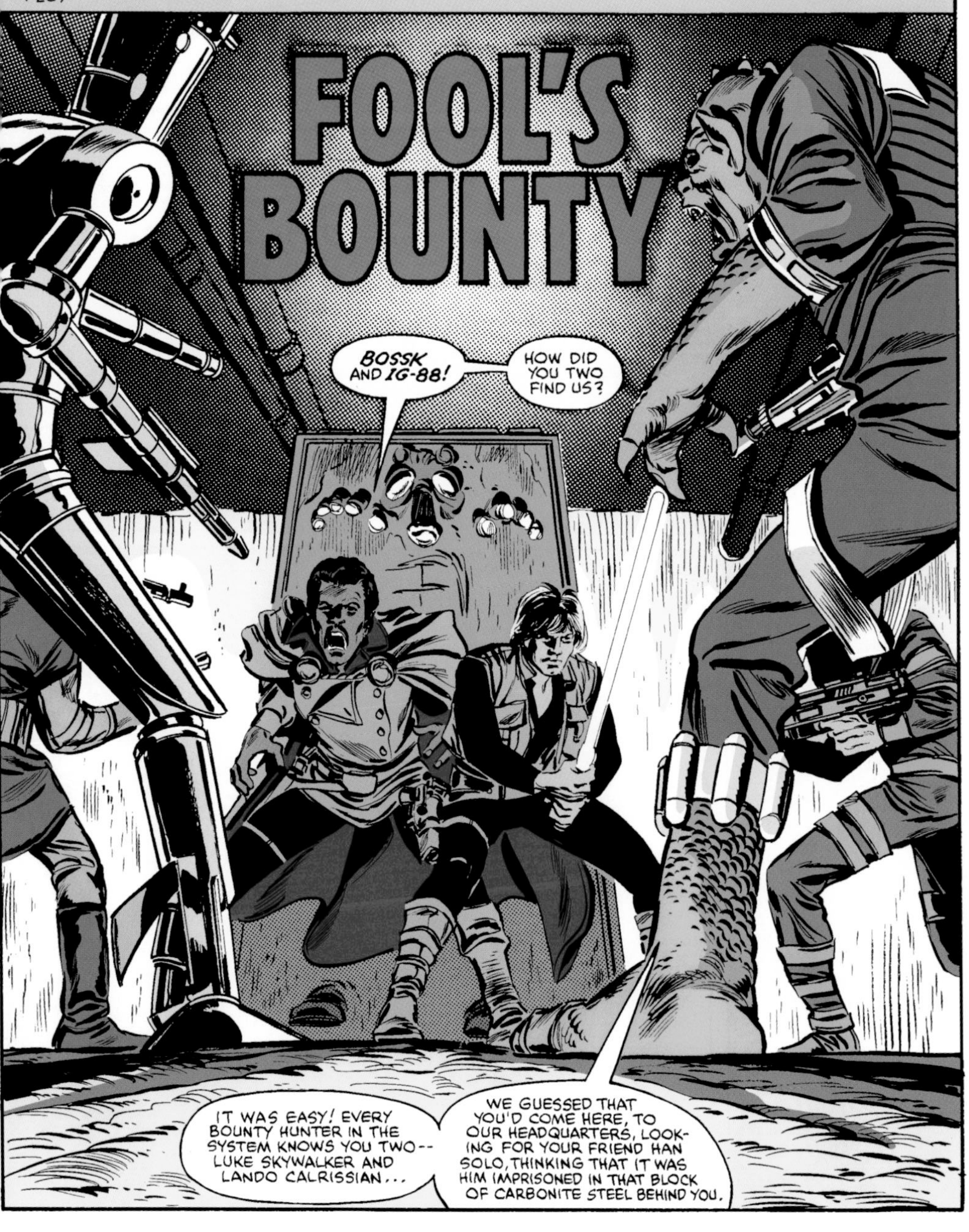

I'VE NEVER EVEN MET THAT CREATURE IN THE CARBONITE! WHO IS HE?
IT DOESN'T MATTER. ALL THAT MATTERS NOW IS THAT YOU'RE GOING TO END UP THE SAME WAY HE HAS.

OH, NO THEY'RE NOT!!
WHO ARE YOU?!
RIK DUEL AND DANI!

LUCKY FOR YOU WE REALIZED WE'D LOST YOU AND FOLLOWED YOUR TRAIL HERE, LUKE!
I'D SAY WE ARRIVED JUST IN TIME!

DON'T WORRY! WE'RE HERE NOW TO PROTECT YOU!
NO ONE'S GOING TO HARM ANYONE AS CUTE AS YOU WHILE I HAVE ANYTHING TO SAY ABOUT IT!

LUKE, I APPRECIATE THE LAST MINUTE RESCUE, BUT JUST WHO ARE THESE PEOPLE?
FRIENDS OF CHIHDO-- THE GUY IN THE CARBONITE BLOCK!
IT'S HIM THEY'RE HERE TO RESCUE!

OH.

NOW I'VE-- HEY. WHAT ARE YOU...?

WHO TAUGHT YOU TO JUMP LIKE THAT?!
THE SAME PERSON WHO GAVE ME THIS!

A LIGHT-SABER! YOU'VE DESTROYED MY BLASTER!
VORP

HEY, WATCH IT, YOU GUYS!
THAT STRAY BLASTER FIRE CAN'T BE DOING OL' CHIHDO MUCH GOOD!

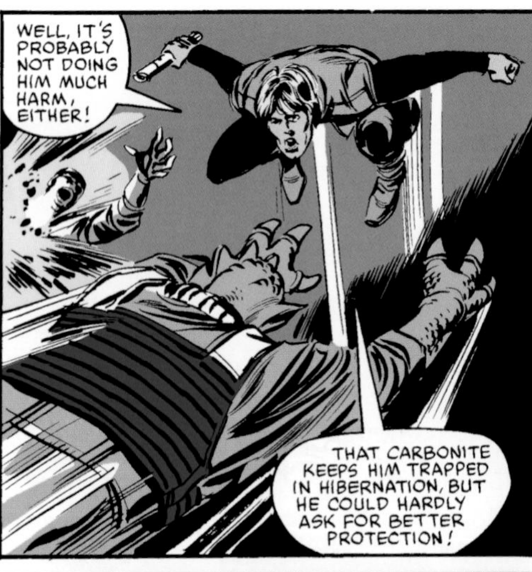
WELL, IT'S PROBABLY NOT DOING HIM MUCH HARM, EITHER!
THAT CARBONITE KEEPS HIM TRAPPED IN HIBERNATION, BUT HE COULD HARDLY ASK FOR BETTER PROTECTION!

BLAST YOU, HOLD--
--STILL!

WELL, THAT ABOUT TAKES CARE OF THESE BOUNTY HUNTERS. NOW WE CAN SEE TO TRANSPORTING YOUR FRIEND IN THE BLOCK OUT OF HERE!

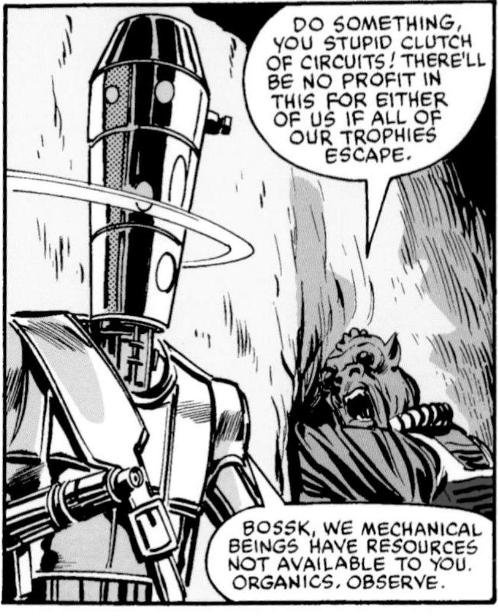
DO SOMETHING, YOU STUPID CLUTCH OF CIRCUITS! THERE'LL BE NO PROFIT IN THIS FOR EITHER OF US IF ALL OF OUR TROPHIES ESCAPE.
BOSSK, WE MECHANICAL BEINGS HAVE RESOURCES NOT AVAILABLE TO YOU, ORGANICS. OBSERVE.

EEEEEE
EEEEEE
EEEEEE
EEEEEE
EEEEEE
EEEE
E

EEEEEEEEEEEEEEEEE
EEEEEEEEEEEEEEEEE
WHAT IS IT?
IT HURTS!
TURN IT OFF!

WE HEARD THE DROID'S SIGNAL.
WHAT DO YOU WANT?
THEM.
GET THEM FOR US.
UH-OH. THAT ALARM CALLED UP THE REINFORCEMENTS.
WE'D BETTER GET OUT OF HERE!

URK
SOUNDS GOOD TO ME!

RIK, I-- AAIIEEK!
GRAB HER!
I'VE GOT HER!

GET HIM!
PILE ON!
DON'T LET HIM GET AWAY!

CLIK
CLIK
UHHH... MY NAME IS DANI. WHAT'S YOURS?
CLIK
CLIK
CLIK
CLIK

A FEW TWISTS AND TURNS DOWN THESE ALLEYS AND THOSE SCUMSUCKERS WILL NEVER BE ABLE TO FIND US. WE CAN HEAD BACK TO MY PLACE AND REGROUP.
DID EVERY-ONE MAKE IT AWAY OKAY?
LANDO?

LANDO... DANI?
DANI?!
RIK, THEY DIDN'T MAKE IT.
HUNH?

WE HAVE TO GO BACK FOR THEM.
LUKE, DON'T BE STUPID. YOU AND I WERE LUCKY ONCE, BUT I DOUBT WE'D BE LUCKY TWICE.
GO BACK THERE NOW AND IT'S A SURE THING YOU'LL END UP FROZEN IN A BLOCK OF CARBONITE.

TAKE YOUR HANDS OFF ME. I'M NOT GOING TO WASTE TIME THINKING ABOUT MY OWN SAFETY.
NOT IF IT MEANS SACRIFICING TWO OF OUR FRIENDS.

THREE OF OUR FRIENDS. WE LEFT CHIHDO BACK THERE, TOO.
HAD YOU FORGOTTEN?
OR DON'T YOU CARE?

I--!

WE ARE GOING TO COME BACK FOR THEM, AREN'T WE?
OF COURSE WE ARE. AS SOON AS WE COME UP WITH A PLAN.
SOMETHING GOOD AND SNEAKY. LEAVE STUFF LIKE THAT TO ME.
IT'S MY SPECIALTY.

HEY, RIK, YOU'VE BEEN HERE ON STENOS FOR A WHILE... COULD YOU TELL ME SOMETHING?
SURE.
WELL... THE STENAXES AREN'T EXACTLY THE MOST TOLERANT CREATURES I'VE EVER MET... DOESN'T IT BOTHER THEM AT ALL THAT THE EMPIRE'S BOUNTY HUNTERS ARE OPERATING HERE IN THEIR CAPITAL?

KID, LAST TIME I TRIED TO PUT SOMETHING OVER ON THOSE BIG WINGED UGLIES, I CAUGHT ONTO JUST HOW MEAN AND NASTY THEY ARE... BUT I FIGURED OUT SOMETHING ELSE, TOO...
NO ONE'S EVER REALLY FIGURED OUT WHAT MOTIVATES 'EM.
THEY DON'T CARE WHAT WE OFFWORLDERS DO TO EACH OTHER, SO LONG AS WE DON'T MESS WITH THEM OR THEIR CULTURE.

AND WHAT MOTIVATES YOU? I SEEM TO REMEMBER YOU, DANI AND CHIHDO POSING AS BOTH REBELS AND IMPERIALS, AND THEN DOUBLE-CROSSING EVERYBODY TO MAKE A PROFIT.
THIS TIME YOU SEEM TO BE SINCERE ABOUT HELPING THE REBELLION. WHY THE CHANGE OF HEART?
WHAT HAPPENED TO CHIHDO--AND SOLO--IS PART OF IT.
THE REST IS SIMPLE ECONOMICS.
WHEN EVERYBODY IS GOVERNED BY A BIG MONOLITHIC POWER STRUCTURE, THE FREE ENTERPRISE SYSTEM HAS TO BREAK DOWN.

YOU CHEAT SOMEBODY, AND WIND UP DEAD, OR ENSLAVED, OR TRAPPED IN CARBONITE, 'CAUSE YOUR VICTIM'S GOT FRIENDS IN HIGH PLACES.
THIS GALAXY WON'T BE A SAFE PLACE FOR CON MEN TO OPERATE IN UNTIL WE WIPE OUT THAT KIND OF ABUSE.

HMMM...

WAIT, I'VE GOT TO USE THE COM-LINK TO CONTACT THE SHIP. LANDO AND I LEFT CHEWBACCA AND ONE OF THE DROIDS THERE...

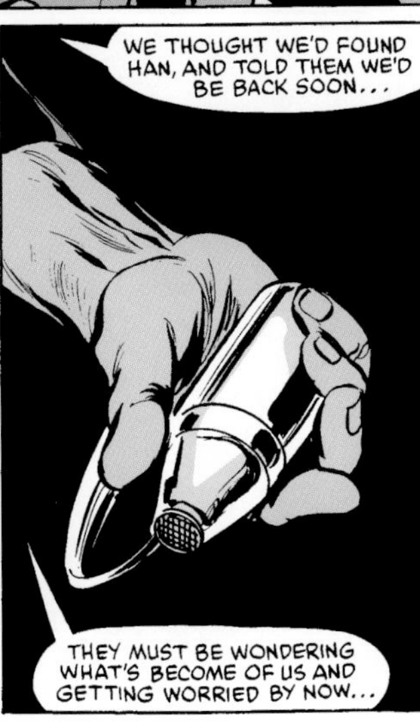
WE THOUGHT WE'D FOUND HAN, AND TOLD THEM WE'D BE BACK SOON...
THEY MUST BE WONDERING WHAT'S BECOME OF US AND GETTING WORRIED BY NOW...

THIS IS LUKE SKYWALKER CALLING THE *MILLENNIUM FALCON.* CHEWBACCA...? ARTOO-DETOO, DO YOU READ ME?
CHEWIE... ARTOO? ARE YOU THERE?

I GUESS THEY DON'T HEAR ME... THEY MUST HAVE STEPPED OUT OF THE SHIP, OR SOMETHING.
GRONK
BA-BEEP

HHHHIIISSSS

HHHHRRRR
BOOP

GRUMPH
BIP-BOOP

PUH-
WHEET!

HHHISSS
GGGRRRR

HHHRRRR!!

GRONK!

BEEP
BIP-BIP
BLURP
HHSSS

OOOH, LANDO... LANDO, I'M SO FRIGHTENED! WHAT'S GOING TO HAPPEN TO US?
NOTHING GOOD, I'M AFRAID.
AT LEAST I'M NOT FACING IT ALONE... I HAVE YOU HERE...

A MAN-- A BIG, STRONG MAN...
...TO TAKE CARE OF ME AND PROTECT ME.

REALLY?
I'M GLAD YOU FEEL THAT WAY...
THAT IS... I'M GLAD YOU KNOW YOU CAN RELY ON ME... TO BE OF SOME COMFORT TO YOU...

BESIDES, LOOK ON THE BRIGHT SIDE. OUR SITUATION MAY NOT BE AS BAD AS WE THINK IT IS.
AFTER ALL, I AM A MAN OF MEANS ...AND THE WHOLE POINT OF BEING A BOUNTY HUNTER IS TO BUY AND SELL PEOPLE FOR A PROFIT...

SO, ALL I HAVE TO DO IS MAKE IT MORE LUCRATIVE FOR OUR GUARD HERE TO FREE US THAN TO SELL US...
...AND I'M SURE HE'LL MAKE THE SENSIBLE CHOICE.

HE'LL DO NO SUCH THING!
HUNH?

DREBBLE!
THAT'S RIGHT, CALRISSIAN--THE MAN WHO'S BUYING YOU. THE RICHEST OFFWORLDER ON THIS MISERABLE HEAP OF SAND. THE MAN WHO'LL PAY DOUBLE ANY BRIBE YOU OFFER THE GUARD...
...FOR YOU, AND FOR ANYONE FOOLISH ENOUGH TO CALL YOU HIS FRIEND.

I'LL BE WAITING RIGHT HERE WHILE THEY PACKAGE YOU FOR TRANSPORT BACK TO MY PLANET--
--WHERE WE CAN DISCUSS, UNINTERRUPTED, THE LITTLE MATTER OF HOW YOU CHEATED ME LAST TIME WE MET.

WHAT A SWEET FELLOW!
MOVE IT ALONG, YOU TWO.

THIS IS IT--WE'RE DOOMED!
WE'RE GOING TO DIE! WE'RE REALLY GOING TO DIE! I'M SO FRIGHTENED.

OH, PLEASE!
OH, HELP ME, PLEASE! I DON'T WANT TO DIE!
I'LL DO ANYTHING YOU SAY!

ANYTHING!

GET AWAY FROM ME! I'VE HEARD ABOUT YOU ZELTRONS...
...AND I DON'T WANT TO GO ROLLING WITH ANY RED-SKINNED FREAK!

THEN WE'LL JUST HAVE TO DANCE INSTEAD!

NICE MOVE, YOU ALMOST TOOK HIS HEAD OFF WITH THAT KICK.

YEAH, TOO BAD HE'S WEARING SUCH A STURDY HELMET.

I'LL JUST GET HIS GUN, AND WE CAN BE ON OUR--!
STOP, CHEAT!!

OH, NO!
GET THEM!

STUN THEM, SHOOT THEM IN THE LEGS, DO WHATEVER IT TAKES--
--BUT DON'T LET THEM GET AWAY!!

RUN!!
ON SECOND THOUGHT, LET'S FORGET THE GUN.

GRUPH
WHAT IS ALL THAT COMMOTION INSIDE?

SOUNDS LIKE TROUBLE WITH THE NEW PRISONERS.
NEW PRISONERS?
YEAH...THE BOSSES CAUGHT SOME GUYS, WHO'RE WORTH A FORTUNE IN REWARD MONEY THEMSELVES, TRYIN'A FREE ONE OF THE OTHER CAPTIVES...

THEY MAY HAVE SOME TROUBLE GETTIN' 'EM ALL LOCKED UP, BUT I CAN GUARANTEE YOU THIS, PAL--
--THERE'S GONNA BE A LOT OF PEOPLE LEAVIN' THIS DUSTBALL A LOT COLDER'N WHEN THEY ARRIVED.

rrrrrrrrrr

ARE YOU SURE THIS IS THE BEST WAY IN?
KEEP YOUR VOICE DOWN, LUKE.

WE DON'T WANT THE WHOLE PLANET TO KNOW WE'RE UP HERE.
IT DOESN'T REALLY MATTER, DOES IT? THE NATIVES CAN SEE EVERY MOVE WE MAKE.

LIKE I TOLD YOU BEFORE, THE STENAXES DON'T CARE. IT DOESN'T MATTER WHAT THEY SEE OR HEAR, SO LONG AS IT DOESN'T CONCERN THEM DIRECTLY.

NOW, COME ON, HELP ME GET THESE BARS OUT...

THEN WE CAN PUT *YOUR* SHARE OF THE PLAN INTO OPERATION.

SHREE

HHHIISSSS!

HHHHRROWR!

TUHWHEE!

BLEEP
HRONK

BIBBLE

HHHSS!
PING

THIS DOOR'S LOCKED!

WHERE TO NOW?
ANYWHERE OUR PURSUERS ***AREN'T!***
FROM THE SOUND OF THINGS, THEY'RE STILL TOO CLOSE FOR MY LIKING.

COME ON. WE CAN GET OUR BEARINGS AND CATCH OUR BREATH LATER.
THIS DOOR IS OPEN.

GOOD.

OH, LANDO...
OH, NO!
LET'S GET OUT OF HERE!
TOO LATE.
STEP RIGHT IN, MR. CALRISSIAN... AND THE LADY.
DON'T YOU THINK WE'VE BEEN CLEVER? ONCE WE REALIZED YOU WERE GOING TO BE TIRESOME, AND SPEND THE WHOLE NIGHT RUNNING AROUND LOOKING FOR AN EXIT...
WE DECIDED IT WOULD BE SIMPLER TO LET YOU FIND YOUR OWN WAY HERE.
START WITH HER.
TAKE YOUR HANDS OFF HER!
NO WAY.
COME ON, HONEY.
DREBBLE WANTS US TO MAKE SURE THE CARBONITE FREEZING SYSTEM IS WORKING OKAY BEFORE WE USE IT ON YOU.

THEN TELL HIM TO TEST IT ON HIMSELF!!
LUKE!

OH, GOOD!

OH, NO!

OH LUKE...

WHAT'S EVERYONE STANDING AROUND FOR?!
RIK! YOU WERE SUPPOSED TO BACK ME UP...

I'D HAVE BEEN HAPPY TO...
...EXCEPT THAT THESE GUYS DECIDED TO BACK ME UP!

GET IN THERE!

GET DOWN!!
WHAT THE HECK IS GOING ON HERE?!

SPEARS? BUT ONLY THE STENAXES USE--AAGH!
KEEP YOUR HEAD DOWN, DANI.
WOULD YOU GET OFF ME?!

BOSS! DO SOMETHING!

DON'T WORRY! WE WILL!
SELF PRESERVATION: A MOST SENSIBLE COURSE OF ACTION!

RROOARR!
SMASH

IT'S CHEWBACCA AND THE STENAXES!
YOU BET IT IS, KID! I SAW YOUR WOOKIEE PAL HIDING BEHIND THE DOOR JUST BEFORE THE GUARDS GOT THE DROP ON ME!

NO, PLEASE!!
LET US GO!!
A WOOKIEE? NO ONE SAID ANYTHING ABOUT US HAVING TO FIGHT A WOOKIEE!

NNNOOO

PLEASE!!!

FOOSH

NICE WORK, CHEWIE...

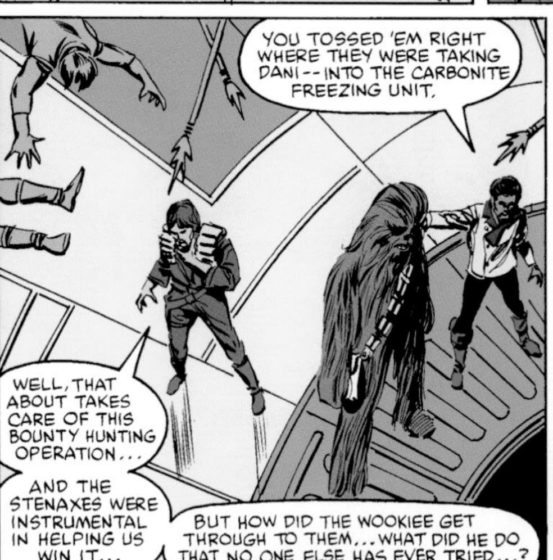
YOU TOSSED 'EM RIGHT WHERE THEY WERE TAKING DANI--INTO THE CARBONITE FREEZING UNIT.
WELL, THAT ABOUT TAKES CARE OF THIS BOUNTY HUNTING OPERATION...
AND THE STENAXES WERE INSTRUMENTAL IN HELPING US WIN IT...
BUT HOW DID THE WOOKIEE GET THROUGH TO THEM... WHAT DID HE DO THAT NO ONE ELSE HAS EVER TRIED...?

BAROOT BLEEP
PUHWHEET PUHWHEET PUHWHEET

CHEWIE... WE'RE SORRY WE DISAPPOINTED YOU... GETTING YOUR HOPES UP WHEN WE THOUGHT WE'D FOUND HAN...
WE KNOW WE'VE LET YOU DOWN... AND LET HAN DOWN...
BUT WE DID THE BEST WE COULD...

GGGRRRRRRRRR
CHEWIE...?
YOU... DO FORGIVE US... DON'T YOU?

H-HEYY--! TAKE IT EASY!
URK
OF COURSE... IT MUST BE BECAUSE THE WOOKIEE'S AN EXPERT AT THE ONE THING THE STENAXES REALLY RESPECT AND UNDERSTAND--
VIOLENCE!
IF I COULD JUST GET THEM WORKING FOR ME...
I'D GET THOSE CREEPS TO SHOW ME HOW TO UNFREEZE CHIHDO, AND...

WHAT A FIGHTING FORCE THEY'D MAKE...
THIS PLAN'S GOT POSSIBILITIES...

WHAT DO YOU THINK, LUKE? WILL RIK EVER GET THE STENAXES TO WORK FOR HIM?
I KIND OF DOUBT IT.

ME, TOO, BUT YOU CAN'T IMAGINE HOW HARD IT IS TO MAKE RIK ABANDON ONE OF HIS SCHEMES UNTIL IT ACTUALLY BLOWS UP ON HIM...
HUNH?!

SO I DECIDED NOW WOULD BE A GOOD TIME TO TAKE A VACATION... WITH YOU.
D-DANI...!
WHERE WILL WE GO FROM HERE?

NEXT: LAHSBANE!

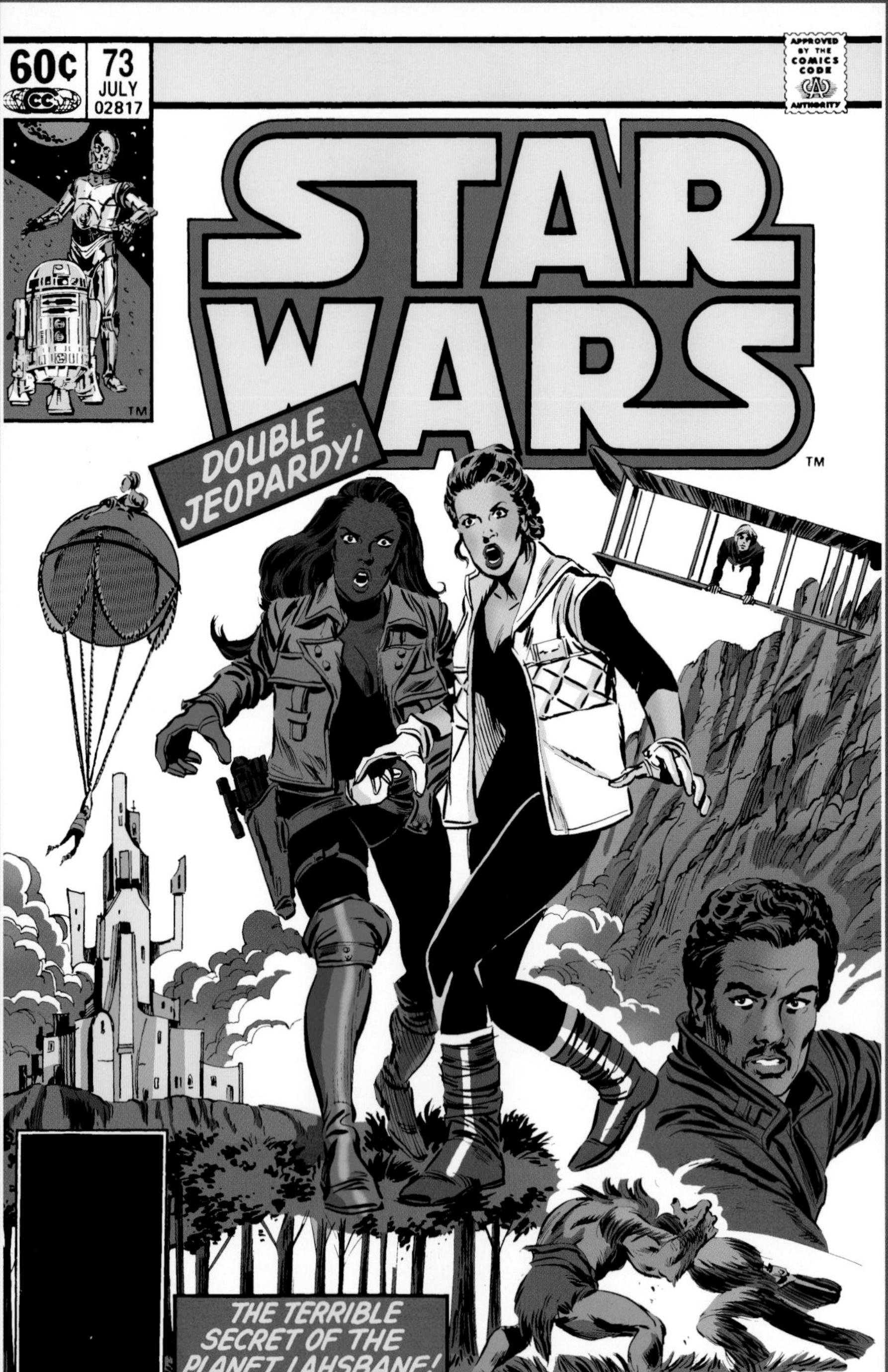

60¢ 73
JULY
02817

APPROVED BY THE COMICS CODE AUTHORITY

STAR WARS™

DOUBLE JEOPARDY!

THE TERRIBLE SECRET OF THE PLANET LAHSBANE!

FRENZ & PALMER

Long ago in a galaxy far, far away. . .there exists a state of cosmic *civil war*. A brave alliance of *underground freedom fighters* has challenged the tyranny and oppression of the awesome *Galactic Empire*. This is their story!

Lucasfilm PRESENTS: STAR WARS™ *THE GREATEST SPACE FANTASY OF ALL!*

JO DUFFY SCRIPT/PLOT · RON FRENZ BREAKDOWNS · TOM PALMER FINISHES · JOE ROSEN LETTERS · GLYNIS WEIN COLORS · LOUISE JONES EDITOR · JIM SHOOTER EDITOR-IN-CHIEF

WE DON'T SEEM TO BE GETTING THROUGH TO THESE *LAHSBEES* AT ALL, *SEE-THREEPIO*. ARE YOU SURE YOU'RE TRANSLATING EVERYTHING I SAY CORRECTLY?
ABSOLUTELY, MASTER *LUKE!* THEY QUITE READILY ADMIT THAT ONE OF THE MISSING REBEL PILOTS WE'RE SEARCHING FOR--*YOM ARGO*--CRASHLANDED AND DIED HERE ON LAHSBANE.
THE PROBLEM ISN'T WITH THEIR UNDERSTANDING, SIR. IT'S THEIR ATTITUDE.
LAHSBANE

WELL, THERE WAS A DROID IN ARGO'S SHIP WITH HIM... AND IT SHOULD HAVE BEEN KEEPING RECORDS OF SOME SORT-- PROBABLY TAPES OF THE MISSION THEY WERE ON...
KEEP YOUR MINDS ON ME! CONCENTRATE!

I AM CONCENTRATING.
NOT YOU, DANI...
THREEPIO, MAKE THEM STOP GIGGLING.

TEE-HEEE
HUHKS HUHKS
TEE-HEE
HUHKS HUHKS
TEE-HEE

I'M BEGINNING TO THINK YOU GUYS AREN'T TAKING THIS SERIOUSLY.

BUT IT'S GOING TO GET PRETTY SERIOUS FOR ALL OF US, IF THE FORCES OF THE GALACTIC EMPIRE COME HERE.
THE IMPERIALS PROBABLY ALREADY KNOW ABOUT ARGO'S CRASH, AND IF THEY SUSPECT THAT RECORDS OF HIS MISSION MIGHT EXIST--
--LIKE OUR LEADERS IN THE REBEL ALLIANCE DO-- THEY MAY COME LOOKING FOR THEM. AND THEY WON'T ASK NICELY. THEY'LL BRING STORM TROOPERS!

SIR, THEY SAY THAT THERE *ARE* RECORDS FROM THE DROID...
THE RECORDS ARE STORED, IN FACT, IN THAT CITY ON THE OTHER SIDE OF THE CANYON...
HOWEVER, THEY HAVE NO INTENTION OF RELINQUISHING THE TAPES TO US.
THAT'S JUST GREAT!

BUT WHY NOT?! DO THEY PLAN TO MAKE A DEAL WITH THE EMPIRE?
IT APPEARS THEY NEITHER KNOW NOR CARE WHAT THE TAPES ARE ACTUALLY FOR... BUT ONE OF THEIR MOST HONORED CITIZENS WAS HELPING LIEUTENANT ARGO...
...HE DIED IN THE CRASH, TOO, AND THEY ARE KEEPING THE TAPES AS A SORT OF MEMORIAL TO HIM!

SO THERE *ARE* TAPES... AND THEY'RE JUST IN THAT CITY OVER THERE! IT MIGHT AS WELL BE ON THE FAR SIDE OF THE GALAXY!

IF ONLY WE'D KNOWN, FOR SURE, BEFORE WE LANDED *HERE*... AND THE *MILLENNIUM FALCON* DEVELOPED ENGINE TROUBLE!

WE SHOULDN'T BE HERE AT ALL! WE SHOULD BE CONTINUING OUR SEARCH FOR *HAN SOLO*, TRYING TO FREE HIM FROM THE BOUNTY HUNTERS WHO CAUGHT HIM.
IT MADE SENSE WHEN OUR LEADERS DIVERTED US HERE... WE WERE CLOSEST TO LAHSBANE, AND ARGO'S MISSION WAS VITAL...
...AND THEY PUT OTHERS TO WORK LOOKING FOR HAN...
BUT WE'RE THE ONES WHO SHOULD BE DOING *IT*!
RESCUING HAN SOLO ISN'T THE REBELLION'S BUSINESS, IT'S OURS!
HAN IS OUR FRIEND!
HOW ARE THE REPAIRS TO THE SHIP GOING, LANDO?
SO FAR--THEY AREN'T, LEIA... BECAUSE WE CAN'T FIND ANYTHING WRONG WITH HER!

HOW THOROUGHLY HAVE YOU CHECKED?
NOT THOROUGHLY ENOUGH, OBVIOUSLY. RIGHT NOW, *CHEWBACCA* AND I ARE REALLY GETTING DOWN INTO THE WORKS OF THE ENGINE...
...AND *ARTOO-DETOO* IS GOING OVER ALL THE CIRCUITRY...

BUT, IF I DIDN'T KNOW BETTER, I'D SWEAR SHE JUST PICKED UP A BAD CASE OF BUGS...

WELL, THAT WOULDN'T SURPRISE ME. THE SHIP HAS BEEN PICKING UP ALL SORTS OF UNDE-SIRABLE LITTLE THINGS LATELY.
HI, YOU GUYS.
BOY, I HOPE THE REPAIRS ON THE SHIP HAVE BEEN GOING BETTER THAN MY ATTEMPTS AT DIPLOMACY...
!!!!!!!!!!!!!!!
HUHKS
HEE-HEE-HEE

PLEASE EXCUSE ME.
DANI, LANDO, LEAVE US ALONE, OKAY?
LEIA, WAIT!

WHY ARE YOU ACTING THAT WAY ABOUT DANI? YOU KNOW I HAVEN'T BEEN DOING ANYTHING TO ENCOURAGE HER...
AND YOU SAID YOURSELF, ZELTRONS CAN'T HELP BEING THE WAY THEY ARE...
NO, LUKE, I...

IS IT BECAUSE OF OUR FAILING TO FIND HAN...?
WE HAVEN'T GIVEN UP ON HIM!

I...

MASTER LUKE, SIR! PRINCESS LEIA! I'VE JUST BEEN CONTINUING MY CON-VERSATION WITH THE LAHSBEES' LEADERS! THEY REALLY ARE CREATURES WITH A FASCINATING LIFE CYCLE!
WHY, DID YOU KNOW THAT THEY--

COULD YOU TELL US ABOUT IT LATER, THREEPIO?...
WE'RE DISCUSSING SOMETHING IMPORTANT.

NEVER MIND, LUKE.

IT DOESN'T REALLY MATTER.
HEY, THREEPIO!
BA BOOP BA BOOP

IF YOU'RE SO ANXIOUS TO TALK TO SOMEONE, WHY DON'T YOU COME OVER HERE AND TRANSLATE WHAT ARTOO'S SAYING?
IT SOUNDS LIKE HE'S FOUND OUT WHAT'S WRONG WITH THE FALCON.

THAT IS CORRECT, SIR. ARTOO SAYS THAT THE AIR HERE IS FILLED WITH SOME KIND OF VERY FINE POLLEN...
...WHICH HAS CLOGGED ALL THE INTAKE VALVES
ARTOO SAYS THAT HE CAN PROBABLY HAVE THEM CLEAR BY TOMORROW IF HE WORKS ALL NIGHT.

SAY, THREEPIO, COULD YOU EXPLAIN SOMETHING TO ME? ALL THROUGH THAT CONVERSATION WITH THE LAHSBEES, I KEPT CATCHING ONE WORD-- *HUHKS*--OVER AND OVER.
WHAT DOES IT MEAN?
THAT'S WHAT I WAS TRYING TO--!

BARR
ROOOM

UH-OH, I WAS AFRAID OF THIS.
WE'VE GOT COMPANY.
IMPERIAL COMPANY.

IT WAS ONLY A MATTER OF TIME. THE IMPERIALS WERE IN HOT PURSUIT OF ARGO WHEN HE TOOK SHELTER HERE. ONCE WORD OF THAT CRASH GOT OUT...
THE REAL QUESTION IS--DOES THE EMPIRE KNOW THAT HIS DROID WAS KEEPING RECORDS.

PROBABLY NOT... THAT'S A RELATIVELY SMALL CONTINGENT OF TROOPS... AND ONLY ONE OFFICER...
THEY'RE PROBABLY HERE TO MAKE AN INQUIRY... SEE IF A BIGGER FORCE IS WARRANTED...

THEY'LL DECIDE IT'S WARRANTED FAST ENOUGH--
--IF THEY EVER SUSPECT WE'RE HERE!
RIGHT.
IT'S A GOOD THING WE PREPARED FOR TROUBLE AS SOON AS WE LANDED.

IT'LL JUST TAKE US A FEW MINUTES TO PASS THOSE CAMOUFLAGE MATS UP TO CHEWBACCA...
WHAT REALLY WORRIES ME IS--CAN WE TRUST YOUR LITTLE FRIENDS NOT TO TELL THAT OFFICER ABOUT US?

OF COURSE WE CAN... THEY ALL SEEM TO HATE ADVANCED TECHNOLOGY...
AND THEY'VE SEEN ENOUGH IN PREVIOUS ENCOUNTERS WITH THE EMPIRE TO BE CONVINCED THAT IMPERIAL ADVANCEMENT REPRESENTS ENFORCED TECHNOLOGICAL ADVANCEMENT.
(((((((((((((((((((((((((((((((

OH.
((((((((((((((((((((((((((((((((((((
HUHKS
YOU FELLOWS CAN FEEL FREE TO HELP US WITH THIS, IF YOU GET BORED JUST WATCHING.

HOW DO YOU LIKE THAT! THEY'VE FORGOTTEN ALL ABOUT ME!
AND ME!
WHAT LUKE AND LANDO ARE DOING IS IMPORTANT...
I'M NOT LETTING IT BOTHER ME THAT THEY'VE FORGOTTEN ME, TOO--

WELL, I'M GOING TO FIND SOME-PLACE TO HIDE. I DON'T WANT ANY IMPERIAL OFFICER FINDING ME HERE.
I HAVE THE DEATH SENTENCE IN SIX STAR SYSTEMS.
AS MANY AS THAT? I DIDN'T KNOW THERE WERE SO MANY PLACES WHERE WHAT YOU DO IS STILL ILLEGAL.

PLEASE... PRINCESS... MISTRESS DANI...
I WAS REFERRING TO STEALING! MY PARTNERS--RIK DUEL AND CHIHDO--AND I HAVE ROBBED AND CONNED SOME VERY IMPORTANT PEOPLE IN OUR DAY!
OH, REALLY?

YOU MADE A THOROUGH MESS OF THE ONLY CAPER I EVER SAW YOU WORK! YOUR "CLIENT" NEARLY KILLED YOU!
WE FOOLED YOU PRETTY WELL!
AND ANOTHER THING...
DANI...

I HEAR YOU TALKING ABOUT YOUR RANK AND THROWING YOUR TITLE AROUND... BUT I'VE NEVER SEEN YOU DO ANYTHING TO JUSTIFY HAVING THEM! WHY DON'T YOU PROVE YOUR WORTH TO THIS PRECIOUS REBELLION OF YOURS?
WHAT WOULD YOU SUGGEST?!
YOUR HIGHNESS...

HOW ABOUT GETTING THOSE TAPES BACK?
YOU'RE THE BIG-TIME THIEF! WHY DON'T YOU HELP ME?
TONIGHT?!
AS SOON AS IT'S DARK!
OH, DEAR! OH, DEAR...

LUKE SAID THAT THE LAHSBEES' DISLIKE OF COMPLICATED MACHINERY IS WHAT'S MADE THEM FRIENDLIER TOWARD THE REBELLION THAN THE EMPIRE...
BUT I WISH THEY WENT IN FOR SOMETHING A LITTLE MORE SOPHISTICATED-- AND SAFER--THAN THESE BALLOONS.
THAT'S JUST BECAUSE YOU'RE A NOVICE. I KNOW MY WAY AROUND PRIMITIVE FLIGHT EQUIPMENT PRETTY WELL.
IT'S A SIMPLE MATTER OF PICKING THE RIGHT BALLOON... TOO SMALL AND WE PLUMMET TO OUR DEATHS.
TOO BIG AND WE WAFT RIGHT STRAIGHT UPWARD... AND NEVER COME DOWN.
WHERE DID YOU LEARN SO MUCH ABOUT THIS?
RIK, CHIHDO AND I OPERATED ON STENOS FOR A LONG TIME... EVERYONE THERE HAS WINGS...
IF YOU DON'T WANT TO BE A TOTAL PARIAH AMONG PEOPLE WHO KNOW HOW TO FLY, YOU PICK UP A LOT OF AERODYNAMIC EXPERTISE VERY QUICKLY!
"...AND THEN THE NASTY METAL THING HIT A TREE AND KILLED HIM... AND THE TREE..."?! ARE YOU SURE THAT'S WHAT THEY SAID?!
SOMEONE'S COMING!
I'LL GO SEE WHO IT IS!
STAY RIGHT HERE.

IMPERIALS! AND THEY'RE HEADING RIGHT FOR LEIA!
AS REQUESTED, SIR, I AM DELIVERING A VERBATIM TRANSLATION OF THE CREATURES' WORDS...
MMMM...THE LITTLE VERMIN DO SEEM TO BE COOPERATING, TO THE BEST OF THEIR EXTREMELY LIMITED CAPABILITIES..
A PITY...BUT I SUPPOSE WE'LL NEVER KNOW FOR SURE WHETHER OR NOT ARGO HAD LEARNED ANYTHING OF VALUE...EXAMINING THE WRECK PROVED NOTHING...
WE'D BEST BE OFF AS SOON AS WE UNCLOG OUR SHIP'S INTAKES!

HELLO THERE!
EH?

I HOPE I'M NOT DISTURBING YOU!
A- A ZELTRON! YOU DIDN'T TELL ME YOU HAD ANY ZELTRONS ON THIS PLANET!
HEE-HEE-HEE-HEE

I LOVE THE FOREST IN THE MOONLIGHT! IT MAKES ME FEEL SO FULL OF...OF...
SIGH
SIGH

YOU'RE FULL OF IT, ALL RIGHT... JUST SO LONG AS YOU KEEP THEIR ATTENTION FOCUSSED ON YOU UNTIL THEY'RE SAFELY--!

YOU KNOW, I DID A TOUR OF DUTY ON ZELTROS ONCE... IN MY YOUNGER DAYS...
IT WAS QUITE AN EXPERIENCE...
YES, SIR.
QUITE AN EXPERIENCE!
YES, SIR!
HOW COME I NEVER GET ASSIGNED TO ANY OF THE FUN PLANETS?

IT'S OKAY! LEIA
THEY'RE GONE!
LEIA?
OVER HERE!

BUT--! LEIA, I TOLD YOU TO STAY RIGHT WHERE YOU WERE!
I'M GOING TO KILL YOU FOR THIS.

NEVER MIND... IF I CAN JUST GET A RUNNING START OFF THIS KNOLL...
HANG ON!

OOF
I'M TRYING TO!

THEY'RE DOING WHAT?!?

GREAT. JUST GREAT!
CAN I LOOK ON THIS AS A SAMPLE OF YOUR "AERODYNAMIC EXPERTISE"?

STOP COMPLAINING AND HELP ME STEER!
HOW AM I SUPPOSED TO DO THAT?!

NEVER MIND. THE WIND'S TAKING US RIGHT WHERE WE WANT TO GO!
I THINK EVERYTHING'S GOING TO BE FINE!

I WISH YOU HADN'T SAID THAT!

HOW COULD YOU LET THEM DO IT, THREEPIO? DIDN'T YOU REALIZE HOW DANGEROUS IT IS?
I TRIED TO TELL THEM, MASTER LUKE. I WARNED THEM ABOUT THE DANGER...
AND OF COURSE I TOLD THEM HOW DISPLEASED YOU WOULD BE, WHEN YOU REALIZED THAT THEY'D ENTERED THE FORBIDDEN CITY...

BUT SOMETIMES I DON'T THINK ANYONE LISTENS TO ME...
LUKE! JUST WHAT ARE YOU PLANNING TO DO WITH THAT?

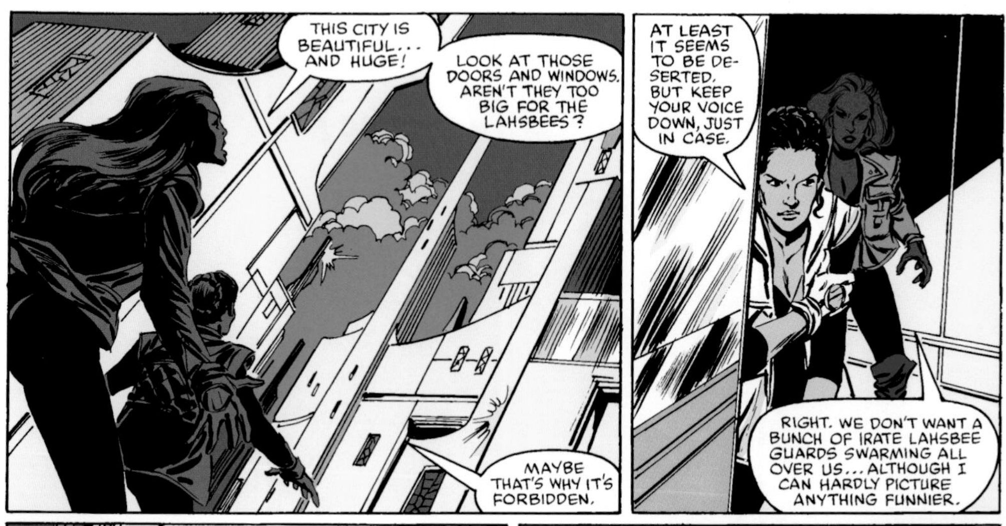
THIS CITY IS BEAUTIFUL... AND HUGE!
LOOK AT THOSE DOORS AND WINDOWS. AREN'T THEY TOO BIG FOR THE LAHSBEES?
MAYBE THAT'S WHY IT'S FORBIDDEN.
AT LEAST IT SEEMS TO BE DESERTED, BUT KEEP YOUR VOICE DOWN, JUST IN CASE.
RIGHT. WE DON'T WANT A BUNCH OF IRATE LAHSBEE GUARDS SWARMING ALL OVER US... ALTHOUGH I CAN HARDLY PICTURE ANYTHING FUNNIER.

NOW ALL WE HAVE TO DO IS FIGURE OUT WHERE THEY'D BE LIKELY TO HIDE THEIR VALUABLES.
THAT'S SIMPLE. JUST LOOK BEHIND THE FIRST LOCKED DOOR.

OKAY. IF IT'S LOCKED, HOW DO WE GET PAST IT?
LEAVE THAT TO ME. I'VE NEVER YET ENCOUNTERED THE LOCK I COULDN'T PICK.

WELL, DANI, FOR ONCE I HAVE TO ADMIT YOU WERE AS GOOD AS... YOUR ...WORD...
OOOOHH... LEIA--!

LUKE...YOU'RE NOT REALLY GOING TO TRY TO CROSS THE CANYON ON THAT GLIDER, ARE YOU?
WHY NOT? THE MECHANICS OF IT SEEM PRETTY SIMPLE... AND I'D TRUST THIS A LOT SOONER THAN I WOULD ONE OF THOSE BALLOONS.

BUT YOU DON'T KNOW WHAT YOU'RE DOING!
SO, I'LL DO THE BEST I CAN... AND TRUST THE FORCE FOR THE REST!

LUKE... I BELIEVE YOU WHEN YOU SAY YOU'RE IN TOUCH WITH THE FORCE... AND I'VE SEEN YOU DO SOME PRETTY AMAZING THINGS WITH IT...
BUT DO YOU REALLY PLAN TO TRUST YOUR LIFE TO A MYSTIC ENERGY FIELD YOU CAN'T EVEN SEE?
YUP.

WELL, GOOD LUCK!
EXCUSE ME, MASTER LANDO... MR. CALRISSIAN... SIR....
I REALLY THINK IT WOULD BE ADVISABLE IF WE WERE TO LEAVE AT ONCE...
MOST ADVISABLE!

SIR...?
THE FORCE...!
OH, WHY DOES NO ONE EVER LISTEN TO ME?

WHAM
I DID TRY TO WARN YOU, SIR.
BUT... BUT... ONLY A WOOKIEE COULD HAVE HIT ME AS HARD AS THAT!
WHY WOULD CHEWIE WANT TO HIT ME?
OH, IT WASN'T CHEWBACCA THAT HIT YOU, SIR. IT WAS THAT.
WHAT IS "THAT"?
THAT'S A HUHK, SIR.
OH, NO.

!!!!!!!!!!!!!!
GROOONK
THERE'S CHEWBACCA, SIR. HE AND ARTOO MUST HAVE FINISHED CLEANING THE POLLEN OUT OF THE SHIP.
AS YOU CAN SEE, A WOOKIEE IS CONSIDERABLY SMALLER THAN A HUHK.
B-BUT...WHERE DID THAT THING COME FROM?
THAT'S THE FORM ALL LAHSBEES TAKE ON... WHEN THEY REACH MATURITY. I TRIED TO EXPLAIN EARLIER, SIR...
ALL--? BUT WE HAVEN'T SEEN ANY LIKE THAT!
OF COURSE NOT, SIR. THE HUHKS ALL LIVE IN THE CITY, SIR. THAT'S WHY IT'S FORBIDDEN--FOR REASONS OF SAFETY.
THE LASHBEES TELL ME THAT ON THE RARE OCCASION A HUHK DOES WANDER BACK TO THE FOREST...
...WELL, SIR, THE CONSEQUENCES FOR ANY CREATURE IT MEETS ARE MOST UNPLEASANT.
COME ON, PULL ME UP! WE'VE GOT TO HELP CHEWIE...
WHILE THERE'S STILL TIME!

IT CERTAINLY DIDN'T TAKE YOU LONG TO FIND THOSE TAPES!
I COULD HAVE DONE IT EVEN FASTER IF YOU'D HELPED!
I TOLD YOU BEFORE, SOMEONE HAD TO ACT AS SENTRY!
AFTER ALL, WE DON'T KNOW FOR SURE THAT WE'RE REALLY...

AAARRRRH

LET'S GET OUT OF HERE!
HOW? THIS CORRIDOR'S A DEAD END.

WHY DON'T YOU SHOOT THEM? WHERE'S YOUR BLASTER?
I LEFT IT ON THE CLIFFSIDE! WHERE'S YOURS?
IT FELL INTO THE CANYON!

WHAT DO YOU PROPOSE TO DO, SIR?
I DON'T KNOW... BUT I HAVE TO THINK OF SOMETHING FAST!

grmmph

OR CHEWIE'S HAD IT!
WELL, IF I MIGHT MAKE A SUGGESTION, SIR...

HHHHRRR

?

I HOPE YOU DIDN'T MIND A LITTLE ASSIST FROM THE REAR, CHEWIE...?
ACTUALLY, CHEWBACCA, IT WAS MY IDEA...
KNOWING THE AVERSION THE NATIVES OF THIS WORLD HAVE TO TECHNOLOGY...
...I WAS FAIRLY CERTAIN THAT THEY'D HAVE NO DEFENSE AGAINST BEING STUNNED BY SIMPLE BLASTER FIRE.

PHU WHEET BEEP BEEP
ARTOO! WHAT'S UP?
HE SAYS, SIR, THAT THE MILLENNIUM FALCON IS NOW READY FOR TAKEOFF. UNFORTUNATELY, SO IS THE IMPERIAL SHIP.

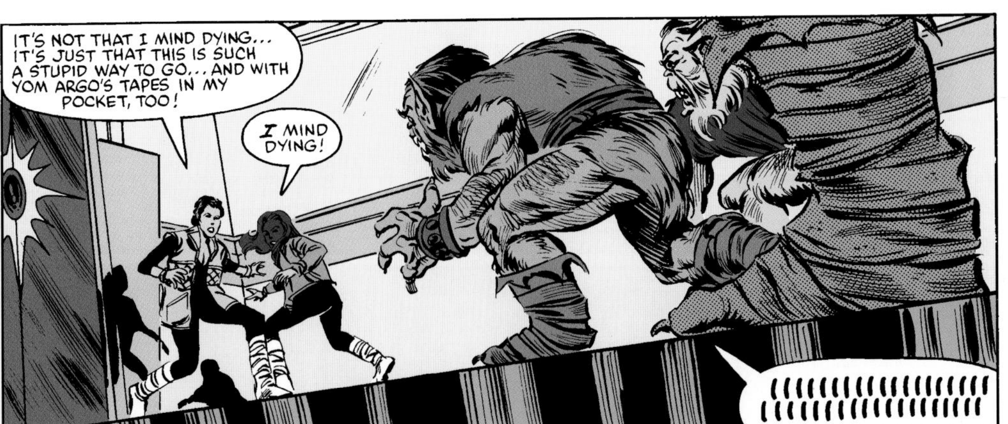
IT'S NOT THAT I MIND DYING... IT'S JUST THAT THIS IS SUCH A STUPID WAY TO GO... AND WITH YOM ARGO'S TAPES IN MY POCKET, TOO!
I MIND DYING!
IIIIIIIIIIIIIIIIIIII IIIIIIIIIIIIIIIIIIII

IIIIIIIIIIIIIIII IIIIIIIIIIIIIIII

?

HELLO.

NOW THAT WE'VE GOT THE TAPES, I GUESS OUR ONLY PROBLEM IS GOING TO BE MAKING IT OUT OF HERE WITHOUT ATTRACTING THE ATTENTION OF THOSE IMPERIALS...
THREEPIO, THE LAHSBEES STILL SEEM KIND OF UPSET. ARE YOU SURE THEY AREN'T ANGRY THAT WE BROKE INTO THEIR CITY...OR THAT WE DON'T INTEND TO GIVE THEM THE TAPES BACK?
QUITE CERTAIN, MASTER LUKE. AS A MATTER OF FACT IT'S THE TAPES THAT ARE UPSETTING THEM.
YOU SEE, THEY NEVER QUITE REALIZED THE PRECISE NATURE OF THOSE TAPES BEFORE...NOW THAT THEY KNOW WHAT THEY'RE FOR--
--AND THAT THEY HAVE SOMETHING TO DO WITH MACHINERY, THEY NO LONGER WANT ANYTHING TO DO WITH THEM.
BLEAH!
BBRZZZZT
HEY! THERE GOES THE IMPERIAL SHIP! THE LAHSBEES SAID THE IMPERIALS WERE STILL OUT ON PATROL.
SO WHO--?
LUKE, I SAW DANI SLIP AWAY, JUST A LITTLE WHILE AGO...BUT WHY WOULD SHE...?
I MADE QUITE A NICE HAUL IN THAT CITY, WHILE LEIA WASN'T LOOKING.
I WONDER IF RIK AND CHIHDO HAVE MISSED ME?
NEXT ISSUE • The ISKALON EFFECT!

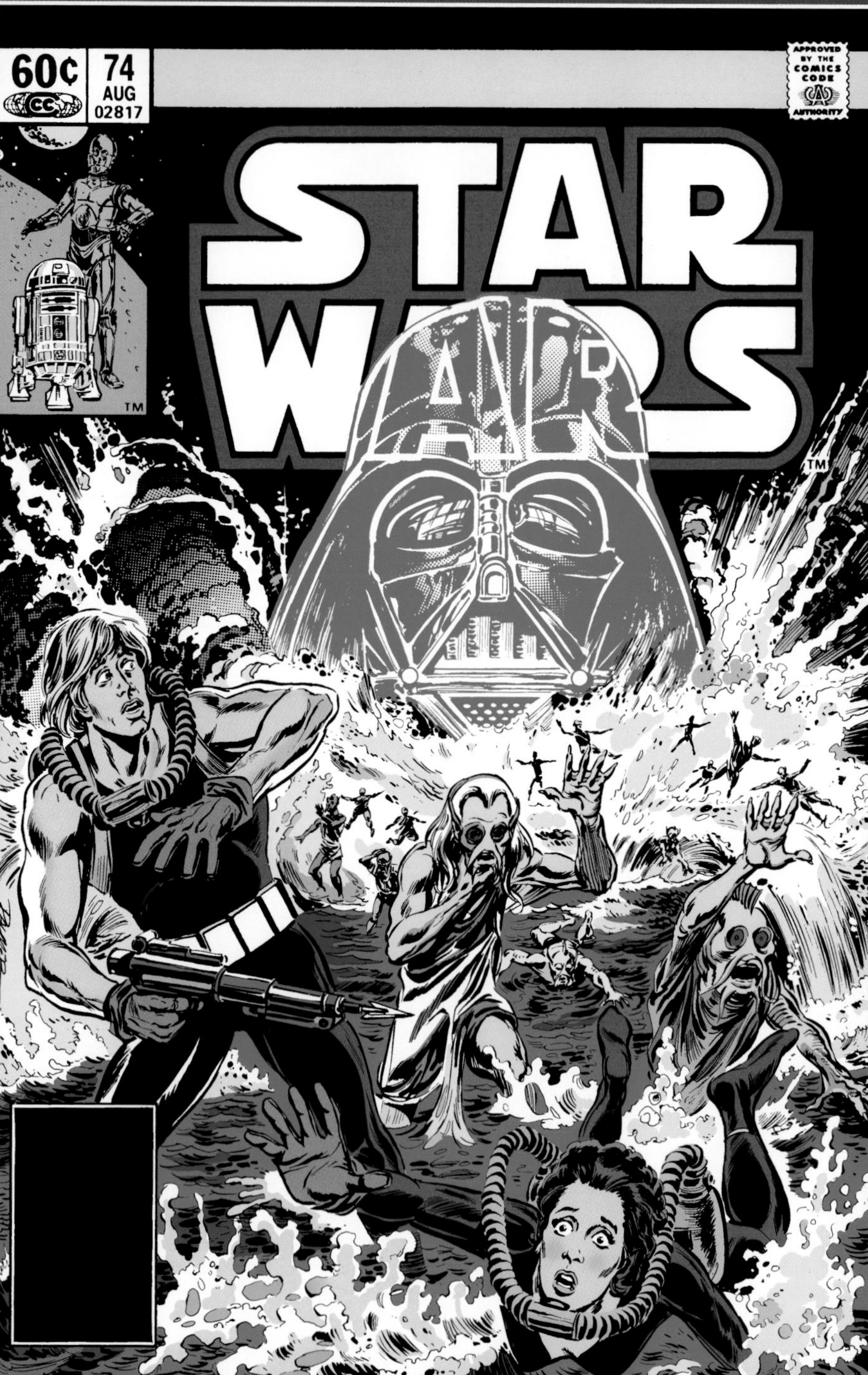

60¢
CC
74
AUG
02817
APPROVED BY THE COMICS CODE AUTHORITY
STAR WARS
TM
TM

Long ago in a galaxy far, far away. . .there exists a state of cosmic *civil war*. A brave alliance of *underground freedom fighters* has challenged the tyranny and oppression of the awesome *Galactic Empire*. This is their story!

Lucasfilm PRESENTS: STAR WARS™ THE GREATEST SPACE FANTASY OF ALL!

JO DUFFY SCRIPT AND PLOT | RON FRENZ LAYOUTS | TOM PALMER FINISHES | JOE ROSEN LETTERS | GLYNIS WEIN COLORS | LOUISE JONES EDITOR | JIM SHOOTER EDITOR-IN-CHIEF

THE ISKALON EFFECT
YOU KNOW, *LEIA*, I'M GLAD OUR ASSIGNMENT FOR *THE REBELLION* TOOK US HERE TO ISKALON.
IT'S BEAUTIFUL!

I MEAN, JUST LOOK AROUND US! IF NOT FOR THIS LANDING PLATFORM WE'RE ON, THERE WOULDN'T BE ANYTHING AT ALL ON THE SURFACE...
JUST OCEAN, AND SKY, AND THE SUN... AND THE OTHER PLANET GAMANDAR...

NOTHING ELSE IN ANY DIRECTION, AS FAR AS THE HUMAN EYE CAN SEE...
I SPENT MY WHOLE LIFE ON TATOOINE-- A DESERT PLANET-- I USED TO DREAM OF LEAVING IT, AND OF SEEING OTHER WORLDS...
BUT I NEVER EVEN IMAGINED THERE COULD BE PLACES LIKE THIS...

GRUMPH
SINCE I MET YOU AND HAN SOLO, AND JOINED THE REBEL ALLIANCE, I'VE TRAVELLED A LOT, AND I'VE GOTTEN USED TO THE IDEA THAT NOT ALL WORLDS ARE DESERTS...
BUT I'VE NEVER SEEN OCEANS LIKE THESE ANYWHERE.

I HAVE, LUKE...
MY HOMEWORLD HAD OCEANS... OH, ALDERAAN WAS SO... I CAN'T EVEN BEGIN TO DESCRIBE WHAT IT WAS LIKE...
UNTIL THE EMPIRE BUILT THE DEATH STAR... AND TESTED IT BY OBLITERATING ALDERAAN...

LEIA...

IF YOU ASK ME, ARTOO, THIS WHOLE PLANET IS NOTHING BUT A BIG DEATHTRAP FOR US DROIDS...
IT'S ALL RIGHT FOR ORGANIC BEINGS... THEY CAN ALWAYS SWIM, IF THEY KNOW HOW, BUT IF YOU OR I EVER STEPPED OFF THIS PLATFORM...
WE'D SINK RIGHT TO THE BOTTOM, AND THAT WOULD BE THE END OF US!

MY HOMEWORLD, MY FAMILY AND FRIENDS... HAN... THE EMPIRE HAS COST ME EVERYONE AND EVERYTHING I'VE EVER REALLY CARED ABOUT...
OH, WHY DO THEY HAVE TO TWIST AND DESTROY EVERYTHING THEY CAN'T CONTROL...?
BECAUSE THAT'S HOW TYRANNY WORKS. THAT'S WHAT WE'RE FIGHTING.

DON'T GIVE UP ON HAN... IT'S NOT THE EMPIRE WHO HAS HIM, IT'S BOUNTY HUNTERS...
AND WHEN OUR LEADERS DIVERTED US HERE, THEY PROMISED THEY'D ASSIGN OTHER PEOPLE TO CONTINUING THE SEARCH FOR HAN...
?
IT DIDN'T SOUND SO BAD, WHEN WE GOT THE MESSAGE... WE WERE THE CLOSEST ONES TO THIS STAR SYSTEM...
BUT THIS MISSION IS TAKING US FROM ONE WORLD TO ANOTHER, WITH NO END IN SIGHT. DO WE JUST FORGET HAN?
DO WE JUST FLY OFF AND FORGET ABOUT THE PEOPLE HERE? I THOUGHT WE JOINED THIS REBELLION BECAUSE WE CARED ABOUT HELPING EVERYONE... NOT JUST THE VICTIMS WE KNEW PERSONALLY, AND NOT JUST WHEN IT WAS CONVENIENT...

SPLOOSH

HELLO, THERE!

YOU LOOKED SO HOT AND MISERABLE... I WAS SURE IT MUST BE ALL THAT FUR OF YOURS...
SO I DECIDED TO HELP YOU COOL OFF! FEEL BETTER?

ROAR!!!
HUNH?
CHEWBACCA, NO!

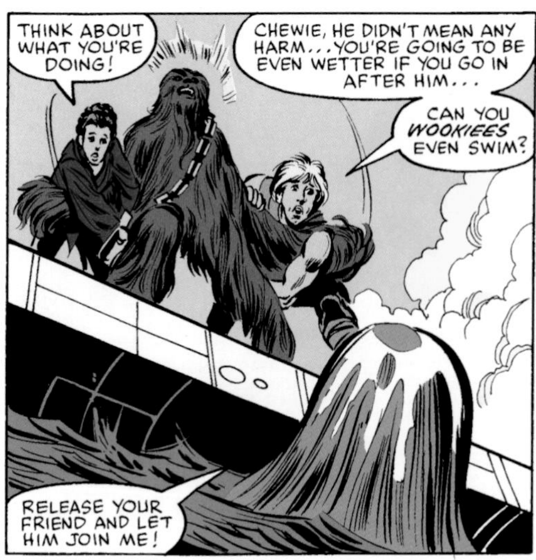
THINK ABOUT WHAT YOU'RE DOING!
CHEWIE, HE DIDN'T MEAN ANY HARM... YOU'RE GOING TO BE EVEN WETTER IF YOU GO IN AFTER HIM...
CAN YOU WOOKIEES EVEN SWIM?
RELEASE YOUR FRIEND AND LET HIM JOIN ME!

HE HAS THE RIGHT IDEA! NO ONE SHOULD BE DRY ON A LOVELY DAY LIKE THIS!
'BYE NOW!

WELL, FOR ONCE IT'S A BLESSING TO BE A DROID AND NOT BE NOTICED! I CAN'T THINK OF ANYTHING NASTIER THAN BEING WET--
--ON THIS OR ANY OTHER DAY!

HOWEVER, IT APPEARS THE PEOPLE HERE SPEAK GALACTIC STANDARD, AND THAT IS A POINT IN THIS WORLD'S FAVOR...
THE LIFE OF A TRANSLATOR DROID CAN BE A WEARY ONE, YOU'VE NO IDEA...

BREEP, DUP DUP
WHAT DO YOU MEAN YOU HAVE EVERY IDEA? WHAT DOES AN ASTRO DROID KNOW ABOUT...
BLOOP
WHAT DO YOU MEAN, I'VE WEARIED YOU?

ARTOO-DETOO, LIVES OFTEN DEPEND ON HOW WELL I TRANSLATE WHAT MASTER LUKE AND PRINCESS LEIA SAY TO PEOPLE...
WHAT DO YOU MEAN, WHAT LIVES? THE LIVES OF THE MISSING REBEL AGENTS WE'RE SEEKING, TO NAME JUST TWO...
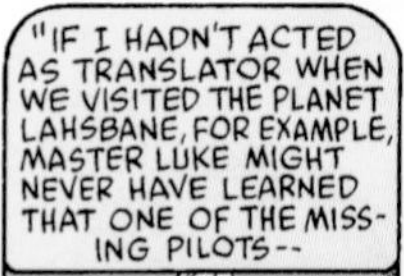
"IF I HADN'T ACTED AS TRANSLATOR WHEN WE VISITED THE PLANET LAHSBANE, FOR EXAMPLE, MASTER LUKE MIGHT NEVER HAVE LEARNED THAT ONE OF THE MISSING PILOTS--

"--YOM ARGO--AND HIS DROID HAD PERISHED IN A CRASH THERE.

"OR THAT TAY VANIS, THE OTHER REBEL, WAS LAST SEEN IN THIS SOLAR SYSTEM... A PLACE THAT'S FIRMLY UNDER IMPERIAL CONTROL."

RUMOR HAS IT THAT THAT AWFUL MAN, LORD DARTH VADER WAS IN THIS SYSTEM JUST RECENTLY, SUPERVISING IMPERIAL OPERATIONS ON ANOTHER WORLD...
IF HE WERE TO RETURN AND CATCH ANY RUMOR OF MASTER LUKE'S PRESENCE HERE...
I SHUDDER TO THINK...
PUH WHEET

IT'S ALL SET!
MASTER LANDO!

I FOUND SOMEONE WHO'S WILLING TO TELL US WHAT WE NEED TO KNOW... OR AT LEAST AS MUCH AS HE KNOWS...
THAT'S GREAT, LANDO!
I WAS JUST ARRANGING OUR WELCOME DOWN BELOW...
BELOW?

OF COURSE BELOW! IT'S THE ONLY PLACE THAT'S FIT TO LIVE!
AND ANY FRIENDS OF THE GREAT *LANDO CALRISSIAN* ARE WELCOME BELOW... EVEN IF THEY ARE CRABBY, STUFFY, FURRY OLD AIR-BREATHERS!
TACTFUL AS EVER, EH, *MONE?* NICE TO SEE YOU AGAIN!

WE'LL TALK AFTER MY FRIENDS AND I DESCEND.
LANDO, I KNOW YOU'VE BEEN HERE BEFORE... BUT ARE YOU SURE ABOUT THIS?

TRUST ME.
YOU, TOO, SEE-THREEPIO.
WHAT DID I TELL YOU, ARTOO? A DEATHTRAP!

IMPRESSIVE, ISN'T IT? THE ISKALONIANS HAVE BUILT THESE TANK/LANDING PORT COMBINATIONS IN SEVERAL PLACES ON THEIR PLANET FOR THE CONVENIENCE OF OFF-WORLDERS...
SOMETIMES THEY EVEN DON WATER TANKS AND JOIN THE AIR-BREATHERS INSIDE FOR BRIEF PERIODS... THEY'RE A VERY FRIENDLY PEOPLE...
THE PLACE WE'RE ENTERING NOW--PAVILLION--IS THE LARGEST ON THEIR PLANET, ABOUT THE SIZE OF A TOWN...

WE'RE SURROUNDED BY WATER ON ALL SIDES! ONLY THE TANKS ARE HOLDING IT BACK... ON TATOOINE, MOISTURE WAS SO SCARCE...
...WE HAD TO FARM FOR IT, JUST TO STAY ALIVE...

AND NOW... THIS!

THERE ARE COMMUNICATIONS TRANSCEIVERS SET INTO THE WALL EVERY COUPLE OF YARDS, SO YOU CAN COMMUNICATE NATURALLY WITH THE SWIMMERS ON THE OTHER SIDE OF THE BARRIER...

LANDO?
PRIMOR!
THESE ARE THE FRIENDS I WAS TELLING YOU ABOUT--CHEWBACCA, LUKE SKYWALKER, AND PRINCESS LEIA ORGANA.

PRIMOR IS... WELL, I GUESS YOU'D CALL HIM THE RULER HERE.
NONSENSE! YOU MAKE ME SOUND LIKE SOME KIND OF MONARCH!

BUT THEY ALL FOLLOW YOUR WILL...
THE SCHOOL FOLLOWS ITS OWN WILL...BUT SOMEONE MUST EVER BE THE FIRST TO SWIM...
MY PEOPLE FOLLOW ME BECAUSE I NEVER TRY TO TAKE THEM AGAINST THE DRIFT OF THEIR OWN INCLINATIONS...
HELLO AGAIN!
HELLO.
I GATHER YOU'VE ALREADY ENCOUNTERED MY GRACELESS OFFSPRING. THAT LOVELY CREATURE WITH HIM IS KENDLE, HIS WIFE...
LET'S KEEP MOVING AS WE TALK... IT'S NOT NATURAL, BEING SO STILL...
BUT... IS IT SAFE TO TALK HERE ...IT'S SO... PUBLIC!
WHAT IS "PUBLIC"?
YES, ARTOO, IT'S DRY NOW ...BUT IF THAT BARRIER EVER GAVE WAY!
HOW CAN WE DISCUSS THE REBELLION, WHEN SOMEONE MIGHT HEAR?
IT DOESN'T MATTER IF THEY HEAR. THEY WON'T LISTEN, UNLESS IT INTERESTS THEM.
LIKE LIFE IN A FISHBOWL!
WE KNOW WE ARE "FISH," LANDO ...BUT WHAT IS A BOWL?
UH...ACTUALLY ...IT'S WHAT WE'RE IN!

LOOK OUT THERE!
OH, NO!

WHAT?
OH, THEM!

SILLY LOOKING, AREN'T THEY? BUT THE EMPIRE HAS INSISTED ON ADAPTING THEIR STORM TROOPERS TO EVERY CLIMATE IN THIS SOLAR SYSTEM...
...EVER SINCE THEY REALIZED THAT SOMEONE--YOUR FRIENDS TAY VANIS AND YOM ARGO, TO BE PRECISE--HAD BEEN FOMENTING REBELLIOUS SENTIMENTS AMONG THE PEOPLE HERE ...NOT THAT IT TOOK MUCH FOMENTING...

TAKE YOUR HAND OFF YOUR BLASTER... HAVE YOU CONSIDERED WHAT WOULD HAPPEN TO THE BARRIER, IF YOU FIRED AT THOSE TROOPERS?
SORRY...
TELL THEM, PRIMOR!
TELL THEM WHAT WE'VE ENDURED!

TELL THEM ABOUT THE CITADEL ON GAMANDAR!
TELL THEM ABOUT MY BROTHER AND THE REST OF THE DIPLOMATS!
AND ABOUT TELFREY!

VANIS AND ARGO WERE FROM THIS SYSTEM--FROM THE PLANET TELFREY. THEY WERE HERE BECAUSE THEIR FAMILIES HAD TOLD THEM OF A GREAT DEAL OF RECENT IMPERIAL ACTIVITY IN THIS SECTOR...

TAY SUSPECTED THAT THE EMPIRE WAS WORKING ON SOME GREAT PLAN OR WEAPON NEARBY... AND HE MAY HAVE BEEN RIGHT...

BECAUSE THE EMPIRE ACTED WITH SPEED AND DREADFUL FORCE WHEN THEY REALIZED THERE WAS UNREST HERE...

OUR TWIN PLANET, GAMANDAR, WAS TOTALLY SUBJUGATED. THE EMPIRE HAS BUILT AN ENORMOUS FORTRESS THERE AND COMPLETELY ENSLAVED THE POPULACE.

WHAT HAPPENED TO TELFREY WAS THE WORST, THOUGH... THE TELFREYANS REBELLED OUTRIGHT ...THEY WERE A PROUD PEOPLE...

IT WILL BE MANY GENERATIONS BEFORE THE SURFACE OF TELFREY WILL AGAIN SUPPORT LIFE...

WHEN WORD REACHED US HERE OF WHAT HAD HAPPENED TO TELFREY, WE THOUGHT IT MIGHT BE PRUDENT TO SEND AMBASSADORS TO THE FORTRESS, TO TELL THE EMPIRE OF OUR DESIRE FOR PEACE...
OUR AMBASSADORS SENT BACK HORROR TALES OF MASS EXECUTIONS... THAT WAS THE LAST WE HEARD FROM THEM...
IT'S LIKE ALDERAAN ALL OVER AGAIN!
THE RULER OF THE FORTRESS SENT US WORD SOON AFTER... OUR AMBASSADORS' WATER TANKS HAD BEEN SMASHED, AND THEY WERE ALL LEFT TO SUFFOCATE.
THAT, HE TOLD US, WAS THE ONLY *PEACE* OUR PRESUMPTUOUS ATTEMPTS AT DIPLOMACY WOULD YIELD.
YOU MUST HELP US!
WE KNOW YOU CAN! ARGO CALLED YOU HEROES!
AND, BEFORE HE DISAPPEARED, TAY VANIS SPOKE YOUR NAMES OFTEN, WITH DEEP ADMIRATION!
NOW, NOW... REMEMBER, NOTHING GOOD IS EVER ACCOMPLISHED IN THOUGHTLESS HASTE... A BAD ACTION CAN ONLY CREATE A WORSE REACTION...
THOSE ARE THE PRINCIPLES WE LIVE BY HERE ON ISKALON... NO ONE IS CLOSER TO THE LAWS OF CAUSE AND EFFECT THAN WE...
DO NOT URGE OUR FRIENDS TO IGNORE THEM...

IF ONLY SOMEONE COULD TELL US WHERE TO LOOK FOR VANIS...
DOESN'T HIS DROID KNOW?
I'M SURE IT DID...BUT THE DROID WAS WITH ARGO WHEN HE CRASHED ON LAHSBANE. IT WAS COMPLETELY DESTROYED...

OH, I DIDN'T MEAN YOM'S DROID...
TAY HAD ONE OF HIS OWN.

HE STORED ALL THE INFORMATION HE'D GATHERED ABOUT THE EMPIRE'S SECRET PLANS IN HIS K3PX UNIT.
WHY DON'T YOU ASK K3 WHERE HE'S GONE?

WE WILL!
AS SOON AS YOU TELL US WHERE THE DROID IS!

OH...I DON'T KNOW...THE LAST TIME I SAW K3, HE WAS ACCOMPANYING TAY AND YOM ON A MISSION...
TO THE FORTRESS...
OH.
THAT'S WONDERFUL, KENDLE. THANKS FOR THE ADVICE.

BLIP
TYPICAL, ISN'T IT, ARTOO?
DEPEND ON YOUR DROID FOR EVERYTHING, AND THEN LEAVE HIM BEHIND LIKE SO MUCH LUGGAGE, IN SOME HIDEOUS PLACE!

THIS IS THE FIRST SOLID PIECE OF INFORMATION WE'VE GOTTEN SINCE ARGO'S TAPES LED US HERE. YOU KNOW WHAT IT MEANS, DON'T YOU?
UH-HUNH. SOMEONE HAS GOT TO GO TO GAMANDAR.

ZOOM
ZOOM
ZIP
ZIP
WHAT...? AFTER ALL WE'VE TOLD YOU OF THE ATROCITIES, TO OUR PEACEFUL DELEGATION...?
LANDO, MY FRIEND, PLEASE RECONSIDER...

THERE'S NOTHING TO RECONSIDER... AND IT WILL HAVE TO BE CHEWBACCA AND I WHO GO... THE OTHERS ARE TOO WELL KNOWN...
THEY MIGHT PASS UNNOTICED ON AN ORDINARY PLANET, BUT NOT A MAJOR IMPERIAL BASE...
GUESS I'VE HEARD ENOUGH...

SIR, IN THE INTERESTS OF THE REBELLION-- AND FOR THE SAKE OF OUR FELLOW DROID, K3PX--ARTOO-DEETOO AND I WOULD LIKE TO--!
IT'S OKAY, THREEPIO. YOU'RE BOTH COMING WITH US.
WE MAY NEED A TRANSLATOR... AND AN ASTRO-DROID.

AND I WILL GO WITH YOU ALSO! I KNOW GAMANDAR, AND YOU DO NOT.
MONE!

THIS CANNOT BE MY FOOLISH, PLEASURE-SEEKING OFFSPRING WHO SPEAKS! YOU HAVE ALWAYS BEEN THE LEAST POLITICAL OF CREATURES... THE LEAST CONCERNED WITH THE GOOD OF THE SCHOOL!
DON'T YOU SEE THAT THERE IS DANGER? REBELLION IS NOT SOME GAME THE FRY PLAY--!

FATHER, THIS IS NOT A QUESTION OF GAMES OR POLITICS. IT IS A MATTER OF FRIENDSHIP.
FOR VANIS'S SAKE-- AND FOR LANDO'S-- I WILL GO TO GAMANDAR WITH LANDO

FAIR WEATHER TO YOU, SON!
THANK YOU, FATHER... KENDLE, ARE YOU SURE YOU'LL BE ALL RIGHT WHILE WE ARE GONE?
I HAVE BUSINESS WITH SOME OF THE OTHER AIR-BREATHERS IN PAVILLION... I'LL CONDUCT THAT TODAY, WHILE YOU'RE AWAY...

THE SEA IS A LONELY PLACE FOR ME, WHEN YOU ARE NOT IN IT.

THEY HAVE NO CONCEPT OF PRIVACY... OR SHYNESS...
IT'S WONDERFUL...
OH... HAN... IF ONLY YOU WERE HERE WITH ME NOW.

GOODBYE, ISKALON! HELLO, IMPERIAL PROMOTION!

GOOD LUCK, LANDO, CHEWIE ... MONE...
FAREWELL...

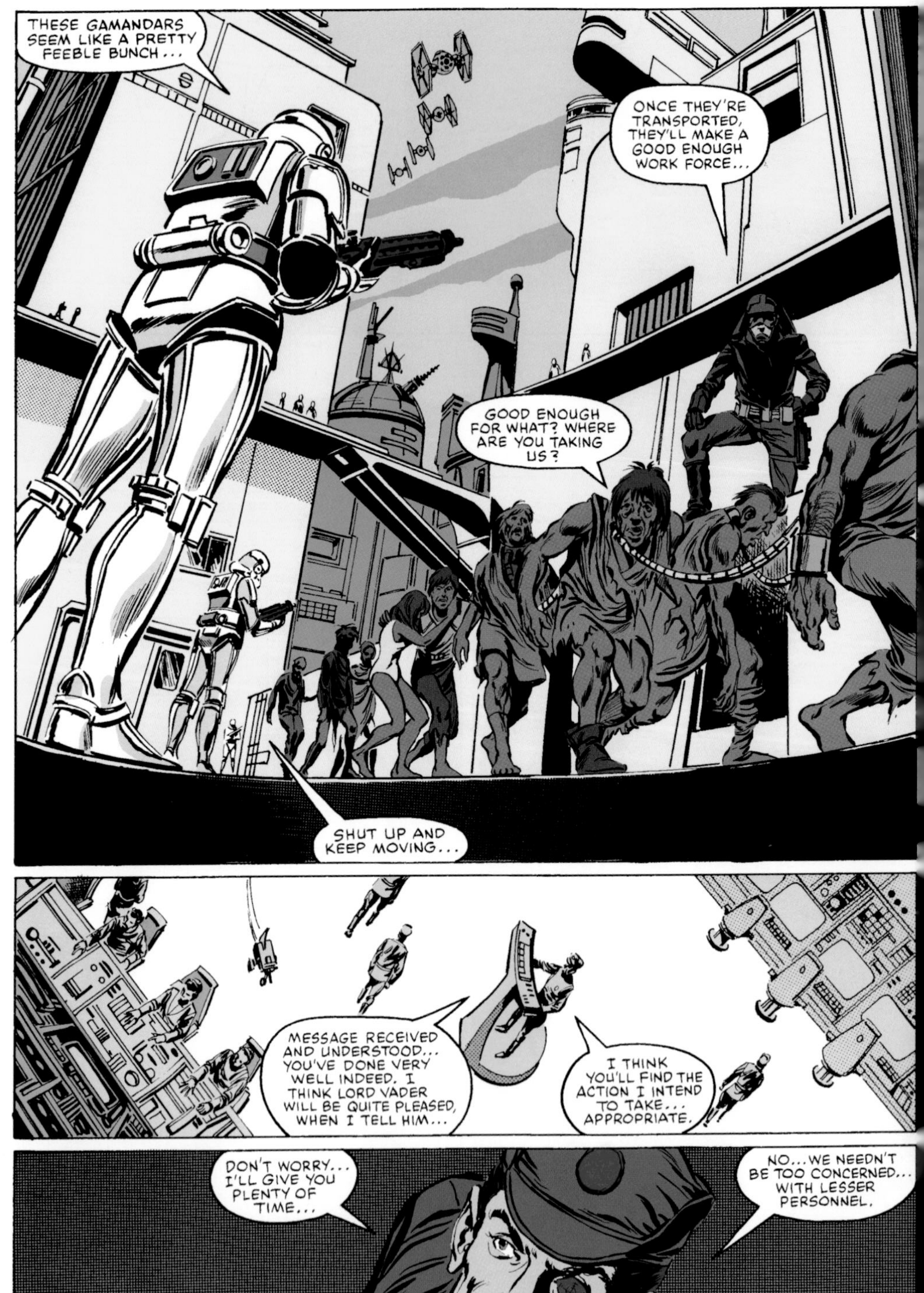
THESE GAMANDARS SEEM LIKE A PRETTY FEEBLE BUNCH...
ONCE THEY'RE TRANSPORTED, THEY'LL MAKE A GOOD ENOUGH WORK FORCE...
GOOD ENOUGH FOR WHAT? WHERE ARE YOU TAKING US?
SHUT UP AND KEEP MOVING...
MESSAGE RECEIVED AND UNDERSTOOD... YOU'VE DONE VERY WELL INDEED. I THINK LORD VADER WILL BE QUITE PLEASED, WHEN I TELL HIM...
I THINK YOU'LL FIND THE ACTION I INTEND TO TAKE... APPROPRIATE.
DON'T WORRY... I'LL GIVE YOU PLENTY OF TIME...
NO... WE NEEDN'T BE TOO CONCERNED... WITH LESSER PERSONNEL.

I DIDN'T THINK I'D FEEL SO... CUT OFF WHEN THEY ALL TOOK OFF IN THE MILLENNIUM FALCON AND LEFT US ALONE HERE...
I KNOW. IT'S HITTING ME THE SAME WAY, TOO... I'M JUST NOW REALIZING HOW UNTENABLE AN AIR-BREATHER'S LIFE COULD BE HERE, IF ANYTHING EVER REALLY WENT WRONG.

FAIR WEATHER TO YOU BOTH. I'LL SEE YOU LATER.
GOODBYE, KENDLE.
NOW WE'RE REALLY ALONE!

NOT ALONE, LEIA. WE HAVE EACH OTHER...

LEIA, I--!
HELLO, THERE!
PRIMOR...
MAY I HELP OR ENTERTAIN YOU UNTIL OUR FRIENDS RETURN?

I KNOW! COME, AND I WILL SHOW YOU OUR WORLD AS YOM ARGO AND TAY VANIS SAW IT.
YOU WILL BE FITTED FOR TANKS, AND YOU WILL LEARN TO LIVE IN OUR WORLD AS WE DO!

PRIMOR...WE APPRECIATE, THIS, REALLY... BUT DON'T YOU THINK WE'D BE BETTER OFF...?
I THINK *THIS* IS A GOOD IDEA... YOU ARE CONCERNED ABOUT SECRECY... AND NO OTHER AIR-BREATHER WILL EVER KNOW WHO YOU ARE WHILE YOU WEAR YOUR TANKS AND MASKS!
SO... FORGET EVERYTHING YOU THINK YOU KNOW ABOUT MOVEMENT! YOU ARE VERY SMALL FRY AGAIN, NEWLY HATCHED, AND I AM YOUR TEACHER...
DON'T BE NERVOUS, LUKE... WE'LL STAY CLOSE TO PAVILLION WHILE YOU ARE STILL LEARNING...

THANK YOU FOR BEING NICE TO HIM, PRIMOR... HIS WORLD WAS POOR IN WATER... THE SENSATION OF TOTAL IMMERSION IS STILL ALIEN TO HIM.
I SUSPECTED AS MUCH...

BUT I ALSO SUSPECT THAT, SOON, HE WILL SURPASS YOU.
AND IN TIME, BECOME LIKE ONE OF US... THE BOY LEARNS VERY QUICKLY.

AND NOW, THERE'S SOMETHING I MUST SHOW YOU BOTH...
NOT ALL PREDATORS ON ISKALON WEAR STORM TROOPERS' ARMOR...
AND NOT ALL OF THE INHABITANTS ARE FRIENDLY, OR INTELLIGENT.

WE CALL THESE WEAPONS STINGERS. THEY ARE MORE POWERFUL THAN YOUR BLASTERS, BUT UNDERWATER THE RANGE IS NOT GREAT.
IF ANYTHING IS TRYING TO EAT YOU, LET IT GET IN CLOSE, AND TRY TO MANEUVER SO THAT PAVILLION IS BEHIND YOU. THEN FIRE.

COME...YOU ARE DOING SO WELL, WE'LL TRY A SHORT EXPEDITION AWAY FROM THE SAFETY OF THE GLASS...
I APPRECIATE THIS, LANDO...I ALWAYS ENJOY A CHANCE TO TRAVEL UP INTO THE HEAVENS, AMONG THE STARS...
OH, COME OFF IT, MONE. YOU DIDN'T REALLY WANT TO LEAVE ISKALON, EVEN FOR A LITTLE WHILE. WHEN YOU'RE OUT OF THE OCEAN YOU'RE LIKE A FI--!
YOU REALLY FEEL OUT OF PLACE. I KNOW THIS IS A FAVOR, AND I APPRECIATE IT!
WE ARE ALL OF ONE BIOSPHERE, ALL INTERCONNECTED. HOW CAN I NOT DO THINGS FOR MY FRIENDS?
MMM...YOUR FATHER TELLS ME THAT AFTER VANIS LOST HIS FAMILY IN THE TELFREY HOLOCAUST, YOU AND KENDLE SPENT A LOT OF TIME WITH HIM, KEEPING HIM COMPANY...
HE WAS BEREAVED... IT MADE HIM HAPPY TO HAVE A NEW FAMILY TO GATHER AROUND HIM...
Y'KNOW...FOR AN IRRESPONSIBLE PLEASURE SEEKER, YOU SURE SPEND A LOT OF TIME LOOKING OUT FOR THE WELFARE OF OTHERS.
NATURALLY, LANDO. THAT IS MY PLEASURE.

I'VE BEEN LOOKING FORWARD TO THIS DAY FOR A LONG TIME...

EVER SINCE THAT IMBECILIC AMBASSADOR EXPLAINED HIS PEOPLE'S PHILOSOPHY, AND WARNED ME ABOUT THE ISKALON EFFECT...
I KNEW THAT THE TIME WOULD COME WHEN THEY'D GIVE ME A REASON TO SET IT OFF...

IT'S TIME, SIR. OUR AGENT HAS JUST SENT WORD THAT HE'S PASSED THE HALFWAY MARK BETWEEN GAMANDAR AND ISKALON.

GOOD.

COMMIT...

WELL, SO FAR MY LITTLE FRY HAVE ACQUITTED THEMSELVES VERY WELL FOR A FIRST DAY IN THE WATER...
NOW THAT YOU'RE A BIT MORE PROFICIENT, HOW WOULD YOU LIKE ME TO TAKE YOU TO SOME OF TAY VANIS'S FAVORITE GROTTOES?

THANK YOU, THAT SOUNDS--!
WAIT A MINUTE, PRIMOR... SOMETHING SEEMS WRONG IN ONE SECTION OF PAVILLION, BUT I CAN'T QUITE SEE... MAY I SWIM OVER AND--?

KENDLE!!
OH, NO!
WHAT'S HAPPENED TO HER TANKS!?
IT DOESN'T MATTER WHAT! SHE WILL SUFFOCATE ...HELP CANNOT POSSIBLY REACH HER IN--!
OH, YES IT CAN!

HRONK
I SEE IT, CHEWIE! I SEE IT!
BUT IF THE MILLENNIUM FALCON WEREN'T THE SHARPEST SHIP IN THIS WHOLE SYSTEM, I'D NEVER HAVE GOTTEN OUT OF ITS WAY IN TIME.

WHAT WAS IT, LANDO?
I DON'T KNOW... IT WAS MOVING TOO FAST FOR ME TO TELL...

WELL, IT'S BAD NEWS FOR SOMEONE, YOU CAN BE CERTAIN OF THAT!
BOOP

PLEASE HURRY!

SHE'S STILL ALIVE! WE'VE GOT TO CARRY HER BACK TO THE SURFACE FAST!

IF ONLY THERE WERE SOME MORE DIRECT WAY OF GETTING HER BACK INTO THE OCEAN!
KENDLE! KENDLE!

DON'T WORRY, PRIMOR! EVERYTHING'S GOING TO BE OKAY!

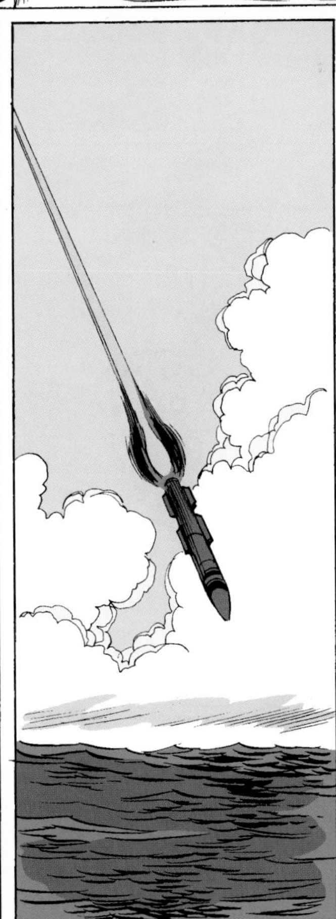

WHAT WAS THAT FLASH?
AN EXPLOSION ...A BIG ONE, MILES AWAY...
LUKE... WHY IS THE TANK VIBRATING?

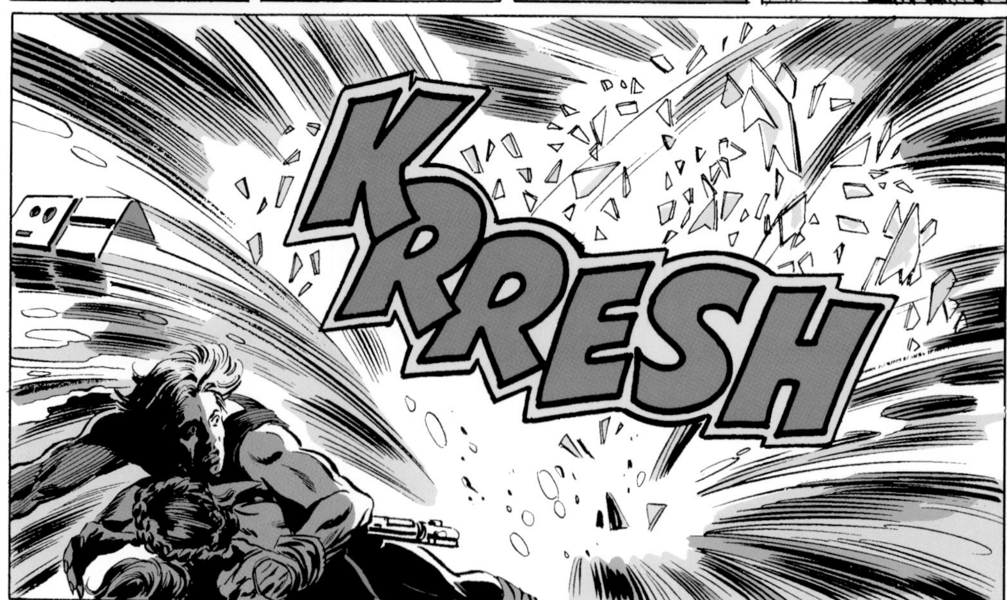

NEXT: The story we could only call:

TIDAL

60¢
75
SEPT
02817
APPROVED BY THE COMICS CODE AUTHORITY
STAR WARS
TM

Long ago in a galaxy far, far away. . .there exists a state of cosmic *civil war*. A brave alliance of *underground freedom fighters* has challenged the tyranny and oppression of the awesome *Galactic Empire*. This is their story!

Lucasfilm PRESENTS: STAR WARS™ THE GREATEST SPACE FANTASY OF ALL!

JO DUFFY *SCRIPT/PLOT* RON FRENZ *LAYOUTS* TOM PALMER *INKS* JOE ROSEN *LETTERS* GLYNIS WEIN *COLORS* LOUISE JONES *EDITOR* JIM SHOOTER *EDITOR-IN-CHIEF*

LEIA, KENDLE, LOOK OUT! SOME KIND OF EXPLOSION IS RUPTURING THE TANK!
LUKE, WHAT--?!?

TIDAL

AND THAT MEANS THE OCEAN IS GOING TO FLOOD THIS ENTIRE CITY --FAST!

BUT, WHAT CAUSED IT?!

LUKE, HELP ME!

LEIA!

LUKE!

HOLD ON, LEIA!

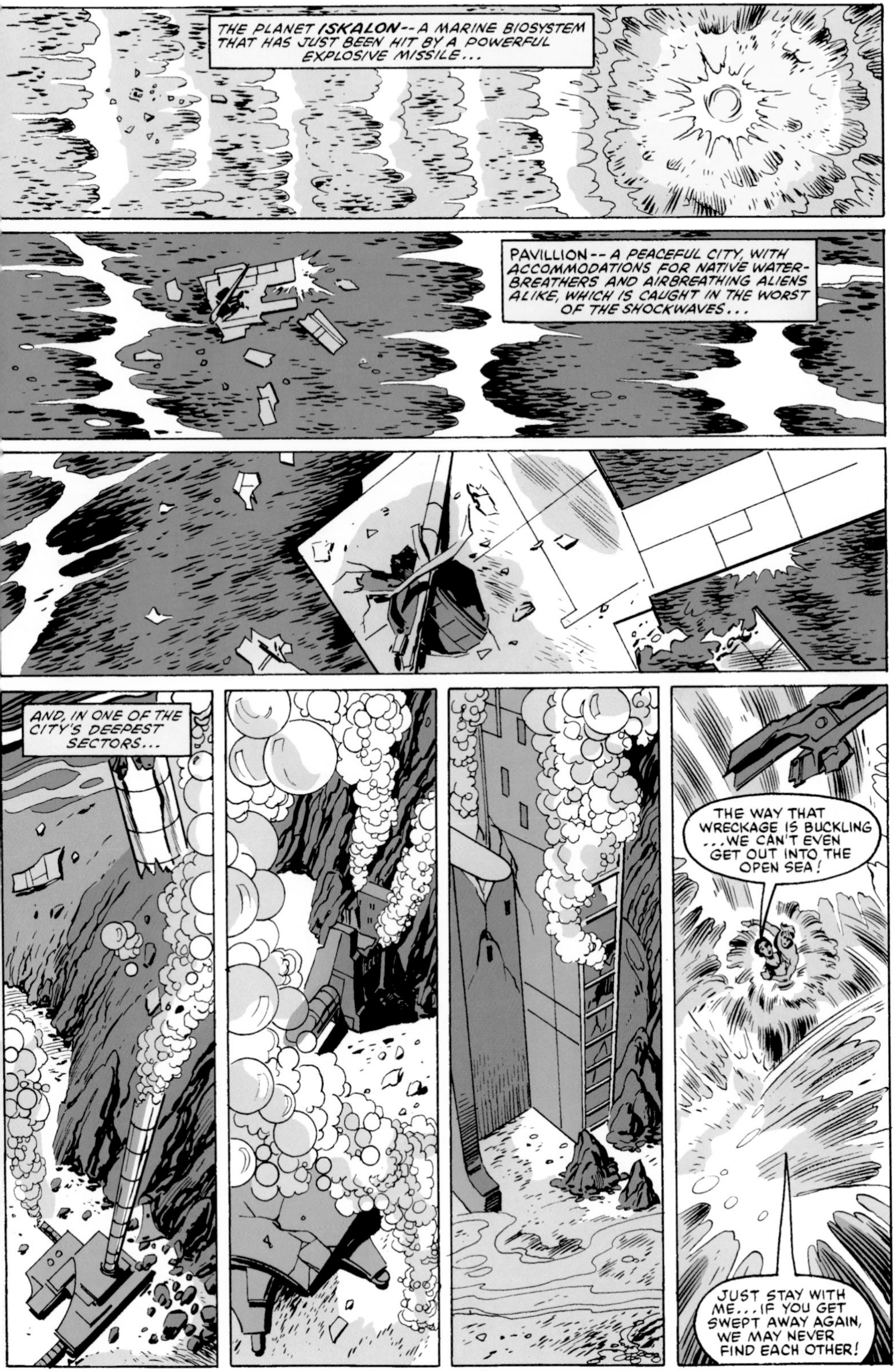

THE PLANET ISKALON--A MARINE BIOSYSTEM THAT HAS JUST BEEN HIT BY A POWERFUL EXPLOSIVE MISSILE...

PAVILLION--A PEACEFUL CITY, WITH ACCOMMODATIONS FOR NATIVE WATER-BREATHERS AND AIRBREATHING ALIENS ALIKE, WHICH IS CAUGHT IN THE WORST OF THE SHOCKWAVES...

AND, IN ONE OF THE CITY'S DEEPEST SECTORS...

THE WAY THAT WRECKAGE IS BUCKLING ...WE CAN'T EVEN GET OUT INTO THE OPEN SEA!
JUST STAY WITH ME...IF YOU GET SWEPT AWAY AGAIN, WE MAY NEVER FIND EACH OTHER!

KENDLE WAS UN-CONSCIOUS WHEN THE EXPLOSION HIT...
HER WATER TANKS HAD BEEN SMASHED SOME-HOW, AND THE AIR INSIDE PAVILLION WAS SUFFO-CATING... HER...
WHO KNOWS WHERE THE WATER MAY HAVE CARRIED HER?!
HEY! WAIT A MINUTE...

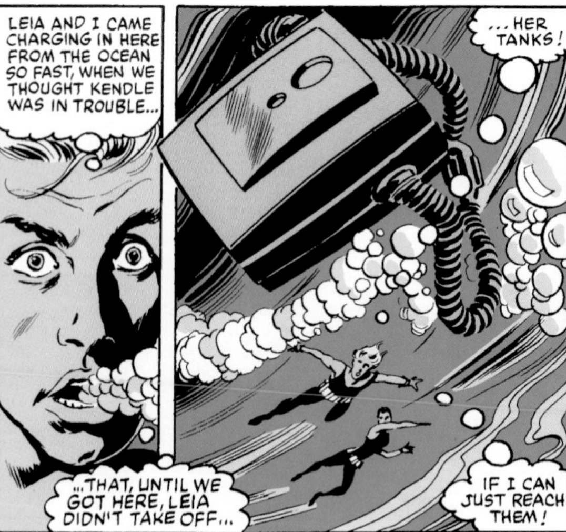
LEIA AND I CAME CHARGING IN HERE FROM THE OCEAN SO FAST, WHEN WE THOUGHT KENDLE WAS IN TROUBLE...
...THAT, UNTIL WE GOT HERE, LEIA DIDN'T TAKE OFF...
...HER TANKS!
IF I CAN JUST REACH THEM!

HERE... WE'RE GOING TO HAVE TO SHARE THE AIR, BUT YOU TAKE THE TANKS...
THEY'RE YOURS, ANYWAY. BESIDES YOU'LL NEED THE AIR MORE THAN I DO...
MY TRAINING AS A JEDI KNIGHT DIDN'T SPECIFICALLY COVER SITUATIONS LIKE THIS ONE...

BUT I'M PROBABLY A LOT BETTER AT THINGS LIKE BREATH CONTROL THAN A PRINCESS FROM ALDERAAN WOULD BE...
THAT'S IT, LEIA... TAKE IT NICE AND EASY ...YOU'RE DOING FINE...

JUST LET ME GUIDE YOU...
WE'RE GOING TO HAVE TO FIND OUR WAY THROUGH WHAT'S LEFT OF PAVILLION, AND OUT INTO THE OPEN SEA, IF WE EVER HOPE TO MAKE IT TO THE SURFACE.

IT'S KENDLE! THANK THE FORCE, THE BLAST OF WATER SEEMS TO HAVE REVIVED HER!
IT'S KENDLE! DID LUKE KNOW SHE WAS STILL HERE, OR WAS HE JUST...?
SHE SEEMS TO WANT US TO FOLLOW HER...
SHE...SHE SEEMS TO KNOW WHICH WAY WE SHOULD GO!
MAYBE WE'LL BE ALL RIGHT...
WHY'S SHE STOPPING?
KENDLE!
COME BACK! DON'T LEAVE US HERE ALL...
...ALONE.

ELSEWHERE...

ATTENTION, SHIP... PLEASE REPEAT IDENTIFICATION AND REQUEST...

THIS IS THE *MILLENNIUM FALCON*, UNDER THE COMMAND OF *MONE*, SON OF PRIMOR OF THE PAVILLION SECTOR OF ISKALON... REQUESTING PERMISSION TO LAND IN ONE OF THE FORTRESS'S DESIGNATED AREAS.

LANDO... THIS IS FAR WORSE THAN ANYTHING I EVER EXPECTED! THE WAY NATURE HAS BEEN WANTONLY DESTROYED...
REPLACED BY MACHINES, WHERE THERE HAS BEEN NO NEED...
THE OPPRESSION OF THE PEOPLE ...OF THE WORLD ITSELF...

THAT'S WHAT HAPPENS WHEN THE EMPIRE CONQUERS A CITY, OR A WORLD, OR A STAR SYSTEM, MONE...
STOPPING IT IS WHAT THIS REBELLION WE'RE FIGHTING IS ALL ABOUT...
BUT *PLEASE* LOWER YOUR VOICE WHEN YOU MAKE REMARKS LIKE THAT...OR OUR FLIGHT IS GOING TO BE CUT VERY SHORT...

LANDO, MY FRIEND, I AM SO SORRY... BUT IT MAKES ME FEEL SO HELPLESS... AND USELESS...
I OFFERED TO COME ALONG WITH YOU BECAUSE THIS WORLD, *GAMANDAR*, TWIN TO MY OWN ISKALON, IS FAMILIAR TO ME...

I THOUGHT I COULD HELP YOU BLEND IN, AND SHOW YOU THE LOCAL WAYS AND PLACES...
BUT *THIS* GAMANDAR I NO LONGER KNOW!

YOU CAME ALONG FOR FRIENDSHIP, AND THAT'S GOOD ENOUGH FOR CHEWBACCA AND ME...
AND YOU'VE ALREADY DONE US A VERY VITAL SERVICE, USING YOUR NAME AND YOUR FATHER'S INFLUENCE TO GET US IN HERE, BY PRETENDING YOU'D BOUGHT OUR SHIP.

THE *MILLENNIUM FALCON* IS TOO WELL KNOWN A SHIP FOR US TO HAVE TRIED TO SNEAK IT IN HERE UNDER A NEW NAME...
AND IF CHEWIE OR I HAD USED OUR OWN NAMES --OR MENTIONED THE REAL OWNER, *HAN SOLO*...
WE'D BE IN THE NEAREST BRIG BY NOW... OR STRAPPED TO AN IMPERIAL INTERROGATOR...
GRONK
...OF ANYONE WHO COMES TO HIM, CLAIMING TO BE FROM THE REBELLION.
HE KNOWS YOU, AND HE'LL TRUST YOU WHEN YOU SAY WE'RE ALL RIGHT.

BESIDES, THERE'S ANOTHER LITTLE JOB YOU MAY HAVE TO DO FOR US.
GRUPH
IF WE EVER FIND THE MISSING PILOT, *TAY VANIS*, WELL, THINGS BEING WHAT THEY ARE HERE IN CITADEL, HE'S BOUND TO BE VERY SUSPICIOUS...

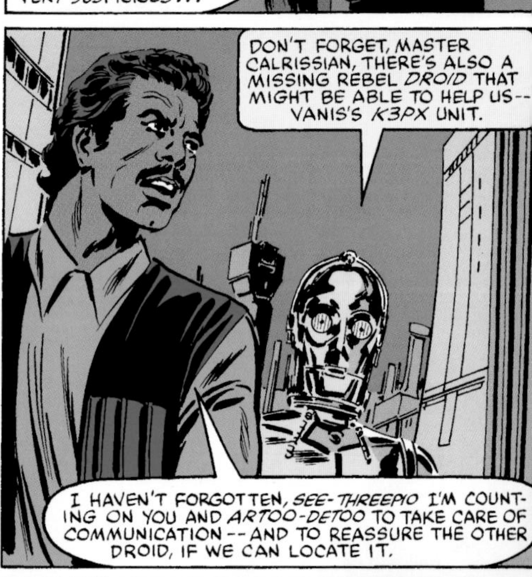
DON'T FORGET, MASTER CALRISSIAN, THERE'S ALSO A MISSING REBEL *DROID* THAT MIGHT BE ABLE TO HELP US-- VANIS'S *K3PX* UNIT.
I HAVEN'T FORGOTTEN, *SEE-THREEPIO* I'M COUNTING ON YOU AND *ARTOO-DETOO* TO TAKE CARE OF COMMUNICATION --AND TO REASSURE THE OTHER DROID, IF WE CAN LOCATE IT.

OH, YOU MUSTN'T COUNT ON ARTOO FOR THIS, SIR. I CAN DEAL WITH IT, IF IT ARISES...
I AM A PROTOCOL DROID, SIR, EQUIPPED TO HANDLE ANY AWKWARD SITUATION THAT MAY ARISE INVOLVING HUMANS, CYBORGS, MY FELLOW DROIDS...OR ANY COMBINATION THEREOF.

I AM ALSO FLUENT IN SIX MILLION FORMS OF COMMUNICATION.
ARTOO IS JUST AN ASTRODROID.

LET'S DUCK DOWN THIS CUL-DE-SAC FOR A MOMENT. NOW SEEMS LIKE AS GOOD A TIME AS ANY...

TO BRIGHTEN UP THIS ENSEMBLE OF MINE WITH A FEW ACCESSORIES.
I DO NOT UNDERSTAND HOW THIS CHANGE OF COSTUME IS GOING TO HELP US. IT DOESN'T DISGUISE YOU. YOU ARE STILL LANDO...

AH, BUT I'M GOING TO BE A MUCH SMARMIER, UNTRUSTWORTHY-LOOKING LANDO IN JUST A FEW MINUTES.
REMEMBER, WE'RE HERE AS WAR PROFITEERS, IMPERIAL COLLABORATORS HOPING TO MAKE A FEW CREDITS AT THE EXPENSE OF THE EMPIRE'S VICTIMS.

WHEN YOU OFFER A DESPICABLE COVER LIKE THAT, NO ONE IS LIKELY TO THINK IT'S A PRETENSE.
OUR STORY IS THAT WE'RE DEALING IN ANY READILY MARKETABLE GOODS--LIKE DROIDS...

AND I HAVE A PERSONAL VENDETTA AGAINST VANIS. HE OWES ME MONEY, OR AT LEAST THAT'S WHAT I'LL BE CLAIMING.
PEOPLE ARE ALWAYS SMALL ENOUGH TO HELP A STRANGER WITH A MOTIVE LIKE THAT, EVEN WHEN HE'S GOT NO PROOF.

BEEP?

BAROOT BIP!

GRONK!
CHEWIE, I'M SORRY IF YOU DON'T LIKE IT.
I KNOW IT'S NOT THE WAY YOU AND HAN WOULD HAVE HANDLED THINGS, BUT I'M NOT HAN.
THAT FULL-SPEED-AHEAD-AND-BASH-THEM-IN-THE-TEETH APPROACH MAY WORK VERY WELL FOR A WOOKIEE AND A CORELLIAN...
BUT IT'S NOT A TECHNIQUE THAT WORKS FOR ME.
MY PLANS INVOLVE SECRECY...SUBTLETY ...SUBTERFUGE...
LANDO, I'VE NEVER HEARD WORDS LIKE THAT BEFORE. THEY HAVE A GRAND SOUND! WHAT DO THEY MEAN...?
WELL, THEY'RE ...THEY'RE WHAT THEY SOUND LIKE ...THEY'RE... YOU KNOW...

SIR, IF I MIGHT SUGGEST...THE ISKALONIANS ALL LIVE TOGETHER, IN SCHOOLS, IN THE OPEN... PERHAPS HE DOESN'T KNOW...
GREAT. THEN HOW DO WE EXPLAIN?
BY TRANSLATING THE *CONCEPTS* INTO ISKALONIAN IMAGERY...

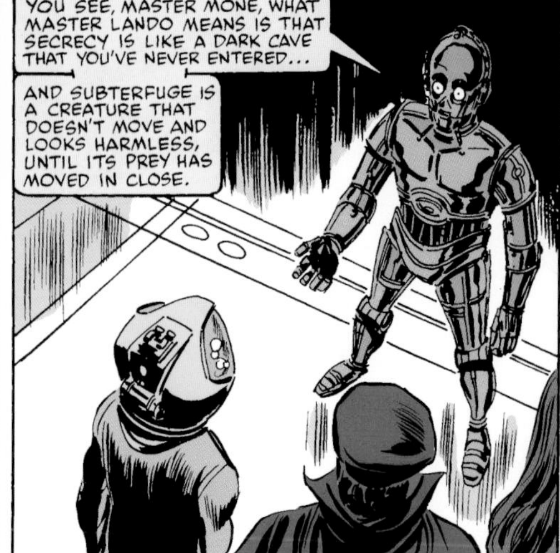

YOU SEE, MASTER MONE, WHAT MASTER LANDO MEANS IS THAT SECRECY IS LIKE A DARK CAVE THAT YOU'VE NEVER ENTERED...
AND SUBTERFUGE IS A CREATURE THAT DOESN'T MOVE AND LOOKS HARMLESS, UNTIL ITS PREY HAS MOVED IN CLOSE.

REMARKABLE! AND ARE THERE REALLY CREATURES THAT LIVE BY SUCH PRINCIPLES?
VIRTUALLY EVERY CIVILIZATION IN THE GALAXY DOES EXCEPT YOURS, MONE.
IT'S A PRETTY GOOD WAY TO LIVE, MOST OF THE TIME. BUT IT DOES HAVE ITS DARKER SIDE, AND ABUSES.

THEY'RE WHAT LEADS TO THINGS LIKE WHAT YOU SEE AROUND US.
WHERE DID ARTOO GET TO?

ONLY THE MAKER KNOWS... WHEREVER WE GO, HE ALWAYS TAKES THE FIRST OPPORTUNITY TO CONVERSE WITH THE CITY COMPUTERS AND SEE WHAT HE CAN LEARN...
HHHRRR
REALLY, HE HAS A DEPLORABLE FONDNESS FOR LOW COMPANY!

YOU THERE! THE ASTRODROID! I'M TALKING TO YOU! WHAT WORK DETAIL ARE YOU ON!
BAWHOOOP

VIP VIP VIP TOK
OH, FINISHED, HUH?
WELL, GET YOURSELF OVER TO SHIPPING AND UNLOADING. THEY'RE SHORT AN INVENTORY CHECKER ANYWAY.

PUH-WHEET
FIRST COURTYARD ON YOUR LEFT.
AND DON'T STOP TO TALK TO STRANGERS!

YAAAWN THAT'S VERY INTERESTING, MISTER...?
DREBBLE. DREBBLE, THEY CALL ME. "DREBS" TO MY FRIENDS.
SEE, ADMIRAL TOWER, THE WAY I GOT IT FIGURED IS, A MAN WANTS TO DO BUSINESS IN A NEW PLACE, FIRST THING HE OUGHTTA DO IS DROP IN ON THE GUY IN CHARGE, AND--!

REALLY? AND DO MANY PEOPLE CALL YOU "DREBS"?
OH...UH...SURE! DON'T YOU WORRY ABOUT ME! I GOT ALL THE FRIENDS I NEED...
ALL THE FRIENDS A DISCREET CHARACTER WITH A LOT OF CASH CAN BUY. KNOW WHAT I MEAN?
I'M BEGINNING TO KNOW A GREAT DEAL MORE THAN YOU MIGHT IMAGINE.

SEE, TOWER, WHAT WE'D LIKE IS TO DO BUSINESS HERE.
YOU DON'T MIND IF I CALL YOU TOWER, DO YOU?
OF COURSE NOT, MR. DREBBLE.

THE WAY MY PARTNERS AND I HAVE HEARD IT, THE EMPIRE DOESN'T MIND A LITTLE FREE ENTERPRISE...
SO LONG AS A GUY NEVER FORGETS WHO'S IN CHARGE... AND ALWAYS COMES ACROSS WITH THE BEST FOR HIS IMPERIAL BUDDIES, NATURALLY...

NATURALLY, MISTER DREBBLE. AND JUST WHAT CAN WE INTEREST YOU IN WHILE YOU'RE HERE... ASIDE FROM THE USUAL CONTRABAND, OF COURSE?
OH, DROIDS, DRUGS, SPICE... AND INFORMATION ABOUT AN OLD ACQUAINTANCE OF MINE--TAY VANIS. AND, LET ME TELL YOU, HE'S NOT A GUY WHO'D CALL ME "DREBS."

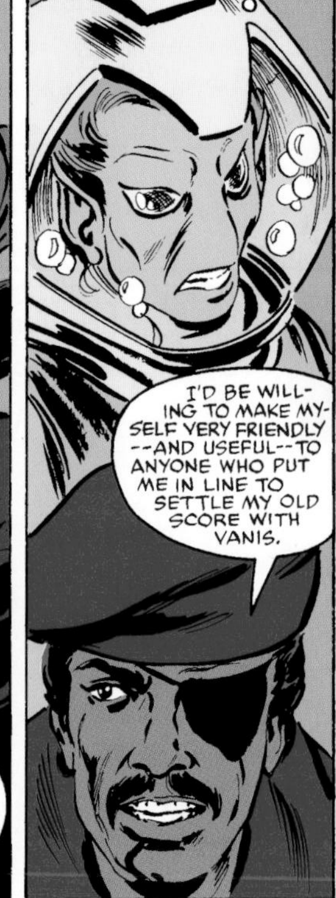

I SHOULD HOPE NOT! REALLY, THIS "SUBTERFUGE" IS VERY BEWILDERING...
I'D BE WILLING TO MAKE MYSELF VERY FRIENDLY --AND USEFUL--TO ANYONE WHO PUT ME IN LINE TO SETTLE MY OLD SCORE WITH VANIS.

REALLY. YOU KNOW, YOU'RE NOT THE ONLY ONE WHO HAS A SCORE TO SETTLE WITH TAY VANIS. AT ONE TIME, HE WAS QUITE A BOTHER TO THE IMPERIAL FORCES IN THIS SYSTEM.

BUT LET ME SHOW YOU--

DARTH VADER!

WHAT IS IT? IT LOOKS SO...EVIL.

IT IS.

HOWWWL

JUST A SIMPLE HOLOGRAM. LORD VADER IS ONE OF THE EMPIRE'S GREAT HEROES.

IN FACT, HE MASTERMINDED THE SUBJUGATION OF THIS SYSTEM, AND THE CONSTRUCTION OF THIS FORTRESS.

I'M SURE HE'D TAKE IT AS A PERSONAL FAVOR --PERHAPS EVEN CALL YOU "DREBS" --IF YOU SETTLED HIS SCORE WITH VANIS, AT THE SAME TIME AS YOUR OWN...

SETTLED IT PERMANENTLY. AND THEN INFORMED US, OF COURSE.

OF COURSE.

BELIEVE ME, TOWER, IT'LL BE A VERY GREAT PLEASURE TO ME, ONCE I'VE GOT TAY VANIS SECURELY IN MY CLUTCHES, TO LET YOU AND LORD VADER KNOW ABOUT IT.

THINGS ARE GOING PRETTY WELL TODAY.
LOOKS LIKE WE'LL BE FINISHED EARLY FOR A CHANGE.
THAT NEW ASTRODROID SURE IS A HARD WORKER, ISN'T HE?

NICE OF 'EM TO FINALLY FIGURE OUT AT HEAD-QUARTERS THAT THIS DETAIL'S ALWAYS SHORT-HANDED.

I STILL HAVEN'T FIGURED OUT WHO OWNS THAT ARTOO UNIT. EITHER OF YOU KNOW WHERE HE COMES FROM?

WELL, HE JUST... THAT IS... AHEM I'VE *ALWAYS* BEEN PLEASED WITH HIS PER-FORMANCE.

GOOD AFTERNOON, MEN! CARE TO DO A LITTLE BUSINESS?
WITH WHOM?

NOBODY IN PARTICULAR... JUST A HUMBLE DEALER IN SECONDHAND DROIDS --WHO WAS REFERRED HERE BY *ADMIRAL TOWER.*
SINCE YOU PUT IT THAT WAY, WHAT ARE YOU IN THE MARKET FOR?

OH... ANYTHING NICE IN THE 3P SERIES. YOU MIGHT SAY I COLLECT THEM. WHAT DO YOU HAVE?

ACCORDING TO THE MANIFEST, RIGHT NOW WE'VE GOT AN A3 THAT'S ABOUT READY FOR THE FURNACES, TWO C3S IN FAIR CONDITION...

AND THAT K3PX UNIT OVER THERE. THE BLACK ONE. AS YOU CAN SEE, IT'S PRACTICALLY NEW. NO ONE KNOWS WHAT BECAME OF THE ORIGINAL OWNER.
IT'S A BEAUTY, ALL RIGHT. WRITE ME UP A BILL AND WE'LL BE ON OUR WAY WITH IT.

ALL RIGHT, K3, WE'VE JUST PURCHASED YOU, SO YOU'LL BE COMING WITH US.
JUST ACT NATURALLY UNTIL WE'RE OUT OF EARSHOT...
DON'T SAY OR DO ANYTHING SUSPICIOUS.

SUSPICIOUS?
YOU KNOW PERFECTLY WELL WHAT I MEAN. YOU *ARE* THE DROID THAT USED TO BELONG TO TAY VANIS, AREN'T YOU?
THAT IS THE CORRECT NAME.

HOW DO YOU DO? I AM C3PO, HUMAN-CYBORG RELATIONS, AND MAY I WELCOME YOU, AND SAY WHAT A PLEASURE IT WILL BE TO WORK WITH A FELLOW 3P SERIES DROID?
YOU MAY NOT.
I HAVE NOTHING TO SAY TO ANY OF YOU.

NO, CHEWBACCA! I KNOW IT'S A WRETCHED SNOB, BUT THINK--IT CAN'T TELL US ANYTHING IF YOU SMASH IT!
LOOK, I UNDERSTAND ...WORKING WITH AN IMPORTANT REBEL AGENT LIKE TAY VANIS, YOU HAVE TO BE SUSPICIOUS OF EVERYONE AND EVERYTHING...
BUT MONE HERE IS A FRIEND OF VANIS'S...

COME BACK WITH US TO ISKALON--MONE'S WORLD. THERE ARE SOME PEOPLE THERE WHO'LL CONVINCE YOU.
THEY'RE IMPORTANT REBEL LEADERS... YOU MUST HAVE HEARD OF THEM--PRINCESS LEIA ORGANA, AND COMMANDER LUKE SKYWALKER!

SKYWALKER? LUKE SKYWALKER WAS ONE OF THE REBELS OF ISKALON?!

OH, LUKE! WE'RE TRAPPED!
MY AIR HOSE!
THE TANKS--!
GASP
FORGIVE ME, LEIA...
BUT HE'S IN CHARGE NOW, WHOEVER HE IS.

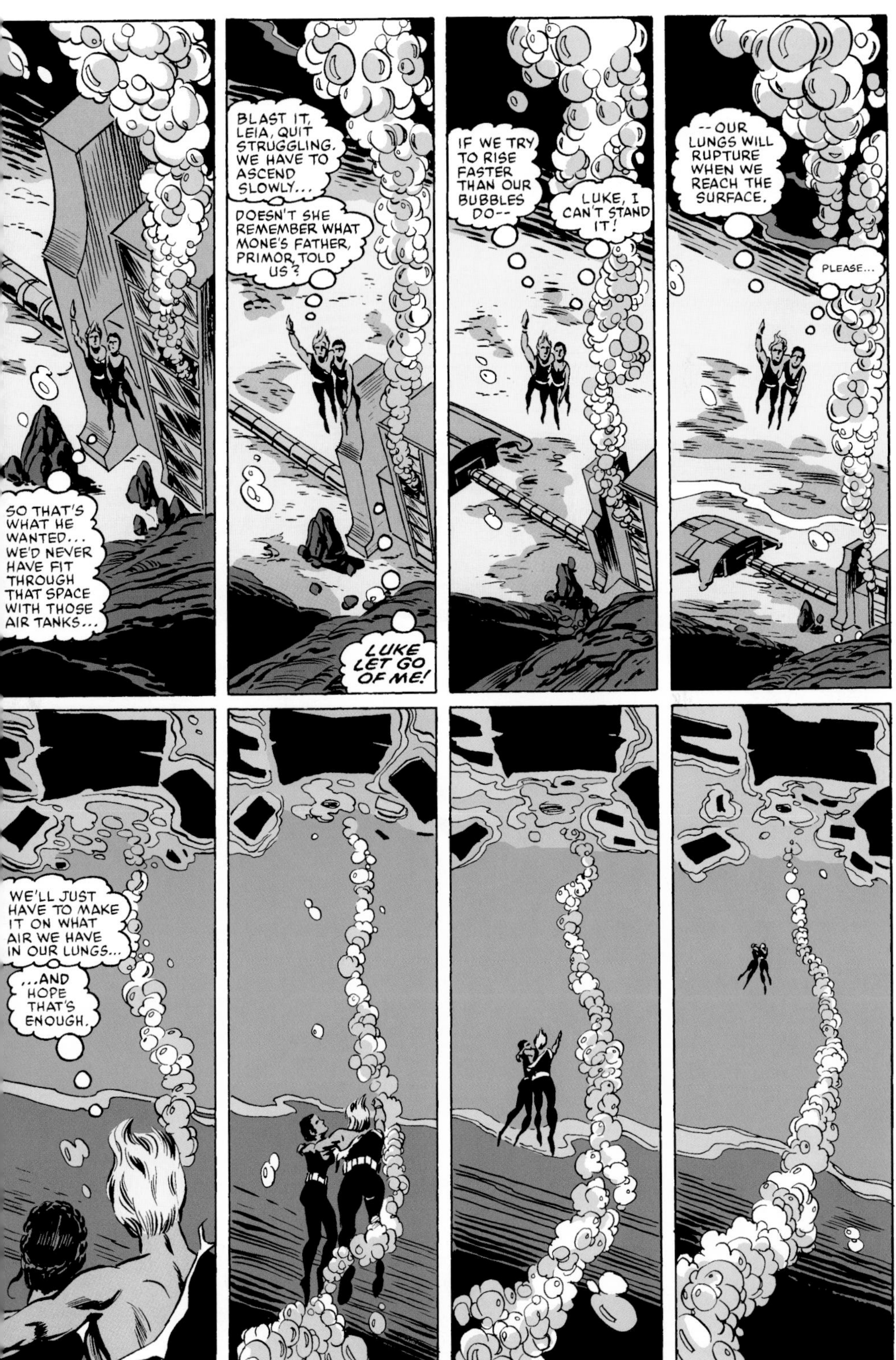
SO THAT'S WHAT HE WANTED... WE'D NEVER HAVE FIT THROUGH THAT SPACE WITH THOSE AIR TANKS...
BLAST IT, LEIA, QUIT STRUGGLING. WE HAVE TO ASCEND SLOWLY...
DOESN'T SHE REMEMBER WHAT MONE'S FATHER, PRIMOR, TOLD US?
LUKE LET GO OF ME!
IF WE TRY TO RISE FASTER THAN OUR BUBBLES DO--
LUKE, I CAN'T STAND IT!
--OUR LUNGS WILL RUPTURE WHEN WE REACH THE SURFACE.
PLEASE...
WE'LL JUST HAVE TO MAKE IT ON WHAT AIR WE HAVE IN OUR LUNGS...
...AND HOPE THAT'S ENOUGH.

GASP
GASP

LUKE...FORGIVE ME...FOR STRUGGLING...I...DIDN'T KNOW... WHAT YOU WERE...DOING...
S'...S' OKAY. LEIA... ME...NEITHER...

LOOK AT PAVILLION...IT'S GONE! DESTROYED! SO MUCH DESTRUCTION...AND SO MANY DEAD...
...WHO WOULD HAVE SET OFF THE ISKALON EFFECT LIKE THAT?

THERE'S ONLY ONE ANSWER... LEIA, YOU KNOW IT AS WELL AS I DO. ONLY THE EMPIRE HAS THAT MUCH POWER, OR DESTROYS THINGS THAT WANTONLY.

BUT... THERE WERE NO REAL REBELS ON ISKALON... THE PEOPLE HERE WOULDN'T BE ABLE TO GRASP A CONCEPT LIKE STEALTH...
ALL THEY KILLED WERE INNOCENT MERMEN, AND A LOT OF THEIR OWN STORMTROOPERS, TOO! WHY?

I GUESS THEY'D COUNT THE ISKALONIANS--AND THEIR OWN PEOPLE--AS EXPENDABLE...
IF IT GAVE THEM A CHANCE AT A TARGET THEY'VE BEEN AIMING AT FOR A LONG TIME...
A TARGET LIKE...
US.
OH, NO!

BUT OUR ASSIGNMENT HERE WAS A LAST MINUTE CHANGE OF PLANS! HOW WOULD THE EMPIRE HAVE EVEN FOUND OUT THAT WE'RE ON ISKALON?
I DON'T KNOW! LEIA, LOOK OVER THERE!

IT'S PRIMOR! IS HE--?
I'M AFRAID SO.

POOR PRIMOR.
AND POOR MONE!
HE WAS WATCHING THROUGH THE GLASS WHEN WE WENT TO RESCUE KENDLE.
THE IMPACT MUST HAVE THROWN HIM AGAINST PAVILLION, FULL FORCE.

NO! NOT MY HUSBAND'S FATHER! NOT FOR MY SAKE!
OH, KENDLE...
WE'RE SO SORRY...

OH, PRIMOR... PRIMOR, I CANNOT BEAR THIS!
LEIA...
OH, LUKE... I FEEL SO...
...RESPONSI-BLE...

NO! NO ONE IS RESPONSIBLE!

NO ONE BUT HER!

KIRO!!
KENDLE!

HOLD IT A SECOND!
JUST WHAT DO YOU THINK YOU'RE GOING TO DO WITH THAT?

JUST WHAT DO YOU THINK YOU'RE DOING? GET OUT OF MY WAY!
AND LET YOU KILL KENDLE? UH-UH!

WHY DO YOU KEEP PROTECTING HER? I'D HAVE KILLED HER BEFORE... EXCEPT THAT KENDLE AND I SMASHED EACH OTHER'S TANKS IN PAVILLION WHILE WE STRUGGLED...
AND WHILE I WENT TO GET MORE WATER, SO I WOULDN'T SUFFOCATE ALONG WITH THE TRAITRESS, YOU HELPED HER!

AND, WHEN SHE WOULD HAVE LED YOU INTO A TRAP IN THE WRECKAGE AWAY FROM THE SURFACE, YOU *STILL* PROTECTED HER, AND I HAD TO SAVE YOU MYSELF!
AND NOW YOU PROTECT HER AGAIN! ***WHY?!?***
WHY NOT? WHY SHOULD WE BELIEVE THESE ACCUSATIONS?
WHAT'S KENDLE DONE TO WARRANT ALL THIS ANIMOSITY?

LOOK AROUND YOU! ISN'T THIS CAUSE ENOUGH?
OH, COME ON. YOU CAN'T BE BLAMING KENDLE FOR ALL THIS!

SHE TOLD THE LEADER ON GAMANDAR--TOWER, SHE CALLED HIM--THAT YOU TWO WERE HERE. I GUESS SHE DIDN'T REALIZE THEY'D SACRIFICE OUR ENTIRE WORLD TO GET YOU.
ARE YOU SURE?
I HEARD HER SEND THE MESSAGE!

NEXT: ARTOO STANDS ALONE!

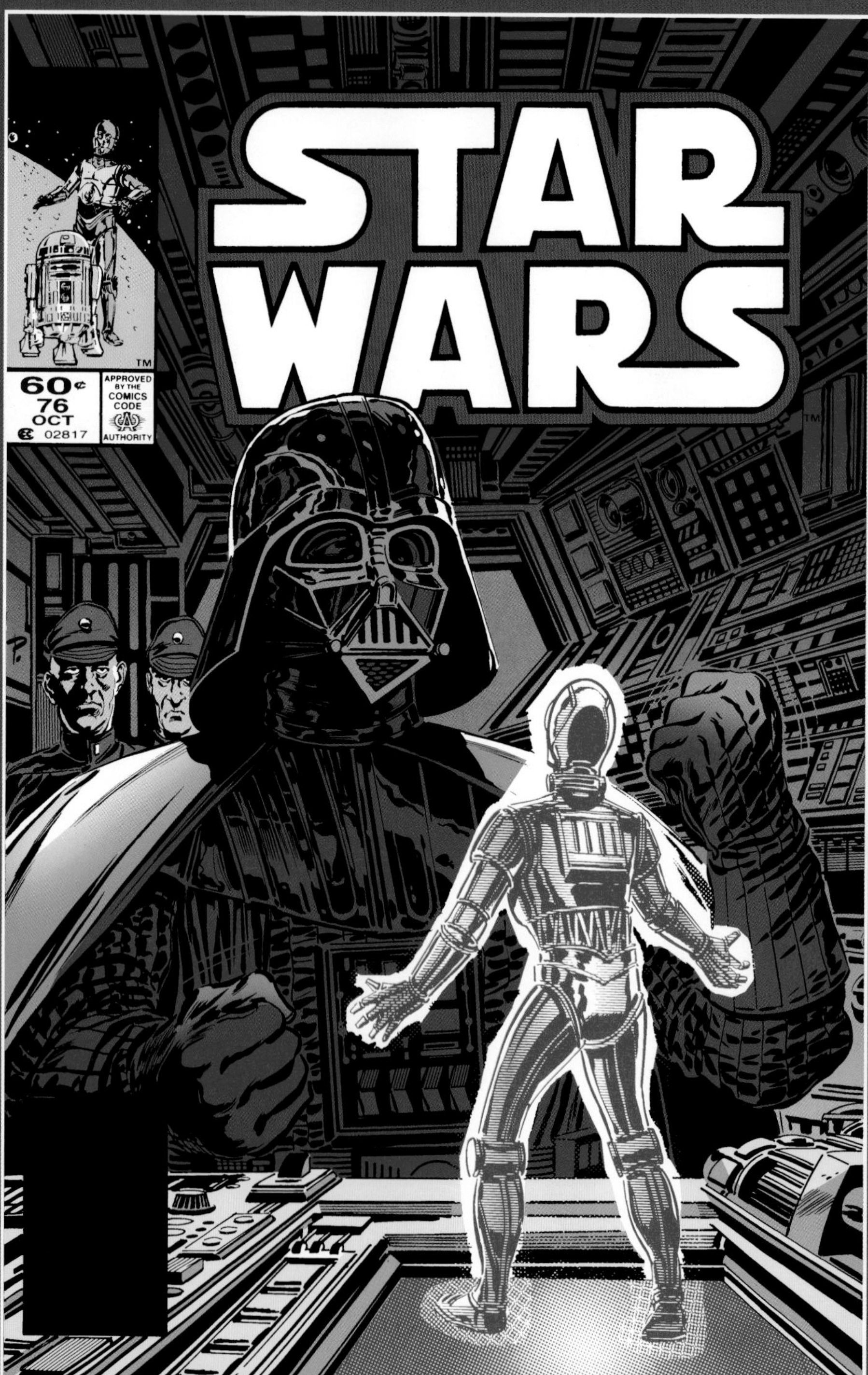
STAR WARS
TM
60¢
76
OCT
02817
APPROVED BY THE COMICS CODE AUTHORITY

Long ago in a galaxy far, far away. . .there exists a state of cosmic *civil war*. A brave alliance of *underground freedom fighters* has challenged the tyranny and oppression of the awesome *Galactic Empire*. This is their story!

Lucasfilm PRESENTS: STAR WARS™ THE GREATEST SPACE FANTASY OF ALL!

JO DUFFY *SCRIPT/PLOT* RON FRENZ *BREAKDOWNS* TOM PALMER *FINISHES* JOE ROSEN *LETTERS* GLYNIS WEIN *COLORS* LOUISE JONES *EDITOR* JIM SHOOTER *EDITOR-IN-CHIEF*

THIS REBELLION AGAINST THE EMPIRE MUST BE CRUSHED--IT WILL BE CRUSHED...
THAT IS WHY WE ERADICATED ALL LIFE ON THE PLANET TELFREY --TO MAKE AN EXAMPLE OF WHAT HAPPENED TO THOSE WHO OPPOSE US...
THAT IS WHY WE ENSLAVED THE POPULACE OF GAMANDAR, AND BUILT OUR FORTRESS THERE...
AND THAT IS WHY WE MUST WATCH THE WATER PLANET, ISKALON, FOR ANY SIGNS OF OVERT OR COVERT REBEL ACTIVITY...
THE EMPIRE WILL BE MAKING ITS FINAL ASSAULT AGAINST THE REBEL FORCES VERY SOON NOW... AND THERE MUST BE NO MISTAKES!
YES... YESSIR, LORD VADER...
WE UNDERSTAND, SIR...
DO YOU?
YOU... NEEDN'T HAVE ANY FEARS ABOUT GAMANDAR AND ISKALON, SIR, AND NEITHER NEED THE EMPEROR...
ADMIRAL TOWER, THE MAN YOU LEFT IN COMMAND OF THE FORTRESS, IS MOST CAPABLE...
TOWER IS AN ARROGANT FOOL, AND A BRUTE...
UH... YES, SIR.
UM... THE FORCES OF GAMANDAR INFORM US THAT THEY ARE VERY CLOSE TO LOCATING TAY VANIS-- THE REBEL WHO DISAPPEARED AFTER STEALING CERTAIN OF OUR VITAL DOCUMENTS...
ONCE TOWER LOCATES HIM AND THE THREAT TO OUR PROJECT IS ELIMINATED...
TOWER SHOULD BE LESS BUSY IN MATTERS THAT DO NOT CONCERN HIM...
VANIS WILL BE DEALT WITH ...IN TIME...
B-BUT, SIR...

B...BUT LORD VADER...
WE'VE DIVERTED DOZENS OF OUR BEST MEN TO SEARCHING FOR VANIS, AND THEY'VE FOUND NO SIGN OF HIM...
AND OUR INTELLIGENCE NETWORK REPORTS THAT THE REBELS HAVE HAD NO BETTER LUCK IN FINDING...
L-LORD VADER...?
WHY HAVE YOU INTERRUPTED US, CORPORAL?
DID YOU NOT HEAR MY ORDERS THAT NOTHING WAS TO DISTURB US DURING THIS CONFERENCE?
I...I...I...FORGIVE ME, SIR...A HOLOGRAPHIC MESSAGE HAS JUST COME IN FOR YOU...FROM THE FORTRESS...
AND...IT...THE DROID SAID THAT YOU...
A DROID IS CALLING ME FROM THE FORTRESS... AND YOU INTERRUPTED US FOR THAT?
VERY WELL. I WILL SPEAK TO IT.
WE WILL CONTINUE WHEN I AM THROUGH.
I AM HERE, K3PX. YOU MAY MAKE YOUR REPORT. HOW IS THE SITUATION ON GAMANDAR?
I DID NOT CONTACT YOU ABOUT GAMANDAR. THERE HAVE BEEN SERIOUS DEVELOPMENTS ON OUR TWIN WORLD--ISKALON.
HAS THERE BEEN ANY REBEL ACTIVITY ON THE WATER PLANET?
THERE HAS BEEN. TOWER DEALT WITH IT, BEFORE I COULD INFORM YOU--HE DEVASTATED THE WORLD WITH A MISSILE...
WE DO NOT KNOW YET IF THERE WERE ANY SURVIVORS...
TOWER HAS OVERSTEPPED HIMSELF.
THERE IS MORE, SIR...ONE OF THE REBELS ON ISKALON WAS NAMED SKYWALKER.
WHAT?!?
LUKE SKYWALKER WAS ON ISKALON?!

ELSEWHERE...
OH, THIS IS HORRIBLE...
SO MUCH DESTRUCTION ...SO MANY DEAD, AND SO MANY WOUNDED...
I... HOPE WE'RE DOING THE RIGHT THING FOR THEM... THE PHYSIOLOGY OF YOU WATER BREATHERS IS SO STRANGE TO US...
OH, KIRO, HOW YOU MUST HATE US...
I SAVE MY HATE FOR MY ENEMIES, PRINCESS LEIA. WHY WOULD I FEEL HATE FOR YOU AND LUKE?
BECAUSE, IF WHAT WE SUSPECT IS TRUE, ALL OF THIS DESTRUCTION WAS SET OFF BY THE EMPIRE IN HOPES OF KILLING ME AND LEIA, AFTER THEY'D GOTTEN WORD THAT WE'RE SAFE HERE ON ISKALON...
WE OF THE SCHOOL ARE CLOSER TO OUR BIOSYSTEM--
--MORE IN TOUCH WITH THE LAWS OF CAUSE AND EFFECT THAN YOU AIR-BREATHERS, LUKE...
AND THE FORCES OF THE IMPERIALS ARE NOT THE ONLY PREDATORS WE'VE EVER FACED!..
WHAT IS THAT?!

TALK LATER! FOR NOW, LET ME HAVE YOUR STINGER!
RRIIEE--!
KEEP YOUR WEAPON CLOSE, LUKE! IF YOU SEE ANYTHING MOVE, ASSUME IT IS HOSTILE AND BLAST IT!
BUT... WHAT WAS THAT THING?
THE CHIAKI. MOST OF THE CITIZENS OF THIS CITY--PAVILLION--ARE NOW DEAD...
THE BLOOD HAS DRAWN THE MONSTERS, WHO WILL CLEAR AWAY THE BODIES...
...AND IF THE MONSTERS' HUNGER ISN'T SATED BY THE DEAD...
...IT WILL BE VERY BAD FOR THE WOUNDED, THE WEAPONLESS, AND THE FEEBLE!

CAN'T WE DO SOMETHING TO PREVENT IT... TO SAVE THE PEOPLE?
THE THREE OF US? STOP THE CHIAKI, IN ALL THEIR NUMBERS, WHEN THE FEEDING FRENZY IS UPON THEM?
AS WELL TO TRY AND STOP THE TIDES WITH YOUR HANDS, LUKE... WE CAN ATTEMPT IT, IF YOU WISH...
BUT WE'LL BE LUCKY TO SURVIVE THIS NIGHT, AND OUTLAST THEIR APPETITES OURSELVES...
YOU... LOOK SORT OF BUSHED, LEIA. IF YOU WANT TO GET SOME SLEEP, I CAN TAKE THE WATCH.
YOU, TOO, KIRO...
THIS IS MY WORLD... I WILL SEE WHAT THE BOMB AND THE CHIAKI HAVE LEFT OF PAVILLION AND OF THE PEOPLE OF ISKALON BY THE DAWN.
THEN I WILL SLEEP.
NO, LUKE... THERE MAY STILL BE SOMETHING I CAN DO FOR THE VICTIMS... EVEN IF IT'S JUST TO WAIT OUT THE END WITH THEM. I'D LIKE TO DO IT...
THEN... I GUESS WE'LL ALL SEE THE DAWN TOGETHER.
THEY ARE THE ONES! THEY BROUGHT THEIR REBELLION HERE AND BROUGHT DOWN THE WRATH OF THE EMPIRE UPON US!!
WHAT--?
KENDLE!

I AM THE MATE OF MONE, SON OF PRIMOR! ALL OF THE SCHOOL SWAM IN THE WAYS AND DIRECTION OF PRIMOR'S CHOOSING ...TILL THE BOMBS KILLED HIM!
UNTIL THE EMPIRE RE-LEASES MONE, I WILL SPEAK FOR THE SCHOOL...
...AND I SAY THAT THESE THREE ARE RESPONSIBLE, AND MUST PAY...
STAY BACK, ALL OF YOU! WE DON'T WANT ANY TROUBLE!
THINK ABOUT WHAT YOU'RE DOING!
BLAST! THIS ISN'T GOING TO WORK... THE PEOPLE OF ISKALON ARE SO USED TO THINKING AS A COLLECTIVE...
I'LL NEVER BE ABLE TO STEM THE MOMENTUM THAT KENDLE HAS STARTED... HAVE TO TRY SOMETHING ELSE...
OH! WHAT'S IT DOING?
THE WRECKAGE IS MOVING THROUGH THE AIR AT US, UNDER ITS OWN POWER!
I SAW IT, BUT I DON'T UNDERSTAND IT! LEIA, WHAT DID LUKE DO?
NOW, YOU TWO! RUN!!
LUKE HAS TRAINED AS A JEDI KNIGHT, KIRO. IT GIVES HIM PARTIAL MASTERY OVER THE FORCE--AN ENERGY FIELD GENERATED BY ALL LIVING THINGS...
WE'RE NOT ALL AS OUT OF TOUCH WITH OUR ENVIRONMENTS AS YOU THINK...
THAT WAS MIGHTY, AND IMPRESSIVE!
I HOPE IT IM-PRESSED KENDLE.
WITHOUT THE ELE-MENT OF SURPRISE, I DOUBT THAT TRICK WILL SUCCEED TWICE!

ELSEWHERE...

THESE ARE GREAT DAYS FOR AN IMPERIAL OFFICER TO BE ALIVE! WE'VE GOT GAMANDAR RIGHT UNDER OUR THUMB, THE INDUSTRIALIZATION AND THE EXPORT OF SLAVES IS PROCEEDING WELL...

...WE'VE GOT SECURITY, WITH A BATTLE FLEET RIGHT IN THIS SYSTEM...AND LORD DARTH VADER HAS PAID US A SURPRISE INSPECTION VISIT AT A TIME WHEN ALL THE NEWS IS GOOD ANYWAY!

THAT NEW ARTOO-DETOO DROID UNIT HAS CERTAINLY MADE LIFE EASIER FOR EVERYONE SINCE HE JOINED THIS WORK DETAIL! I'VE NEVER SEEN SUCH AN AMBITIOUS, COOPERATIVE LITTLE MACHINE!

BOOP

BAP

Y'KNOW...HE'S BEEN SECURITY CLEARED FOR TOP INFORMATION STORAGE AND RETRIEVAL SYSTEMS...AND I DON'T EVEN KNOW WHO OWNS HIM!

WHY...HE... HE'S BEEN WITH ME, SINCE HE ARRIVED ON GAMANDAR...

YEAH, OR MAYBE, SINCE NO ONE ELSE SPOKE UP, YOU WANNA EARN POINTS BY TAKING CREDIT FOR SOMEONE ELSE'S HARDWORKING DROID, HUH?

OH... MY ACHING HEAD...
WHAT ARE WE DOING IN AN IMPERIAL SECURITY CELL?!

OH... YEAH, I REMEMBER NOW...
MONE'S WIFE, KENDLE, SENT US HERE TO GAMANDAR, TO FIND THE K3PX UNIT THAT USED TO BELONG TO TAY VANIS...
AND WE FOUND THE DROID, AND IT LOOKED LIKE EVERY-THING WAS GONNA TURN OUT FINE...
AND THEN THE ROTTEN THING TURNED AROUND AND BLASTED ALL FOUR OF US!

CHEWBACCA? CHEWIE? ARE YOU OKAY?
WURF
YEAH, WELL... YOU'RE LUCKY YOU WOOKIEES HAVE SUCH THICK HEADS!

IT LOOKS LIKE SOMEONE SHUT OFF SEE-THREEPIO... TAKE CARE OF HIM, WILL YOU? I WANT TO SEE HOW MONE'S DOING.
I AM... AS WELL AS ONE CAN BE, UNDER THE CIRCUM-STANCES, LANDO... IT HAS BEEN TOO LONG SINCE I CHANGED THE WATER IN MY BREATHING TANKS...
IT IS GETTING STALE... SOON IT WILL BE COMPLETELY FOUL, AND THEN I WILL NOT BE ABLE TO BREATHE AT ALL.

ALL WE CAN DO IS EXPLAIN THAT TO THE IMPERIALS IF YOU GET TOO BAD, MONE, AND HOPE THEY'LL BE LENIENT...
BUT I HAVE A BAD FEELING THAT NONE OF US IS GOING TO BE BREATHING AT ALL FOR MUCH LONGER...
MASTER LANDO, I CANNOT TELL YOU HOW UPSET I AM BY ALL THIS...
TO THINK THAT ONE OF MY FELLOW DROIDS--!
WHO PUT US HERE IS THE LEAST OF OUR WORRIES, THREEPIO. WHAT CONCERNS ME IS THAT THE WAY THIS THING WAS SET UP, IT'S LIKE THEY WERE EXPECTING US FROM THE START...
BUT...WHY? HOW COULD THEY HAVE BEEN?
BECAUSE ONE OF YOUR FRIENDS BETRAYED YOU, OF COURSE!
IN FACT, IT WAS YOUR LITTLE WIFE, FISH-MAN!
SHE WAS HOPING TO BUY YOUR LIFE, AND THE LIFE OF YOUR FATHER, BY TURNING THE REBELS OVER TO US, AND BUYING OUR FRIENDSHIP...
TOO BAD IT WORKED AGAINST HER. WE TOOK CARE OF ISKALON, AND ALL THE REBELS ON IT...SET OFF THE ISKALON EFFECT.
I WISH I COULD HAVE BEEN THERE TO SEE THE WAVE OUR MISSILE SET OFF...BUT ACCORDING TO OUR SCANNERS, THERE'S VIRTUALLY NOTHING LEFT OF THE CITY OF PAVILLION--OR YOUR FRIENDS, I'LL WAGER...
KENDLE... BETRAYED US?
HOW COULD SHE...HOW COULD SHE USE SUBTERFUGE? THAT IS THE WAY OF AIR-BREATHERS ...NOT OF THE SCHOOL!
MONE, I'M SO SORRY...
GGRRRR
CHEWBACCA, PLEASE...I SHARE YOUR FEELINGS, BUT DO THINK BEFORE YOU DO ANYTHING--

-- RASH. OH, DEAR, OH DEAR...
CHEWIE, NO!

HE WANTED YOU TO GO FOR HIM! THAT DOOR IS PROBABLY...
KLIK
...BOOBY-TRAPPED.
HOWWL

TOWER, YOU FILTHY COWARD--!

AH...SO OUR MR. DREBBLE... OR DREBS... OR LANDO... OR WHATEVER YOUR REAL NAME IS... DOES HAVE A BACKBONE AFTER ALL...
THAT'S GOOD. THAT'S VERY GOOD.
WE'LL BEGIN INTENSIVE INTERROGATIONS RIGHT AWAY... STARTING WITH THE WOOKIEE. ORDER THE COMPUTER TO UNLOCK THE CELL DOOR.

EH...? K3PX, WHAT ARE YOU DOING HERE? I DIDN'T ASK FOR YOU, OR THAT OTHER CONTINGENT OF STORM TROOPERS. WE WON'T NEED THEM...
THE FORCE FIELD HAS TAKEN ALL THE FIGHT OUT OF THE WOOKIEE...
YOU WILL COME WITH ME.

DON'T BE RIDICULOUS. I'M ABOUT TO QUESTION THESE REBELS. ONE OF THEM MAY KNOW WHAT BECAME OF TAY VANIS.
VANIS IS NO CONCERN OF YOURS. YOU WILL COME TO THE HOLOGRAM PROJECTION AREA AT ONCE. THERE IS A COMMUNICATION FOR YOU.
DON'T BE RIDICULOUS. WHOEVER IS BROAD-CASTING, THE MESSAGE CAN WAIT.

THE MESSAGE IS BEING BEAMED IN FROM LORD DARTH VADER.
VADER? WELL, WHY DIDN'T YOU SAY SO? THIS IS EXCELLENT. HE'S GOING TO BE MOST PLEASED WHEN HE LEARNS WHAT I'VE...

LORD VADER KNOWS. HE IS MOST DIS-PLEASED.
YOU ARE UNDER ARREST.
VADER?
ARREST... BUT HE CAN'T. YOU CAN'T MEAN...? GUARDS, STOP THIS LUNATIC MACHINE!

COME ON, TOWER. YOU'RE UNDER ARREST...
B-BUT-BUT-BUT--?
LORD DARTH VADER'S ORDERS.

CAN...CAN YOU HEAR WHAT THEY ARE DOING OUT THERE?
I-I'M NOT SURE, MONE... I THOUGHT I HEARD SOMEONE OPENING THE CELL DOOR, BUT HE STOPPED BEFORE THE COMPUTER HAD FINISHED UNLOCKING IT...

WHY WOULD ANYONE--?

NO, WAIT A MINUTE! I WAS RIGHT. THE CELL DOOR IS OPENING. BRACE YOURSELVES FOR--

ARTOO! WHAT ARE YOU DOING HERE?
BAWHEET BEEP BABOOP BIP BIP
NEVER MIND... I GUESS WE GET THE MESSAGE. THANKS.

WELL DONE, ARTOO! I ALWAYS KNEW YOU HAD IT IN YOU!
CAN YOU LEAD US TO THE SHIP... IF CHEWIE AND MONE CAN MAKE IT, THAT IS?

CRUNCH
THERE SHE IS! THE MILLENNIUM FALCON HAS NEVER LOOKED MORE BEAUTIFUL TO ME THAN SHE DOES RIGHT NOW...
MASTER LANDO, ARTOO INFORMS ME THAT BEFORE HE...ER...TENDERED HIS RESIGNATION TO THE IMPERIAL FORCES...
...HE GAVE THE CITADEL'S COMPUTERS STRICT ORDERS THAT IT WAS TO LET US STRICTLY ALONE...AND INTERFERE WITH ANY PURSUIT.
BEAUTIFUL!
TOWER, YOU HAVE ACTED IN HASTE AND INDULGED YOURSELF AT THE EXPENSE OF THE EMPIRE FOR THE LAST TIME...
BUT, SIR! LORD VADER, I WAS ONLY...
I AM FULLY AWARE OF WHAT YOU WERE GOING TO DO...
JUST AS I AM AWARE OF WHAT YOU HAVE DONE... MORE AWARE OF IT THAN YOU ARE YOURSELF...
THERE WAS NO NEED FOR YOU TO SET IN MOTION THE ISKALON EFFECT WITHOUT FIRST CONSULTING ME...
BUT... THERE WERE REBELS IN PAVILLION...THEY MIGHT HAVE BEEN ALLIES OF TAY VANIS.
YOUR MOTIVES DO NOT CONCERN ME. WHAT DOES IS THAT YOUR HASTY ACTION MAY HAVE ENDED THE LIFE OF ONE PARTICULAR REBEL...
A MAN BOTH THE EMPEROR AND MYSELF HAVE BEEN AFTER FOR SOME TIME...
LORD VADER, WE'VE BEGUN GETTING REPORTS FROM THE REMAINS OF OUR FORCES ON ISKALON. THERE ARE SURVIVORS IN PAVILLION!
THANK THE FORCE.

THE FORCE IS NOT WITH YOU, TOWER. IT IS WITH ME.
PREPARE MY PERSONAL CRAFT. I SHALL JOURNEY TO ISKALON AT ONCE...
AS SOON AS I HAVE SETTLED WITH THIS FOOL...
LORD VADER...BACK IN DETENTION AREA...THERE ARE SOME REBEL PRISONERS. P-PERHAPS ONE OF THEM COULD BE...
THE MAN I SEEK IS NOT AMONG THEM. WHOEVER THEY ARE, THEY SHALL KEEP UNTIL MY RETURN.
GUARDS, EXECUTE ADMIRAL TOWER. TRANSMISSION ENDS.
WHAT SHIP IS THAT, ANYWAY?
I DON'T KNOW... BUT ACCORDING TO THE FORTRESS'S COMPUTERS, IT'S GOT FULL CLEARANCE FOR TAKEOFF...
LET'S GET BACK, FAST... COMPUTER SAYS THERE'S SOME KIND OF TROUBLE IN THE FORTRESS, AND WE'RE NEEDED.

WELL, IT COULD BE WORSE... WE'RE OUTNUMBERED, BUT THESE STINGERS ARE FULLY CHARGED...
...AND WE'RE IN A SHELTERED AREA. WE DON'T HAVE TO WORRY ABOUT THEM COMING AT US FROM THE WATER, OR RUSHING OUR BLIND SIDE IN FORCE...

SO... WE'RE SECURE FOR THE MOMENT... UNLESS THEY TAKE IT INTO THEIR HEADS TO TRY ONE MASSIVE SUICIDAL RUSH...
I GUESS IT DEPENDS ON HOW BADLY THEY REALLY WANT US...
BEWARE OF COMPLACENCY, LUKE. THE SCHOOL THINKS AS ONE, AND THEY ARE LETTING KENDLE DO THEIR THINKING FOR THEM...
IF SHE DECIDES THAT MANY OF THEM SHOULD DIE, TO KILL THE THREE OF US...

LOOKS LIKE SOME OF THE STORM TROOPERS SURVIVED... IF THEY DON'T MIND THAT THE EMPIRE WAS WILLING TO SACRIFICE THEM TO GET US...

THEY MIGHT MANAGE TO CONVINCE KENDLE THAT A MASS CHARGE IS THE BEST WAY...

WATCH THEM... THEY ARE GETTING TOO CLOSE...

THE RUSH IS STARTING!

FIRE!!!

KEEP SHOOTING, LEIA. CUT THEM ALL DOWN BEFORE THEY GET TOO CLOSE.

DO WE HAVE TO KILL THEM ALL?

YES! WITH THE SCHOOL, IT IS THE ONLY WAY. OTHERWISE, THEY MAY NEVER STOP...

WAIT...THEY ARE SLOWING DOWN. NO, STOPPING. THEY'VE GONE BACK TO JUST ISOLATED BURSTS OF SNIPER FIRE...
LOOKS LIKE WE'RE SAFE AGAIN.
YOU AND LEIA ARE SAFE, LUKE. FOR ME, YOUR SECURE SPOT IS A TRAP... IF I CANNOT FIGHT MY WAY BACK TO THE OPEN SEA BEFORE THE WATER IN MY BREATHING TANKS GOES FOUL...
WE WON'T LET YOU DIE, KIRO...

WE'LL FIGHT OUR WAY OUT OF THIS CORNER BEFORE THAT HAPPENS.
YOU ARE GOOD COMRADES. I CAN SEE WHY MONE AND PRIMOR LIKED YOU.
MONE--! IF ONLY WE KNEW FOR SURE WHAT HAD HAPPENED TO LANDO AND THE OTHERS, ON GAMANDAR...

KILL THEM! KILL THE ALIENS, AND THAT EVIL LITTLE TRAITOR! THEY ARE TO BLAME FOR THIS CARNAGE ...AND FOR THE DEATH OF PRIMOR...

...AND FOR THE LOSS OF MY MONE!
COME ON! MAYBE THEIR STINGERS AREN'T WELL ENOUGH CHARGED TO WITHSTAND ANOTHER RUSH!

OH-UH . . . LOOKS LIKE THEY'RE GETTING READY FOR A SECOND WAVE ASSAULT . . .
THAT'S IT, HONEY . . . JUST KEEP WATCHING THAT GROUP AHEAD OF YOU FOR ANOTHER MINUTE . . .
LEIA, BEHIND YOU--! LOOK--
--OUUARRK--!
KIRO!!
OH, KIRO, NO . . .
HE . . . HE . . . RIGHT THROUGH THE TROOPER'S ARMOR . . .
. . . WITH KIRO'S BLADE!

WHO'S NEXT?
KIRO'S NEXT, IF WE CAN'T GET HIM INTO THE OCEAN, AND FAST.
WH-AAT?!
HE'S ALIVE, LUKE. THAT BLAST JUST SHATTERED HIS FACEPLATE.

THEN WE'LL HAVE TO CARRY HIM TO THE SEA, RIGHT NOW.
BUT, WE'LL NEVER MAKE IT. KENDLE AND THOSE TROOPS ARE BETWEEN US AND THE WATER...
I-AM-NOT-GOING-TO-STAND-HERE-AND-WATCH-ANOTHER-OF-MY-FRIENDS-DIE!

YOU GRAB THAT STINGER AND FOLLOW ME!

LOOK! OVER THERE!
IT'S--!
THE CHIAKI!
OH, NO...
IT'S DIVING --AT US! GET OUT OF THE WAY!

RRRIIIIEEE..!

VORP VORP VORP VORP

THE MILLENNIUM FALCON...

LANDO...

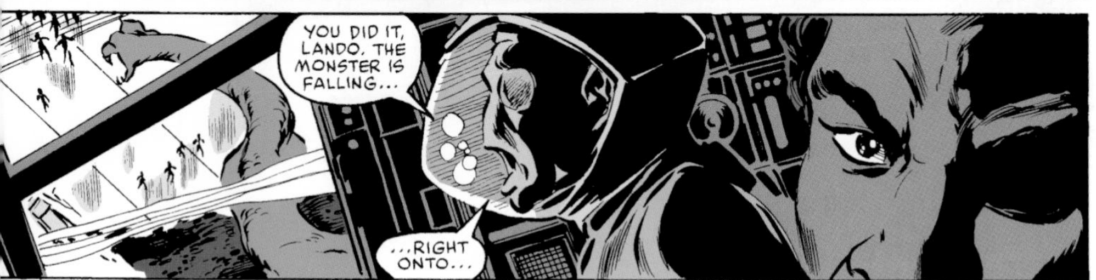

KENDLE... LUKE, WHEN THE CREATURE FELL, SHE... SHE COULDN'T... SHE DIDN'T...
DON'T DWELL ON IT, LEIA... AT LEAST WE MANAGED TO SAVE KIRO... I THINK...

YOU KEPT YOUR PROMISE ABOUT NOT LETTING ME DIE IN THE AIR, LUKE.
THANK YOU...
NO PRIMOR... NO KENDLE... WHOM DO WE FOLLOW?
WHAT SHALL WE DO?

YOUR HIGHNESS, ARTOO AND I WOULD LIKE TO EXPRESS OUR RELIEF AT--!
YOU SAVED OUR LIVES... AND WE THOUGHT YOU WERE DEAD! I'VE BEEN SO WORRIED ABOUT YOU--!
ME, TOO, LEIA.
GRONK
KENDLE...

WHY... WHY, BELOVED? WHY?!

LUKE, LANDO, WE MUST SAY FARE-WELL, NOW.
AND, WHEN YOU RETURN TO THE PLANETS OF THE AIRBREATHERS, TELL YOUR FELLOW REBELS THAT NONE OF THEM IS WEL-COME HERE...
I AM THE SON OF PRIMOR, AND THE SCHOOL WILL FOL-LOW ME. I SHALL LEAD IT INTO THE DEPTHS...
THERE SHALL BE NO MORE PAVILLIONS, NO MORE TANKS, NO MORE LIVING IN TWO WORLDS, NOT SO LONG AS THERE IS AN EMPIRE.

FIN

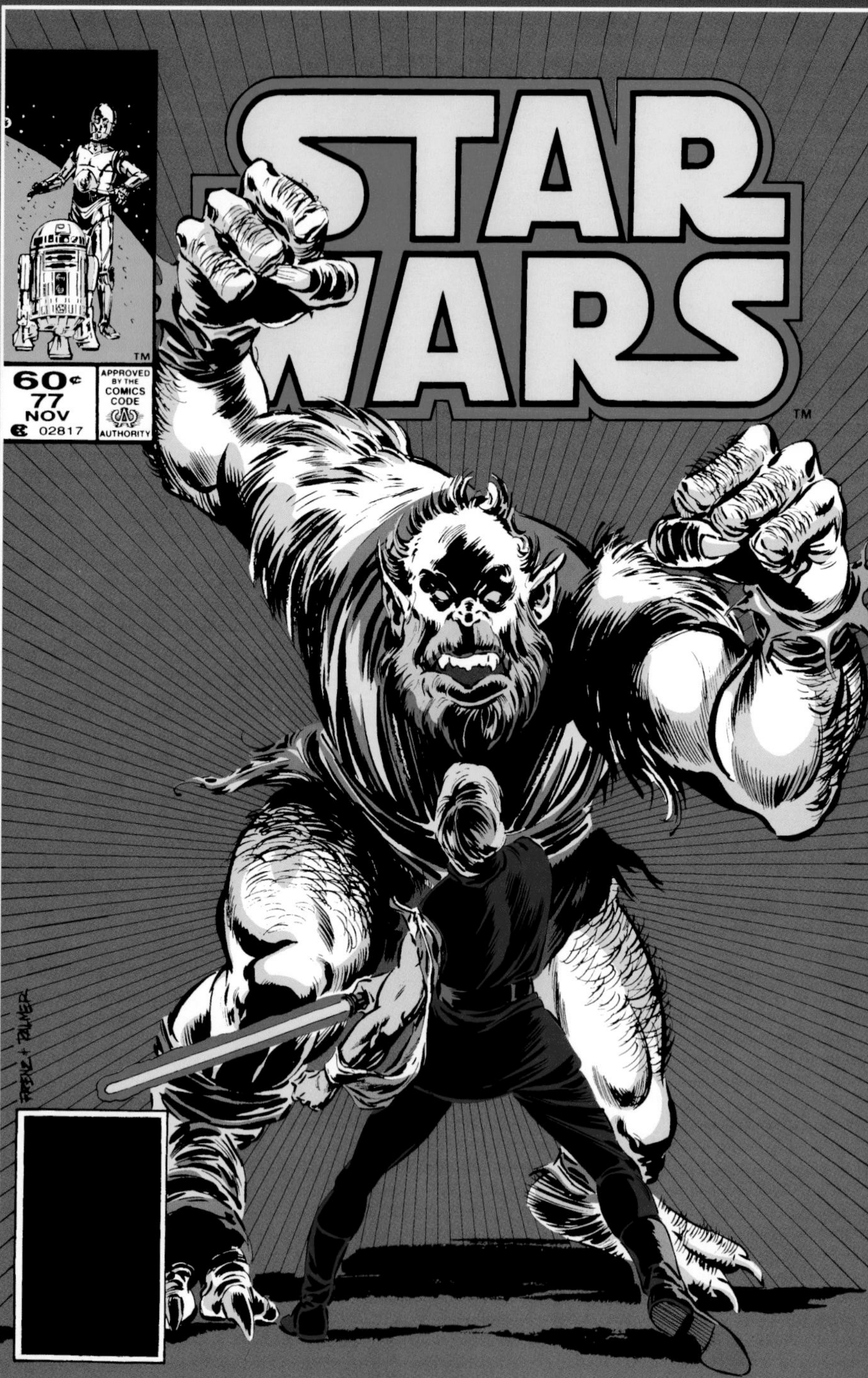

STAR WARS
TM
60¢
77
NOV
02817
APPROVED BY THE COMICS CODE AUTHORITY
TM

Long ago in a galaxy far, far away. . .there exists a state of cosmic *civil war*. A brave alliance of *underground freedom fighters* has challenged the tyranny and oppression of the awesome *Galactic Empire*. This is their story!

Lucasfilm PRESENTS: STAR WARS™ THE GREATEST SPACE FANTASY OF ALL!

JO DUFFY *SCRIPT AND PLOT BREAKDOWNS* RON FRENZ TOM PALMER *FINISHES* JOE ROSEN *LETTERS* GLYNIS WEIN *COLORS* LOUISE JONES *EDITOR* JIM SHOOTER *EDITOR-IN-CHIEF*

SHOO! NOO! GET AWAY FROM ME, YOU NASTY LITTLE BEASTS...YOU VERMIN...YOU HOOJIBS!
YOU'RE GOING TO CONSUME ALL OF MY ENERGY AND LEAVE ME DRAINED...
CHANTEUSE of the STARS...

CALM DOWN, SEE-THREEPIO. PLIF AND HIS FRIENDS ARE JUST GREETING YOU... YOU KNOW IN ALL THE TIME WE'VE BEEN HERE ON ARBRA THEY'VE NEVER EATEN THE ENERGY OF ANY REBEL DROID...
B... BUT, MASTER LUKE, SIR...
YOUR HIGHNESS, COMMANDER SKYWALKER, ALL OF YOU... WELCOME BACK.
IT'S A RELIEF TO BE BACK.
HOW DID THE MISSION GO?
NOT WELL, I'M AFRAID... NOT WELL AT ALL...
YOU HEARD ABOUT WHAT HAPPENED ON ISKALON...?
GGGRRRR
...HOW THE EMPIRE COMMITTED GENOCIDE AGAINST THE POPULACE... AND THE SURVIVORS HAVE ALL GONE INTO HIDING?
THEY DON'T WANT US BACK THERE, AS LONG AS OUR PRESENCE MAY ATTRACT IMPERIAL REPRISALS...
THERE'S MORE, TOO... OUR SEARCH FOR THE MISSING REBEL PILOT-- TAY VANIS --AND THE VITAL INFORMATION HE WAS CARRYING ENDED IN TOTAL FAILURE...
WE FOLLOWED THE TRAIL FOR WEEKS...BUT IT TURNED INTO A DEAD END AT ISKALON...
WE'RE SORRY, GENERAL...
DON'T BLAME YOURSELF, PRINCESS LEIA... I KNOW THAT YOU, AND LUKE, AND THE OTHERS DID THE VERY BEST YOU COULD...

WHILE YOU WERE RETURNING FROM ISKALON IN THE *MILLENNIUM FALCON*, WE RECEIVED NEW INFORMATION... INFORMATION THAT COULD DRAMATICALLY RESTRUCTURE OUR PRIORITIES...
INFORMATION SO INCREDIBLE THAT...
WHAT IS IT, SIR?

THAT'S JUST IT... I DON'T THINK YOU'D BELIEVE ME IF I SIMPLY TOLD YOU.
I WANT ALL OF YOU TO SEE THIS FOR YOURSELVES.

NOW, AS ALL OF YOU KNOW, YOU'VE SPENT THE PAST FEW WEEKS SEARCHING FOR TWO MISSING REBEL SPIES-- *TAY VANIS* AND *YOM ARGO*.
TOGETHER, THE PAIR OF THEM HAD UNCOVERED POSITIVE INFORMATION ABOUT THE NATURE AND LOCATION OF THE EMPIRE'S NEW SECRET WEAPON...
ARGO WAS KILLED ON THE PLANET *LAHSBANE*, AND VANIS WAS LAST SEEN SOMEWHERE IN THE REGION OF THE TWIN PLANETS OF ISKALON AND *GAMANDAR*...
HOWEVER, WE RECENTLY INTERCEPTED A TOP-SECRET IMPERIAL TRANSMISSION THAT WAS BEAMED TO THEIR FLEET FROM ONE OF THE CITY COMPUTERS IN THE *FORTRESS* THEY SET UP AFTER CONQUERING GAMANDAR.

IMPERIAL REPORTS INDICATE THAT ANOTHER REBEL HAD UNCOVERED THE SAME INFORMATION THAT ARGO AND VANIS HAD...
THE TRANSMISSION INCLUDED A HOLOGRAPHIC PROJECTION IDENTIFYING THAT REBEL...

?

HAN SOLO!
GROWR
H-HAN...
BUT IT CAN'T BE!
CHEWBACCA... HAN WAS YOUR PARTNER... SO LEVEL WITH ME. DID HE DO ANY ESPIONAGE WORK WHILE THE TWO OF YOU WERE TOGETHER...
...OR WERE YOU TWO EVER SEPARATED LONG ENOUGH FOR HIM TO HAVE LEARNED THE EMPIRE'S SECRET ALONE?
gruph
THAT'S WHAT I THOUGHT... BUT DO HAN AND ALL OF US A FAVOR AND KEEP YOUR WOOKIEE MOUTH QUIET ABOUT IT, OKAY?
EVEN IF WE DON'T BELIEVE THE REPORT, THE CHANCE TO MOBIL-IZE THE SEARCH FOR HAN AGAIN IS TOO GOOD TO PASS UP!
IT SURE IS GOOD TO SEE OL' HAN AGAIN, EVEN IF IT'S ONLY LIKE THIS, HUH, LEIA?
OOHH... OH, YES...

COMMANDER, NO ONE IS AS ANXIOUS TO FIND CAPTAIN SOLO AS I... *WE* ARE... BUT WE CANNOT LET OUR FEELINGS BLIND US TO THE TRUTH.
HE'S BEEN A PRISONER OF BOUNTY HUNTERS-- ENCASED IN A BLOCK OF CARBONITE-- EVER SINCE LANDO CALRISSIAN JOINED US AT THE PLANET *BESPIN*...

I'M AWARE OF THAT, PRINCESS LEIA... BUT SO IS THE EMPIRE.
IT WAS THEY, AFTER ALL, WHO ACTUALLY HANDED CAPTAIN SOLO OVER TO HIS CAPTORS...
IF THEY BELIEVE THAT CAPTAIN SOLO CONSTITUTES A THREAT TO THEIR SECURITY, WE CAN ONLY ASSUME THAT THEY HAVE RECENT INFORMATION WHICH WE ARE NOT YET PRIVY TO.

LEIA... MAKING THAT SPEECH WAS THE BRAVEST, MOST UNSELFISH THING I'VE EVER SEEN YOU DO...
THEN... WHAT ARE WE GOING TO DO?

I PROPOSE THAT WE DIVIDE OUR FORCES... WE HAVE NEW LEADS ON BOTH MISSING MEN... YOUR HIGHNESS, I'D LIKE YOU AND COMMANDER SKYWALKER TO CONTINUE THE SEARCH FOR VANIS...
WELL, IF ANYONE'S GOING TO GO LOOKING FOR HAN, IT'LL BE ME AND CHEWBACCA... NO ONE HAS A BETTER RIGHT TO GO AFTER HIM THAN WE DO...

PRECISELY MY FEELINGS ON THE MATTER, LANDO.
I'LL BRIEF YOU ON WHERE YOU'RE GOING AS SOON AS LUKE AND THE PRINCESS ARE ON THEIR WAY TO THEIR DESTINATION... *KABRAY*...
THE ONLY PROBLEM IS... WE'RE NOT SURE OF WHAT THE BEST WAY OF GETTING THEM IN THERE UNOBTRUSIVELY IS...

EXCUSE ME, MY DEAR FELLOW, IF I INTERJECT A THOUGHT... BUT AS A TELEPATH, I CANNOT HELP BUT BE AWARE OF THE PRECISE NATURE OF YOUR PROBLEM...
AND, AS SPOKESMIND FOR ALL OF THE HOOJIBS, I THINK I SEE A SIMPLE SOLUTION TO IT...

I'M GLAD THEY LET US TAKE THE FALCON... I GUESS THEY FIGURED LANDO AND CHEWIE WERE TOO LIKELY TO BE RECOGNIZED IF ANY OF HAN'S ENEMIES SAW THEM FLYING HAN'S SHIP...
BUT I WISH THEY'D LET US TAKE ONE OF THE DROIDS, TOO...
I DO, TOO... BUT THEY NEEDED THREE-PIO TO HELP WITH DE-BRIEFING ARTOO...

ARTOO WAS HOOKED UP TO THE IMPERIAL COMMUNICA-TIONS SYSTEMS THE WHOLE TIME HE WAS ON GAMANDAR ...WHO KNOWS WHAT KIND OF VITAL INFORMATION HE MAY HAVE COME INTO CONTACT WITH?
WE'RE COMING UP ON KABRAY NOW... SURE ISN'T MUCH TO LOOK AT, IS IT?
RIGHT... IT'S ONE OF THE MOST PERFECT-LY USELESS AND NEUTRAL SPACE STA-TIONS IN EXISTENCE...

THAT'S WHAT MAKES IT A PERFECT PLACE FOR EMBASSIES AND DELEGATIONS TO CONVENE...
IN THE DAYS BEFORE THE EMPIRE IT WAS THE HUB OF THE GALAXY... EVEN NOW IT STILL GETS PRETTY LIVELY SOMETIMES...
PLIF, WE REALLY APPRECIATE YOU AND YOUR PEOPLE LEAVING ARBRA AND COMING ALONG TO HELP US...

THINK NOTHING OF IT, LUKE. WE ARE HAPPY TO EXPAND OUR HORIZONS WITH THIS SHORT EXCURSION...
ESPECIALLY IN THE NAME OF FRIENDSHIP...
THROUGH THE THOUGHTS OF YOU AND YOUR FRIENDS...ES-PECIALLY HER HIGHNESS... WE HAVE LEARNED A GREAT DEAL ABOUT WHAT KIND OF MAN CAPTAIN SOLO IS. WE FEEL HE'S WORTH SOME RISK.
OH.
DON'T BE EMBARRASSED, MY DEAR. ANY MALE WOULD BE PLEASED TO KNOW HE'D INSPIRED SUCH FEELINGS IN A LADY.

WELL, WE WERE CLEARED FOR LANDING WITH NO TROUBLE. LET'S HOPE THE REST OF THE MISSION GOES AS SMOOTHLY...

OH, **NO!** IT CAN'T BE--!

HELLO THERE, DARLING!
WERE YOU LOOKING FOR ME?

EURK
GET HOLD OF YOURSELF, LUKE. THAT ISN'T *DANI*, IT'S SOME GIRL YOU'VE NEVER SEEN BEFORE.
I TOLD YOU WHEN YOU MET DANI NOT TO TAKE HER FRIENDLINESS TOO SERIOUSLY. ALL *ZELTRONS* ARE LIKE THAT!
GEE... I ALWAYS THOUGHT DANI LIKED ME PERSONALLY... A LITTLE...

UH... NO, I'M AFRAID I WASN'T REALLY LOOKING FOR ANYONE...
THEN, AREN'T WE LUCKY YOU FOUND US!
HHMMPH
WHAT IS IT?
THOSE ZELTRONS! THEIR... ENTHUSIASMS MAKE THEM NATURAL BORN PARTY MIXERS...
MARK MY THOUGHTS, PLIF, YOU CAN ALWAYS TRUST THEM TO OVERRUN ANY EMBASSY PARTY...

...JUST LIKE A LOT OF...
...LIKE...

UH... LIKE...
DON'T TAKE IT PERSONALLY LEIA.

YES...? AND JUST WHO ARE YOU?
WE'RE NEWLY ARRIVED HERE... FROM THE PLANET ARBRA...
YAWN HOW ENCHANTING, I'M SURE...
AND JUST WHAT IS THERE ABOUT YOU THAT SHOULD CONVINCE THESE STORM TROOPERS AND ME TO LET YOU PROCEED ANY FURTHER INTO THE ROOM?

AND JUST WHAT QUALIFICATIONS DO YOU HAVE--OUTSIDE OF OFFICIOUSNESS, BOORISHNESS, AND MISGUIDED SNOBBERY--FOR ANY DUTY WHATSOEVER?
WHEN THE YOUNG LADY AND THE GENTLEMAN AGREED TO JOIN THE DELEGATION I LEAD, I ASSURED THEM THEY WOULD BE SUBJECTED TO NO UNPLEASANTNESS...
MAKE A LIAR OF ME AGAIN, AND I ASSURE YOU, THE IMPERIAL GOVERNOR OF THIS SATELLITE SHALL HEAR OF IT!

WELL DONE, PLIF!
UNDER THE CIRCUMSTANCES, IT SEEMED LIKE THE BEST WAY TO PROCEED.
INDEED!
VERILY!

YOU KNOW... I DON'T FEEL LIKE THIS MUCH ANY MORE THESE DAYS... BUT ALL OF A SUDDEN, IT'S LIKE I'M A KID FRESH OFF THE DESERT MOISTURE FARM AGAIN...
...LIKE I STILL HAVE SAND IN BOTH MY EARS...
BEFORE THE EMPEROR DISBANDED THE SENATE, I REPRESENTED MY HOME PLANET...
I FEEL RIGHT AT HOME IN GATHERINGS LIKE THIS...
GEE, THAT BLONDE GUY IS CUTE!
TEE-HEE

BUT, WHATEVER YOU DO, DON'T EAT ANYTHING YOU DON'T RECOGNIZE... REMEMBER, ONE RACE'S DELICACY IS ANOTHER RACE'S POISON...
FOOD'S THE LAST THING ON MY MIND RIGHT NOW...
AND WE DON'T INTEND TO EAT ANYTHING WE'RE NOT SUPPOSED TO, EITHER...

WE'D BETTER SPLIT UP NOW... TAKE THE BEST OPPORTUNITY TO SLIP AWAY AND FIND THE MESSAGE VANIS IS SUPPOSED TO HAVE LEFT HERE...
RIGHT.

DID YOU HEAR THAT AT THE VERY LAST MINUTE, THE REPRESENTATIVES OF ISKALON WITHDREW THEIR ACCEPTANCE AND REFUSED TO ATTEND?
THE SCANDAL HAS BEEN SIMPLY...

HHHHSSSS!
NO, REALLY, I'M NOT SAYING IT JUST TO FLATTER YOU! WOMEN FIND MEN WITH WINGS INCREDIBLY SEXY...
TEE-HEE
HUHKS

CAN YOU IMAGINE? THIS YEAR, THEY'RE ACTUALLY ADMITTING DELEGATES FROM THE PLANET LAHSBANE!
BUT ONLY THE VERY YOUNG ONES, FORTUNATELY!
GOODNESS, YES! IF YOU COULD SEE WHAT THEY'RE LIKE AFTER THEY REACH PUBERTY!

HELLO, THERE! I'VE NEVER SEEN A MAN AS BEAUTIFUL AS YOU IN MY LIFE! WANT TO HAVE SOME FUN?
NOT REALLY.
WELL, WE DO! DON'T BE SELFISH!
UH... BYE.

WHEW
NO, SERIOUSLY... I HAVE IT IN THE STRICTEST CONFIDENCE THAT THE AMBASSADOR FROM PURSIN HAS HAD A SECRET MEETING WITH THE GOVERNOR...
HE PROPOSED THAT IF THE GOVERNOR SETTLED THEIR DISPUTE WITH THE PLANET YUGAMI IN PURSIN'S FAVOR, THEN THE PURSIANS WOULD RULE YUGAMI AS AN IMPERIAL SATRAP!
DO YOU KNOW WHAT THEY DECIDED?

LUKE SLIPPED OUT THE DOORWAY THAT LEADS TO WHERE THE PRIVATE ROOMS ARE LOCATED...
I WONDER WHAT'S BACK HERE...

THIS AREA IS RATHER SQUALID... AND ALL THAT EQUIPMENT...
OH, I SEE... THIS MUST BE WHERE THE ENTERTAINERS' ROOMS ARE LOCATED...
IT CAN'T HURT TO LOOK AROUND... FOR ALL WE KNOW, VANIS WAS HERE MASQUERADING AS AN EMPLOYEE AND NOT A DELEGATE!

BUT, SHIRLEY! YOU'RE OUR HEADLINER... OUR STAR! THE GOVERNOR IS LOOKING FORWARD TO--! ÷EEP÷
NOW, LISTEN UP, MORTI, AND LISTEN GOOD! I MEANT WHAT I TOLD YOU WHEN I TOOK YOU ON AS MY AGENT--
--I DON'T WORK FREAK SHOWS!

WELL, PLIF, THIS IS WHERE THE PRIVATE ROOMS ARE LOCATED.
IF VANIS WAS HERE WITH ONE OF THE DELEGATES, HE MAY HAVE LEFT SOME MESSAGE ABOUT HIS NEXT DESTINATION IN ONE OF THE ROOMS.

HELLO, THERE!
OH, NO.

ARE YOU LOOKING FOR SOMETHING?
ARE YOU LOST?
ARE YOU LOOKING FOR US?
NO!!

LUKE... I THOUGHT YOU MIGHT LIKE TO KNOW... FROM WHAT I CAN PICK UP OF THE ZELTRONS' THOUGHTS AND FEEINGS...
IT ISN'T JUST THEIR NATURAL TENDENCIES AT WORK TONIGHT.
IT'S SOMETHING ABOUT YOU, PERSONALLY.
GREAT.
TOO BAD.
HAVE YOU SEEN ANYTHING NICER SINCE WE GOT HERE?
NO.
THEN WHAT ARE WE WAITING FOR?
I ALSO FEEL YOU OUGHT TO KNOW...
...THAT THOSE TWO GIRLS ARE IN HOT PURSUIT AND GAINING ON US.
WHAT?! IS THIS ROOM EMPTY?
YES.
GOOD.
PANT PANT PANT
THE DRESSING ROOMS WERE A WASHOUT. BUT TAY VANIS COULD HAVE SERVED ON THE KITCHEN STAFF...
THEY CERTAINLY DO SERVE SOMETHING FOR EVERY TASTE HERE...

JUST AS MY MASTER LIKES IT-- SO FRESH IT'S STILL WARM!
ICK!

AND JUST WHAT DO YOU THINK YOU'RE DOING, SNOOPING AROUND MY KITCHENS?
WELL? I'M WAITING...

I'M HERE... IN THE INTERESTS OF MY MASTER... THE GREAT PLIF, OF THE HOOJIBS OF ARBRA...
YOU SEE, PLIF IS VERY PARTICULAR ABOUT WHAT HE EATS...
VERY PARTICULAR... YOU CAN'T IMAGINE HOW PARTICULAR HE IS...
YOU REALLY CAN'T!

WHEW
FINICKY UPSTART!

OH, NO! HERE COMES SOMEONE ELSE... AND I CAN'T THINK OF A SINGLE GLIB EXPLANATION FOR WHY I'M DOWN HERE ON ALL FOURS!

JUST WAIT TILL THAT DOUBLECROSSER GETS A TASTE OF THIS SOUP!

WELL, AT LEAST WE PICKED A GOOD TIME TO SEARCH... WITH THE BANQUET AND SHOWS GOING ON, MOST OF THE ROOMS ARE EMPTY...
WE'VE LOOKED IN THIRTEEN SUITES SO FAR. HOW MANY MORE ARE YOU GOING TO CHECK?
AS MANY AS IT TAKES... ALL OF THEM IF NECESSARY...

AT LEAST, WORKING WITH THIS SCANNER, IT DOESN'T TAKE ME MUCH TIME TO LOOK...

...FOR...
FOR WHAT?

FOR THAT!
PLIF! WE'VE DONE IT! WE'VE FOUND VANIS'S MESSAGE...

AFTER ALL THESE WEEKS OF SEARCHING!

HUNH?
I'D SUGGEST WE CONCEAL OURSELVES AT ONCE...THE TENANT OF THIS ROOM IS ABOUT TO FIND US!

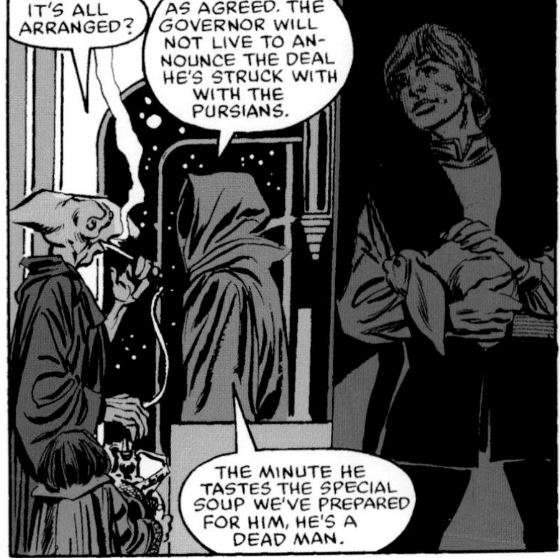
IT'S ALL ARRANGED?
AS AGREED. THE GOVERNOR WILL NOT LIVE TO ANNOUNCE THE DEAL HE'S STRUCK WITH WITH THE PURSIANS.
THE MINUTE HE TASTES THE SPECIAL SOUP WE'VE PREPARED FOR HIM, HE'S A DEAD MAN.

WHAT?!

NICE EMBASSY THIS IS!
COME ON, PLIF. NO ONE LIKES IMPERIALS LESS THAN I DO, BUT I CAN'T JUST STAND AROUND WHILE A MURDER IS COMMITTED...
ESPECIALLY NOT A MURDER THAT'S LIKELY TO SET OFF A WAR.

LET ME KNOW IF THEY BEGIN TO SUSPECT WE'RE ON TO THEM!

STOP RIGHT WHERE YOU ARE! WE HAVE YOU SURROUNDED!

EEK!
NOW, BE A GOOD BOY AND STOP BREAKING OUR HEARTS!
SAY YOU'LL COME BACK TO OUR SUITE WITH US.
LOOK, I'M SORRY, BUT I--

--I-YI-YI!
STORM TROOPERS!
PLOP
I'D LIKE TO PASS ON THE HOT TUB... JUST FOR A LITTLE WHILE. I WAS ON MY WAY BACK TO TO THE MAIN BALLROOM TO CATCH THE NEXT SHOW...

DOESN'T THAT SOUND LIKE FUN?
TEE-HEE-HEE-HEE
NO.
ONE SIDE, LAHSBEE.
BUT WE'LL GO, TO MAKE YOU HAPPY...
IF YOU PROMISE YOU'LL MAKE US HAPPY, LATER.

WELL, THE EMPLOYEES' QUARTERS DON'T SEEM TO HAVE BEEN WHERE VANIS SPENT HIS TIME ...I'VE CHECKED THEM PRETTY THOROUGHLY...
I HOPE LUKE AND PLIF HAD BETTER LUCK...
NOW, ALL I HAVE TO DO IS MAKE IT BACK TO THE MAIN BALLROOM WITHOUT ATTRACTING ANY ATTENTION...
YOU'RE SURE SHE'S HIDING OUT BACK HERE?
POSITIVE. I SAW HER MYSELF, SKULKING ABOUT...
OH, NO!
HOW WILL YOU HANDLE HER, ONCE WE'VE CAUGHT HER?
DON'T WORRY. THERE ARE WAYS!
WE SAW YOU DUCK IN HERE! COME OUT, OR WE'LL COME IN AFTER YOU!
THE GOVERNOR DOESN'T LIKE TO BE KEPT WAITING!
HOW DO I HIDE? WHAT CAN I DO?!
AH, SHIRLEY... I'M SO GLAD YOU'VE COME TO YOUR SENSES AND DECIDED TO BE REASONABLE ABOUT ALL THIS...
I WOULD SO HAVE HATED TO HAVE TO GET NASTY... AND INVOKE THAT CLAUSE IN YOUR CONTRACT!
BUT... I DON'T... I'M NOT...
I THOUGHT YOU WERE--!

I UNDERSTAND, SWEETIE. IT'S YOUR FIRST GOVERNOR. A LITTLE STAGE FRIGHT IS NORMAL, BUT YOU DON'T HAVE TIME TO STAND AROUND AND INDULGE YOURSELF!
BUT YOU DON'T UNDERSTAND...
EXPLAIN IT TO ME LATER, CHICKIE! THE SHOW STARTS IN FIVE MINUTES...
BUT, I TELL YOU, I'M NOT...

AND YOU'RE GOING TO HAVE TO SPEND ALL THAT TIME IN DRESSING... LET ME PICK YOU OUT SOMETHING NICE...
I MEAN, THAT RAG YOU HAVE ON WILL NEVER, BUT NEVER DO! WHERE'D YOU PICK IT UP, ANYWAY?
TACKY! TACKY! TACKY!

ISN'T THE FIRST COURSE READY YET?
THEY'RE BRINGING IT FROM THE KITCHEN NOW, GOVERNOR...
GREAT, PLIF! DID YOU HEAR THAT? AND I STILL HAVEN'T FIGURED OUT ANY WAY I CAN PREVENT HIM FROM DRINKING IT... AT LEAST NOT WITHOUT ATTRACTING ATTENTION...
YOU PROMISE? RIGHT AFTER THE SHOW?
THAT'S A VERY STRANGE THING FOR YOU TO BE WORRIED ABOUT UNDER THE CIRCUMSTANCES...
AT LEAST, REST ASSURED THE REST OF US HAVE DONE EXACTLY AS YOU ASKED...
I CAN'T WAIT!
I REALLY CAN'T WAIT! LET'S GO BACK TO MY ROOM NOW!

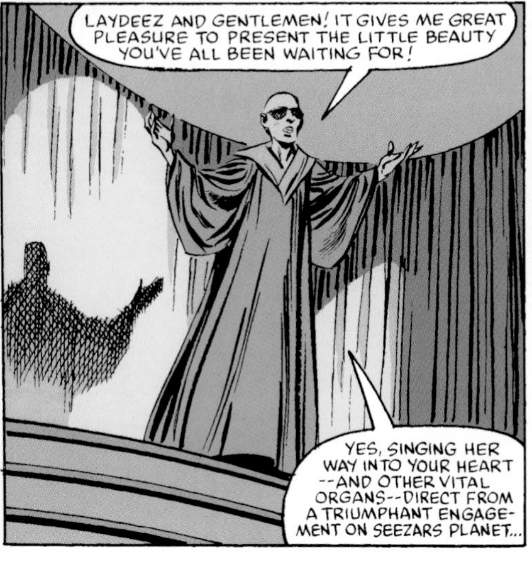
LAYDEEZ AND GENTLEMEN! IT GIVES ME GREAT PLEASURE TO PRESENT THE LITTLE BEAUTY YOU'VE ALL BEEN WAITING FOR!
YES, SINGING HER WAY INTO YOUR HEART --AND OTHER VITAL ORGANS--DIRECT FROM A TRIUMPHANT ENGAGEMENT ON SEEZARS PLANET...

THE CHANTEUSE OF THE STARS!

IT'S LEIA!
HELP.
COME ON, BABY! SING IT!
I... SUPPOSE I MIGHT AS WELL.

SIGH

L-LIKE A METEOR CUTTING ACROSS A STARLESS NIGHT...
BRAVO!

...HE BRIGHTENS UP MY DARKEST HOUR...
YOUR SOUP, GOVERNOR.
PLIF, LOOK!
SOUP'S ON!

I'VE RUN OUT OF CHOICES! I'VE GOT TO ACT, NOW, AND THEN ACCEPT THE CONSEQUENCES!
WELL, IT'S ABOUT TIME!
GEE... ARE YOU LITTLE FELLOWS ANY FUN?
♪ HE'S GENTLE AND HE'S TRUE...♫
♪ NEVER TRIES TO FORCE ME, OH, NO...♫
EEP
!!!!!!!!!!!!!!!
HUHK!
HUHK!!!
!!!!!!!!!!!!!!!
OH, NO! WHAT IS IT?!
BUT HOW COULD THAT HAPPEN?
ONE OF THE LAHSBEES HAS JUST REACHED PUBERTY!
I THINK HE WAS OVER-STIMULATED!

HERE'S MY CHANCE!
LET ME THROUGH! THE GOVERNOR MUST BE PROTECTED AT ALL COSTS!

ESPECIALLY FROM THE POISON IN THAT DISH YOU'RE SERVING.
WHOOPS! SORRY...

?
!!!!!!!!!!!
UH-OH.

ONE SIDE, HONEY!
COWARDS AND AMBASSADORS FIRST!
OH, NO! IT'S GOING AFTER LUKE!

GET BEHIND US!

THREATS TO THE GOVERNOR ARE OUR BUSINESS. OUR BLASTERS WILL TAKE CARE OF THAT THING!
I NEVER THOUGHT THE DAY WOULD COME WHEN IMPERIAL STORM TROOPERS WOULD BE PROTECTING ME!

HEY... MY BLASTER ISN'T WORKING!
NEITHER IS MINE! WHAT'S GOING ON HERE?

OH, NO! THIS IS MY FAULT!
I HAD THE HOOJIBS DRAIN THE ENERGY FROM EVERY TROOPER'S BLASTER, WHILE THEY WERE CIRCULATING AROUND THE PARTY, IN CASE LEIA AND I RAN INTO TROUBLE...
AND NONE OF THE OTHER DELEGATES ARE PERMITTED TO CARRY ANY SORT OF WEAPON!

!!!!!!!!!!!

PRINCESS LEIA! YOUR HIGHNESS, YOU MUST FINISH YOUR SONG AT ONCE!

MY SONG--? BUT, LUKE'S...
YOU MUST TRUST ME! I KNOW WHAT IS ON THAT ENORMOUS CREATURE'S MIND! YOUR VOICE IS THE ONLY HOPE LUKE HAS!

♪ A-AND... SO I FOLLOW HIM... ♫

♫ ... LIKE THE TAIL OF ♪ A COMET...

NEXT: LANDO CALRISSIAN AND CHEWBACCA THE WOOKIEE, STARRING IN--

THE BIG CON!

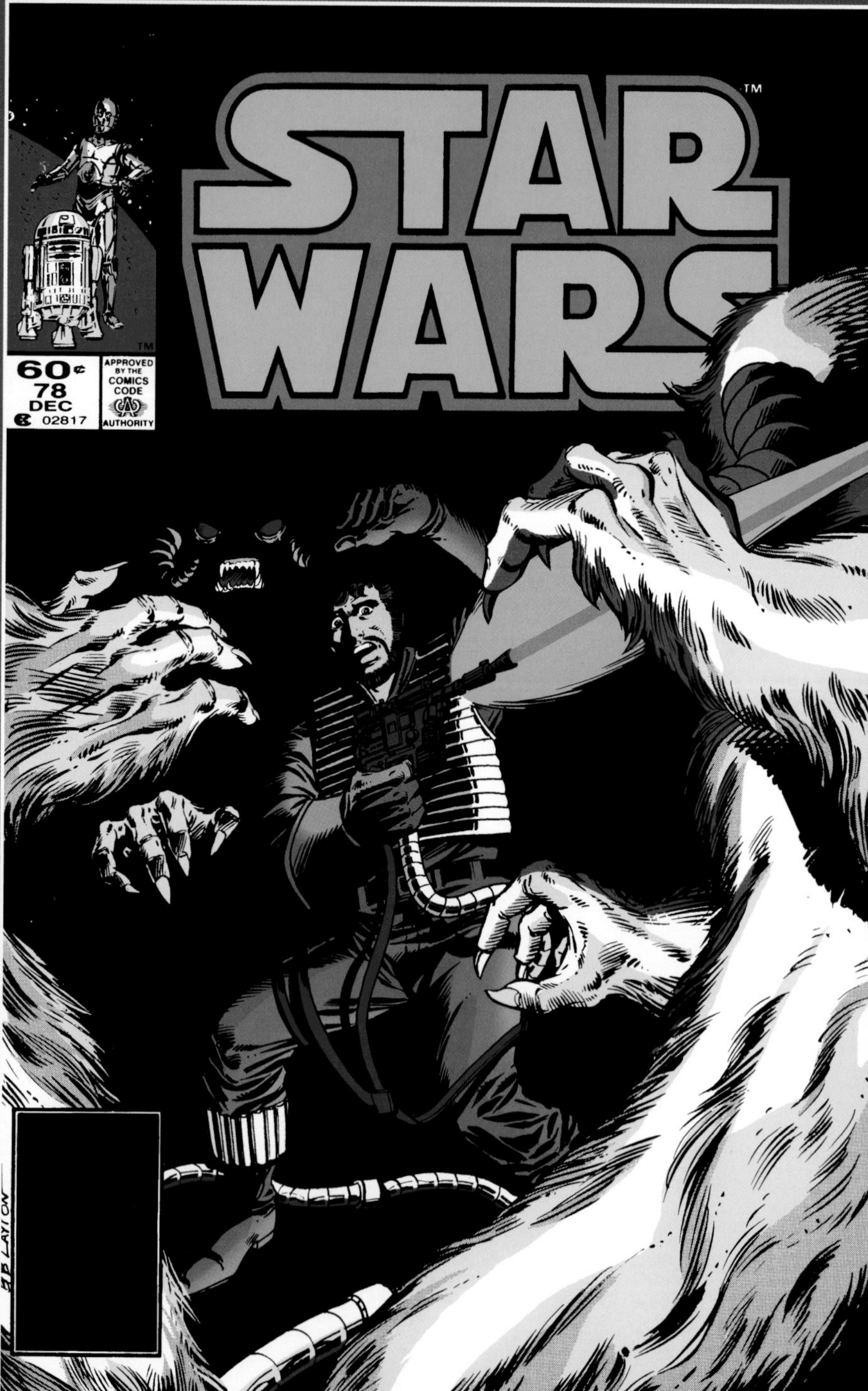
STAR WARS
60¢
78
DEC
02817
APPROVED BY THE COMICS CODE AUTHORITY

As *Luke Skywalker* and *Princess Leia* continue their search for their friend and ally, *Han Solo*, their thoughts drift back to another missing colleague and an even-more-desperate rescue mission...

Lucasfilm PRESENTS: STAR WARS™ THE GREATEST SPACE FANTASY OF ALL!

DAVID MICHELINIE PLOT / SCRIPT · LUKE McDONNELL PENCILS · BOB LAYTON PLOT/INKS · JOE ROSEN LETTERS · GLYNIS WEIN COLORS · LOUISE JONES EDITOR · JIM SHOOTER AT-AT/ITOR

HOTH STUFF!

HOURS AGO, A SLEEK STARSHIP HAD ROCKETED FROM A SECRET BASE ON THE PLANET ARBRA, CARRYING ITS CREW OF THREE ON A MISSION OF DESPERATE SEARCH.
NOW, IN AN ISOLATED QUADRANT OF THE UN-EXPLORED GALAXY, THAT SEARCH IS ABOUT TO END!
THERE'S THE TRANSPORT CRUISER OUR LONG-RANGE SCANNERS PICKED UP! IT'S WEDGE'S SHIP!
IT'S GOTTA BE!

LUKE, YOU REALLY SHOULDN'T GET YOUR HOPES UP TOO HIGH.
THE PRINCESS IS RIGHT, COMMANDER--
--THE TRAJECTORY OF THAT TRANSPORT MAY INDICATE THAT IT CAME FROM *HOTH*, BUT THERE'S NO EVIDENCE THAT *WEDGE ANTILLES* IS ON BOARD.
I MEAN, THINGS GOT PRETTY HOT ON THAT ICE PLANET WHEN THE EMPIRE SHOWED UP. AND SINCE WEDGE HASN'T BEEN HEARD FROM SINCE, THERE'S NO SOLID REASON TO BELIEVE THAT HE ESCAPED...
...OR THAT HE'S EVEN ALIVE!
BUT HE *IS* ALIVE! I *KNOW* HE IS! HE... WELL...
...HE *HAS* TO BE!

SLOWLY, PRECISELY, THE Y-WING FIGHTER MOVES CLOSER TO THE TRANSPORT'S DOCKING BAY. AND SOON--

--AS COMMANDER LUKE SKYWALKER, PRINCESS LEIA ORGANA AND LIEUTENANT BARLON HIGHTOWER CLAMBER ABOARD...
WEDGE! HEY, WEDGE!
COME ON, GUYS, WE'VE GOT TO SEARCH THE SHIP! EVERY INCH!

TAKE IT EASY, LUKE! YOU'RE NOT THINKING STRAIGHT! WE CAN ACCOMPLISH THE SAME PURPOSE MUCH FASTER BY TAKING A LIFE SCAN!
THEN DO IT!
I-I MEAN, UH... "PLEASE."

CALMLY, PRINCESS LEIA ACTIVATES A SHIPBOARD SENSOR CONSOLE, TAPS OUT A COMMAND FOR COMPREHENSIVE LIFE READINGS, AND FINDS...
NOTHING. THERE'S NO LIFE ON THIS SHIP AT ALL, EXCEPT FOR US.
IT'S A DERELICT, LUKE. I'M SORRY.

I DON'T BELIEVE IT. I WON'T BELIEVE IT!
I WON'T...

SAY, PRINCESS, I HOPE I'M NOT OUT OF LINE, BUT WHAT'S SO SPECIAL ABOUT ONE WARRIOR?
HE'S NOT JUST A WARRIOR, LIEUTENANT--

--HE'S LUKE'S OLDEST *FRIEND!* THEY GREW UP TOGETHER ON TATOOINE, THEY FOUGHT THE DEATH STAR TOGETHER... AND WHEN WEDGE DIDN'T SHOW UP AT THE RENDEZVOUS AFTER THE BATTLE ON HOTH, LUKE WAS CRUSHED.
MOST *BROTHERS* AREN'T AS CLOSE AS THEY WERE.
I SEE.

THAT'S WHY LUKE JUMPS AT ANY HOPE, EVEN ONE AS SLENDER AS THIS TRANSPORT. AND THAT'S WHY IT HURTS SO MUCH WHEN THAT HOPE PROVES TO BE AS HOLLOW AS--
--WAIT A MINUTE! THE SHIP'S *LOG TAPES!*

THEY'RE NOT MUCH, BUT MAYBE THEY CAN AT LEAST TELL US WHERE THE TRANSPORT CAME FROM! I'LL JUST PUNCH IN THE STANDARD PLAYBACK CODE AND--

HI, FOLKS! IF YOU'RE HEARIN' THIS, I GUESS YOU'RE ALIVE!
SURE WISH *I* WAS!
WEDGE! TH-THAT'S *WEDGE'S* VOICE!

THIS IS *WEDGE ANTILLES*, AND I *GUESS* I MIGHT AS WELL TELL MY STORY. NOT THAT IT MATTERS MUCH, BUT I DON'T HAVE ANYTHING BETTER TO DO. AND BESIDES--
--I ALWAYS DID LIKE SPINNIN' A GOOD YARN! SO--

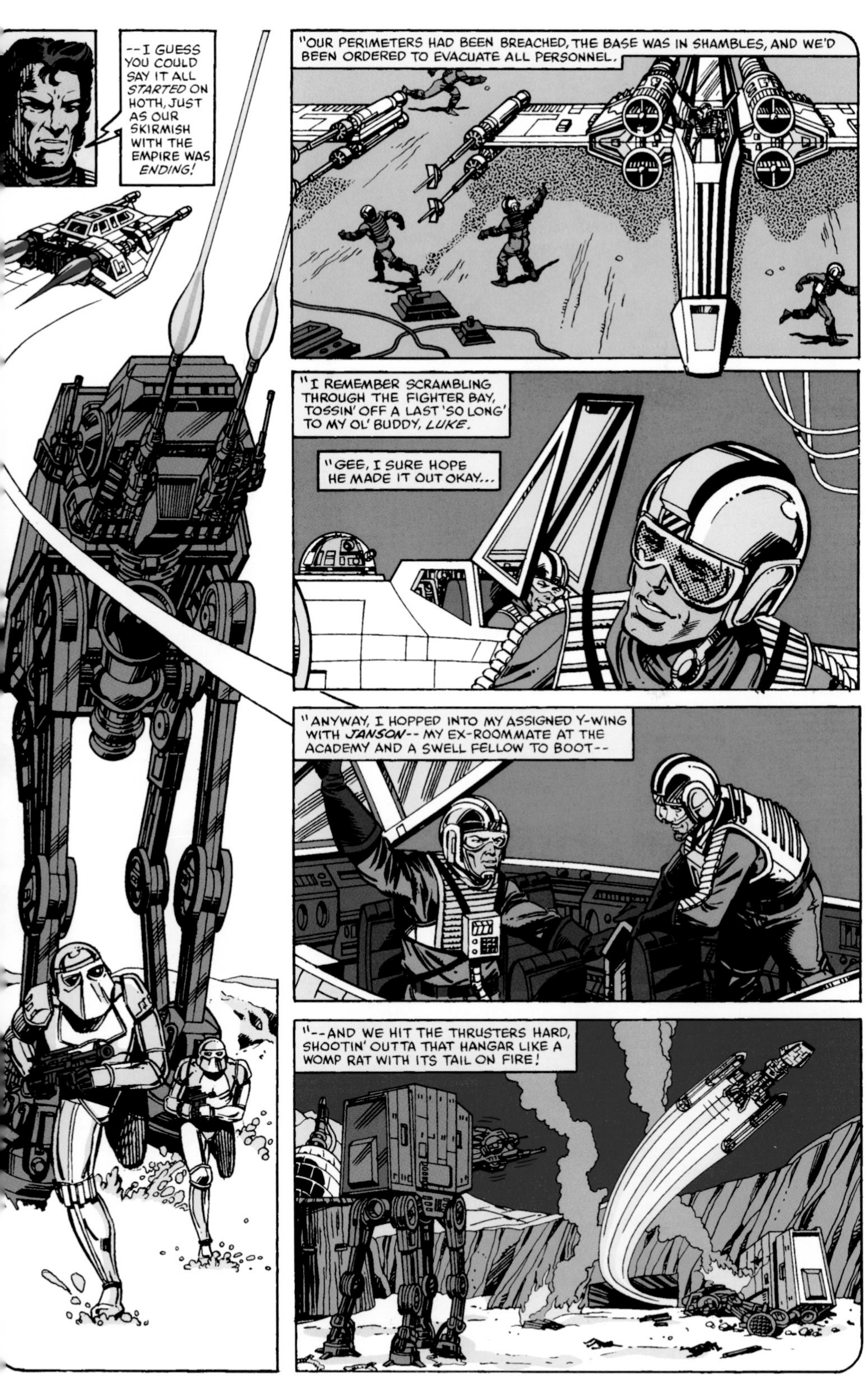
--I GUESS YOU COULD SAY IT ALL *STARTED* ON HOTH, JUST AS OUR SKIRMISH WITH THE EMPIRE WAS *ENDING*!
"OUR PERIMETERS HAD BEEN BREACHED, THE BASE WAS IN SHAMBLES, AND WE'D BEEN ORDERED TO EVACUATE ALL PERSONNEL.
"I REMEMBER SCRAMBLING THROUGH THE FIGHTER BAY, TOSSIN' OFF A LAST 'SO LONG' TO MY OL' BUDDY, *LUKE*.
"GEE, I SURE HOPE HE MADE IT OUT OKAY...
"ANYWAY, I HOPPED INTO MY ASSIGNED Y-WING WITH *JANSON*-- MY EX-ROOMMATE AT THE ACADEMY AND A SWELL FELLOW TO BOOT--
"--AND WE HIT THE THRUSTERS HARD, SHOOTIN' OUTTA THAT HANGAR LIKE A WOMP RAT WITH ITS TAIL ON FIRE!

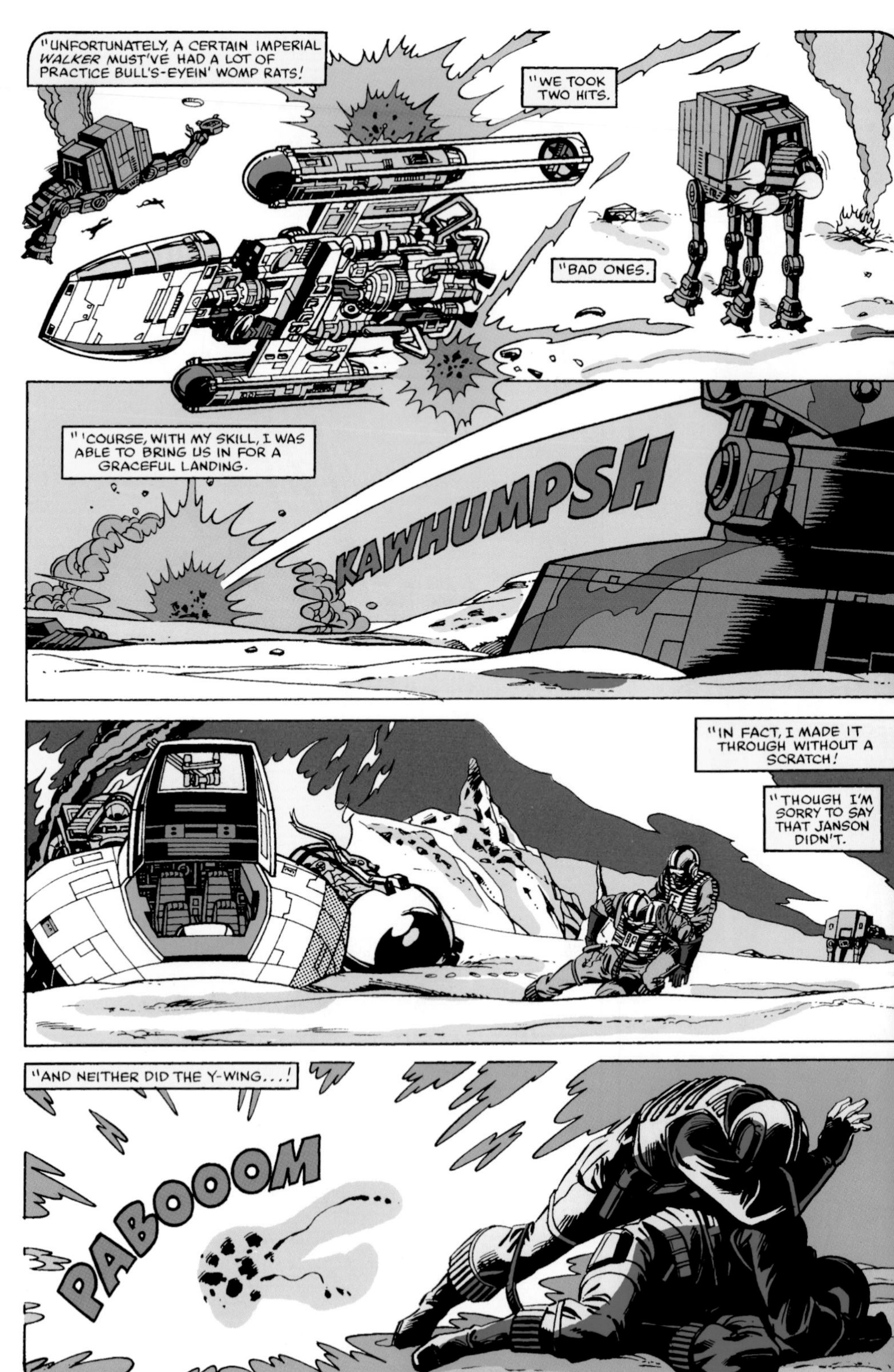
"UNFORTUNATELY, A CERTAIN IMPERIAL *WALKER* MUST'VE HAD A LOT OF PRACTICE BULL'S-EYEIN' WOMP RATS!
"WE TOOK TWO HITS.
"BAD ONES.
"'COURSE, WITH MY SKILL, I WAS ABLE TO BRING US IN FOR A GRACEFUL LANDING.
KAWHUMPSH
"IN FACT, I MADE IT THROUGH WITHOUT A SCRATCH!
"THOUGH I'M SORRY TO SAY THAT JANSON DIDN'T.
"AND NEITHER DID THE Y-WING...!
PABOOOM

"THE BATTLE WAS ALMOST OVER THEN, BUT WITH THE IMPERIALS SWARMING AROUND LIKE MYNOCKS ON A POWER GENERATOR, WE STILL NEEDED A PLACE TO HIDE--
"--SO WE HEADED FOR THE AT-AT LUKE HAD TAKEN OUT WITH A PROTON GRENADE!

"LUCKILY, THE CREW WAS TOO BUSY BEIN' DEAD TO NOTICE!

"ONCE INSIDE, WE BIDED OUR TIME UNTIL SUNSDOWN, WHILE STORMTROOPERS PICKED OUR OLD BASE APART, LIKE THEY WERE LOOKIN' FOR SOMETHING SPECIAL.
"BUT SINCE THEY DIDN'T SEEM TOO CONCERNED ABOUT THEIR OWN CASUALTIES, WE WERE SAFE ENOUGH IN THE WALKER.

"SO, AFTER TENDING TO JANSON AS BEST I COULD, AND BREAKING OUT A HEAT STICK FROM MY EMERGENCY PACK, I SETTLED DOWN FOR THE COLDEST NIGHT I EVER WANT TO SPEND!

"NOT THAT MORNING WAS MUCH BETTER--BUT AT LEAST THE SUNS WERE OUT TO MAKE THINGS *SEEM* WARMER.

"BUT EVEN THEY COULDN'T TAKE THE CHILL OFF A BATTLEFIELD LITTERED WITH FROZEN CORPSES, WRECKED WALKERS AND ABANDONED SNOWSPEEDER VADER AND HIS GANG HAD LEFT FAST, WITHOUT EVEN PICKING UP THE PIECES!

"WHATEVER THE SITH LORD WAS AFTER MUST'VE BEEN *REAL* IMPORTANT!

"BUT AT LEAST THEY WERE GONE, AND THAT MEANT THAT JANSON AND ME COULD RETURN TO THE BASE.

"MY IDEA WAS TO SET UP SHOP IN THE *ION CANNON TURRET.* THAT WOULD GIVE US PROTECTION FROM THE ELEMENTS--
"--AS WELL AS PROVIDE A VANTAGE POINT FOR SPOTTING ANY RESCUE EFFORTS.

"IT SOUNDED LIKE A GOOD PLAN, AND IT WAS. UNTIL WE ACTUALLY GOT INSIDE THE BASE AND HEARD--

GRRRAARRGGGH!
"--*WAMPAS!* THOSE BIG NATIVE BEASTIES WITH THE RAZOR-SHARP CLAWS!
"SEEMS THEY HADN'T WASTED ANY MORE TIME THAN VADER HAD!

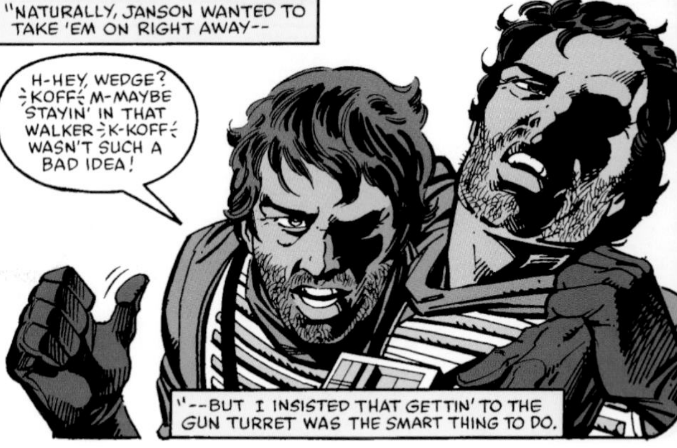

"NATURALLY, JANSON WANTED TO TAKE 'EM ON RIGHT AWAY--
H-HEY, WEDGE? *KOFF* M-MAYBE STAYIN' IN THAT WALKER *K-KOFF* WASN'T SUCH A BAD IDEA!
"--BUT I INSISTED THAT GETTIN' TO THE GUN TURRET WAS THE SMART THING TO DO.

"THE LIFTS WERE OUT, SO WE HAD TO CLIMB OVER A LOT OF DEBRIS IN THE BACK-UP STAIRWAY, BUT THE TURRET ITSELF WAS IN GOOD SHAPE.

"THE CONTROL ROOM WOULD KEEP THE WIND OFF US FINE AND, WITH THE HELP OF A PORTABLE HEAT GENERATOR, WOULD KEEP US WARM ENOUGH TO STAY ALIVE.

"SO, AFTER MAKIN' JANSON AS COMFORTABLE AS I COULD-- AND GETTIN' HIM TO PROMISE NOT TO RUN OUT AND TAKE ON THE WHOLE EMPIRE WHILE I WAS GONE--I SET OFF TO TAKE INVENTORY OF OUR NEW HOME-SWEET-HOME.

"LUCKILY, THERE WERE STILL A FEW CARTONS OF FOOD CONCENTRATE LEFT IN THE SUPPLY ROOM, SO I KNEW WE WOULDN'T STARVE.
"AT LEAST, NOT RIGHT AWAY.

"BUT THE BIG FIND CAME WHEN I STUMBLED INTO THE COMMUNICATIONS CENTER--

"--AND FOUND THAT IT WAS NOT ONLY INTACT, BUT WAS STILL FUNCTIONING!

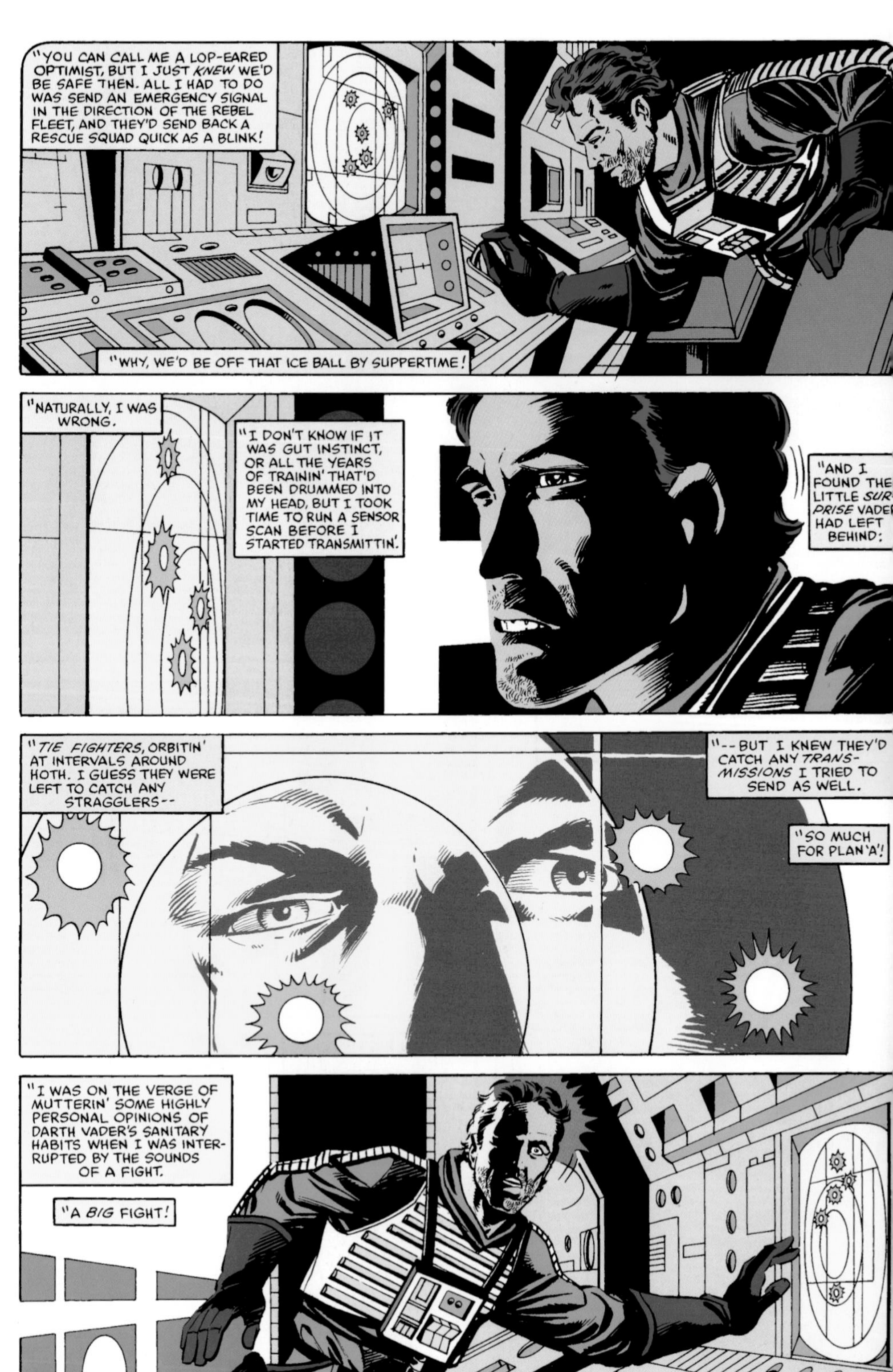
"YOU CAN CALL ME A LOP-EARED OPTIMIST, BUT I JUST KNEW WE'D BE SAFE THEN. ALL I HAD TO DO WAS SEND AN EMERGENCY SIGNAL IN THE DIRECTION OF THE REBEL FLEET, AND THEY'D SEND BACK A RESCUE SQUAD QUICK AS A BLINK!
"WHY, WE'D BE OFF THAT ICE BALL BY SUPPERTIME!
"NATURALLY, I WAS WRONG.
"I DON'T KNOW IF IT WAS GUT INSTINCT, OR ALL THE YEARS OF TRAININ' THAT'D BEEN DRUMMED INTO MY HEAD, BUT I TOOK TIME TO RUN A SENSOR SCAN BEFORE I STARTED TRANSMITTIN'.
"AND I FOUND THE LITTLE SURPRISE VADER HAD LEFT BEHIND:
"TIE FIGHTERS, ORBITIN' AT INTERVALS AROUND HOTH. I GUESS THEY WERE LEFT TO CATCH ANY STRAGGLERS--
"--BUT I KNEW THEY'D CATCH ANY TRANSMISSIONS I TRIED TO SEND AS WELL.
"SO MUCH FOR PLAN 'A'!
"I WAS ON THE VERGE OF MUTTERIN' SOME HIGHLY PERSONAL OPINIONS OF DARTH VADER'S SANITARY HABITS WHEN I WAS INTERRUPTED BY THE SOUNDS OF A FIGHT.
"A BIG FIGHT!

"FOR A MINUTE, I THOUGHT JANSON HAD BROKEN HIS PROMISE! BUT THEN I HEARD THE GROWLS...
"...THE ANIMAL SCREAMS...
"...AND THE SMELL HIT ME-- THE SHARP STINK O' THE STUFF I STARTED SLIPPIN' IN AS I GOT NEAR THE STOCK PENS.
"BLOOD!
"BUT EVEN THAT DIDN'T SET ME FOR WHAT I SAW WHEN I ENTERED THE PLACE--DEAD *TAUNTAUNS* WERE PILED ALL OVER!
"AND THERE WAS ONE LIVE ONE, ITS EYES LOOKIN' BIGGER'N PLANETS, CAUGHT SMACK BE- TWEEN TWO *REAL* DETERMINED WAMPAS!
"THE POOR BEAST DIDN'T STAND A CHANCE.

"AND I SOON KNEW EXACTLY HOW HE FELT!
"I GUESS HUMAN FLESH IS EVEN TASTIER THAN TAUNTAUN MEAT TO THOSE NASTIES!
"ANYWAY, I TOOK ONE OUT WITH MY BLASTER AS THEY CHARGED--
"--BUT THE OTHER TOOK *ME* OUT WITH A BACKHAND THAT FELT LIKE A RETRO BLAST FROM A STAR DESTROYER!
"SO I PLAYED DEAD.
"HE FELL FOR IT.
"AND THAT LITTLE MISTAKE COST HIM THE GAME!
"ALONG WITH, I'M HAPPY TO ADD, A GOODLY PORTION OF HIS SCRUFFY-LOOKIN' *SKULL*!
"ALL-IN-ALL, THE FIGHT LASTED LESS THAN A MINUTE. BUT IT TOOK *HOURS* TO CALM THAT TAUNTAUN DOWN.
"EVEN WHEN DOMESTICATED, THEY'RE MIGHTY SKITTISH
"BUT I FINALLY GOT THE BEASTIE BREATHIN' NORMAL AGAIN, AND TETHERED HER NEAR THE GUN TURRET.

AND THAT'S WHEN THE REAL ORDEAL BEGAN. THE IMMEDIATE DANGER WAS OVER, BUT A SUBTLE, SNEAKIER ENEMY POPPED UP:
BOREDOM.

"JANSON WAS HURT WORSE THAN I'D THOUGHT, HURT INSIDE WHERE I COULDN'T HELP HIM.
"IT TOOK A LOT OUT OF HIM TO TALK, SO EVENTUALLY HE JUST STOPPED.

"AND THAT LEFT ME WITH A LOT OF QUIET, AND A LOT OF MEMORIES. MOSTLY, I THOUGHT OF BELINA, AND THE TIME WE'D SPENT TOGETHER IN THE COOL, DRY NIGHTS OF TATOOINE.
"AND THAT PROBABLY HURT ME AS MUCH AS JANSON'S WOUNDS HURT HIM. BUT I COULDN'T STOP...
"...EVEN IF I'D WANTED TO.

"MONTHS PASSED, AND SUPPLIES RAN LOW.
"I SUPPLEMENTED OUR LARDER BY HUNTIN' ICE SCRABBLERS-- Y'KNOW, THOSE FURRY RODENTS WHO'RE EATEN BY TAUNTAUNS, WHO'RE EATEN BY WAMPAS, WHO'RE EATEN BY NO ONE 'CAUSE THEY'RE TOO MEAN?
"YEAH, THOSE'RE THE ONES...

"ANYHOW, THAT'S ABOUT ALL I HAD TO DO--
"--'CEPT TELL JANSON MY LIFE STORY A COUPLA DOZEN TIMES. I DON'T THINK HE COULD EVEN HEAR, THEN, BUT IT HELPED ME TO TALK.

"AND ALL THE WHILE THOSE IMPERIAL FIGHTERS KEPT GOIN' 'ROUND...
"...AND ROUND...
"...AND 'ROUND.

"LIFE WAS DULL, SURE, BUT LOOKIN' BACK, I ALMOST WISH IT HADN'T CHANGED...
"...LEASTWAYS NOT IN THE WAY IT *DID* CHANGE THAT DAY I CAME BACK FROM A SUCCESSFUL HUNT--
"--AND FOUND A SCENE THAT DROPPED MY BODY TEMP LOWER THAN THE SNOW AND SLUSH I'D JUST BEEN GALLOPIN' THROUGH!
"THE CANNON TURRET WAS WRECKED. ELECTRONIC COMPONENTS HAD BEEN TORN OUT O' THE CONSOLES, SUPPLIES HAD BEEN SCATTERED ALL OVER THE FLOOR. AND JANSON...
...POOR JANSON, A HELPLESS MAN WHO WAS DYIN' ANYWAY...
"...HAD BEEN *SLAUGHTERED!* CARVED UP AND LEFT TO ROT BY SOMEONE WHO KNEW THEIR BUSINESS--
"--AND OBVIOUSLY *ENJOYED* IT!

"I CAN'T SAY WHEN I'VE BEEN AS ANGRY. WHY, I WAS SO MAD THAT I ALMOST MISSED THE TRACKS-- A DOZEN MEN, SEVERAL VEHICLES.
"BUT FIND 'EM I DID.

"AND I FOLLOWED 'EM-- THROUGH BATTLEFIELDS STRIPPED OF USEFUL EQUIPMENT, OF ANYTHING ELECTRONIC, ANYTHING EVEN REMOTELY VALUABLE.
"AND IT BEGAN TO DAWN ON ME JUST WHO I WAS UP AGAINST.

"WHEN I HEARD SOUNDS, I SLOWED DOWN, DISMOUNTED, CREPT FORWARD...
"...AND THE INHUMAN LAUGHTER, THE WORDS THAT SLID OFF ALIEN TONGUES LIKE COLD GREASE, TOLD ME I'D BEEN RIGHT.

"THOUGH I WISHED WITH ALL MY HEART THAT I HADN'T BEEN.

"*SCAVENGERS!*

" THE SCUM OF THE GALAXY, MISFITS WHO FOLLOW THE PATHS OF BATTLE, STEALIN' ANYTHING THEY CAN SELL, MAKIN' A PROFIT FROM THE PAIN OF WAR.

"HECK, MOST'D SHOOT THEIR OWN MOTHERS FOR A SECOND-HAND DROID MOTIVATOR!

"BUT THAT WASN'T THE *BIG* SURPRISE.
"WHEN I FOCUSED MY MACRO-BINOCULARS ON THE GROUP'S TRANSPORT, I SAW--
"--*ARNS GRIMRAKER!*
"A CHIEF SCAVENGER THE REBELLION'D DEALT WITH BEFORE, WHEN WE HADN'T ANY CHOICE.
"I DOUBT YOU COULD FIND A CRUELER, MORE SOULLESS MAN IN THE WHOLE UNIVERSE.
"AND I SUDDENLY KNEW JUST WHO'D SENT JANSON ON HIS FINAL JOURNEY...!
"BUT I WAS OUTNUMBERED, OUTGUNNED, SO I REMOUNTED AND HEADED BACK TO BASE--
"--WITH MY STOMACH FEELING AS HOLLOW AS THE CORE OF A BLACK HOLE.
"THE REST OF THE DAY WAS SPENT CLEANIN' UP, AND BURYIN' JANSON BENEATH THE SNOW.
"I SAID A FEW WORDS OVER THE GRAVE, BUT IN ALL HONESTY...MY HEART WASN'T IN IT.
"I WAS THINKIN' MORE OF ME, OF HOW I'D GET BY WITH JANSON GONE.
"AND I KNEW I WOULDN'T.
"IN TOTAL ISOLATION, WITH NO ONE TO EVEN TALK TO, I'D GO INSANE.
"I KNEW THEN THAT I'D HAVE TO STEAL A SHIP AND GET OFF HOTH. I'D HAVE TO FACE THE SCAVENGERS. IT WAS THE ONLY WAY I COULD SURVIVE. AND BESIDES...
"...I WANTED TO *NAIL* THOSE SLIME-LICKERS!

"SO, THE NEXT DAY, I WENT BACK TO THE SCAVENGERS' CAMP--AND FOUND GRIMRAKER AND HIS CREW IN THE PROCESS OF PACKIN' UP.
"I GUESS THEY'D FINISHED STRIPPIN' HOTH OF EVERYTHING WORTH TAKIN'.
BUT AT LEAST THE GUARDS WERE PREOCCUPIED--EITHER BY BEIN' BORED OR BY MENTALLY COUNTIN' THEIR SHARE O' THE TAKE--
"--AND I WAS ABLE TO MAKE MY WAY TO THE GUN TUGS THE SCAVS USED TO ESCORT THEIR TRANSPORT SHIP.
"I FIGURED THEY MUST'VE DOPED OUT THE TIE FIGHTER PATTERNS IN ORDER TO GET TO AND FROM HOTH SAFELY--
"--SO I PROCEEDED TO DO A LITTLE CREATIVE PROGRAMMIN' ON THE TUGS' NAVIGATIONAL COMPUTERS!
"AFTER THAT I SLIPPED OVER TO ONE OF THE MLC-3 UNITS THEY HAD SITTIN' AROUND--
"--AND JURY-RIGGED ITS MOTION AND ATTACK CIRCUITS TO OPERATE AUTOMATICALLY ON A TIME PROGRAM.
"THEN I SPRINTED FOR THE TRANSPORT AS, RIGHT ON CUE--

"--THAT LITTLE MLC STARTED ROLLIN' AND FIRIN', TAKIN' OUT EQUIPMENT AND PERSONNEL AT RANDOM--
SSASHOW
HUH--?!
"--GIVIN' ME THE DIVERSION I NEEDED TO GET ABOARD THE TRANSPORT, AN' BUYIN' ME THE TIME TO FIGURE OUT WHICH BUTTONS TO PUSH--
"--TO GET HER OFF THE GROUND!
GLIK THE SHIP! GLIK-BZT TAKING OFF! BZT-GLIK
OH, FLOTT!
DON'T JUST STAND THERE, YOU IDIOTS! GET TO THE GUN TUGS!
NOBODY STEALS FROM ARNS GRIMRAKER --AN' LIVES!

"AS I'D HOPED, THE FLIGHT PATTERN THAT AVOIDED THE IMPERIAL PATROLS HAD BEEN PRE-PROGRAMMED INTO THE TRANSPORT'S NAVCOMP.
"SO ALL I HAD TO DO WAS LOCK IT IN, TRIGGER THE SHIP'S THRUST BOOSTERS--

"--AND JUST LIKE THAT, A DREAM CAME TRUE.
"I WAS OFF OF HOTH!

"THE SCAVENGERS FOLLOWED, AS EXPECTED--BUT THEY FOLLOWED THE AVOIDANCE MAZE IN THEIR COMPUTERS INSTEAD OF FOLLOWING ME!
"SO THEY NEVER REALIZED THAT I'D *CHANGED* THAT MAZE--

"--UNTIL THE TIE SQUAD THEY RAN RIGHT INTO STARTED BLOWIN' 'EM APART!

"AS I WATCHED THE BLIPS OF THE GUN TUGS FLASH AND DISAPPEAR FROM MY SENSOR SCREEN, I SMILED.
"AND I COULDN'T HELP THINKIN' THAT, SOMEWHERE, JANSON WAS GRINNIN' WITH ME...

"BUT WOULDN'T YOU KNOW IT--THE SCAVS STILL GOT IN A LAST LAUGH. 'CAUSE SOON AFTER I HAD LEFT THE HOTH QUADRANT, AND WAS WELL OUT OF RANGE OF THE IMPERIAL FIGHTERS--
"--THE TRANSPORT'S ENGINES UP AND STOPPED!
"SEEMS ONE OF THE SCAVENGERS' STRAY SHOTS HAD SEVERED THE EXTERIOR ION LINK--
"--LETTIN' ALL OF THE SHIP'S FUEL LEAK OUT INTO SPACE!
"AND SINCE THE TRANSPORT WAS INTENDED TO BE TOWED BY TUGS, THE ONLY PROVISIONS ABOARD WERE EMERGENCY RATIONS FOR A SINGLE MAINTENANCE OFFICER!
"NEEDLESS TO SAY, THEY DIDN'T LAST VERY LONG...
"SO THERE YOU HAVE IT. WHOEVER YOU ARE, I HOPE YOU ENJOYED MY LITTLE BEDTIME STORY.
"I ONLY WISH I WAS STILL AROUND TO TELL IT IN PERSON!
"BUT WITH NO FOOD, AND NO FUEL, I GUESS IT'S JUST--"
--A MATTER OF TIME...
"A MATTER OF TIME"?! BUT HOW MUCH TIME?

WE DON'T EVEN KNOW WHEN THAT TAPE WAS MADE! WEDGE COULD'VE BEEN DEAD FOR DAYS! FOR WEEKS! FOR--

FOR CRYIN' OUT LOUD!
GASP
HUH...?

LEIA? BARLON? WH-WHAT'S THE MATTER? WHAT'RE YOU STARING A--

--HIM!
I-IT'S HIM!
WEDGE!
HE'S MOTIONING TOWARDS THE AIRLOCK! COME ON!

BABBLING WITH JOY AND AMAZEMENT, THE THREE STARTLED WARRIORS CLAMBER DOWN CORRIDORS, MOVING TOWARDS THE GIANT SPACESHIP'S LOWER-LEVEL AIRLOCKS.
WHILE NEARBY, A FOURTH--AND EQUALLY *SURPRISED*--REBEL FLOATS GENTLY TOWARDS SAME.

AND SOON, ONCE ALL HAVE BEEN RE-UNITED INSIDE, AND RATIONS FROM THE Y-WING FIGHTER HAVE BEEN PASSED AROUND--

--QUESTIONS ARE EAGERLY, FINALLY, ANSWERED...

THAT'S RIGHT, LUKE. I GOT PRETTY HUNGRY BEFORE I REALIZED THAT I WAS SITTIN' RIGHT ON *TOP* OF EVERYTHING I NEEDED!

WITH A HOLD FULL OF SCAVENGED PARTS, ALL I HAD TO DO WAS SCROUNGE UP A NEW ION LINK, THEN DRAIN OFF FUEL FROM SALVAGED ENGINE UNITS, AND I COULD PILOT THIS BARGE TO THE NEAREST SETTLEMENT FOR RESTOCKING!

THE WHOLE PROCESS TOOK A COUPLE OF DAYS, AND I DIDN'T HAVE TIME TO UPDATE THE LOG, BUT I FIGURED THE END RESULT WOULD BE WORTH THE EFFORT. MATTER OF FACT, I WAS OUTSIDE INSTALLIN' THE NEW LINK WHEN YOU GUYS SHOWED UP.
I SAW YOU ARRIVE, BUT IT TOOK ME A WHILE TO WORK MY WAY AROUND TO THE CONTROL ROOM TO LET YOU KNOW I WAS HERE.

I HOPE I DIDN'T WORRY YOU TOO MUCH.

WEDGE, WE'LL FORGIVE YOU THIS TIME. BUT PLEASE--

--*DON'T* LET IT HAPPEN AGAIN!

SOON AFTER, THE TWO STARCRAFT MOVE OUT, SLOWLY AT FIRST, THEN BUILDING SPEED, CARRY-ING FOUR SMILING REBELS AND A SHIPLOAD OF MUCH-NEEDED EQUIPMENT TO ARBRA--
--AND TO A CELEBRATION THAT WILL LAST, QUITE POSSIBLY, FOR DAYS...

WAR IN THE ICE TRENCHES OF HOTH!

WALKER SCOUTS IN ACTION--AS VISUALIZED BY MICHAEL GOLDEN!

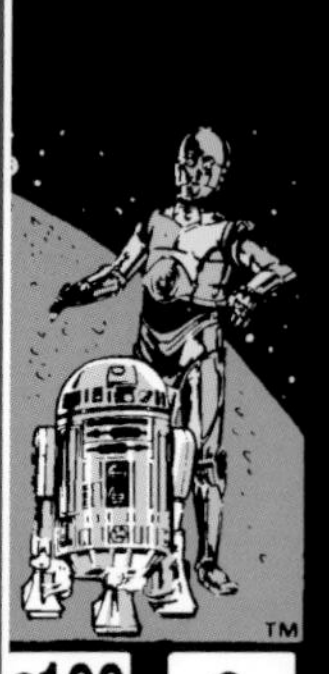

STAR WARS™

ANNUAL

$1.00
U.K. 50p
CAN. $1.25

3
1983

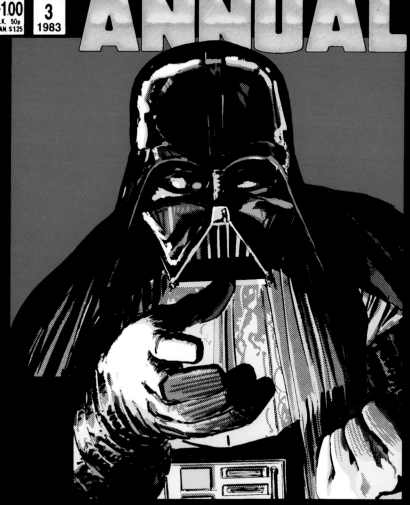

JO DUFFY
WRITER
KLAUS JANSON
ARTIST & COLORIST
JOE ROSEN
LETTERER
LOUISE JONES
EDITOR
JIM SHOOTER
EDITOR IN CHIEF

WE WON'T, MY LORD. REST ASSURED WE WON'T.
YOU SPEAK VERY DRAMATICALLY OF OUR MISSION AND THE IMPORTANCE OF THIS PLANET, LORD VADER...
...BUT, OF COURSE YOU ARE EXAGGERATING.

I EXAGGERATE NOTHING, GENERAL ANDRID.
THE WORK THAT GOES ON ON THE PLANET BELDERONE IS VITAL TO IMPERIAL PLANS--

--BOTH FOR THE CONQUEST OF NEW PLANETS AND SYSTEMS--
--AND FOR THE FINAL CRUSHING OF THIS REBELLION WHICH HAS CONTINUED TO FLOURISH--

--DESPITE THE BEST EFFORTS OF YOU AND MEN LIKE YOURSELF TO CRUSH IT.
I REPEAT, GENTLEMEN. FAIL ME HERE, FAIL THE EMPEROR HERE, AND YOU WON'T GET THE OPPORTUNITY TO FAIL AGAIN...

REBELLIOUS SENTIMENTS IN THIS SYSTEM HAVE BEEN GROWING OF LATE... OUR INTELLIGENCE INFORMS US OF IT...
AND MY MASTER HAS SENSED IT, AS WELL...
HE IS ONE WITH THE FORCE, AND HE KNOWS WHEN SOMETHING--LIKE THE GROWING UNREST IN THIS SECTOR--THREATENS HIM...
AND I, TOO, HAVE SENSED TROUBLE BREWING AMONG THE MAJORITY OF THE POPULATION OF KULTHIS--THE THIRD PLANET OF THIS STAR SYSTEM...
AS SOON AS THE WORK ON BELDERONE HAS REACHED THE PROPER STAGE... VERY SOON NOW, GENTLEMEN...
--YOU AND YOUR FORCES WILL SWEEP ACROSS KULTHIS, AND CRUSH THE REBELLION THERE, ONCE AND FOR ALL!
LORD VADER, I WOULD BE THE LAST ONE TO BELITTLE YOUR FAITH IN THAT MYSTIC ENERGY FIELD YOU REFER TO AS THE FORCE...
...OR TO IMPLY THAT THE TRAINING YOU RECEIVED DURING YOUR DAYS AS A JEDI KNIGHT HAD MADE A ROMANTIC OF YOU--!

THEN DON'T! I HAVE MORE IMPORTANT THINGS TO CONCERN ME THAN THE PETTY POSTURINGS OF A LITTLE MAN LIKE YOURSELF, ANDRID...
...BUT DO NOT PRESUME TOO MUCH, NOR TEMPT ME TOO FAR...

...OR I SHALL...
I HAVE MORE IMPORTANT THINGS TO CONCERN ME.
THERE IS MORE AT STAKE HERE THAN YOU REALIZE... MORE THAN ANYONE REALIZES...

FAR MORE THAN THE FATE OF BELDERONE, OF KULTHIS, OR A DOZEN SUCH INSIGNIFICANT PLANETS...

IMPORTANT ELEMENTS WILL COME INTO PLAY HERE, VERY SOON...

WE MUST BE READY!

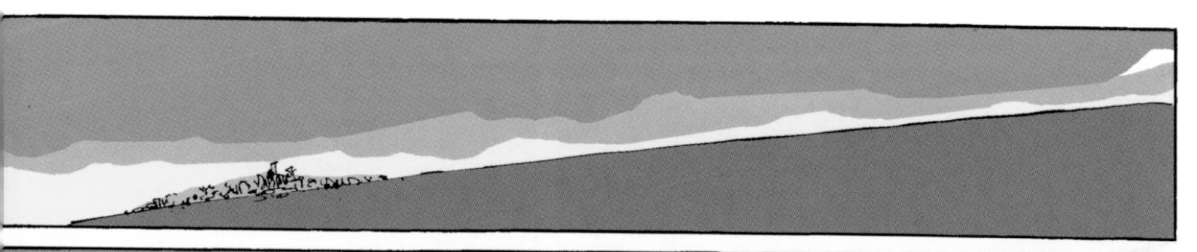

FLINT! FLINT?
WHERE ARE YOU?!
BARNEY?!
HEY, BARNEY, COME ON! BARNEY?

YOU'VE GOT TO COME AND SEE THIS! SOMETHING NEAT IS HAPPENING!
BARNEY, I KNOW YOU'RE IN THERE...

NO I'M NOT. I'M WHERE ANY SENSIBLE MAN WOULD BE--
--SOMEPLACE WHERE I CAN TAKE A NAP WITHOUT HAVING SOME MANIAC WAKING UP MY ENTIRE NEIGHBORHOOD AND ANTAGONIZING THE NEIGHBORS.

THEM! EVEN IF THEY DID GET MAD AT US, I'D LIKE TO SEE YOUR NEIGHBORS TRY ANYTHING. THEY WOULDN'T HAVE THE ENERGY.
WHAT'S THIS "US" STUFF?
COME ON!
COME ON, WHERE?

I TOLD YOU, SOMETHING NEAT IS HAPPENING! THERE'S A SHIP LANDING OVER BY THE SPACE-PORT...
OH, A SHIP LANDING. WELL, THAT'S TERRIBLY IMPORTANT, OF COURSE...
WHAT IS IT TODAY... ARE THEY DROPPING OFF ANOTHER NEW LOAD OF SUPER-VISORS? OR PICK-ING UP SOME MORE OF THE COMPLETED PRODUCTS?
NOTHING LIKE THAT! THIS IS SOME-THING IMPORTANT... THIS SHIP ISN'T FROM THE EMPIRE...
IT'S SOMETHING DIFFERENT... I KNOW IT. I CAN FEEL IT!
COME ON! WE OUGHT TO GO AND SEE IT...
OH, SURE! IT'S OUR SWORN DUTY AS THE GUARDI-ANS AND PROTECTORS OF BELDERONE...
HEY, I HEARD YOUR MOTHER CALLING YOU A MINUTE AGO... SHOULDN'T WE GO SEE HER FIRST?
AND MISS THIS? WHAT FOR? MOM ALWAYS WANTS SOME-THING...
FLINT! FLINT!!
UH-OH! I KNEW IT!

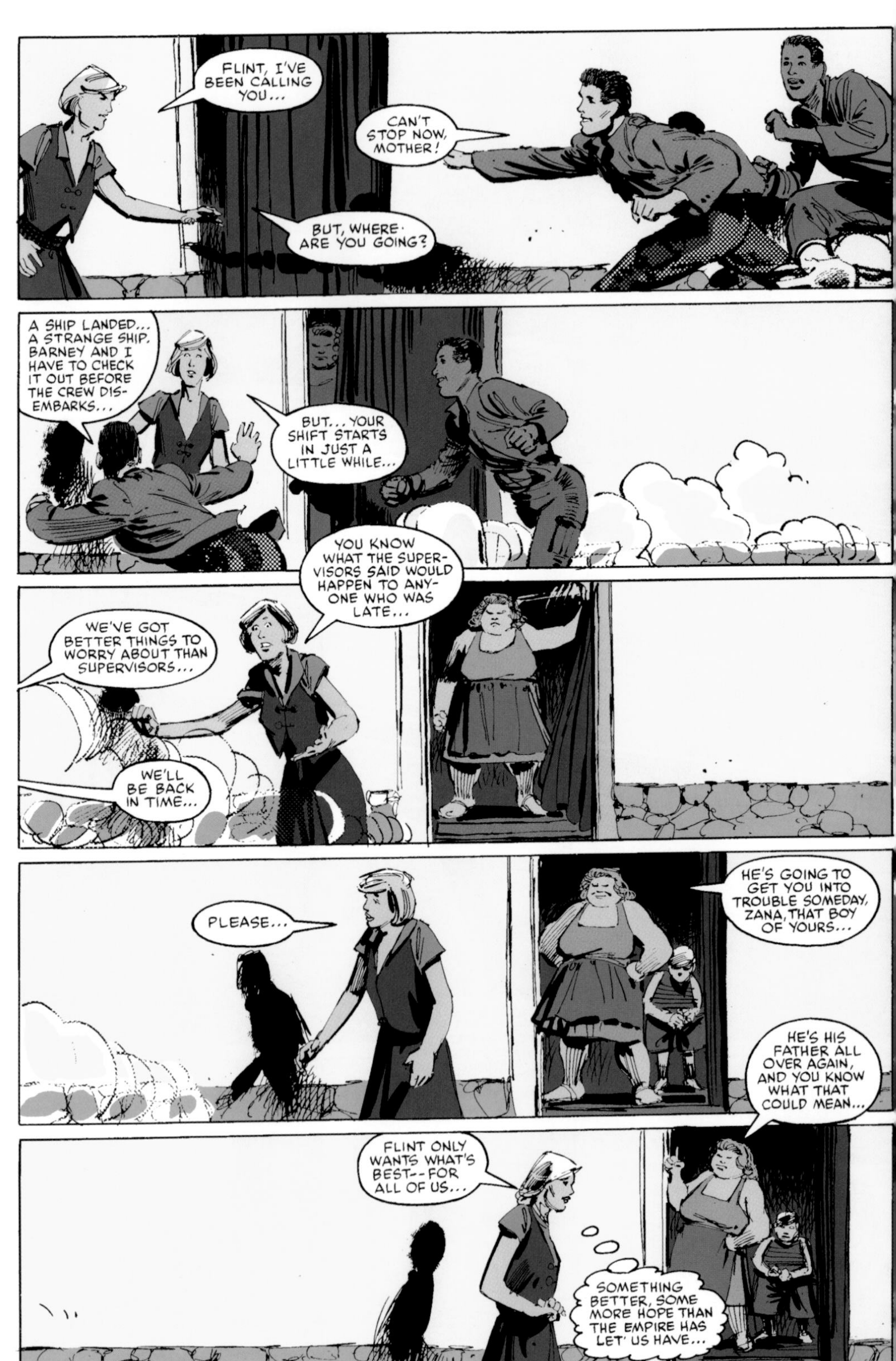
FLINT, I'VE BEEN CALLING YOU...
CAN'T STOP NOW, MOTHER!
BUT, WHERE ARE YOU GOING?
A SHIP LANDED... A STRANGE SHIP. BARNEY AND I HAVE TO CHECK IT OUT BEFORE THE CREW DIS-EMBARKS...
BUT... YOUR SHIFT STARTS IN JUST A LITTLE WHILE...
YOU KNOW WHAT THE SUPER-VISORS SAID WOULD HAPPEN TO ANY-ONE WHO WAS LATE...
WE'VE GOT BETTER THINGS TO WORRY ABOUT THAN SUPERVISORS...
WE'LL BE BACK IN TIME...
PLEASE...
HE'S GOING TO GET YOU INTO TROUBLE SOMEDAY, ZANA, THAT BOY OF YOURS...
HE'S HIS FATHER ALL OVER AGAIN, AND YOU KNOW WHAT THAT COULD MEAN...
FLINT ONLY WANTS WHAT'S BEST--FOR ALL OF US...
SOMETHING BETTER, SOME MORE HOPE THAN THE EMPIRE HAS LET US HAVE...

THEY SAY SHE'S CALLED THE *MILLENNIUM FALCON...*

THERE IT IS! WHAT DID I TELL YOU? WE *HAD* TO CHECK THIS OUT!

HEY... THIS SHIP HAS GOT REALLY TERRIFIC LINES. WHAT'S IT CALLED?

SO, THIS IS BELDERONE, EH? WELL, IT LOOKS CHARMING. ABSOLUTELY CHARMING...

BARNEY... LOOK AT THAT GUY. LOOK AT WHAT HE'S WEARING!
HUH? WHAT... *WHERE?!*
LOOK AT HIS WEAPON!

HE'S WEARING A *LIGHT-SABER!*
YOU KNOW WHAT THAT MEANS, DON'T YOU? HE MUST BE A *JEDI KNIGHT...*
JUST LIKE MY FATHER WAS!

LOOK AT THAT ONE... THE WAY SHE'S DRESSED, AND HOW SHE'S ACTING...
THE WAY *HER MAJESTY* IS FLAUNTING HERSELF, SHE MIGHT AS WELL BE A QUEEN...
OR A SOLDIER. NO NICE BELDERON WOULD GO AROUND LOOKING AND ACTING LIKE THAT!

I THINK SHE'S BEAUTIFUL!
NO ONE ASKED YOU!
YOU GROW UP TO BE LIKE THAT, AND NO MAN WOULD HAVE YOU!

WHAT BRINGS YOU ALL TO BELDERONE? WE DON'T GET MANY VISITORS HERE, EXCEPT WHEN THEY COME ON BUSINESS...
OH, BUT WE HAVE COME ON BUSINESS... WE REPRESENT A TRADING FLEET...
BUT THE ONLY GOODS WE MANUFACTURE HERE ARE THE--ACK!
WE HAVE A TRADE AGREEMENT FOR MOST OF OUR LOCAL PRODUCE TO BE SUPPLIED TO THE EMPIRE. THEY FLATTER US WITH THEIR CUSTOM...

WELL, AT LEAST THE INHABITANTS HERE SPEAK *GALACTIC STANDARD*, SO MY SKILLS AS A TRANSLATOR *DROID* WON'T BE CALLED UPON...
BA-BLIP!
WHAT DO YOU MEAN, "WHAT SKILLS?" *ARTOO-DETOO*, YOU KNOW PERFECTLY WELL THAT I...
HEY, MISTER, WHERE DID YOU GET THE *LIGHTSABER*?
MY LIGHTSABER?
ARE YOU A JEDI KNIGHT?

MY... MY LIGHT-SABER? IT WAS LEFT TO ME BY MY... GIVEN TO ME BY A FRIEND OF MY FATHER'S.
I KNEW IT! YOUR FATHER WAS A JEDI, WASN'T HE?
MY DAD WAS ONE OF THEIR REAL HEROES!
NO... MY FATHER WAS ...NAVIGATOR ON A SPICE FREIGHTER.
WHAT HAVE YOU BROUGHT TO TRADE WITH?
THAT DEPENDS ON WHAT YOU HAVE TO OFFER...
AFTER ALL, WE CAN'T JUST GIVE AWAY WHAT WE HAVE IN OUR HOLD. YOU KNOW HOW IT IS.
WHERE HAVE YOU COME FROM, ANYWAY?
FROM HERE AND THERE, REALLY. ALL OVER. MOST RECENTLY, WE'RE FROM KULTHIS.
KULTHIS?!
WOULDN'T YOU JUST KNOW IT...
GOT TO BE GOING...
MENTIONING KULTHIS GOT AN EVEN BIGGER RE-ACTION THAN WE EXPECTED. IT SEEMS OUR INTELLIGENCE REPORTS WERE CORRECT.
MMM... VISITORS FROM KULTHIS AREN'T TOO POPULAR THESE DAYS... I WONDER WHY NOT...
MAYBE WE'D BETTER PRESENT OURSELVES OFFICIALLY TO WHOEVER'S IN CHARGE BEFORE WE OFFEND SOMEONE ELSE...
DON'T LET THEM BOTHER YOU, MISTER...?
CALRISSIAN. LANDO CALRISSIAN. AND THESE ARE MY FRIENDS, LUKE AND LEIA. AND THAT BIG FELLOW IS CHEWBACCA, THE WOOKIEE...
NO ONE'S REALLY IN CHARGE HERE, ANYWAY. WE'RE RUN BY THE EMPIRE, JUST LIKE EVERYTHING ELSE IS.

BUT, IF YOU WANT TO COME INTO THE VILLAGE AND MEET PEOPLE, SO YOU CAN GET ON WITH YOUR TRADING, MY MOTHER RUNS A TAVERN THAT'S AS GOOD A PLACE AS ANY...
THANKS, BUT WHAT ABOUT THE FALCON... WE'VE LOCKED IT, OF COURSE, BUT IS THERE ANYWHERE WE SHOULD MOVE IT TO?

NO, IT'LL BE FINE HERE. JUST SO IT'S NOT IN TOWN PROPER.
AND IT'LL BE SAFE. NO ONE HERE WOULD HAVE THE NERVE OR THE IMAGINATION TO THINK OF TRYING TO STEAL ANYTHING...
MY, YOU'RE A BIG ONE, AREN'T YOU?
GGGRRRRPH

JUST TO BE ON THE SAFE SIDE, WE CAN LEAVE OUR DROIDS--SEE-THREEPIO AND ARTOO-DETOO--HERE WITH THE SHIP. WE WON'T BE TRADING THEM, ANYWAY.
THANK THE MAKER FOR THAT!
BOOP
HEY, IF YOU WANT SOMEONE TO STAY HERE JUST TO BE SURE, I CAN...
BUT YOURS IS FINISHED FOR THE DAY! OKAY!
YOU CAN STAY HERE!
ME? HEY, WAIT A MINUTE...
FLINT! YOUR SHIFT BEGINS IN A LITTLE WHILE!

IT'S JUST UNTIL WE'VE LOOKED AROUND. THANK YOU SO MUCH...?
ULP B-B-BARNEY...
AND I'M FLINT. COME ON, IT'S THIS WAY!

WELL, THEY CERTAINLY DIDN'T LIKE THE MENTION OF KULTHIS, DID THEY?
IT MAKES ME WONDER WHAT WE COULD BE UP AGAINST IF THE BELDERONS EVER FIND OUT WHY WE'RE REALLY HERE...
I THINK MAYBE THEY WILL FIND OUT, LEIA...

LUKE, WHAT IS IT...?
LEIA, WHATEVER IS GOING ON HERE... I THINK IT'S A BIG THREAT TO OUR BASE IN KULTHIS... IN FACT, TO THE ENTIRE REBELLION...
DARTH VADER IS HERE, SOMEWHERE NEARBY...
THAT'S WHAT OUR INTELLIGENCE REPORT INDICATED. THAT'S WHY WE'VE COME HERE... WHAT MAKES YOU SO CERTAIN OF IT NOW...?

I CAN FEEL HIS PRESENCE, THROUGH THE FORCE.
AND, LEIA...

I'M SURE HE SENSES ME, AS WELL.

FLINT... WHAT IS IT? WHERE HAVE YOU BEEN?
IT'S ALIENS! ALIEN CUSTOMERS! GIVE 'EM THE FULL TREATMENT. BELDERONE HOSPITALITY, OKAY?
BUT... BUT, FLINT, YOU'RE DUE AT WORK... YOU'LL BE LATE!

MOM! **HEY, MOM!** YOU'LL NEVER GUESS WHAT I'VE BROUGHT YOU! YOU'VE GOT TO COME OUT AND SEE!

SOME DAY YOU'LL HAVE AN ACCIDENT...
THE WAY I DRIVE? NEVER FEAR!
MOTHER! I ***SAID*** NEVER FEAR, AND I ***MEANT*** IT! BYE!

WE'RE SO SORRY TO BE IMPOSING ON YOU... IF IT'S A PROBLEM, PERHAPS YOU COULD DIRECT US SOMEWHERE ELSE...
WHAT? OH. I'M SORRY.

NO, FLINT WAS ABSOLUTELY RIGHT. WE DO WELCOME CUSTOMERS HERE...
IT'S JUST THAT, WELL, THINGS HAVEN'T BEEN ENTIRELY EASY FOR US HERE ON BELDERONE, WITH THE REBELLION GETTING SO CLOSE...
I FORGOT MY MANNERS, THAT'S ALL...

I UNDERSTAND... YOUR SON MUST BE QUITE...TIRING AT TIMES...
HE CERTAINLY DOESN'T SEEM TO MIND HAVING A REBEL WORLD-- IF THAT'S WHAT KULTHIS REALLY IS--SO CLOSE...
HELLO?
HELLO, GENERAL? DO YOU COPY?
SO...YOU'RE SURE THERE'S A BLACK MAN AND A WOOKIEE WITH THEM? THEN THE BOY AND THE GIRL CAN ONLY BE ***PRINCESS LEIA ORGANA*** AND ***COMMANDER LUKE SKYWALKER***...
THIS IS GOING TO BE QUITE A FEATHER IN MY CAP...

NO. I SEE NO REASON TO INFORM LORD VADER OF THIS...

I HAVE OTHER AGENTS ON BELDERONE. THEY CAN HANDLE THIS...

WELL, WHATEVER IS GOING ON, IT MAKES THE LOCAL PEOPLE VERY UNEASY WHEN YOU TRY TO TALK ABOUT IT...
HRONK!
YOU NOTICED IT, TOO? THEY ALL TALK ABOUT THEIR JOBS, BUT THEY'RE CAREFUL NEVER TO MENTION JUST WHAT THEY DO HERE.

WELL, THE FORCES ON KULTHIS ARE PRE-PARED. THEY'VE GOT SEVERAL SQUADRONS OF SINGLE-PILOT FIGHTERS STAND-ING BY.
IF THEY GET WORD FROM US THAT ANYTHING'S SERIOUSLY WRONG, THEY'LL MOBI-LIZE...

BLEAH
HOW CAN WE TELL THEM SOMETHING NO ONE WILL TELL US? THOUGH, I GUESS THE SIMPLE FACT THAT EVERYONE HERE'S SO EDGY IS A PRETTY BIG CLUE...

MORE ALE, SIR?
BUT, FLINT...YOU HEARD WHAT HE SAID. HIS FATHER WAS A NAVIGATOR ON A...
OH, COME ON, BARNEY! HE HAD TO SAY THAT! HE'S A JEDI! HE'S GOT TO BE...
HE'S EVERYTHING WE'D LIKE TO BE... EVERYTHING WE'RE GOING TO BE, SOMEDAY.
NOW, ACT CASUAL. WE DON'T WANT HIM TO KNOW WE KNOW!

LUKE... HAVEN'T YOU NOTICED?
NOTICED WHAT?
YOU'VE PICKED UP SOME LOCAL ADMIRERS...
YEAH... BUT IT'S PROBABLY NOT JUST ME. IT'S ALL OF US.
I KNOW WHAT WHAT IT'S LIKE. MY HOMEWORLD-- TATOOINE--WAS A LOT LIKE THIS ONE.
YOU BEGIN TO GO CRAZY FOR SOME DIVERSION, ANYTHING THE LEAST BIT FOREIGN OR EXOTIC...
IT'S NOT US, LUKE. IT'S YOU, PERSONALLY, AND YOU KNOW IT!
COME ON. ADMIT IT. DON'T THEY REMIND YOU OF ANYONE? JUST THE LEAST LITTLE BIT?
NO. SHOULD THEY?
OH, GIVE THEM A BREAK, LUKE. ALL KIDS NEED HEROES.
WE'RE HERE ON A MISSION. I HAVE OTHER THINGS TO TAKE CARE OF... THINGS THAT MATTER...
MA'AM... ZANA? I THINK MY FRIEND HERE COULD USE SOME MORE ALE...

WE'LL TAKE CARE OF IT, MOM!

GO GET SOME MORE ALE, BARNEY...
ME?! WHY SHOULD I BE THE ONE TO...?

YOUR FRIEND DOESN'T SEEM TO LIKE THE LOCAL FOOD, SIR...

IT'S NOT THAT HE INTENDS ANY INSULT, ZANA... IT'S JUST THAT WOOKIEES' TASTES RUN MORE TO THE...
AAROOOO

AAIIEE!
FLINT! DID YOU SEE THAT?! HE GOT ONE!
WE WANT TO TALK TO YOU...
AND I'VE GOTTEN NUMBER TWO!
COME ON, CHEWIE! I COUNTED THREE OF THEM!

NO...
DON'T...
WELL, I DOUBT THAT THIS IS A NORMAL PART OF THE LOCAL NIGHT LIFE... WE'RE LUCKY YOU REACTED SO FAST, LUKE.
YOU KNOW WHAT THIS MUST MEAN, DON'T YOU?
THE EMPIRE KNOWS WE'RE HERE.
DID YOU SEE THAT? DID YOU SEE THE WAY HE MOVED? HOW FAST HE WAS...
AND HE SHOT LIKE... LIKE NOTHING I'VE EVER SEEN BEFORE! IT WAS UNCANNY...
IT WAS THE FORCE...
HE USED THE POWER OF THE FORCE TO SENSE THEIR PRESENCE... IT GUIDED HIM...
...AND HE TRIED TO DENY BEING A JEDI!
NOT JUST A JEDI! DIDN'T YOU HEAR WHAT LEIA SAID?!
THEY'RE REBELS, TOO!
HELLO? GENERAL ANDRID, DO YOU COPY? THIS IS URGENT...

I UNDERSTAND. THANK YOU...

GENTLEMEN... ONE OF MY SPIES ABOARD THIS CRUISER HAS JUST INTERCEPTED A MOST INTERESTING MESSAGE...
YOU REFER TO A REBEL TRANSMISSION, MY LORD?

I DO NOT, COLONEL MALDROD. THE TRANSMISSION I REFER TO WAS SENT FROM AN IMPERIAL AGENT... TO ONE OF YOU HERE

GENERAL ANDRID! PERHAPS YOU WOULD BE INTERESTED TO LEARN THAT ALL OF YOUR ASSASSINS ARE DEAD, ONE OF THEM BY HIS OWN HAND. YOU HAVE ENSURED THAT THE REBELS KNOW WE ARE AWARE OF THEM!
BUT! BUT I--!

I HAD TO ACT QUICKLY! LUKE SKYWALKER IS AMONG THE REBELS HERE!
HAD WE WAITED, HE MIGHT HAVE SLIPPED THROUGH OUR FINGERS!

IF HE HAS SLIPPED THROUGH OUR FINGERS, ANDRID, IT IS DUE TO YOUR STUPIDITY... AND THE EGOTISM THAT LED YOU TO THINK THAT YOU COULD TAKE SKYWALKER ALONE!
I HAVE BEEN AWARE OF HIS PRESENCE FROM THE MOMENT HE ENTERED THIS SYSTEM...
AWARE OF HIM, THROUGH THE POWER OF THE FORCE...

YOU MOCKED THE POWER OF THE FORCE ONCE, IN MY PRESENCE...
NOW, FEEL WHAT IT CAN DO!
URK
GENTLEMEN, I PROPOSE A TOAST...
TO OUR COMRADE... THE LATE GENERAL ANDRID...
TELL THEM TO HAVE MY PERSONAL TRANSPORT STANDING BY...
BECAUSE OF THAT FOOL'S PRECIPITOUS ACTION, WE MUST MOVE AGAINST THE REBELS ON KULTHIS AT ONCE, BEFORE THEY CAN PREPARE...
I SHALL GO TO BELDERONE WITH ONE OF YOU AND SUPERVISE THE MOBILIZATION PERSONALLY.

I REALLY DON'T LIKE LEAVING YOU TWO HERE LIKE THIS, ALONE...

LUKE, WE DON'T HAVE ANY OTHER CHOICE...

YOU TOLD ME YOURSELF THAT DARTH VADER ALREADY KNEW WE WERE HERE...

THAT ATTACK TONIGHT PROVES THEY MUST BE READY TO MOVE AGAINST KULTHIS, THAT SECRECY IS NO LONGER NEEDED...

SOMEONE HAS TO TAKE THE FALCON, GET TO OUR FORCES ON KULTHIS AND WARN THEM SO THEY CAN STRIKE HERE FIRST...

BUT I DON'T WANT TO LEAVE YOU AND LANDO HERE...

LUKE, IT HAS TO BE YOU WHO GOES WITH CHEWBACCA, OR VADER WILL ONLY FIND US AGAIN...

SOMEONE HAS TO STAY HERE, AND SEE IF WE CAN'T STILL FIND OUT EXACTLY WHAT THE EMPIRE IS UP TO, BEFORE THE FIGHTERS FROM KULTHIS ARRIVE...

WE CAN'T ABANDON OUR ENTIRE MISSION JUST BECAUSE THINGS HAVE GOTTEN COMPLICATED...

I GUESS YOU'RE RIGHT!

OF COURSE WE'RE RIGHT!

HHOOOWL

LOOK AT IT THIS WAY! WE STILL MIGHT BE ABLE TO REALLY THROW THE EMPIRE'S PLANS OUT OF WHACK BEFORE YOU GET BACK!

WELL, I GUESS THAT'S IT... IT'S UP TO US NOW, TO FIND OUT WHAT THE EMPIRE'S DOING HERE, AND WHAT THEY'VE GOT IN STORE FOR KULTHIS.
IF WE CAN!
YOU CAN, IF YOU'LL LET US HELP YOU.

WHAT ARE YOU TWO DOING HERE?
LANDO, PLEASE...
WE'RE SORRY WE FOLLOWED YOU... BUT IT'S BECAUSE WE WANT TO HELP!
PLEASE LET US!
WE'RE PART OF THE WORK FORCE... EVERY-ONE WHO LIVES HERE HAS TO PITCH IN... NOT THAT THE WORK WE'RE DOING EVER BENEFITS BELDERONE...
EXCEPT THAT BY COOPERAT-ING, WE KEEP THE EMPIRE OFF OUR BACKS A LITTLE LONGER...

PLEASE... YOU'VE GOT TO GIVE US THIS CHANCE, LET US HELP YOU... BELDERONE IS OUR WORLD, AFTER ALL...
IT'S WHAT WE'VE DREAMED OF, ALL OUR LIVES, ESPECIALLY SINCE THE EMPIRE GOT HERE...
TO HELP SOMEHOW... TO BE THE ONES WHO MAKE A DIFFERENCE IN WHAT HAPPENS...
YOU MENTIONED A WORK FORCE ...JUST WHAT IS IT YOU'RE WORKING ON?
COULD YOU SHOW US?
IT'S OUTSIDE OF TOWN... THERE'D NEVER BE ROOM FOR IT IN THE VILLAGE...

THIS IS WHERE YOU ENTER IT...
THE MAIN WORKS, AND THE MACHINES WE'RE BUILDING, THEY'RE ALL BELOW GROUND...
MY L---SIR! IT'S THEM. THE REBELS! THEY'RE HERE!
HAVE NO FEAR, COLONEL MALDROD... ALL IS IN READINESS. OUR FORCES WILL BE READY TO SWEEP TO THE FAR SIDE OF THE VILLAGE, WHERE OUR BULK CRUISERS WILL PICK THEM UP, FOR TRANSPORT TO KULTHIS...
WE ARE NEEDED TO SUPERVISE THEM. THESE FEW PUNY REBELS CAN PRESENT NO REAL THREAT TO US...
SKYWALKER IS NOT AMONG THEM...
THIS IS COMMANDER SKYWALKER. ALL PLANES, DO YOU COPY?
WE'RE MAKING OUR ASSAULT ON THE CAPITAL CITY OF BELDERONE UPON ARRIVAL, UNLESS WE RECEIVE OTHER ORDERS BEFORE THEN...
WELL, WHAT ARE THEY?
AND WHERE ARE THEY? WHAT DID YOU BRING US OUT ALL THIS WAY FOR?
WE'LL TAKE YOU BELOW AND SHOW YOU!
YOU'D NEVER BELIEVE US IF WE JUST TOLD YOU... IT'S MUCH MORE IMPRESSIVE IF YOU CAN JUST SEE FOR YOURSELVES...

WHAT THE HELL ARE THOSE THINGS?!
IMPERIAL WALKERS... THEY'RE CALLED ATATs... THE EMPIRE USED THEM TO DRIVE US OFF HOTH...
I'VE NEVER SEEN ANYTHING LIKE WHAT THEY DID THERE!

AND THAT'S WHAT THEY'RE PLANNING TO LAUNCH AGAINST KULTHIS?
WE'VE GOT TO PUT A STOP TO THIS... IMPEDE THEM, SOMEHOW...

FLINT... WHERE ARE THEY GOING TO GO?
WHERE CAN THEY GO... BUT TO TOWN?

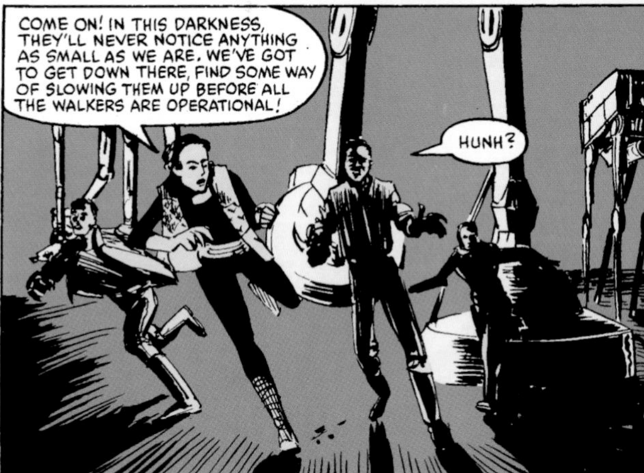
COME ON! IN THIS DARKNESS, THEY'LL NEVER NOTICE ANYTHING AS SMALL AS WE ARE. WE'VE GOT TO GET DOWN THERE, FIND SOME WAY OF SLOWING THEM UP BEFORE ALL THE WALKERS ARE OPERATIONAL!
HUNH?

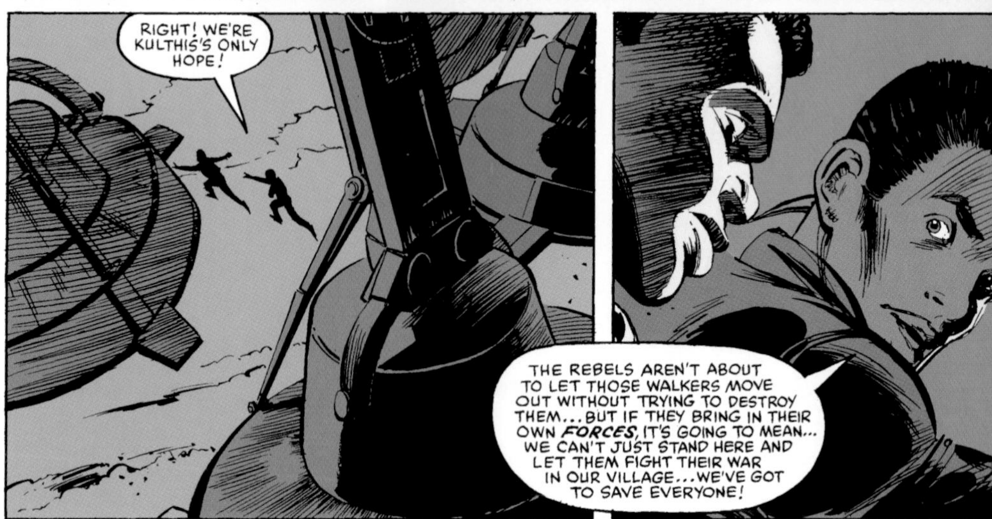
RIGHT! WE'RE KULTHIS'S ONLY HOPE!
THE REBELS AREN'T ABOUT TO LET THOSE WALKERS MOVE OUT WITHOUT TRYING TO DESTROY THEM... BUT IF THEY BRING IN THEIR OWN FORCES, IT'S GOING TO MEAN... WE CAN'T JUST STAND HERE AND LET THEM FIGHT THEIR WAR IN OUR VILLAGE... WE'VE GOT TO SAVE EVERYONE!

WE'VE GOT TO WARN MY MOTHER!!
SHOULDN'T WE HAVE TRIED TO STOP THEM...?
WHAT FOR? THEY ARE INSIGNIFI-CAN'T! THEY MEAN NOTHING, AND THEY CAN ACCOMPLISH NOTHING!

COME! WE MUST BE SURE THE BULK CRUISERS ARE READY TO ACCOMMODATE THE WALKERS AS SOON THEY HAVE DEALT WITH ANY RESISTANCE FROM THE VILLAGE...
AND WITH WHATEVER ADVANCE FORCES THE PLANET OF KULTHIS WILL UNDOUBTEDLY HAVE SENT AGAINST US BY NOW...
YES, MY LORD ...SIR.
HOW ARE WE DOING?
NOT GOOD! THERE'S ONLY ONE OF THEM COMING, BUT IT'S GAINING A LOT OF GROUND ON US, EVERY TIME IT PUT ITS BIG FOOT DOWN...
I NEVER DREAMED WHEN THE PARTS WERE ALL PUT TOGETHER, THEY'D ADD UP TO ANYTHING LIKE THAT!
WELL, BARN, DON'T WORRY. WE'RE GOING TO MAKE IT, WE HAVE TO!
THERE'S NO ONE ELSE WHO CAN!

YOU'RE RIGHT, WE ARE. BUT THOSE ATAT WALKERS AREN'T UNBEATABLE. WE HAVEN'T GOT THE RAW POWER TO BEAT THEM, BUT IT CAN BE DONE WITH STRATEGY...
GO FOR THEIR WEAK POINTS, AND DON'T ANYONE TAKE FOOLISH CHANCES...
ANYONE WHOSE SHIP IS EQUIPPED WITH A CABLE AND TOW LINE, FLY AROUND A WALKER AND EN-TANGLE ITS LEGS...
THEN, LET SOMEONE ELSE FINISH IT FOR YOU, ONCE IT'S DOWN...
COMMANDER, WASN'T IT ATATS THAT DROVE YOU FROM THE BASE ON THE ICE PLANET, HOTH?
YEAH... BUT THE NUMBERS ARE IN OUR FAVOR HERE. WE WERE OUT-MANNED ON HOTH...
ALSO WE WERE TRYING TO PROTECT A GROUND BASE... HERE, IT'S THE EMPIRE WHO ARE TRYING TO DEFEND THEIR BASE!

NOW WHAT?
I... THINK IT MAY BE OKAY... ONE OF THOSE LITTLE FIGHTERS IS AFTER THE BIG...

IT'S NO GOOD, THE WALKER GOT IT...
THEN IT'S ALL UP TO US...
FLINT! BE CAREFUL! YOU NEARLY CRASHED US JUST THEN!
WE HAVE TO GET THERE FAST!
MOTHER? *MOTHER!*
FLINT, BE--

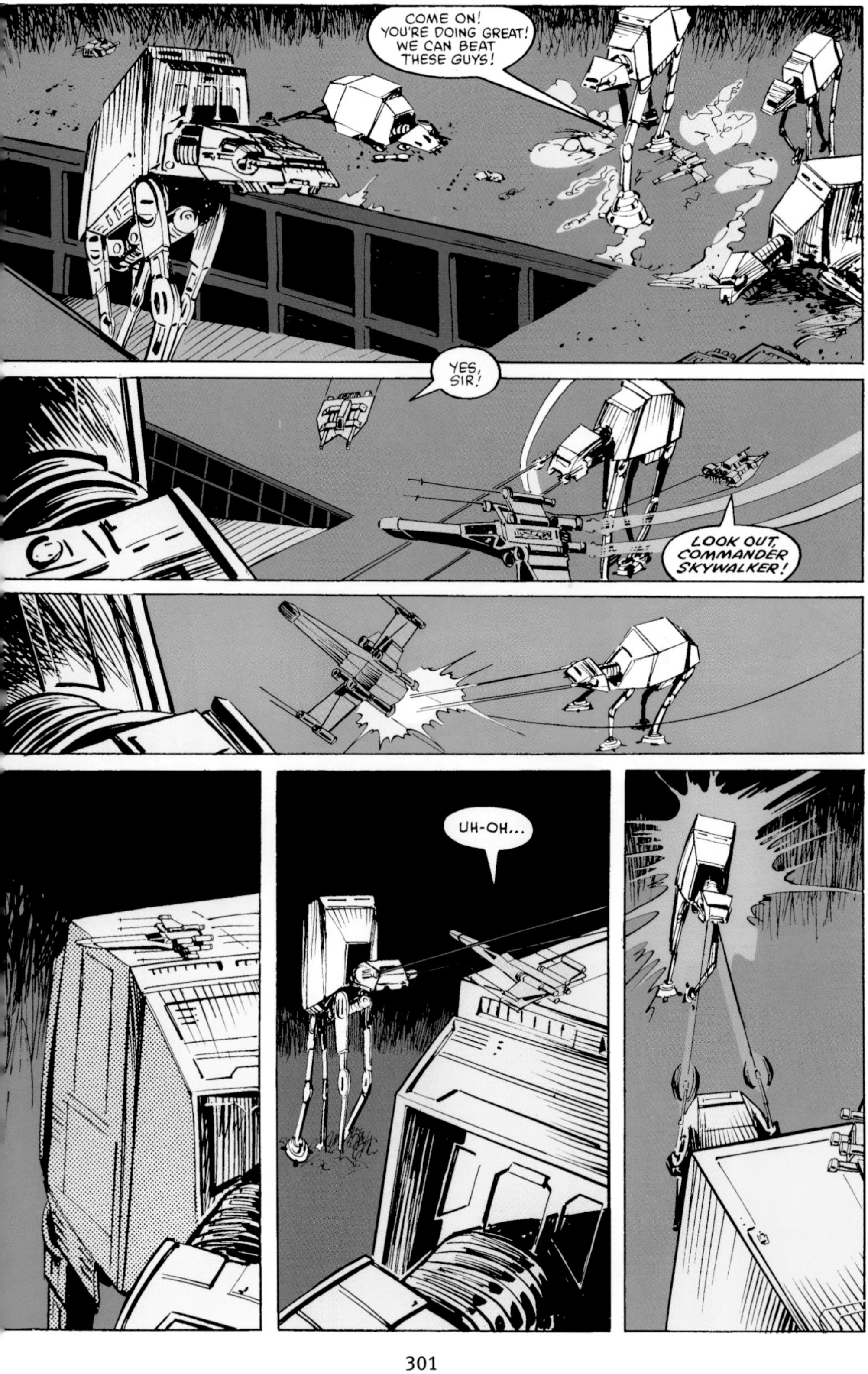

COME ON! YOU'RE DOING GREAT! WE CAN BEAT THESE GUYS!

YES, SIR!

LOOK OUT, COMMANDER SKYWALKER!

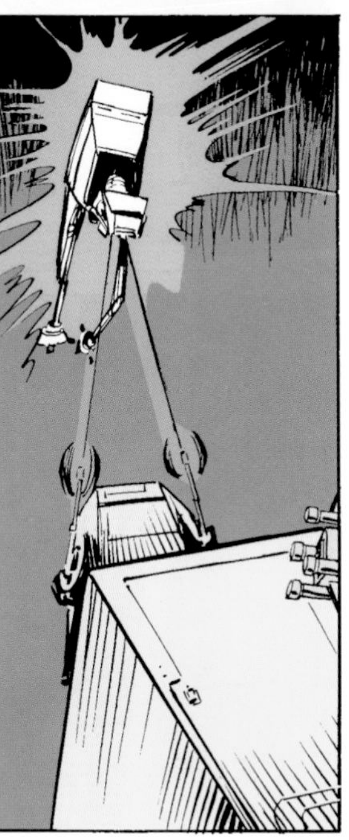

HUHN?
DON'T BE SO SURPRISED, LUKE...AND DON'T WORRY ABOUT A THING... IT'S US!

US?
LANDO AND LEIA!
NOW, WHERE CAN WE DROP YOU BEFORE WE USE THIS THING TO INFLICT SOME REAL DAMAGE ON THE IMPERIALS?
WE MANAGED TO OVERPOWER THE CREW OF THIS ONE... SNEAKED INTO THE BASE BEFORE THEY'D ALL TAKEN OFF...
JUST HEAD OVER TOWARD THAT OTHER WALKER...
I HAVE A FEW IDEAS OF MY OWN ON HOW TO INFLICT DAMAGE ON IMPERIALS...

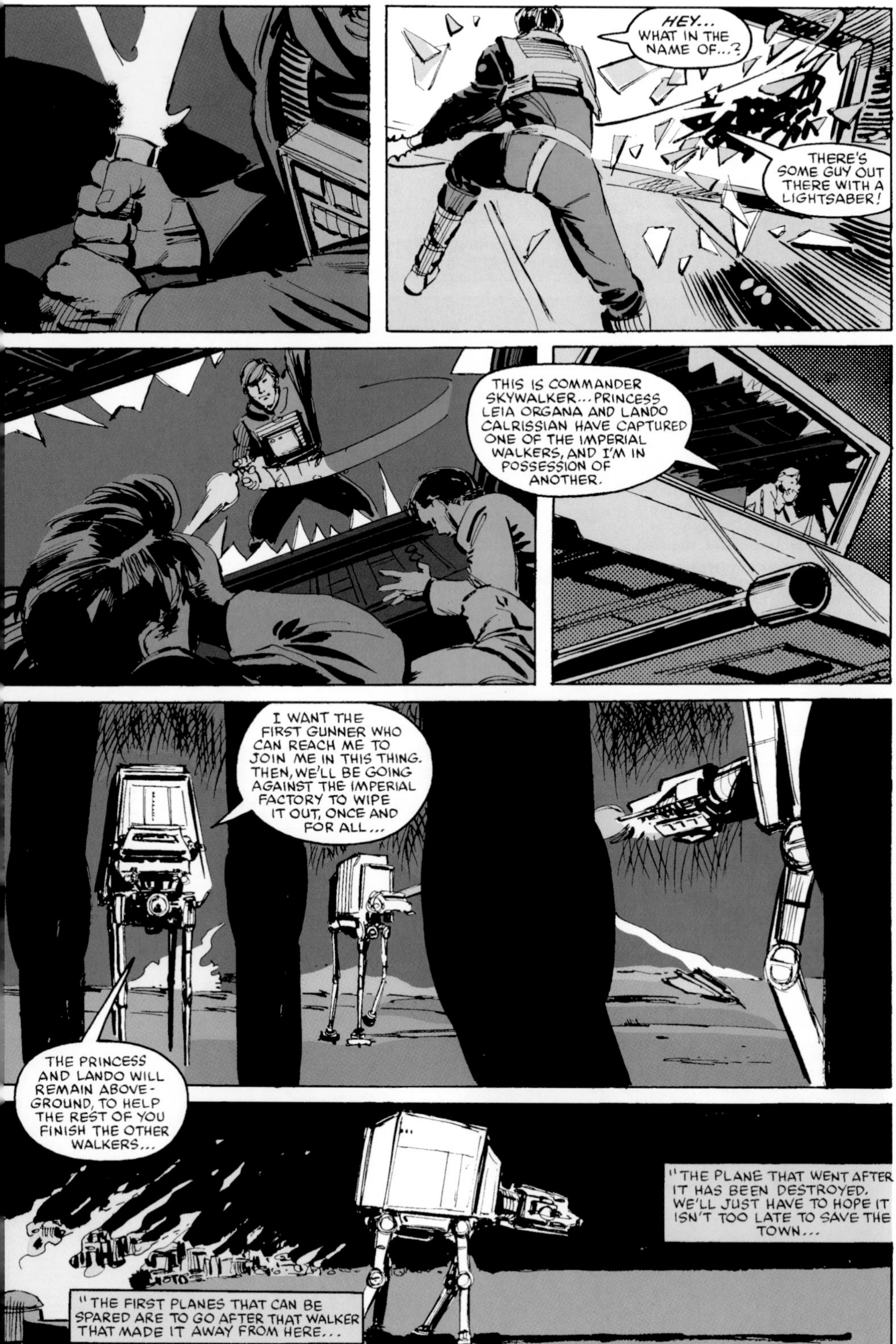

HEY... WHAT IN THE NAME OF...?
THERE'S SOME GUY OUT THERE WITH A LIGHTSABER!

THIS IS COMMANDER SKYWALKER... PRINCESS LEIA ORGANA AND LANDO CALRISSIAN HAVE CAPTURED ONE OF THE IMPERIAL WALKERS, AND I'M IN POSSESSION OF ANOTHER.

I WANT THE FIRST GUNNER WHO CAN REACH ME TO JOIN ME IN THIS THING. THEN, WE'LL BE GOING AGAINST THE IMPERIAL FACTORY TO WIPE IT OUT, ONCE AND FOR ALL...

THE PRINCESS AND LANDO WILL REMAIN ABOVE-GROUND, TO HELP THE REST OF YOU FINISH THE OTHER WALKERS...

"THE FIRST PLANES THAT CAN BE SPARED ARE TO GO AFTER THAT WALKER THAT MADE IT AWAY FROM HERE...

"THE PLANE THAT WENT AFTER IT HAS BEEN DESTROYED. WE'LL JUST HAVE TO HOPE IT ISN'T TOO LATE TO SAVE THE TOWN...

OO-OOHH....
MY... HEAD!
WE'RE LUCKY TO BE ALIVE, BARNEY...
BARN...?
BARNEY! NO! YOU CAN'T BE! I WON'T LET YOU! I... I...
I... WON'T...
MOTHER...?
MOTHER!!!
MOTHER, PLEASE ANSWER ME!
OH...OH, PLEASE, MOTHER, NO...
WHY...?

IT WAS ALL JUST A GAME... WE WERE USELESS ...WE COULDN'T DO A THING...
AND THEY LET US GO ON ...PRETENDING WE COULD HELP...
BUT WE COULDN'T...WE WERE USELESS... I WAS USELESS... AND NOW YOU'RE DEAD...

I SWEAR...I SWEAR TO YOU...I'M GOING TO LEARN ...I'M GOING TO GET THE TRAINING...THE SAME TRAINING MY FATHER HAD...
I'M GOING TO BECOME SOMEONE WHO MATTERS...

AND THEN I'LL SHOW THEM ALL!

I KNOW HOW YOU FEEL... I HAD ALMOST FORGOTTEN WHAT IT WAS LIKE TO FEEL THAT WAY...
IT HAS BEEN SOME TIME SINCE I HEARD ANYONE SPEAK THE WAY YOU DO NOW...

I DID NOT TAKE YOU SERIOUSLY BEFORE, AND I SHOULD HAVE... FOR-GIVE ME.
LET ME MAKE IT UP TO YOU NOW...

I COULD NOT SINGLE YOU OUT FOR SPECIAL TRAINING RIGHT AWAY... YOU WOULD BE JUST ONE OF OUR MEN AT FIRST...
BUT I HAVE SENSED THE POWER IN YOU...IN TIME, I PROMISE YOU, YOU WILL BE TUTORED SPECIALLY...AND IF YOU REALLY WISH IT...
YOU WILL BECOME SOMEONE WHO MATTERS VERY MUCH!

THE WHOLE VILLAGE DESTROYED ...I FEEL SO AWFUL ABOUT THIS...
NEITHER DO WE.
LEIA, IF IT'S ANY CONSOLATION, THE SURVIVORS TELL ME THAT THERE HASN'T BEEN MUCH OF A LIFE HERE FOR ANYONE, SINCE THE EMPIRE SET UP THEIR BASE...
AT LEAST KULTHIS IS SAFE...
YES, UNTIL THE EMPIRE SETS UP ANOTHER ATAT PRODUCTION LINE, SOMEWHERE ELSE... THEY WON'T STOP WITH ONE DEFEAT. THE NEVER DO.
YOU HAVE TO BELIEVE US...WE'RE SO SORRY ABOUT WHAT HAPPENED TO YOU...TO YOUR HOME ...YOUR VILLAGE...
AND WE'RE VERY SORRY ABOUT YOUR FRIEND...
DON'T BE... IT WASN'T YOUR FAULT...
YOU DIDN'T BRING TROUBLE TO US... IT WAS HERE FROM THE DAY THE EMPIRE SET UP THAT FACTORY...
I WISH I COULD BELIEVE FLINT SAW THINGS THE SAME WAY YOU DO...THANKS FOR JOINING US, BARNEY...
WHAT'S TO THANK..? MY ENTIRE FAMILY WAS KILLED, AND I'VE ALWAYS HATED THIS PLACE. THERE'S NOTHING FOR ME HERE...

THIS IS JUST WHAT I'VE DREAMED OF... WHAT I'VE WANTED ALL MY LIFE... EXCEPT THIS TIME IT'S NO GAME...
I'M GOING TO GET MY CHANCE... JOIN THE REBELLION... MAYBE FIND SOMEONE WHO CAN REALLY TRAIN ME AS A JEDI KNIGHT...
LIKE FLINT HAS... Y'KNOW, ONE OF THE NEIGHBORS SAW HIM GO... HEARD HIM TALKIN' TO THAT IMPERIAL LORD... HE SAID FLINT SOUNDED CERTAIN... AND EVEN HAPPY.
MAYBE... MAYBE HE WAS NEVER AS INTERESTED IN THE REBELLION AND THE EMPIRE... OR GOOD AND EVIL... AS HE THOUGHT.
MAYBE ALL HE EVER REALLY WANTED ***WAS*** POWER, AND IT JUST TOOK THIS TO MAKE HIM SEE IT.

ATTENTION ALL STORM TROOPERS. ATTENTION ALL STORM TROOPERS.
THE IMPERIAL FORCES ARE PULLING OUT NOW. REPORT TO YOUR TRANSPORT VESSELS AT ONCE...
"I DON'T KNOW...MAYBE WE'RE ALL WRONG, AND FLINT'S THE ONE WHO'S RIGHT...
"MAYBE, IN THE END, HE IS GONNA BE THE ONE WHO MAKES A DIFFERENCE."

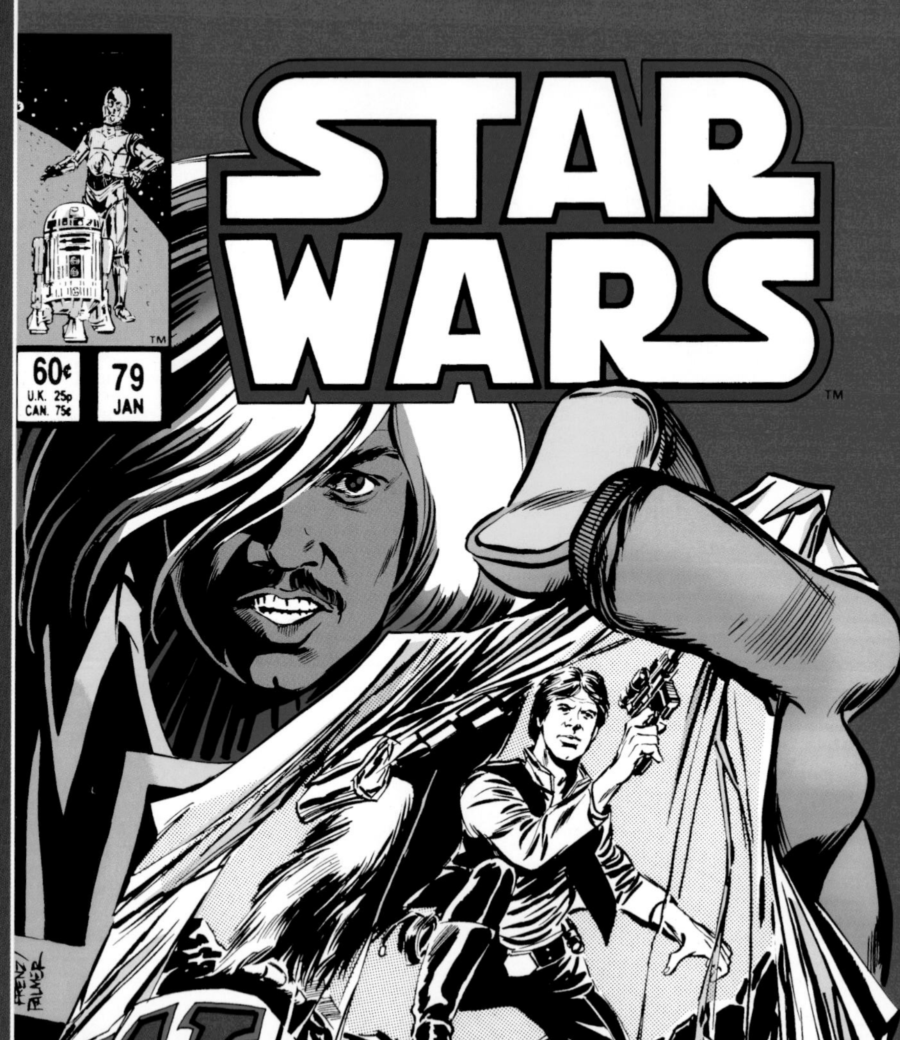

STAR WARS
TM
60¢
U.K. 25p
CAN. 75¢
79
JAN
FRENZ/PALMER

JO DUFFY SCRIPT AND PLOT
RON FRENZ BREAKDOWNS
TOM PALMER FINISHES
JOE ROSEN LETTERS
GLYNIS WEIN COLORS
LOUISE JONES EDITOR
JIM SHOOTER EDITOR-IN-CHIEF
GENTLEMEN--AND LADIES--I GIVE YOU ONE OF THE FINEST SPACE PIRATES WHO EVER FLEW--A SMUGGLER, A CHEAT, A CONFIDENCE ARTIST... ONE OF THE BEST.
LET'S HEAR IT FOR HIM NOW, LIKE WE REALLY MEAN IT!
I WANT EACH AND EVERY ONE OF YOU TO SHOW HOW MUCH YOU ADMIRE-- HAN SOLO!
THE BIG CON

COME ON, EVERYONE, I MEAN IT. LET'S DO IT!
SHOW YOUR APPRECIATION ...FROM THE HEART!

BOOO!
HISSSS
SPLAT

SOLO, YOU JERK!!

Y'KNOW... I GOT ONLY ONE REGRET ABOUT THE BOUNTY HUNTERS FINALLY CATCHING OL' HAN AN' TAKIN' 'IM OUTTA CIRCULATION.
THAT THEY DIDN'T KILL HIM?
NAW... THAT I'M NOT THE GUY WHO COLLECTED THE HUNDRED THOUSAND CREDIT REWARD ON HIS WORTHLESS HEAD!
GOOD RIDDANCE TO THE CORELLIAN CREEP, I SAY!

NOW, NOW, CHILDREN... YOU'RE TAKING A VERY NARROW-MINDED --NOT TO SAY DIM--VIEW OF THIS ENTIRE AFFAIR.

I, FOR ONE, SINCERELY REGRET CAPTAIN SOLO'S PLIGHT... I HATE KNOWING THAT ANY OF OUR BRETHREN HAS FALLEN INTO THE HANDS OF BOUNTY HUNTING SCUM...
AT A TIME WHEN HE MIGHT BE OF SOME USE TO US!

WE'LL NEVER KNOW FOR SURE, OF COURSE. BECAUSE I, FOR ONE, DON'T INTEND TO GO CHARGING OFF ON SOME FOOLISHLY HEROIC, SUICIDAL RESCUE MISSION...
...ONLY TO FIND OUT AT ITS END THAT HAN COULDN'T HELP US.
BUT THE FACT REMAINS THAT WE'RE STUCK HERE... SKULKING IN OUR DEN IN THE...ER...COMMERCIAL DISTRICT OF ARCAN IV...
WITH ONE OF THE SWEETEST CAPERS WE'VE EVER PLANNED LAID OUT BEFORE US... AND WE'RE UNABLE TO PROCEED BECAUSE WE LACK THE ONE VITAL ARTICLE WE NEED TO MAKE IT WORK.

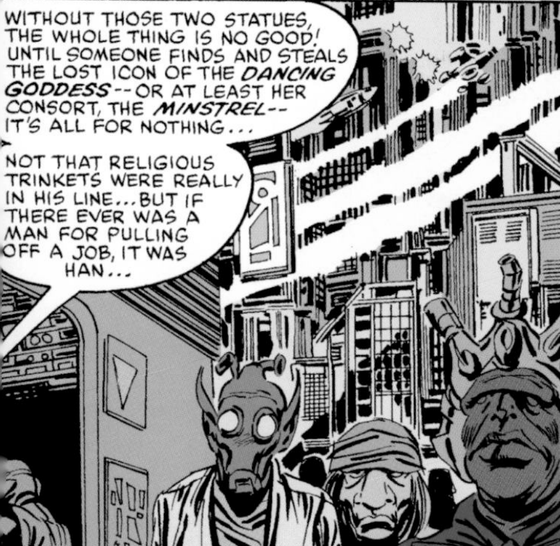
WITHOUT THOSE TWO STATUES, THE WHOLE THING IS NO GOOD! UNTIL SOMEONE FINDS AND STEALS THE LOST ICON OF THE DANCING GODDESS--OR AT LEAST HER CONSORT, THE MINSTREL--IT'S ALL FOR NOTHING...
NOT THAT RELIGIOUS TRINKETS WERE REALLY IN HIS LINE...BUT IF THERE EVER WAS A MAN FOR PULLING OFF A JOB, IT WAS HAN...

CURSE HIS EYES, ANYWAY!
PASS THE BOTTLE.
IT'S EMPTY.

BAM BAM
BAM BAM

WHAT'S THE PASS-WORD?!?
GROOONK

OH...UH, SURE. DO COME RIGHT IN. PLEASE.

O-OH MY GOSH!
DO...DO YOU SEE THAT?
WHO IS THAT?
WHAT IS THAT?
ER...UH...NICE NIGHT... ISN'T IT?
GONNA TRY YOUR LUCK?
ARE YOU CRAZY?! THAT'S A WOOKIEE. WITH A WOOKIEE YOU ONLY GET LUCKY IF YOU'RE UNLUCKY!
EVENING, STRANGER. YOU NEW IN THESE PARTS? WE DON'T GET MANY WOOKIEES IN HERE.
WHAT BRINGS YOU TO ARCAN IV?
I DO!

WHY DO YOU ASK?
OH, UH... NO REASON AT ALL, MISTER... MISTER ...MISTER...?
UH... SIR.
DREBBLE.
CAPTAIN DREBBLE.
"CAPTAIN DREBBLE"?
BRING ME A LARGE BOTTLE OF THE LOCAL RUM... AND ANOTHER ROUND FOR MY FRIEND.

AH...YES, YOUR FRIEND, CAPTAIN DREBBLE...BY THE WAY, WHAT DO YOU CALL YOUR FRIEND?
I CALL HIM A FRIEND. YOU CAN CALL HIM A WOOKIEE.
WE KNOW HE'S A WOOKIEE. WHICH WOOKIEE IS HE?
THE ONLY ONE HERE...SO CALL HIM THAT...OR FIND OUT HOW HE REACTS WHEN PEOPLE CALL HIM THINGS HE DOESN'T LIKE.
AH...AH, YES, CAPTAIN. BUT WE STILL DON'T KNOW WHY YOU'RE HERE.
WHY IS ANYONE ANYWHERE? WE'RE LOOKING FOR A GOOD JOB, SOMETHING PROFITABLE, OF COURSE.
YOU TWO ARE LEMO AND SANDA, RIGHT? I HEARD YOUR GANG WAS MOUNTING A PROJECT, AND MUDDLING IT.
THE WOOKIEE AND I WILL HELP YOU WITH IT...
...FOR A SHARE.
WHAT?!?
YOU CREEP! WE'LL KILL YOU FIRST!
GGRRRR!
YAWN
NO...YOU'D BE TOO SMART TO DO ANYTHING THAT FOOLISH...NOT WHEN I'VE COME HERE, PREPARED TO GIVE YOU SOME FREE ADVICE...
...AS A MARK OF MY GOOD FAITH, AND TO SHOW YOU HOW USEFUL I CAN BE.
BUT, SANDA AND I--!
YES, I'M SURE YOU DO. NOW, PUT YOUR BLASTER AWAY, THERE'S A GOOD FELLOW.

VERY WELL... I'LL HEAR YOU OUT, FOR NOW.
THANKS, LEMO. BLASTERS MAKE ME NERVOUS. YOU HAVE NO IDEA--!
SPEAKING OF IDEAS, YOU SAID YOU'D BROUGHT US ONE. LET'S HEAR IT.
VERY WELL. LET'S SAY THAT THE WOOKIEE AND I HAVE HEARD SOMETHING...

IT DOESN'T MATTER WHERE WE HEARD IT... BUT LET'S SAY THE WOOKIEE AND I KNEW THAT A CERTAIN GROUP OF PEOPLE WERE LOOKING FOR TWO STATUES...
AND THE WOOKIEE AND I ALSO KNEW THAT A FORMER PARTNER OF THE GANG--A FELLOW WHO'D GONE MISSING SOME TIME BEFORE--WAS AN ABSOLUTE GENIUS AT LOCATING LOST ARTIFACTS--
--TRIVIAL TOYS LIKE THE MINSTREL, AND REALLY SIGNIFICANT PIECES LIKE THE DANCING GODDESS.

WELL, IF I WISHED THAT GROUP OF PEOPLE ANY GOOD LUCK AT ALL I'D JUST FEEL MYSELF BOUND TO ASK THEM--
--WHY THE BLAZES YOU BUMBLING AMATEURS HAVEN'T CAPTURED HAN SOLO AND USED THE METHODS THAT SEVERAL OF YOU SPECIALIZE IN TO FORCE HIM TO HELP YOU OUT!

SOLO?
SPECIALIST AT FINDING ARTIFACTS?
WHAT ARE YOU TALKING ABOUT?
WE... WE HADN'T HEARD...

OH, COME ON... I THOUGHT EVERY DISHONEST BUSINESSMAN THIS SIDE OF THE WHEEL HAD HEARD ABOUT WHAT HAPPENED ON STENAX.
WORD IS, IN A WEEK, SOLO MANAGED TO FIND SOMETHING THAT THE NATIVES HAD BEEN SEEKING FOR MILLENNIA--THE LOST GOD OF VOL.
YOU REALLY DO NEED SOME SKILLED GUIDANCE, DON'T YOU?
ARROGANT SCUM, TALKING TO THE CHIEF LIKE THAT! I'LL FIX HIM!

DREBBLE--!

KORUU--!
YOU IDIOT!
NOT WITH US BEHIND HIM!

DIE...

...EEEEEEH?

HE'S DEAD!
WHO THREW THAT KNIFE?
I DIDN'T SEE ANYONE MOVE.

NEITHER DID KORUU.
AND IF ANYONE ELSE GETS CLEVER, HE PROBABLY WON'T SEE ME MOVE EITHER.

YOU'RE FAST, DREBBLE. I'LL GIVE YOU THAT.
LIKE I SAID, BLASTERS MAKE ME NERVOUS.
YOU CAN MAKE IT UP TO ME. YOU PAY FOR OUR DRINKS.

THE WOOKIEE AND I WILL BE AT OUR SHIP, THE COBRA, HANGAR SEVEN OF THE SPACEPORT. LOOK US UP IF YOU WANT TO WORK WITH US.

WHAT DO YOU MEAN YOU THINK I LAID IT ON TOO THICK BACK THERE? FOR THAT CROWD, THERE'S NO SUCH THING AS TOO THICK. THE HOKIER THE BETTER!
BELIEVE ME, THERE ARE ALL SORTS OF CRIME OPEN TO THE RESOURCEFUL. I'VE STUDIED IT. PIRACY ALWAYS ATTRACTS THE ROMANTICS--GULLIBLE ROMANTICS...
GGGRROOWR!
ER... PRESENT COMPANY EXCLUDED, OF COURSE.

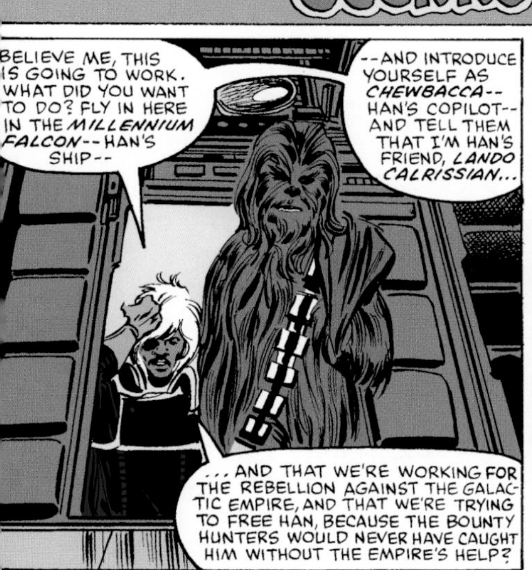
BELIEVE ME, THIS IS GOING TO WORK. WHAT DID YOU WANT TO DO? FLY IN HERE IN THE *MILLENNIUM FALCON*--HAN'S SHIP--
--AND INTRODUCE YOURSELF AS *CHEWBACCA*--HAN'S COPILOT--AND TELL THEM THAT I'M HAN'S FRIEND, *LANDO CALRISSIAN*...
...AND THAT WE'RE WORKING FOR THE REBELLION AGAINST THE GALACTIC EMPIRE, AND THAT WE'RE TRYING TO FREE HAN, BECAUSE THE BOUNTY HUNTERS WOULD NEVER HAVE CAUGHT HIM WITHOUT THE EMPIRE'S HELP?

NO, WE HAVE A BETTER CHANCE AS DREBBLE, SPACE PIRATE, AND THE WOOKIEE WITH NO NAME, LOOKING FOR HAN FOR PERSONAL GAIN AND WILLING TO HURT HIM IN OUR OWN INTERESTS, WITHOUT HESITATION.
THAT'S SOMETHING LEMO AND SANDA AND THEIR GANG WILL ACCEPT. THEY CAN RELATE TO IT!

HROOOF?
WHY DO I KEEP USING "DREBBLE" WHENEVER I NEED AN ALIAS? SIMPLE. DREBBLE'S THE NAME OF AN OLD ENEMY OF MINE.

WHENEVER I'M ON A JOB THAT'S LIKELY TO GET SOMEONE--ESPECIALLY IN THE EMPIRE--MAD AT ME, I USE HIS NAME.
WITH A LITTLE LUCK, MAYBE ONE DAY SOME OF THE PEOPLE I'VE CONNED WILL DECIDE TO LOOK *HIM* UP.
I KNOW IT'S A SLIM CHANCE, BUT THE POSSIBILITIES KEEP ME ENTERTAINED.

BURRAK
REALLY. YOU'D BE SURPRISED HOW GULLIBLE PEOPLE CAN BE.
LIKE THOSE PIRATES BELIEVING MY STORY THAT HAN HAD ANY SPECIAL KNACK FOR FINDING LOST ARTIFACTS, JUST 'CAUSE HE DID IT ONCE.
IF THEY'D BEEN LOOKING FOR A MUSICIAN, I'D HAVE CONVINCED THEM HAN WAS A FAMOUS BANDLEADER...
ANYTHING TO GET THEM INTERESTED IN FINDING HIM.
FFRROWF
YEAH...THESE LITTLE ITEMS THAT I WON IN AN ALL NIGHT CARD GAME, BACK WHEN I MANAGED THAT GAS MINE ON BESPIN...
...THEY'RE OUR BACKUP INSURANCE NOT THAT I EVER REALLY WANTED THEM IN THE FIRST PLACE...
BUT WHO KNOWS? THEY MIGHT BE HANDY NOW.

DREBBLE! WOOKIEE! IT'S US! WE'VE COME TO BUY YOU DINNER!
WE'LL BE RIGHT THERE!
WE CAN JUST TAKE ONE OF THESE WITH US... LEAVE THE OTHER HERE FOR SAFETY.
LET'S GO, CHEWIE!

HRONK!

WHAT? MY--?
OH! RIGHT! MY DISGUISE. BE RIGHT WITH YOU.

OKAY, I'M ALL SET!
FUNNY...IT'S AWFULLY DARK IN HERE, ALL OF A SUDDEN.

BUMP
GRUMPH!

WRONG...WRONG SIDE! OF COURSE I KNEW I HAD IT ON THE WRONG SIDE. WHAT DO YOU THINK I AM, BLIND OR SOMETHING?

SORRY TO HAVE KEPT YOU WAITING.
NOT AT ALL, CAPTAIN. NOT AT ALL. SANDA AND I WERE JUST TALKING ABOUT OUR DEPLORABLE LACK OF MANNERS BEFORE...
AFTER ALL, IF A MAN... ER, TWO MEN... I MEAN, IF A MAN AND A WOOKIEE ARE GOING TO BE OUR PARTNERS, THE LEAST WE CAN DO IS SHOW THEM SOME HOSPI-TALITY...
AND FIND OUT WHY THEY KNOW SO MUCH. AND THEN KILL THEM.
IS THIS WHAT SMILING IS SUP-POSED TO FEEL LIKE? IT HURTS!
LET US TAKE YOU TO OUR FAVORITE LITTLE OUT OF THE WAY BISTRO. I BELIEVE YOU'LL FIND THAT THE NATIVE CUISINE IS QUITE SOMETHING.
JUST HOW "OUT OF THE WAY" IS THIS PLACE YOU'RE TAKING US? NOTHING TOO LONELY AND ISOLATED I HOPE.
HOPE AGAIN, SUCKER.
OH NO... IT DOESN'T TAKE LONG AT ALL TO GET THERE BY HOVER CAR...
NOT THE WAY WE DRIVE.
FLIP
I REALLY HOPE YOU'LL ENJOY YOUR EVENING, CAPTAIN.
WHOOPS!
I EXPECT I WILL.

HERE WE ARE, YOU AND THE WOOKIEE GO ON AHEAD, CAPTAIN. WE'LL PARK THE HOVER CARS...

THIS IS VERY FRIENDLY OF YOU, LEMO...
WHAT WOULD YOU LIKE?
APPETIZERS, THE SPECIALTY OF THE HOUSE, AND THAT BANTHA SWILL YOU CALL WINE. AND MAKE IT FAST, TRAMP!
ER... YES, MISS SANDA. RIGHT AWAY.

WELL, THE APPETIZERS CERTAINLY SMELL GOOD.
I'D ADVISE YOU TO GO EASY, DREBBLE ...THE FOOD ON ARCAN IV IS A LITTLE HOT...

THANKS FOR THE WARNING ...BUT I THINK IT'S DELICIOUS.
I WAS RIGHT ABOUT YOU! YOU ARE A TOUGH MAN, AND I'M SURE THERE'S NO NEED TO WORRY ABOUT YOUR FRIEND...

MUNCH
SNIF SNIF

WURP

CAREFUL!
GLUG GLUG GLUG GLUG

THAT'S NOT WATER IN THAT PITCHER. IT'S DELTRO SPICE WINE, OR HAVE YOU ALREADY FIGURED THAT OUT?
HOOWWL

THAT BIG METAL BOWL--THAT'S THE WATER.
IMPORTED WINE, TOO? JUST THE THING TO COOL A MAN OFF AFTER A HARD DAY!

DREBBLE, I LIKE YOU! YOU'RE TOUGH, AND YOU'VE GOT LOTS OF STYLE!
AND YOU'VE GOT QUITE A HEAD FOR WINE, TOO!
FILL HIS GLASS AGAIN...
RIGHT. ANOTHER ROUND, AND LET'S TOAST OUR NEW PARTNER, AND HEAR HIS IDEAS ON FINDING THE DANCING GODDESS, THE KEY TO ALL OUR DREAMS!
I THOUGHT WE'D AGREED. THE BEST WAY TO FIND THAT STATUE IS TO FIND THE MAN WHO CAN LEAD US TO HER.

FINDING HAN SOLO IS THE KEY TO THE WHOLE THING... THEN WE CAN LEAN ON HIM...
HAVE ANOTHER DRINK.
DON'T MIND IF I DO...
FINDING SOLO'S NOT THE PROBLEM. WE KNOW RIGHT WHERE HE IS, AND HE'S NOT LIKELY TO BE GOING ANYWHERE.

THE TRICKY THING'S GOING TO BE CONVINCING JABBA THE HUTT TO LET US HAVE HAN, WITHOUT BEING FORCED TO CUT HIM IN...
GRRR..?

JABBA?
SURE. I THOUGHT EVERYONE KNEW THAT MUCH. SOLO WAS WORKING FOR THE REBELLION... AND SOME BIG IMPERIAL LORD CAUGHT HIM...
AND HANDED HIM OVER TO THE BOUNTY HUNTER, BOBA FETT.

AND FETT EVENTUALLY HANDED HIM OVER TO JABBA AND COLLECTED THE BOUNTY...
YEAH... THAT'S WHAT CHEWIE AND I'D HEARD, TOO... BUT WE CHECKED OUT JABBA'S HEADQUARTERS ON TATOOINE, AND FETT HADN'T ARRIVED THERE YET...
SO, WE FIGURED MAYBE WE'D HEARD WRONG, AND THERE WAS SOME OTHER BUYER. HAN HAS A LOT OF ENEMIES, AND ÷HIC÷

RIGHT NOW, SO DO YOU!
ME AND MY BIG MOUTH!
÷HIC÷

RRROOAR
WHAT'S THE WOOKIEE DOING?
EEEK!

THEY'RE GETTING AWAY!
HIC
STOP THEM!

NO, IT'S OKAY. THE NIGHT AIR'S CLEARED MY HEAD. I'LL DRIVE. WE HAVE TO GET BACK TO THE SHIP, FAST!
URF!

THERE THEY GO!
THOSE DIRTY DOUBLE-CROSSERS! WE'LL KILL THEM FOR THIS!

GET TO THE OTHER CARS!

NOTHING. NOT ONE LONELY, EVEN MARGINALLY AFFLUENT GENTLEMAN HAS PASSED THIS WAY ALL NIGHT.
I'M HUNGRY. I'M COLD, AND MY FEET ARE KILLING ME IN THESE STUPID SHOES.
IT'S ALL THE FAULT OF THOSE LOUSY OFF-WORLD PIRATES. EVER SINCE THEY MOVED INTO THE COMMERCIAL DISTRICT...

HONEST MEN WON'T. AND THEY BROUGHT THEIR OWN WOMEN WITH THEM, SO NO ONE'S REPLACING MY LOST CUSTOMERS.
ONCE... JUST ONCE, IF THERE WERE ANY JUSTICE IN THIS UNIVERSE, I'D FIND SOME WAY OF GETTING EVEN WITH JUST ONE OF THOSE PIRATES.

EXCUSE ME, MISS, BUT MY FRIEND AND I ARE NEW TO THIS PLANET.
WELL, I'LL BE--! THERE'S JUSTICE IN THE UNIVERSE AFTER ALL!
WE SEEM TO HAVE LOST OUR WAY.
COULD YOU PLEASE POINT OUT THE FASTEST ROUTE BACK TO THE SPACEPORT?

OF COURSE, SIR. IT WILL BE MY PLEASURE!
YOU GO RIGHT ON THE WAY YOU'RE GOING, THROUGH THE FIRST INTERSECTION. WHEN YOU GET TO THE SECOND PURPLE LIGHT, MAKE A LEFT TURN.

THAT WILL TAKE YOU ONTO THE ACCESS ROAD THAT LEADS TO THE MAIN HIGHWAY. YOU CAN'T MISS IT, AND IT LEADS RIGHT TO THE SPACEPORT.
THANKS A LOT. WE APPRECIATE IT.

NOT AT ALL, SIR, MY PLEASURE.

DOPE.

HUNH?!
THERE THEY GO!
I SEE THEM!
DON'T LOSE THEM!

BUT, LEMO, LOOK WHICH ROAD THEY'RE TAKING!
THEY CAN'T MEAN TO GO DOWN THERE!
I DON'T CARE WHAT THEY MEAN! DON'T LOSE THEM!

WELL, CHEWIE, I THINK WE'VE LOST THEM!
HOWL?!
WHAT DO YOU MEAN, CAN'T I SEE WHAT'S UP AHEAD? WHATEVER IT IS...

I CAN'T SEE MUCH OF ANYTHING WITH THIS STUPID DISGUISE ON.

THAT'S BETTER, NOW I'VE GOT SOME VISION...
SO WHAT'S SO IMPORTANT FOR ME TO...

...SEE?
ULP

I SEE MY WHOLE LIFE FLASHING BEFORE MY EYES.

LET'S GET OUT OF HERE BEFORE THEY REACH US!

POIT
SMAK
I DON'T BELIEVE IT.
WE MADE IT. WE'RE STILL ALIVE!

DREBBLE AND THE WOOKIEE HAVE TURNED OFF THE HIGHWAY!
BUT, WE DON'T HAVE TIME TO--

SPAM

AAIIEEE!

VAMPH

THERE YOU SEE, CHEWBACCA? I TOLD YOU I'D LOSE THEM.
PRETTY SMOOTH PLANNING, EH?
GGGGRRR!

VORP
VORP
VORP
YOU COULD BE RIGHT ABOUT THAT.

HRARF
WHAT DO YOU MEAN, IF A WOOKIEE WANTS SOMETHING DONE RIGHT, HE'D BETTER DO IT HIMSELF?

OH, I SEE.
ER...CHIEF... WHAT'S THE WOOKIEE DOING?

NO!
DON'T!
HELP!

GREAT WORK, CHEWIE! JUST FOLLOW ME BACK AT THE SHIP!
KABOOM
HRONK

OOPS. A COUPLE OF LEMO'S MEN STILL WANT TO PLAY...
BUT, FROM WHAT I'VE SEEN, THEY'RE DRIVING A LITTLE FASTER THAN THEIR SKILL SHOULD ALLOW...
I HOPE CHEWIE ISN'T HAVING TOO MUCH TROUBLE SHAKING OFF HIS LAST FEW FRIENDS...

MAYBE, IF I TRY MANEUVERING DOWN A TIGHT SQUEEZE AT HIGH SPEED, AND THEY TRY TO STAY WITH ME...
VASHT
VASHT

AHA! THAT DID IT! GOTCHA, SUCKERS!

I'VE GOTTEN ALL TURNED AROUND, AGAIN. I WONDER WHICH WAY I'M GOING THIS TIME...
OH NO!

SIMULTANEOUSLY...
GRONK

RURF!
CRASH
SMASH

GRONK?

NO! IT CAN'T BE!
CHEWIE, TURN IT AROUND! I'M GOING TOO FAST TO--

BLOOEY!

AGH!
URF
WHAMMO!

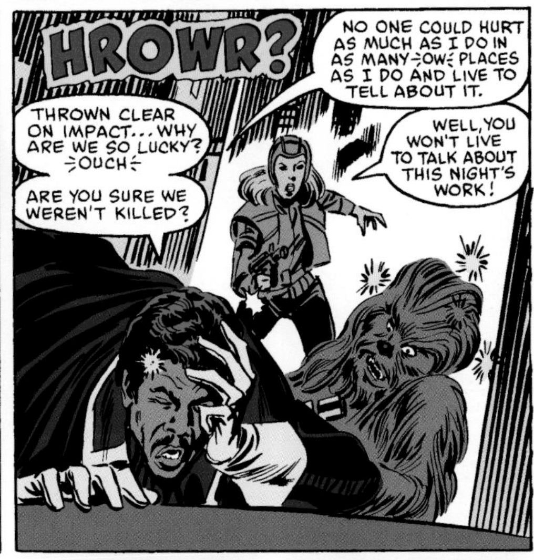

HROWR?
NO ONE COULD HURT AS MUCH AS I DO IN AS MANY -OW- PLACES AS I DO AND LIVE TO TELL ABOUT IT.
THROWN CLEAR ON IMPACT... WHY ARE WE SO LUCKY? -OUCH-
ARE YOU SURE WE WEREN'T KILLED?
WELL, YOU WON'T LIVE TO TALK ABOUT THIS NIGHT'S WORK!

HUH? OH, HELLO THERE, MISS. NICE TO SEE YOU. I'M HAPPY YOU SURVIVED ALL THOSE CRASHES!
LOOK, CAN'T WE TALK OVER THIS BUSINESS OF YOU SHOOTING ME? I'M PHILOSOPHICALLY OPPOSED TO BEING KILLED.
HEY, I'M IN A LOT OF PAIN AS IT IS, LEAVE ME ALIVE TO SUFFER. IT WILL BE CRUELER IN THE LONG RUN ANYWAY.
HROF

-GASP-
YOU'VE GOT IT... AFTER ALL THE MONTHS WE'VE SPENT HUNTING FOR IT.

THERE IT IS! THE LOST MINSTREL!

WITH THIS, I'LL SURELY BE ABLE TO FIND THE DANCING GODDESS... THE OTHER STATUE IS THE KEY TO EVERYTHING... AND THIS ONE PUTS IT IN MY GRASP! MINE! MINE ALONE! ME!
DAFI! YOU CAUGHT THEM! GOOD WORK!
GET AWAY FROM ME, DO YOU HEAR?! THIS IS MINE! MINE, MINE, *MINE!* I'M NOT SHARING IT WITH ANYONE!
SHE'S GONE CRAZY!
CHEWBACCA, THIS SEEMS LIKE AS OPPORTUNE A MOMENT AS THERE WILL EVER BE FOR US TO SLIP AWAY...
AGH!

CHEER UP, WOULD YOU? WE FINALLY FOUND OUT FOR SURE WHERE TO FIND HAN. WE'VE DONE WHAT WE CAME OUT HERE TO DO...

AND IT DIDN'T COST US A THING... EXCEPT FOR SOME HUNK OF ARTISTIC JUNK THAT NEVER MEANT A THING TO ME ANYWAY.
THE ONLY REASON I HAD EITHER OF THESE WAS BECAUSE I KNEW I HAD A WINNING HAND THAT NIGHT, AND THE OTHER GUY INSISTED THEY WERE VALUABLE ENOUGH TO MATCH MY STAKE...

MAYBE SOMEDAY, AFTER HAN'S SAFELY BACK AMONG US, WE CAN FIND OUT JUST WHAT LEMO'S GANG WANTED THE STATUES FOR...
I WONDER WHAT THEY'D HAVE DONE, IF THEY'D KNOWN WE HAD THE MINSTREL--AND THE *GODDESS,* HERE, ALL ALONG.

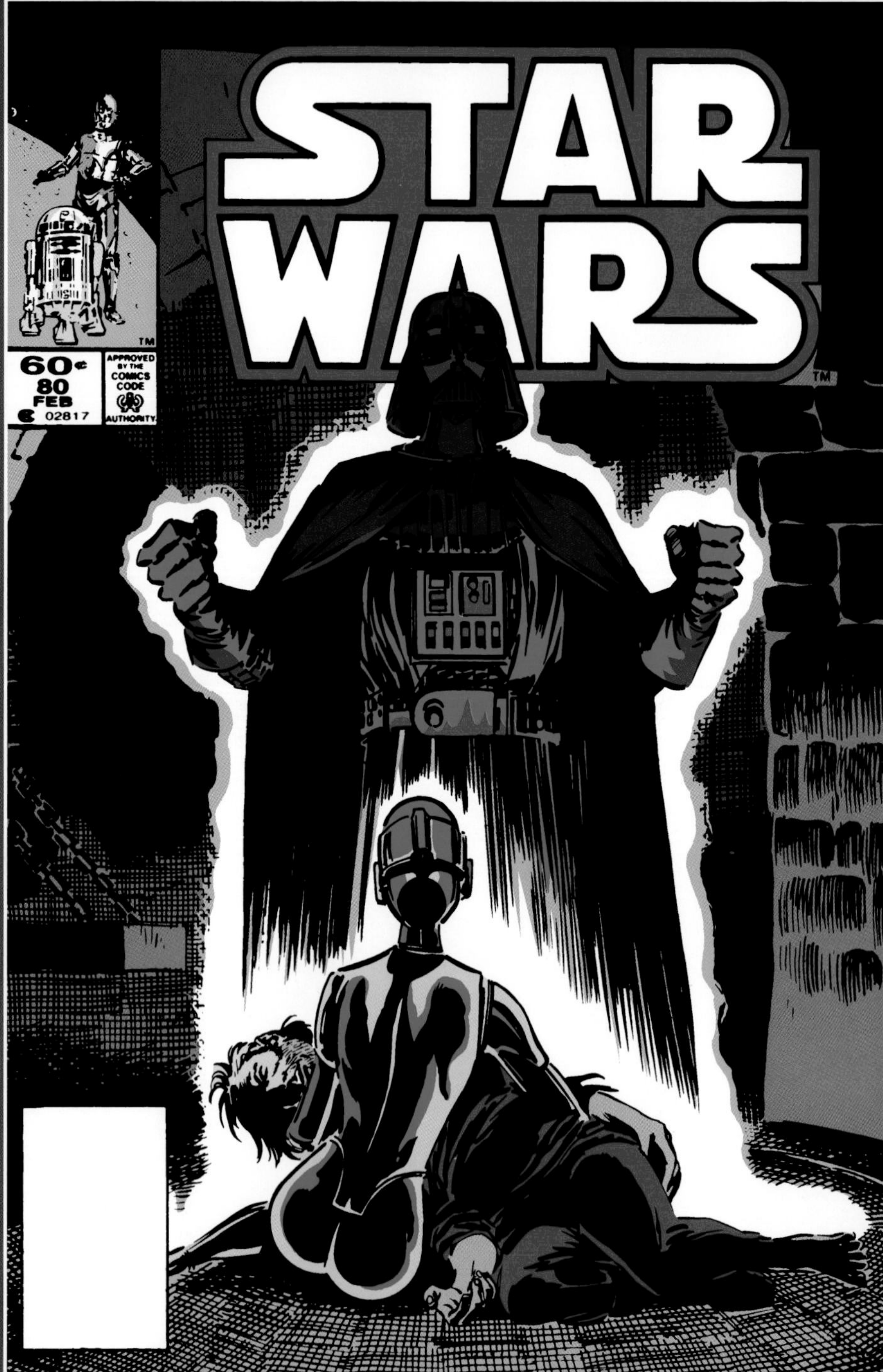
STAR WARS
60¢
80
FEB
02817
APPROVED BY THE COMICS CODE AUTHORITY

JO DUFFY PLOT AND SCRIPT
RON FRENZ BREAKDOWNS
TOM PALMER FINISHER
JOE ROSEN LETTERER
GLYNIS WEIN COLORIST
LOUISE JONES EDITOR
JIM SHOOTER EDITOR-IN-CHIEF
ELLIE

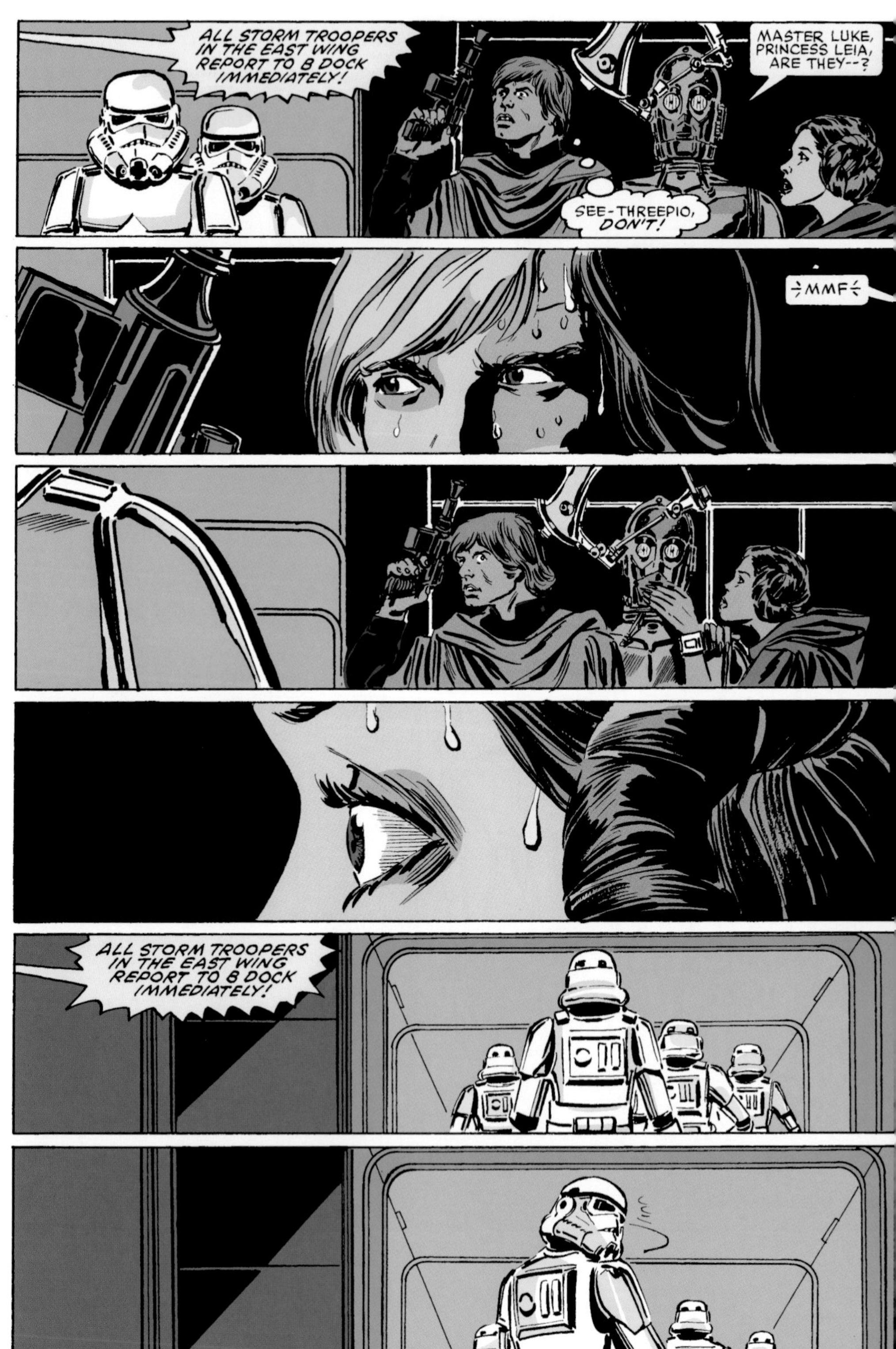
ALL STORM TROOPERS IN THE EAST WING REPORT TO 8 DOCK IMMEDIATELY!
MASTER LUKE, PRINCESS LEIA, ARE THEY--?
SEE-THREEPIO, DON'T!
MMF
ALL STORM TROOPERS IN THE EAST WING REPORT TO 8 DOCK IMMEDIATELY!

YOU, THERE! WHY HAVE YOU FALLEN OUT OF LINE? DIDN'T YOU HEAR THE ANNOUNCEMENT? ALL TROOPS IN THIS SECTOR HAVE BEEN ORDERED TO B DOCK, NOW.
WELL, WHAT IS IT?

SIR, I THOUGHT I HEARD...
WHAT?

I GUESS IT WAS NOTHING.
GOOD.

THAT WAS A LITTLE TOO CLOSE...
I THOUGHT FOR CERTAIN WE WERE FINISHED.
IF THAT TROOPER HAD HEARD YOU, THREEPIO, WE WOULD HAVE BEEN.

COME ON. WE'D BETTER FINISH OUR SEARCH AND GET OUT OF HERE. IF ANY OF THE IMPERIAL GUARDS FIND US, IT WON'T MATTER WHETHER THEY IDENTIFY US AS REBEL AGENTS OR NOT...
THIS AREA'S OFF-LIMITS TO ALL CIVILIANS.

COULDN'T WE JUST TELL THEM THAT WE'D LOST OUR WAY?
IT WOULDN'T HOLD UP. THIS ENTIRE WORLD IS JUST A STORAGE AND TRANSFERRAL POINT FOR THE EMPIRE'S SUPPLIES...
THE CARGO WE BROUGHT IN AS OUR COVER HAS ALL BEEN UN-LOADED AND SIGNED FOR.
WE NO LONGER HAVE ANY BUSINESS ANYWHERE ON THIS BASE.
EXCEPT FOR OUR *REAL* BUSINESS-- LOCATING OUR MISSING AGENT, TAY VANIS.
THE LAST MESSAGE WE HAD FROM HIM INDICATED THAT HE WAS HEADING TO-WARD THIS WORLD, ON THE PRETENSE OF BEING A TRADER.
AND HE WAS CARRYING TAPES THAT SPIES IN THE BOTHAN SYSTEM HAD SMUGGLED TO HIM ...PLANS FOR SOME KIND OF A NEW IMPERIA SUPER WEAPON...
THERE'S NO SIGN THAT ANY ONE'S BEE IN HERE IN MONTHS, LU ...MAYBE WE SHOUL CHECK TH HANGAR BAY...
WELL... THE GROUND CREW SAYS OUR OWN SHIP IS ALMOST REFUELED. WE SHOULD HAVE CLEARANCE TO TAKE OFF IN JUST A LITTLE WHILE...
BUT WE STILL DON'T KNOW WHAT BECAME OF VANIS, HIS SHIP, OR THE MISSING TAPES!
VANIS'S SHIP ISN'T HERE, LEIA. IT WOULD BE EASY ENOUGH TO SPOT IT IF IT WERE...
ACCORDING TO OUR COMMANDER, VANIS ALWAYS FLEW A STANDARD X-WING THAT HE'D MODIFIED TO HIS OWN SPECIFI-CATIONS...
THEN... WE'RE JUST GOING TO HAVE TO TRY OUR ALTER-NATE PLAN... I WAS HOPING WE WOULDN'T HAVE TO TAKE THE RISK...

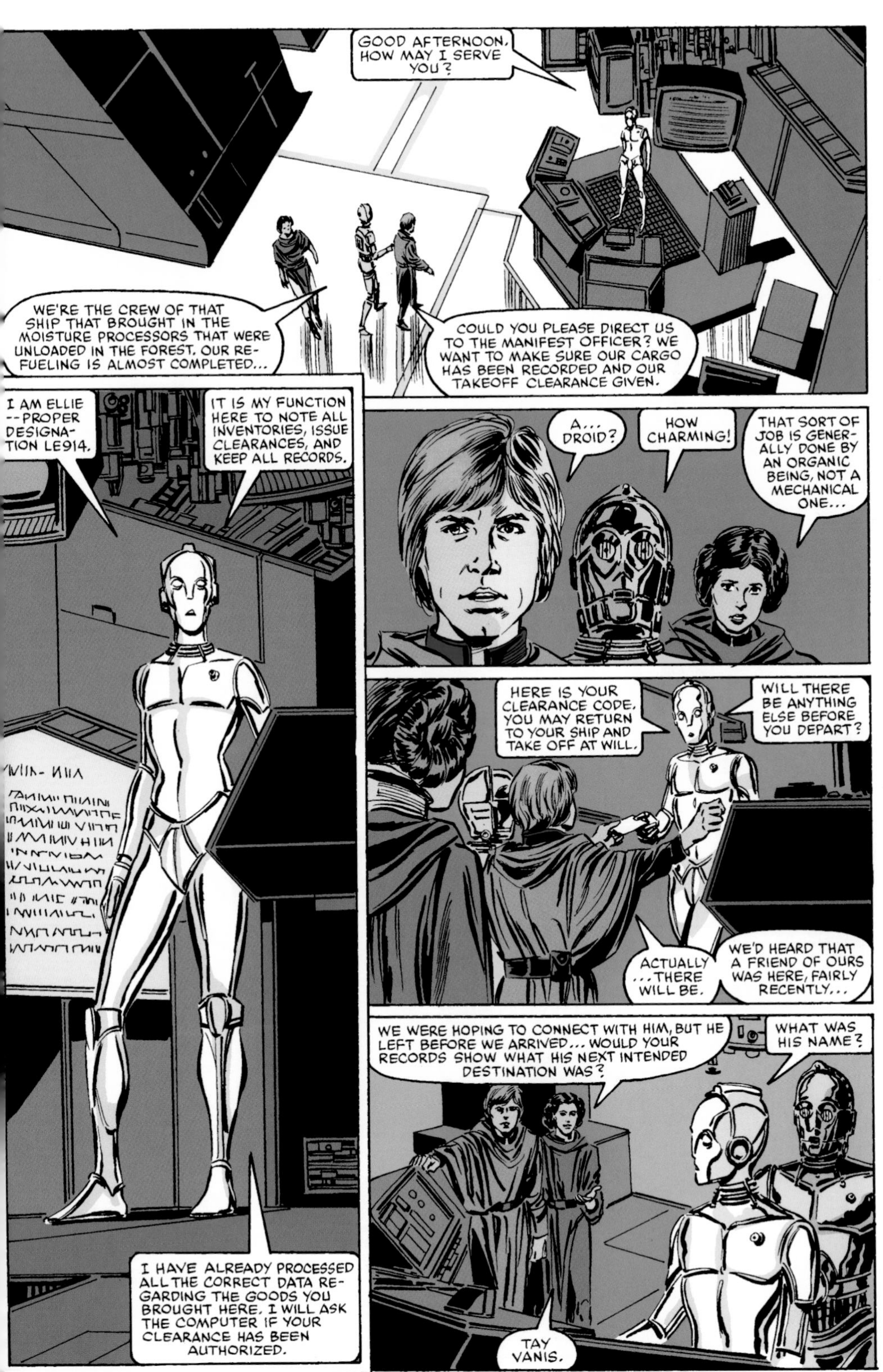
GOOD AFTERNOON, HOW MAY I SERVE YOU?
WE'RE THE CREW OF THAT SHIP THAT BROUGHT IN THE MOISTURE PROCESSORS THAT WERE UNLOADED IN THE FOREST. OUR RE- FUELING IS ALMOST COMPLETED...
COULD YOU PLEASE DIRECT US TO THE MANIFEST OFFICER? WE WANT TO MAKE SURE OUR CARGO HAS BEEN RECORDED AND OUR TAKEOFF CLEARANCE GIVEN.
I AM ELLIE --PROPER DESIGNA- TION LE914.
IT IS MY FUNCTION HERE TO NOTE ALL INVENTORIES, ISSUE CLEARANCES, AND KEEP ALL RECORDS.
I HAVE ALREADY PROCESSED ALL THE CORRECT DATA RE- GARDING THE GOODS YOU BROUGHT HERE. I WILL ASK THE COMPUTER IF YOUR CLEARANCE HAS BEEN AUTHORIZED.
A... DROID?
HOW CHARMING!
THAT SORT OF JOB IS GENER- ALLY DONE BY AN ORGANIC BEING, NOT A MECHANICAL ONE...
HERE IS YOUR CLEARANCE CODE. YOU MAY RETURN TO YOUR SHIP AND TAKE OFF AT WILL.
WILL THERE BE ANYTHING ELSE BEFORE YOU DEPART?
ACTUALLY ...THERE WILL BE.
WE'D HEARD THAT A FRIEND OF OURS WAS HERE, FAIRLY RECENTLY...
WE WERE HOPING TO CONNECT WITH HIM, BUT HE LEFT BEFORE WE ARRIVED... WOULD YOUR RECORDS SHOW WHAT HIS NEXT INTENDED DESTINATION WAS?
WHAT WAS HIS NAME?
TAY VANIS.

ONE MOMENT, PLEASE. I WILL ASK THE COMPUTER.
THIS IS A PLEASANT SURPRISE! I HAD NO IDEA THERE WERE ANY LE SERIES DROIDS IN USE HERE.
I AM THREEPIO-- *SEE* THREEPIO-- HUMAN/CYBORG RELATIONS...
...A TRANSLATOR, FLUENT IN OVER...
WELL, SO FAR, SO GOOD. SHE DIDN'T REACT WHEN WE MENTIONED VANIS'S NAME...
WE'LL HAVE WHAT WE CAME FOR IN JUST A MINUTE.
REEEE!
WE'RE DOOMED.
BETTER DRAW YOUR BLASTER, LEIA. WE'RE ABOUT TO HAVE COMPANY!
WHO SET OFF THAT ALARM?
IT MUST HAVE BEEN THEM!
LOOK OUT. ONE OF THEM GOT A LIGHT SABER!
YOU TAKE CARE OF THEM, LUKE. I'LL COVER THE OTHER CORRIDOR.
RIGHT.
I DON'T UNDERSTAND. HOW DID THE STORM TROOPERS...?
THERE WAS A SIGNA IN THE COMPUTER, SET TO TRIGGER AN ALARM IF ANYONE REQUESTED ACCESS TO INFORMATION REGARDING TAY VANIS.
I AM SORRY. I WAS UNAWARE OF ITS EXISTENCE
GREAT.

BOTH OF YOU, GET BEHIND THE CONSOLE. IT SHOULD SHIELD YOU FROM THE BLASTER FIRE. LEAVE THIS TO US.
OH, DEAR! OH, DEAR!
GET HIM!
AAGHK
VWORP

LOOK OUT! THAT BOLT LUKE DEFLECTE IS RICOCHETING RIGHT TOWARD...
THE CONSOLE! WE'LL BE UNPROTECTED!
ELLIE, WHAT ARE YOU--?
ELLIE!!!
MY GOODNESS!
THAT TAKES CARE OF THIS GROUP, BUT THERE'L BE ANOTHER WAVE OF TROOPERS IN HERE PRETTY FAST. LET'S MOVE OUT BEFORE THEY ARRIVE!

OF COURSE, THE CIRCUMSTANCES ARE APPALLING... BUT I'M SO GLAD YOU'VE DECIDED TO JOIN US...
OUR SHIP, THE MILLENNIUM FALCON, IS RUMORED TO BE ONE OF THE FASTEST--!
IF WE WERE ALL A LITTLE FASTER--AND QUIETER--ELLIE'S CHANCES OF SEEING THE SHIP FOR HERSELF WOULD BE A LOT BETTER, THREEPIO!
THERE SHE IS! NICE OF THE EMPIRE TO FUEL HER FOR US!
IF ONLY OUR TAKEOFF CLEARANCE IS STILL IN EFFECT...
LOOKS LIKE IT STILL CHECKS OUT!
IF ONLY WE KNEW WHERE WE WERE GOING...
I CAN DIRECT YOU.
BEFORE THE COMPUTER OBEYED ITS PROGRAMMING TO BETRAY US, IT GAVE ME TAY VANIS'S DESTINATION.
TAKE HEADING EIGHT-POINT-ONE, STROKE TWELVE.
WHERE WILL THAT TAKE US?
TO THE CASTLE THAT WAS ONCE THIS PLANET'S SEAT OF GOVERNMENT... UNTIL THE EMPIRE CONQUERED THIS WORLD, AND DEPOPULATED IT.

"DEPOPULATED." THAT'S WHAT THEY CALL IT, WHEN THEY MURDER AN ENTIRE WORLD'S PEOPLE...
LIKE WHAT THEY DID TO VANIS'S HOMEWORLD, TELFREY...OR MY OWN PLANET, ALDERAAN...TOTALLY DESTROYED...
IF WE CAN FIND THE BOTHAN TAPE MAYBE WE CAN PREVENT THE NEX TELFREY...OR ALDERAAN.
HER HIGHNESS WAS PRINCESS LEIA ORGANA, OF THE ROYAL FAMILY OF ALDERAAN, AND A MEMBER OF THE IMPERIAL SENATE.
AND MASTER LUKE IS COMMANDER LUKE SKYWALKER, OF THE REBEL ALLIANCE!
LUKE...IF THEY FOLLOW US, CAN YOU LOSE THEM?
IF I STAY CLOSE TO THE TREES, THEY WON'T BE ABLE TO SCAN US... THE RAIN'LL HELP, TOO. AND I'VE HANDLED WORSE PLANETARY WEATHER CONDITIONS THAN THIS...
ELLIE, WAS THERE ANY FURTHER INFORMATION ABOUT TAY VANIS IN THE COMPUTER?
ONLY THAT AT THE TIME OF HIS DISAPPEARANCE, THERE WAS AN IMPORTANT IMPERIAL SITH LORD VISITING THE BASE --DARTH VADER...
VADER!
WOULDN'T YOU JUST KNOW IT?
I-I DIDN'T THANK YOU EARLIER. YOU PREVENTED MY DESTRUCTION.
BUT...HOW DID A MANIFEST DROID COME TO BE BLASTER-PROOF?
BEFORE I WENT INTO SERVICE ON THIS WORLD, I WAS PRIVATELY OWNED.
MY LAST MASTER HAD ME SPECIALLY OUTFITTED FOR HIGH STRESS FUNCTIONS...
LUKE, TURN THE SHIP AROUND, AND LOOK FOR A PLACE TO SET DOWN! I JUST SAW SOMETHING THROUGH THE TREES!
THERE'S AN X-WING CRASHED BACK THERE!

IT'S VANIS'S SHIP, ALL RIGHT. IT LOOKS LIKE THE RECORDER IS STILL INTACT.
IF THERE'S ANYTHING IN IT, I'LL BYPASS THE SAFETY SYSTEMS AND WE'LL TAKE IT BACK TO THE FALCON AND PLAY IT.
WELL, IT'S NOT THE BOTHAN TAPES. THAT'S FOR SURE.
IT LOOKS LIKE SOME KIND OF HOLOGRAPHIC RECORDING!
UH-HUNH. VANIS MUST HAVE LEFT IT FOR US AFTER HE CRASHED.
I AM TAY VANIS. FELLOW REBELS, I THANK THE FORCE THAT YOU'RE HERE TO SEE THIS RECORDING.
I KNOW I ADDRESS MY ALLIES, BECAUSE IF ANYONE ENTERS MY SHIP WITHOUT ACTIVATING THE PROPER CODED SEQUENCE, THIS TAPE WILL BE DESTROYED.
I HOPE YOU HAVE REACHED ME QUICKLY. AFTER MY PARTNER, YOM ARGO, AND I FOUND THE BOTHAN TAPES, AND REALIZED THE EMPIRE WAS ON TO US, WE DECIDED THAT I SHOULD FLEE WITH THE TAPES... PLANET-HOPPING ALONG A COURSE WE AGREED UPON...
...WHILE HE WENT BACK TO THE REBEL FLEET FOR AID.
I KNOW YOM WILL BRING YOU AS QUICKLY AS HE CAN, BUT I HOPE YOU HURRY. DARTH VADER IS CLOSE BEHIND ME, AND I'M ALMOST OUT OF TIME...

I'LL FLEE INTO THE WOODS, AND HOPE I CAN EVADE CAPTURE...
BUT...YOM ARGO NEVER MADE IT BACK TO THE FLEET. HE WAS SHOT DOWN IN LAHSBANE, RIGHT AFTER HE LEFT THE BOTHAN SYSTEM.
VANIS HAD NO WAY OF KNOWING THAT, LEIA.
HE WAS WAITING FOR A RESCUE THAT COULD NEVER COME.
ELLIE? ELLIE 914?
NOW WHERE HAS SHE...?
PRINCESS LEIA, MASTER LUKE...
LATER, THREEPIO.
THERE'S MORE.
I...THINK I HEAR THEM COMING...I'VE GOT TO GO!
BUT DON'T WORRY. EVEN IF THE EMPIRE GETS ME, THEY'LL NEVER RECOVER THOSE TAPES. I DON'T HAVE THEM WITH ME. I LEFT THEM WITH SOMEONE ELSE.
MY DROID HAS BEEN WITH ME FOR YEARS--FROM THE VERY BEGINNING--AND CAN BE RELIED UPON TO FOLLOW MY COMMAND.
IF THERE IS NO WORD OF ME WITHIN TWO PLANETARY DAYS...

...ELLIE 914 WILL DESTROY THE BOTHAN TAPES.
SIGNING OFF.
ELLIE?
WHERE IS SHE?!
THREEPIO, WHY DIDN'T YOU...?
I DID TRY TO APPRISE YOU OF IT THE MOMENT SHE WENT OUT-SIDE, BUT YOU SAID...
NEVER MIND. BLAST IT!
SHE'S LONG GONE, LUKE. NOT A TRACE OF HER.
THIS IS THE SECOND TIME ON THIS MISSION THAT A DROID'S DE-CEIVED US. FIRST THERE WAS THAT K3PX UNIT THAT CLAIMED IT HAD BELONGED TO VANIS...
AND ACTUALLY BELONGED TO DARTH VADER...
AND THEN WE FIND VANIS'S REAL DROID...
AND SHE ACTS LIKE SHE'S AN IMPERIAL.
I'M SO GLAD SHE ISN'T! SHE'S A REBEL! OH, I KNEW I LIKED ELLIE. SHE'S ON OUR SIDE!
THEN WHY DIDN'T SHE CONFIDE IN US?
LET'S GET SUITED UP AND GO CHECK OUT THAT CASTLE. I WANT SOME ANSWERS...
...ABOUT VANIS, ELLIE, AND THOSE TAPES!

MASTER LUKE, SIR, WHY ARE YOU...?
SHHH...LET HIM CONCENTRATE, THREEPIO. THERE'S MORE TO HIS TRAINING AS A JEDI KNIGHT THAN JUST USING HIS LIGHT SABER, YOU KNOW.
IF THERE'S ANYTHING SERIOUSLY WRONG INSIDE THAT CASTLE, LUKE'S SENSITIVITY TO THE FORCE SHOULD MAKE HIM AWARE OF IT.
I...THINK IT'S ALL CLEAR. LET'S GO!
SHHH...
I'M NOT SAYING I WANT TO GET KILLED...BUT I WISH I WERE STATIONED JUST A LITTLE CLOSER TO THE HEART OF THE ACTION.
A MAN DOESN'T WIN DECORATION AND PROMO-TIONS BY WASTING HIS TIME AT A BORING JOB ON A DEAD PLANET LIKE THIS ONE.
DEAD'S THE WORD FOR IT, ALL RIGHT. IF YOU LIKE ACTION, YOU SHOULD HAVE GOTTEN HERE A LITTLE SOONER--WHILE WE WERE KILLING IT
THE NATIVES GIVE YOU MUCH TROUBLE?
BUTCHERS!
RIGHT. LET'S STAY WITH THE SECOND ONE. QUIETLY.

YOU'D BE SURPRISED. WE DIDN'T ORIGINALLY INTEND TO KILL THEM ALL, BUT THEY FORCED US TO.
HOW SO?
AFTER WE'D WIPED OUT THE LEADERS, AND A FEW VILLAGES, THE SURVIVORS TOOK ARMS AGAINST US. CAN YOU IMAGINE?
AFTER THAT, WE WENT AFTER THEM ON A LARGE SCALE.
HOW LONG DID THAT TAKE?
A LONG TIME, CONSIDERING HOW FEW THERE WERE TO BEGIN WITH. THE VERMIN CLUNG TO LIFE VERY TENACIOUSLY. IT WAS RATHER AMUSING.
SORRY I MISSED IT. SEE YOU LATER.
SO... YOU ENJOY KILLING CREATURES WHO ARE OUTGUNNED AND OUTNUMBERED?
WHO... WHO'S THERE?
JUST A FEW FRIENDS... FROM THE REBELLION.
NOW WE CAN ALL HAVE A LITTLE FUN TOGETHER.
B-BUT YOU CAN'T!
WHY NOT?
OH... PLEASE... I'LL DO ANYTHING! TELL YOU ANYTHING...
THERE'S ONLY ONE THING WE WANT. VANIS.
YES! OH, YES! OF COURSE!
THERE'S INFORMATION IN ANOTHER CORRIDOR, A LOCKED ROOM! I'LL TAKE YOU TO IT!
IT'S BEHIND THIS DOOR.
OPEN IT.

LUKE.
DARTH VADER!

LOOK OUT, YOUR HIGHNESS! HE'S STEALING YOUR BLASTER!

THEN I'LL HAVE TO BORROW LUKE'S!

AAAAIIIIEE!

THAT HOLOGRAM... IT'S LIKE IT WAS WAITING FOR US... BUT WHY?

Y THE POWER OF THE ORCE, I HAVE FORESEEN HAT YOU WILL COME... OLLOWING THE TRAIL OF OUR FELLOW REBEL, HE GREAT TAY VANIS.
ONLY YOU HAVE THE SKILL, THE DETERMINATION, AND THE TRAINING TO ENABLE YOU TO FOLLOW A PATH SO COLD, AND TWISTED, AND DANGEROUS. AND POINTLESS.
AS YOU HAVE GUESSED BY NOW, I CAPTURED VANIS, SOME TIME AGO. I CHOSE TO CONCEAL THIS FROM LL BUT MY TROOPS IN THIS VERY INSTALLATION.
IT SUITED MY PURPOSES TO DO SO. BY HIDING THE TRUTH, I MADE CERTAIN THAT NONE OF YOUR REBEL SPIES COULD EVER LEARN IT.
YOU WERE KEPT VERY BUSY, LOOKING FOR A MAN I ALREADY POSSESSED ...AND CERTAIN AMBITIOUS MEMBERS OF THE EMPIRE WERE KEPT EQUALLY BUSY AND HARMLESS AT THE SAME FUTILE TASK.
NOW, I BID YOU FAREWELL. BUT, SO THAT YOUR LONG WEEKS OF SEARCHING WILL NOT HAVE BEEN IN VAIN, I LEAVE YOU, AS A GIFT, THE CONTENTS OF THIS ROOM. ACCEPT THEM WITH MY COMPLIMENTS, YOUNG SKYWALKER.

VANIS.
OH...OH, LUKE...
ALL THIS TIME, WHILE WE'VE SEARCHED FOR HIM...
...NOT EVEN THE EMPIRE KNOWING WHERE HE WAS.. VADER HAD HIM, AND WAS DOING.. THIS.
VADER...
THAT'S IT. FORGET THE MISSION. WE CANNOT LEAVE VANIS HERE LIKE THIS. HE'S STILL...
...HE'S STILL A PERSON. MAYBE... MAYBE WITH MEDICAL ATTENTION... IF WE BRING HIM BACK TO THE FLEET...
JUST SO WE... GET HIM OUT OF HERE...

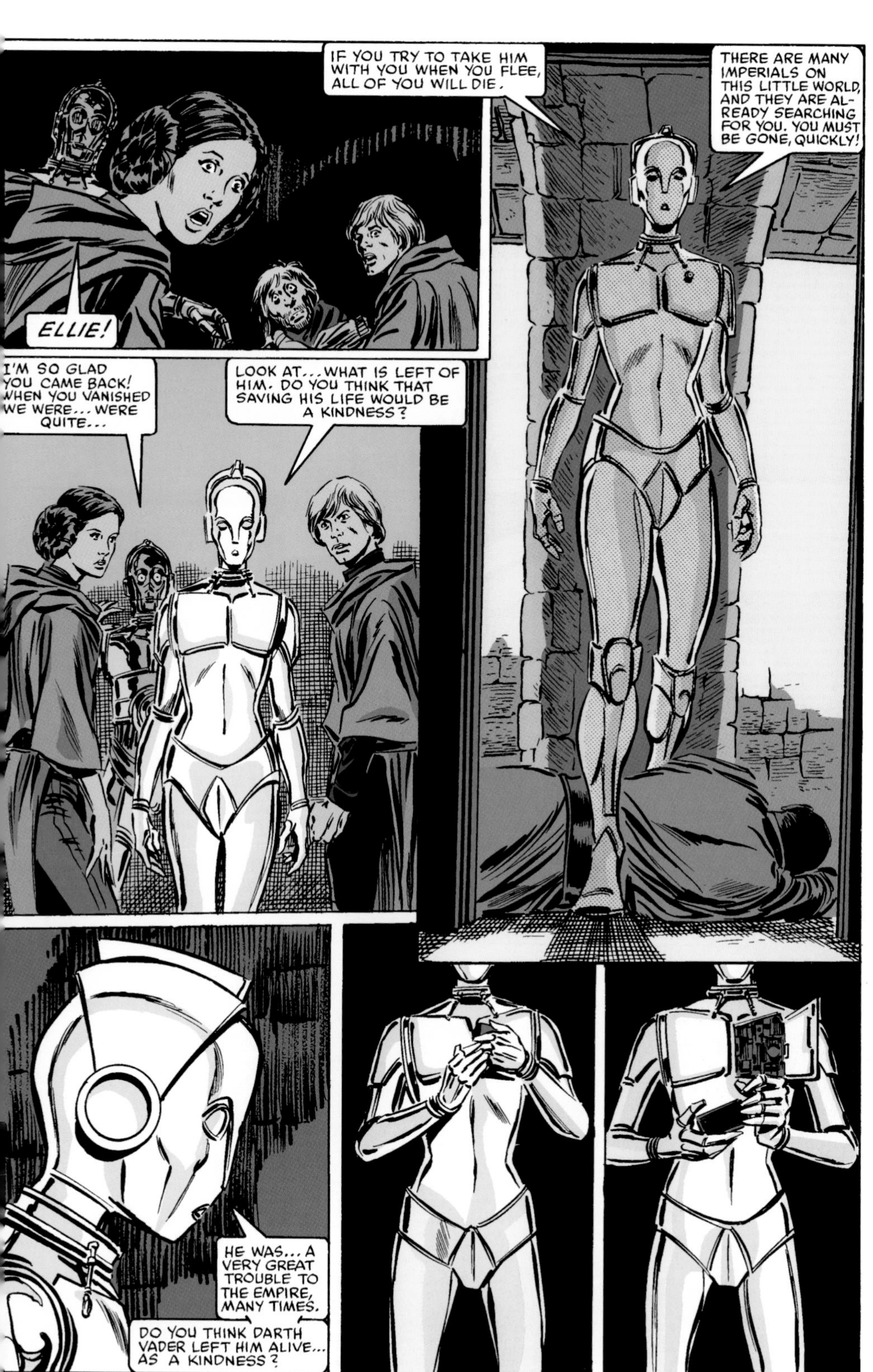
ELLIE!
IF YOU TRY TO TAKE HIM WITH YOU WHEN YOU FLEE, ALL OF YOU WILL DIE.
THERE ARE MANY IMPERIALS ON THIS LITTLE WORLD, AND THEY ARE ALREADY SEARCHING FOR YOU. YOU MUST BE GONE, QUICKLY!
I'M SO GLAD YOU CAME BACK! WHEN YOU VANISHED WE WERE... WERE QUITE...
LOOK AT... WHAT IS LEFT OF HIM. DO YOU THINK THAT SAVING HIS LIFE WOULD BE A KINDNESS?
HE WAS... A VERY GREAT TROUBLE TO THE EMPIRE, MANY TIMES.
DO YOU THINK DARTH VADER LEFT HIM ALIVE... AS A KINDNESS?

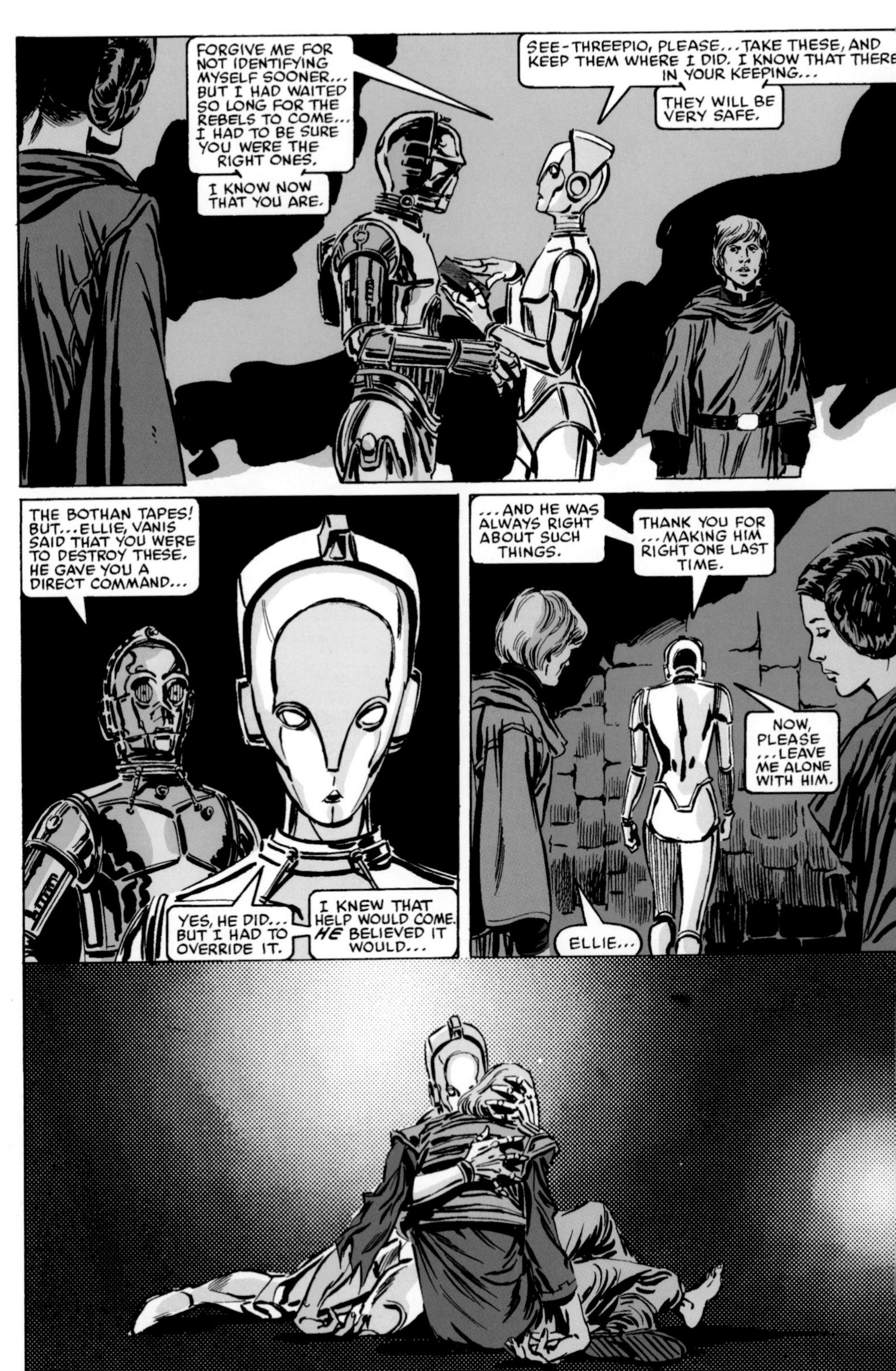
FORGIVE ME FOR NOT IDENTIFYING MYSELF SOONER... BUT I HAD WAITED SO LONG FOR THE REBELS TO COME... I HAD TO BE SURE YOU WERE THE RIGHT ONES.
I KNOW NOW THAT YOU ARE.
SEE-THREEPIO, PLEASE... TAKE THESE, AND KEEP THEM WHERE I DID. I KNOW THAT THERE IN YOUR KEEPING...
THEY WILL BE VERY SAFE.
THE BOTHAN TAPES! BUT... ELLIE, VANIS SAID THAT YOU WERE TO DESTROY THESE. HE GAVE YOU A DIRECT COMMAND...
YES, HE DID... BUT I HAD TO OVERRIDE IT.
I KNEW THAT HELP WOULD COME. HE BELIEVED IT WOULD...
...AND HE WAS ALWAYS RIGHT ABOUT SUCH THINGS.
THANK YOU FOR ...MAKING HIM RIGHT ONE LAST TIME.
NOW, PLEASE ...LEAVE ME ALONE WITH HIM.
ELLIE...

COME ON...LET'S FIND THIS CASTLE'S MAIN POWER STATION BEFORE WE GO.
HE--THEY DESERVE SOME KIND OF MONUMENT.

KARRROM

YES, ADMIRAL... WE'RE ON OUR WAY BACK TO THE FALCON NOW. WE'LL HEAD FOR THE RENDEZVOUS POINT AT ONCE, SIR.
WITH THE BOTHAN TAPES.
NO, SIR. I DON'T THINK OUR TRANS-MISSION'S BEING MONITORED. THERE'S PROBABLY NO ONE LEFT WHO COULD DO IT.

VANIS, SIR...? HE WAS... GONE BEFOR WE REACHED HERE... BUT HE'D LEFT THE TAPES FOR US... IN A VERY SAFE PLACE.
NO, ADMIRAL ACKBAR. THERE WERE ...NO OTHER SURVIVORS.

CLOUD CITY CONFRONTATION!

SEE-THREEPIO WANDERS OFF IN SEARCH OF AN *R2* DROID AND DISCOVERS *IMPERIAL STORMTROOPERS* INSTEAD! RENDERED BY THE X-MEN'S PENCILER AND CO-PLOTTER, JOHN BYRNE!

#1 IN A FOUR-ISSUE LIMITED SERIES

STAR WARS

RETURN OF THE JEDI

THE OFFICIAL COMICS ADAPTATION!

STAN LEE PRESENTS: THE OFFICIAL COMICS ADAPTATION OF

STAR WARS

RETURN OF THE JEDI

Adapted by ARCHIE GOODWIN Art by AL WILLIAMSON & CARLOS GARZON
Lettered by ED KING Colored by CHRISTIE SCHEELE & BOB SHAREN
Edited by MICHAEL HIGGINS & JO DUFFY Editor in Chief JIM SHOOTER

Based on the Story by GEORGE LUCAS
Screenplay by LAWRENCE KASDAN & GEORGE LUCAS.

A LONG TIME AGO IN A GALAXY FAR, FAR AWAY...

Rebel commanders are planning their next move against the evil Galactic Empire. For the first time, all Rebel warships are being brought together to form a single, giant armada.

Luke Skywalker and Princess Leia have made their way to Tatooine to rescue Han Solo from the clutches of the vile gangster, Jabba the Hutt.

Little do they know the Rebellion is doomed. The Emperor has ordered construction of a new armored space station more powerful than the first dreaded Death Star...

COMMAND STATION, THIS IS ST321. CODE CLEARANCE BLUE. ALERT ENDOR MOON BASE TO DEACTIVATE YOUR SECURITY SHIELD FOR APPROACH. SWIFTLY... OUR PASSENGER IS IN NO MOOD TO WAIT.

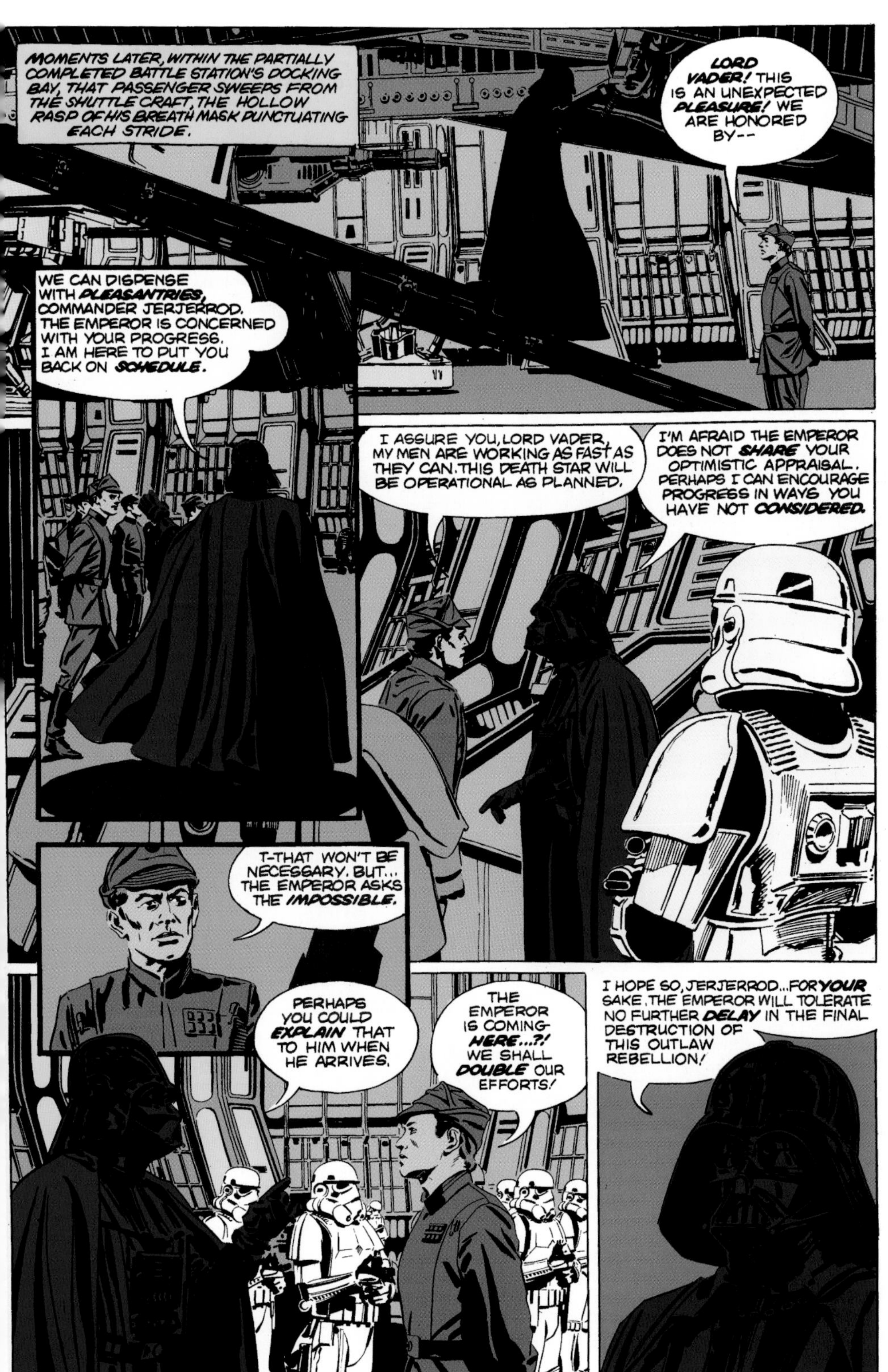
MOMENTS LATER, WITHIN THE PARTIALLY COMPLETED BATTLE STATION'S DOCKING BAY, THAT PASSENGER SWEEPS FROM THE SHUTTLE CRAFT, THE HOLLOW RASP OF HIS BREATH MASK PUNCTUATING EACH STRIDE.
LORD VADER! THIS IS AN UNEXPECTED PLEASURE! WE ARE HONORED BY--
WE CAN DISPENSE WITH PLEASANTRIES, COMMANDER JERJERROD. THE EMPEROR IS CONCERNED WITH YOUR PROGRESS. I AM HERE TO PUT YOU BACK ON SCHEDULE.
I ASSURE YOU, LORD VADER, MY MEN ARE WORKING AS FAST AS THEY CAN. THIS DEATH STAR WILL BE OPERATIONAL AS PLANNED.
I'M AFRAID THE EMPEROR DOES NOT SHARE YOUR OPTIMISTIC APPRAISAL. PERHAPS I CAN ENCOURAGE PROGRESS IN WAYS YOU HAVE NOT CONSIDERED.
T-THAT WON'T BE NECESSARY. BUT... THE EMPEROR ASKS THE IMPOSSIBLE.
PERHAPS YOU COULD EXPLAIN THAT TO HIM WHEN HE ARRIVES.
THE EMPEROR IS COMING HERE...?! WE SHALL DOUBLE OUR EFFORTS!
I HOPE SO, JERJERROD...FOR YOUR SAKE. THE EMPEROR WILL TOLERATE NO FURTHER DELAY IN THE FINAL DESTRUCTION OF THIS OUTLAW REBELLION!

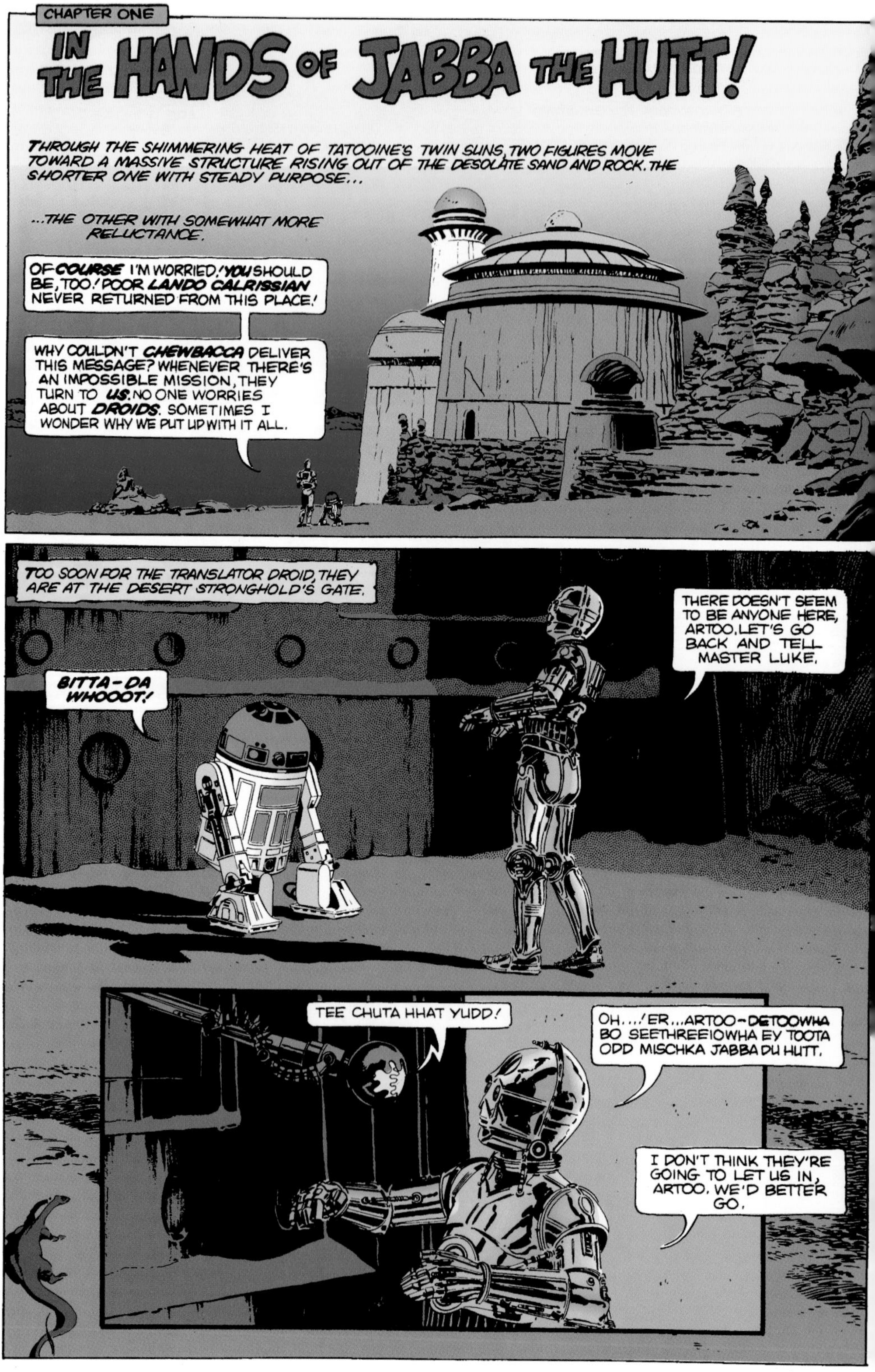

CHAPTER ONE

IN THE HANDS OF JABBA THE HUTT!

THROUGH THE SHIMMERING HEAT OF TATOOINE'S TWIN SUNS, TWO FIGURES MOVE TOWARD A MASSIVE STRUCTURE RISING OUT OF THE DESOLATE SAND AND ROCK. THE SHORTER ONE WITH STEADY PURPOSE...

...THE OTHER WITH SOMEWHAT MORE RELUCTANCE.

OF COURSE I'M WORRIED! YOU SHOULD BE, TOO! POOR LANDO CALRISSIAN NEVER RETURNED FROM THIS PLACE!

WHY COULDN'T CHEWBACCA DELIVER THIS MESSAGE? WHENEVER THERE'S AN IMPOSSIBLE MISSION, THEY TURN TO US. NO ONE WORRIES ABOUT DROIDS. SOMETIMES I WONDER WHY WE PUT UP WITH IT ALL.

TOO SOON FOR THE TRANSLATOR DROID, THEY ARE AT THE DESERT STRONGHOLD'S GATE.

BITTA-DA WHOOOT!

THERE DOESN'T SEEM TO BE ANYONE HERE, ARTOO. LET'S GO BACK AND TELL MASTER LUKE.

TEE CHUTA HHAT YUDD!

OH...! ER...ARTOO-DETOOWHA BO SEETHREEIOWHA EY TOOTA ODD MISCHKA JABBA DU HUTT.

I DON'T THINK THEY'RE GOING TO LET US IN, ARTOO. WE'D BETTER GO.

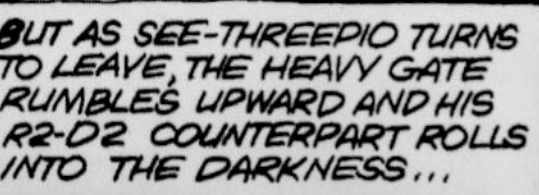
BUT AS SEE-THREEPIO TURNS TO LEAVE, THE HEAVY GATE RUMBLES UPWARD AND HIS R2-D2 COUNTERPART ROLLS INTO THE DARKNESS...

...WHERE SOMEONE WAITS.
W-WE BRING A MESSAGE TO YOUR MASTER, JABBA THE HUTT--
BUH-DEETA KLIK WHRRRRT!

--AND A GIFT. GIFT? WHAT GIFT?
NEE JABBA NO BADDA. ME CHAADE SU GOODIE.
FREEEET WA-DOOT!
I'M TERRIBLY SORRY BUT HE INSISTS OUR MASTER'S INSTRUCTIONS ARE TO GIVE IT--WHATEVER IT IS-- ONLY TO JABBA HIMSELF!

THE TALL AIDE TO THE GALACTIC UNDERWORLD LEADER GLARES FOR A MOMENT AT THE DROIDS. THEN...GESTURES FOR THEM TO FOLLOW HIM.
SOMEDAY, ARTOO, YOUR STUBBORNESS WILL BE OUR UNDOING! NOW JUST DELIVER THIS GIFT AND THE MESSAGE AND GET US OUT OF HERE QUICKLY!
I HAVE A BAD FEELING ABOUT THIS!

"A WRETCHED HIVE OF SCUM AND VILLAINY." THE WORDS OF OBI-WAN KENOBI LEAP THROUGH THREEPIO'S MEMORY CIRCUITS. THEY WERE SPOKEN IN DESCRIPTION OF MOS EISLEY SPACEPORT. THEY APPLY EVEN MORE TO THE CROWDED, NOISY CHAMBER WHERE THE DROIDS ARE LED...
...THE THRONE ROOM OF JABBA THE HUTT.
WE'RE DOOMED!

AND LOOKING UP INTO THE IMPATIENT GLARE OF THE BEING HE AND HIS COMPANION HAVE BEEN SENT TO SEE DOES NOTHING TO DISSUADE THREEPIO OF THAT FEELING!
BO SHUDA!

BO SHUDA!
THE MESSAGE, ARTOO... THE MESSAGE!
FROM HIS DOMED HEAD, THE LITTLE DROID PROJECTS A BEAM OF LIGHT...
...AND WITHIN IT, A TOWERING HOLOGRAM GROWS.
GREETINGS, MIGHTY JABBA! I AM LUKE SKYWALKER, JEDI KNIGHT AND FRIEND OF HAN SOLO.
I SEEK AN AUDIENCE WITH YOUR GREATNESS TO BARGAIN FOR HIS LIFE.
THE NOTION BRINGS RUDE HOWLS AND SNIGGERING FROM MOST GATHERED IN THE CHAMBER EXCEPT FOR ONE WHOSE BUSINESS IT IS NEVER TO UNDERESTIMATE ANY FOE... THE BOUNTY HUNTER BOBA FETT.
I KNOW YOUR ANGER WITH CAPTAIN SOLO IS HUGE, EXALTED ONE, BUT I'M SURE WE CAN DEVISE A MUTUALLY BENEFICIAL ARRANGEMENT. AS A TOKEN OF MY GOOD WILL, I PRESENT TO YOU A GIFT...
THESE TWO DROIDS. BOTH ARE HARDWORKING AND WILL SERVE YOU WELL.
WHAT...? WHAT DID HE SAY?! THIS CAN'T BE! ARTOO, YOU'VE PLAYED THE WRONG MESSAGE!
THE NASTY CHUCKLE THAT FLOWS FROM JABBA'S INCREDIBLE BULK IS NOT ENCOURAGING...

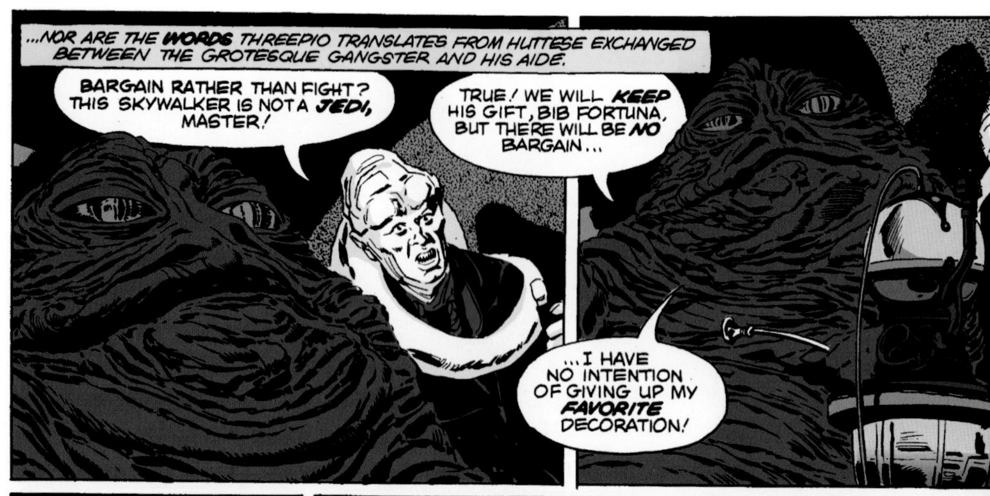
...NOR ARE THE WORDS THREEPIO TRANSLATES FROM HUTTESE EXCHANGED BETWEEN THE GROTESQUE GANGSTER AND HIS AIDE.
BARGAIN RATHER THAN FIGHT? THIS SKYWALKER IS NOT A JEDI, MASTER!
TRUE! WE WILL KEEP HIS GIFT, BIB FORTUNA, BUT THERE WILL BE NO BARGAIN...
...I HAVE NO INTENTION OF GIVING UP MY FAVORITE DECORATION!

AND AS JABBA LAUGHS AT THE FIGURE FROZEN IN GLEAMING CARBONITE...

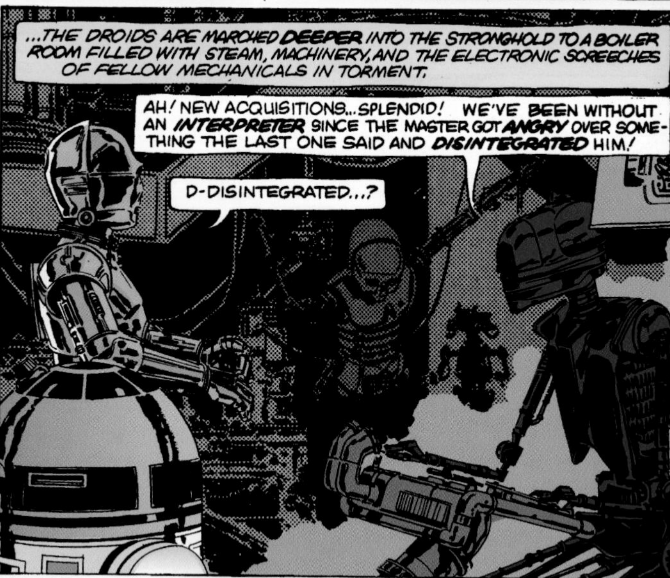
...THE DROIDS ARE MARCHED DEEPER INTO THE STRONGHOLD TO A BOILER ROOM FILLED WITH STEAM, MACHINERY, AND THE ELECTRONIC SCREECHES OF FELLOW MECHANICALS IN TORMENT.
AH! NEW ACQUISITIONS...SPLENDID! WE'VE BEEN WITHOUT AN INTERPRETER SINCE THE MASTER GOT ANGRY OVER SOMETHING THE LAST ONE SAID AND DISINTEGRATED HIM!
D-DISINTEGRATED...?

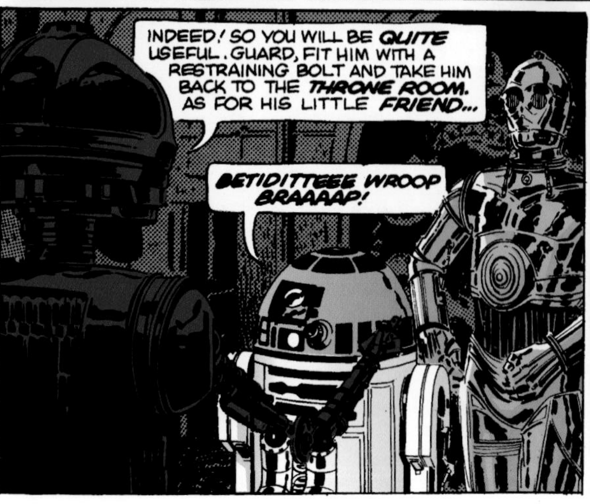
INDEED! SO YOU WILL BE QUITE USEFUL. GUARD, FIT HIM WITH A RESTRAINING BOLT AND TAKE HIM BACK TO THE THRONE ROOM. AS FOR HIS LITTLE FRIEND...
BETIDITTEEE WROOP BRAAAAP!

OH, A FEISTY ONE! I HAVE NEED FOR YOU ON THE MASTER'S SAIL BARGE. SEVERAL OF OUR ASTRODROIDS HAVE DISAPPEARED RECENTLY. YOU'LL FILL IN NICELY...
...AFTER YOU LEARN SOME RESPECT.

BROUGHT ROUGHLY BACK TO THE COURT OF JABBA THE HUTT, THREEPIO FINDS A WILD REVEL IN PROGRESS, WHERE THE NERVOUS DROID RECEIVES A LESSON IN THE SHIFTING MOODS OF HIS NEW MASTER AS THE DANCE OF A SLAVE GIRL ATTRACTS JABBA'S FAVOR...
DA EITHA!
...AND THAT FAVOR IS REJECTED!
NA CHUBA NEGATORIE... NA! NA! NATOOTA --
BOSCKA!
ONE WORD FROM THE HUTT. AND SUDDENLY...
...THE FLOOR BENEATH THE DANCER IS GONE!
WITH SWIFT FORCE, THE TRAP SNAPS SHUT AND TO THE OBSCENE AMUSEMENT OF THE MOTLEY CROWD, A GROWL RISES FROM BELOW...
...FOLLOWED BY A HIDEOUS SCREAM!
BARELY HAVE THREEPIO'S PERCEPTION CIRCUITS RECOVERED FROM THIS SHOCK THAN A SUDDEN HUSH MAKES HIM AWARE OF NEW ARRIVALS IN JABBA'S DOMAIN.
OH, NO...!

...CHEWBACCA!
IN THE HANDS OF A BOUNTY HUNTER... WHO, IN A STRANGE TONGUE ELECTRONICALLY PROCESSED, DEMANDS REWARD FOR THIS PRIZE.

A DEMAND IT FALLS UPON SEE-THREEPIO TO TRANSLATE FOR A LESS THAN-RECEPTIVE MASTER.
FIFTY THOUSAND? FIFTY? TELL HIM TWENTY-FIVE THOUSAND IS ALL I GRANT, TALKDROID...
...PLUS HIS LIFE!

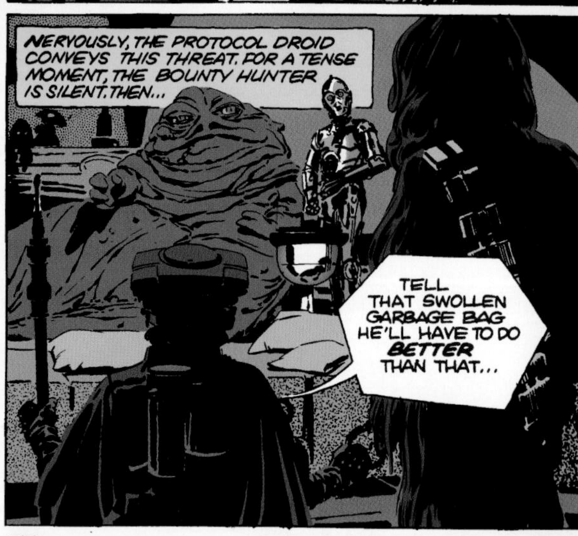

NERVOUSLY, THE PROTOCOL DROID CONVEYS THIS THREAT. FOR A TENSE MOMENT, THE BOUNTY HUNTER IS SILENT. THEN...
TELL THAT SWOLLEN GARBAGE BAG HE'LL HAVE TO DO BETTER THAN THAT...

...OR THEY'LL BE PICKING HIS SMELLY HIDE OUT OF EVERY CRACK IN THE ROOM! I'M HOLDING A THERMAL DETONATOR!

WELL... WHAT DID HE SAY, TALKDROID? OUT WITH IT!
OH, DEAR! YOUR GRANDNESS, HE... AH... RESPECTFULLY DISAGREES WITH YOUR EXALTEDNESS AND BEGS YOU TO... ER... RECONSIDER...
...OR HE'LL RELEASE THE THERMAL DETONATOR HE'S HOLDING!

THERE IS FRANTIC SCURRYING AMONG THE FORMER REVELERS FOR THE CHAMBER'S FAR WALLS. JABBA STARES MALEVOLENTLY, THEN... LAUGHS.
THIS BOUNTY HUNTER IS MY KIND OF SCUM! FORCEFUL AND INVENTIVE. TELL HIM THIRTY-FIVE, TALKDROID... NO MORE! AND WARN HIM NOT TO PUSH HIS LUCK.
AND RELIEF FILLS THE ROOM... AS THE BOUNTY HUNTER NODS ACCEPTANCE.
COME, MY FRIEND, JOIN OUR CELEBRATION! I MAY FIND OTHER WORK FOR YOU!
AGAIN, THERE IS MUSIC AND NOISE, LOUD AND BOISTEROUS. AND THERE ARE JEERS AND TAUNTS AS GUARDS HAUL THE WOOKIEE PRISONER AWAY PAST A THRONG OF TOTALLY HOSTILE STRANGERS...
...WITH PERHAPS ONE EXCEPTION.
NIGHT. SILENCE HAS AT LAST COME TO THE THRONE ROOM OF JABBA'S STRONGHOLD. THE PARTY IS LONG OVER. ONLY SHADOWS REMAIN.
AND ONE OF THEM MOVES... TOWARD A DIM ALCOVE... AND A BLOCK OF GLEAMING CARBONITE.

STEALTHILY, FORCE FIELD CONTROLS ARE TOUCHED, LOWERING THE BLOCK. THEN... THE PROCESS BEGUN IN THE CARBON-FREEZING CHAMBER OF THE BESPIN SYSTEM'S CLOUD CITY MINING COMMUNITY...

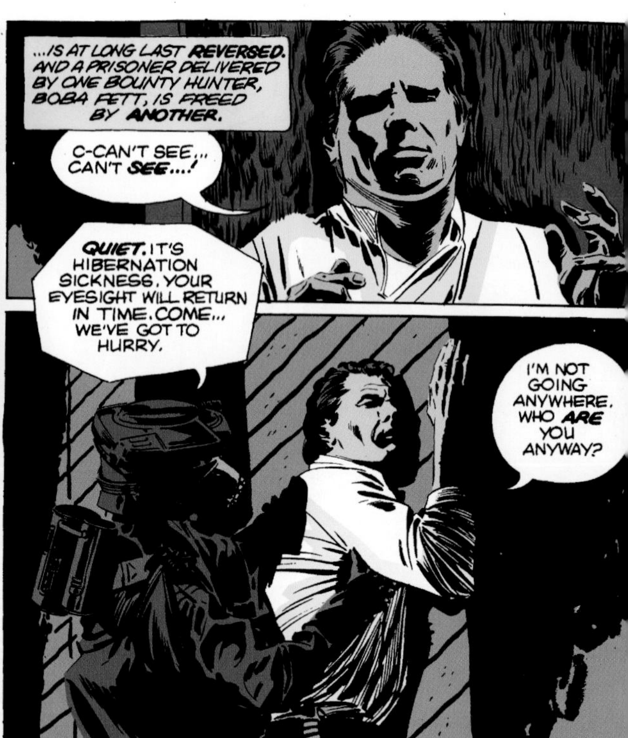

...IS AT LONG LAST REVERSED. AND A PRISONER DELIVERED BY ONE BOUNTY HUNTER, BOBA FETT, IS FREED BY ANOTHER.
C-CAN'T SEE... CAN'T SEE...!
QUIET. IT'S HIBERNATION SICKNESS. YOUR EYESIGHT WILL RETURN IN TIME. COME... WE'VE GOT TO HURRY.
I'M NOT GOING ANYWHERE. WHO ARE YOU ANYWAY?

A HELMET IS REMOVED AND A VOICE, NO LONGER ELECTRONICALLY DISGUISED, SPEAKS WARMLY.

I'M SOMEONE WHO LOVES YOU, HOTSHOT.

BUT WE'RE IN JABBA'S PALACE AND I'VE GOT TO GET YOU OUT OF HERE QUICKLY.

THEY START AWAY. THE CORELLIAN SMUGGLER STAGGERING WEAKLY, SUPPORTED BY THE REBEL LEADER AND PRINCESS OF LONG-DESTROYED ALDERAAN. SUDDENLY, A CURTAIN PARTS...

...ACCOMPANIED BY MOCKING LAUGHTER.

MY, MY, WHAT A TOUCHING SIGHT, HAN, MY BOY, YOUR TASTE IN COMPANIONS HAS IMPROVED... EVEN IF YOUR LUCK HAS NOT.

OON, THE PAIR STAND BEFORE JABBA'S THRONE.
LISTEN, SO I GOT A LITTLE SIDETRACKED FROM REPAYING YOU... WE CAN WORK THIS OUT! YOU'LL GET TRIPLE--
TOO LATE, SOLO! YOU MAY HAVE BEEN THE BEST PILOT IN THE BUSINESS BUT NOW YOU'RE BANTHA FODDER!
PUT HIM WITH HIS WOOKIEE FIRST MATE, I'LL DECIDE HOW TO KILL HIM LATER.
AS FOR HIS OTHER COMPANION... BRING HER TO ME!
OF THE TWO GUARDS NEAR PRINCESS LEIA, ONE HESITATES, ON THE VERGE OF DEFYING THE ORDER.
I'LL BE ALL RIGHT.
I'M NOT SO SURE.
THE WHISPERED EXCHANGE GOES UNNOTICED... AS LEIA IS SHOVED INTO THE UNDERWORLD LEADER'S ARMS!
WE HAVE POWERFUL FRIENDS! YOU'LL REGRET THIS!
PERHAPS! BUT MEANWHILE I WILL THOROUGHLY ENJOY THE PLEASURE OF YOUR COMPANY!
OH, NO... I CAN'T WATCH!
ELSEWHERE, A DUNGEON DOOR WHINES OPEN... AND A REUNION BEGINS.
VOROWWWRRGGG!
ALL RIGHT... IT'S GREAT...! ONLY... YOU'RE CRUSHING ME...!
WHAT'S GOIN' ON AROUND HERE ANYWAY?

IN BARKS AND GROWLS, THE MILLENNIUM FALCON'S CO-PILOT BRINGS HIS BLINDED PARTNER UP TO DATE.
LUKE'S A JEDI KNIGHT... AND EVEN LANDO'S HERE, GOIN' ALONG WITH THE KID'S RESCUE PLAN? I'M OUT OF THINGS A LITTLE WHILE AND EVERY-ONE GETS DELUSIONS!
WELL, PAL, I'LL BELIEVE IT WHEN I SEE IT... IF YOU'LL EXCUSE THE EXPRESSION.
HE COMES. ALONE. UNARMED.
AND THE STONGHOLD'S NORMAL DEFENSES CANNOT HALT OR SLOW THAT COMING.

YOU WILL TAKE ME TO JABBA NOW. YOU SERVE HIM WELL. YOU ARE SURE TO BE REWARDED.
I WILL TAKE YOU TO JABBA NOW. I SERVE HIM WELL. I AM SURE TO BE REWARDED.

TUMULT GREETS LUKE SKYWALKER'S APPEARANCE IN THE THRONE ROOM BUT HE REMAINS CALM... EVEN AT THE SIGHT OF THE REPLACEMENT NOW CHAINED IN THE PLACE OF JABBA'S DANCING GIRL.
I TOLD YOU NOT TO ADMIT HIM! BIB FORTUNA, YOU'RE A WEAK-BRAINED FOOL!

JEDI MIND TRICKS WILL NOT WORK ON ME, BOY. I AM NOT AFFECTED BY YOUR HUMAN THOUGHT PATTERN. I WAS KILLING YOUR KIND WHEN BEING A JEDI MEANT SOMETHING!

I'M TAKING CAPTAIN SOLO AND HIS FRIENDS, JABBA. YOU CAN PROFIT... OR BE DESTROYED. IT'S YOUR CHOICE. I WARN YOU NOT TO UNDERESTIMATE MY POWERS.

HE HUTT ONLY LAUGHS, LOUD AND ASTILY.
THERE WILL BE NO BARGAIN, YOUNG JEDI... ONLY THE ENJOYMENT OF WATCHING YOU **DIE!**

MASTER LUKE! YOU'RE **STANDING** ON A MRRMMPHHH

A GESTURE, SUDDENLY A BLASTER LEAPS FROM A GUARD'S HOLSTER... TO FILL LUKE'S HAND!
BUT BEFORE HE CAN **USE** IT...

BOSCKA!

...THE FLOOR BENEATH HIM **DISAPPEARS!**

LUKE!

GRATES REMAIN OPEN SO THOSE ABOVE CAN WATCH AND APPRECIATE...

...WHAT TRANSPIRES TWENTY-FIVE FEET BELOW.

LUKE RISES, FLINGING ASIDE HIS CLOAK, AS A GATE RUMBLES UPWARD IN THE SIDE OF THE PIT... AND **SOMETHING** LUMBERS FORWARD!

THE RANCOR! CARNIVOROUS. INSATIABLE. HIDE IMPERVIOUS TO BLASTER FIRE. UNTIL NOW, LUKE SKYWALKER THOUGHT SUCH CREATURES WERE LEGEND, HOBGOBLINS TO FRIGHTEN THE CHILDREN OF TATOOINE MOISTURE FARMERS. BUT THE MONSTER THAT STALKS HIM ACROSS THE BONE-LITTERED CAVERN IS ALL TOO REAL!
AND TO THE DELIGHTED HOWLS OF THE AUDIENCE ABOVE, DESPITE JEDI-TRAINED AGILITY, HE SWIFTLY RUNS OUT OF ROOM TO RETREAT.
BUT EVEN AS THE RANCOR'S CLAWS DART TO SEIZE HIM...
...LUKE'S HANDS HAVE FOUND A WEAPON!
WITH IT, HE JABS, HAMMERS, AND THRUSTS...
...WEDGING IT INTO THE RANCOR'S JAWS! PAIN MAKES THE MONSTER DROP HIM... BUT THE DIVERSION IS WORTH ONLY MOMENTS!
...WHILE IT LASTS, LUKE RUNS FOR THE GATE THAT ADMITTED THE CREATURE!

UT PAST THE GATE, THE WAY TO SAFETY IS BARRED...AND THE
ATE'S CONTROLS LIE BEYOND THOSE BARS! AS THE RANCOR,
NGRIER THAN EVER, COMES SNARLING AFTER HIM...
...LUKE HURLS A SKULL SCOOPED FROM THIS HOLDING CAVE'S FLOOR...

...SHATTERING THE CONTROL PANEL AND BRINGING THE MASSIVE GATE THUNDERING DOWN ONTO THE GREAT BEAST'S HEAD!
THE RANCOR DIES...

..BUT THE TRIUMPH IS BRIEF. GRABBED BY OUTRAGED GUARDS, LUKE SOON FINDS HIMSELF
FACING THE HUTT AGAIN. ONLY THIS TIME... HAN AND CHEWBACCA ARE BROUGHT TO JOIN HIM.
ER... FOR YOUR EXTREME OFFENSE, THE GREAT JABBA DEMANDS ALL THREE OF YOU PAY WITH THE MOST TORTUROUS FORM OF DEATH... YOU WILL BE TAKEN TO THE DUNE SEA AND THROWN INTO THE GREAT PIT OF CARKOON...

THAT DOESN'T SOUND TOO BAD...

...NESTING PLACE OF THE ALL-POWERFUL SARLACC! IN ITS BELLY, YOU WILL FIND A NEW DEFINITION OF SUFFERING AS YOU SLOWLY DIGEST FOR A THOUSAND YEARS!
ON SECOND THOUGHT, WE COULD PASS ON THAT.

YOU SHOULD HAVE BARGAINED, JABBA... THIS IS THE LAST MISTAKE YOU'LL EVER MAKE!

TELL THAT TO THE SARLACC, YOUNG JEDI! TAKE THEM AWAY!

THE DUNE SEA! A SKIFF SWINGS OUT OVER THE PIT OF CARKOON, AWAY FROM THE HUGE SAIL BARGE IT ACCOMPANIES. FOR THOSE ON THE BARGE... THIS IS A PLEASURE CRUISE.
FOR THREE ON THE SKIFF...A LAST RIDE!
I THINK MY SIGHT'S GETTING BETTER, KID. INSTEAD OF A BIG, DARK BLUR... I SEE A BIG, BRIGHT BLUR.
BELIEVE ME, HAN YOU'RE NOT MISSING ANYTHING. I GREW UP HERE.
ABOARD THE BARGE... ANTICIPATION GROWS. AND FOR A VERY FEW... CONCERN.
DON'T STRAY TOO FAR, MY LOVELY. AFTER THE AMUSEMENT OUTSIDE ENDS, YOU'LL SOON BEGIN TO APPRECIATE ME.
ARTOO! SO THIS IS WHAT THEY'VE DONE WITH YOU! HOW CAN YOU CALMLY SERVE DRINKS?
THEY'RE GOING TO EXECUTE MASTER LUKE! AND IF WE'RE NOT CAREFUL,... US TOO!
I DON'T MEAN TO SEEM UNGRATEFUL, BUT IF THIS IS YOUR BIG PLAN, LUKE... SO FAR I'M NOT CRAZY ABOUT IT.
JABBA'S PALACE WAS TOO WELL GUARDED. I HAD TO GET YOU OUT OF THERE. JUST STAY CLOSE TO CHEWIE, I'LL TAKE CARE OF EVERYTHING.
I CAN HARDLY WAIT.
AND BELOW... THE SARLACC STIRS!

TO BE CONTINUED

BIB FORTUNA
AIDE TO
JABBA THE HUTT

SY SNOOTLES AND THE REBO BAND
NOW PLAYING IN THE THRONE ROOM
OF JABBA THE HUTT

SALACIOUS CRUMB

IMPERIAL
SHUTTLE

60¢
U.K. 25p
CAN. 75¢
2
NOV

#2 IN A FOUR-ISSUE LIMITED SERIES

STAR WARS

RETURN OF THE JEDI™

THE OFFICIAL COMICS ADAPTATION!

STAN LEE PRESENTS: THE OFFICIAL COMICS ADAPTATION OF

STAR WARS

RETURN OF THE JEDI

Adapted by ARCHIE GOODWIN Art by AL WILLIAMSON & CARLOS GARZON
Lettered by ED KING Colored by CHRISTIE SCHEELE & BOB SHAREN
Edited by MICHAEL HIGGINS & JO DUFFY Editor in Chief JIM SHOOTER

Based on the Story by GEORGE LUCAS
Screenplay by LAWRENCE KASDAN & GEORGE LUCAS.

CHAPTER 2:
THE EMPEROR COMMANDS!
THE HOUR OF EXECUTION! FROM JABBA THE HUTT'S MASSIVE SAIL BARGE COMES THE AMPLIFIED VOICE OF THE UNDERWORLD MONARCH'S RELUCTANT TRANSLATOR, SEE-THREEPIO...
HIS EXCELLENCY HOPES YOU WILL... ER... DIE HONORABLY, BUT SHOULD ANY OF YOU WISH TO BEG FOR MERCY BEFORE BEING THROWN INTO THE SARLACC'S MAW... HE WILL NOW HEAR YOUR PLEAS.
CHEWIE... AM I FACING THE RIGHT DIRECTION?
TELL THAT SLIMY PIECE OF WORM-RIDDEN FILTH HE'LL GET NO SUCH PLEASURE FROM US!
THIS IS YOUR LAST CHANCE, JABBA. FREE US... OR DIE.

E'LL SEE IF YOU'RE
IGHT, MY YOUNG JEDI
RIEND... PUT HIM
IN!
LAUGHTER FILLS THE GREAT BARGE'S MAIN CABIN, CHILLING THE CAPTIVE LEIA ORGANA...
BUT IN THE COMMOTION, NO ONE NOTICES A SERVING DROID JETTISON HIS TRAY AND MAKE FOR THE DECK...
...WHERE HE FACES THE SAND SKIFF BEARING LUKE, HAN, AND CHEWBACCA TO THEIR DEATHS AS A HATCH OPENS ON HIS DOME...
...SO THAT AS HIS YOUNG MASTER IS FORCED OUT OVER THE MOUTH OF THE MONSTROUS OBSCENITY KNOWN AS THE SARLACC...
...SOMETHING IS FIRED THROUGH THE AIR TO HIM.
A LIGHTSABER!
VOWRAAARK!
HEY! WHAT'S GOIN' ON?
SUDDENLY ABOARD THE SMALL FLOATING CRAFT... THERE IS BATTLE! BATTLE JOINED BY A GUARD WHO THROWS OFF HIS HELMET TO REVEAL HIS TRUE IDENTITY!

IN THAT BATTLE, A CREWMAN BENTON, FEEDING THE SARLACC ITS FIRST VICTIM...

...BECOMES ONE INSTEAD AS LUKE AND LANDO CALRISSIAN FIGHT TO FREE HAN AND CHEWBACCA OF THEIR BONDS!

REACTION ABOARD THE SAND BARGE IS SWIFT...AND OUTRAGED! AT JABBA'S ROARING COMMAND, THERE IS A STAMPEDE FOR THE UPPER-DECK.

IN THE LEAD... BOBA FETT!

BUT THE BOUNTY HUNTER DOES NOT STOP THERE AS THE OTHERS DO.

IGNITING HIS BACK PACK ROCKETS, HE SOARS TOWARD THE SAND SKIFF.

WHILE IN THE BARGE'S MAIN CABIN, LEIA DISCOVERS THE TROUBLE OUTSIDE HAS SENT JABBA'S MINIONS SWIRLING AWAY FROM THEIR MASTER...
...AND ACTS!
MOVING SWIFTLY OVER AND AROUND THE GREAT, BLUBBERY HULK THAT IS THE GALACTIC CRIME LORD...
...SHE TURNS THE TETHER THAT KEEPS HER CAPTIVE INTO A WEAPON!
BUT...

EVEN AS HER MONSTROUS CAPTOR QUIVERS AND DIES, THE REBEL PRINCESS FINDS HERSELF STILL BOUND TO HIM...
...ESCAPE STILL TANTALIZINGLY BEYOND HER GRASP...
...UNTIL WHAT SHE HAS DONE IS DISCOVERED.
OUT ON THE SKIFF, BOUNTY HUNTER AND YOUNG JEDI FACE-OFF...
...WHEN A BLAST FROM THE MASSIVE BARGE'S DECK GUN ROCKS THE SMALLER CRAFT!
BOBA FETT FALLS STUNNED, BUT ANOTHER FALLS FARTHER!
LANDO! IT'S HAN! I'M FREE...BUT CHEWIE'S STILL WORKIN' AT HIS BONDS! WHERE ARE YOU?!
ABOUT ONE FRAYED CABLE AWAY FROM BEING THE MAIN COURSE! BUT HAULING ME UP WON'T HELP IF THAT DECK GUN KEEPS SCORING!

AS THE GAMBLER AND ORIGINAL OWNER OF THE MILLENNIUM FALCON SHOUTS, LUKE SKYWALKER IS ALREADY MOVING...
...AS THE DAMAGED SKIFF CAREENS MOMENTARILY CLOSER TO THE SAIL BARGE...
...LANDING HIGH, SOMERSAULTING FORWARD...
...TO LAND AMID ENRAGED AND DETERMINED ENEMIES!

ONE BY ONE, THEY FALL TO THE FLASHING LIGHTSABER! BUT OTHERS APPEAR TO TAKE THEIR PLACE...
...AND THE DECK GUN KEEPS FIRING!

LANDO...? ARE YOU NEAR? CAN YOU GRAB THIS!
IF THE CABLE HOLDS AND YOU DON'T POKE ME IN THE EYE! GET IT CLOSER...! TO MY HAND!

HAN IS NOT ALONE IN TAKING ACTION. BOBA FETT RISES, TAKING AIM AT THE LIGHTBLADE-WIELDING FIGURE ON THE MAIN DECK OF JABBA'S BARGE!

GROWL FROM CHEWBACCA ALERTS HAN! DESPERATELY, HE SWINGS THE SPEAR BEING EXTENDED TO LANDO! BUT...
YOU INTERFERING BLIND GAWK! YOU'RE NEXT!

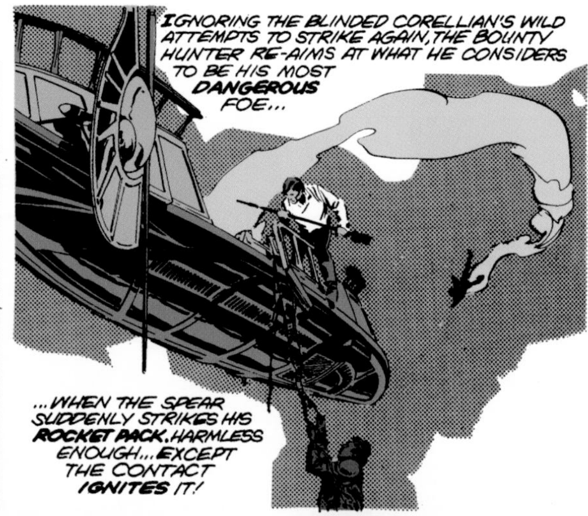
IGNORING THE BLINDED CORELLIAN'S WILD ATTEMPTS TO STRIKE AGAIN, THE BOUNTY HUNTER RE-AIMS AT WHAT HE CONSIDERS TO BE HIS MOST DANGEROUS FOE...
...WHEN THE SPEAR SUDDENLY STRIKES HIS ROCKET PACK. HARMLESS ENOUGH... EXCEPT THE CONTACT IGNITES IT!

THE MAN WHO SOLD HIS SERVICES TO BOTH DARTH VADER AND JABBA THE HUTT SOARS HIGH...
...AND FALLS FAR, TO THE SARLACC'S PLEASURE.

ROWRAAAARK!
I DID THAT...? WISH I COULD HAVE SEEN IT!

BUT ONLY ONE DANGER IS ELIMINATED... AS A BLAST FROM THE DECK GUN OF THE SAIL BARGE REMINDS THEM!

WHILE IN THE BARGE'S MAIN CABIN...
VREE-DITTA TUH-WHOOOOT!
ARTOO! THANK THE FORCE IT WAS YOU WHO FOUND ME! NOW LET'S GET OUT OF HERE!

LEIA RACES FOR THE DECK...WHERE THE UNEQUAL BATTLE IS TURNING AGAINST LUKE SKYWALKER!
THE FINGERS OF HIS MECHANICAL HAND, WHICH REPLACED THE REAL ONE SEVERED BY THE DARK LORD OF THE SITH, STILL FLEX... BUT HIS LIGHTSABER ROLLS ACROSS THE DECK BEYOND HIS REACH.
NO, NO! NOT MY EYES, YOU MISERABLE LITTLE SCAVENGER!
OUTSIDE... ANOTHER RESCUE GOES LESS WELL, AS THE RESULTS OF THE DECK GUN BLAST ADD CONSIDERABLY TO THE DIFFICULTIES IN SAVING LANDO CALRISSIAN.
HAN! IT'S GOT ME!
EASY, BUDDY! MUST BE ALL THE BLOOD RUSHIN' TO MY HEAD... BUT I CAN SEE A LOT BETTER.
GREAT! NOW COULD YOU GROW A FEW INCHES TALLER?!

ABOARD THE LARGER VESSEL, THIS VULNERABLE CHAIN OF WOOKIEE AND HUMANS IS TOO TEMPTING A TARGET FOR THE DECK GUNNER TO PASS UP...
SO TEMPTING HE DOES NOT NOTICE A NEW ELEMENT IN THE BATTLE...UNTIL TOO LATE!
NOW SUDDENLY THE GUN THAT WOULD HAVE FINISHED HAN, LANDO, AND CHEWBACCA...
...BEGINS RAKING THE GREAT CRAFT'S OWN MASTS INSTEAD!
ND IT IS ALL THE DISTRACTION LUKE NEEDS TO CALL BACK HIS LIGHTBLADE.
AIM IT DOWN, LEIA! FIRE AT THE DECK! I'LL BE RIGHT THERE!
ARTOO-DETOO, WHY DID YOU FORCE ME UP HERE? THE FIGHTING IS EVEN WORSE THAN BELOW. THERE'S NO ESCAPE. IT'S MUCH TOO HIGH FOR ME TO JUMP.
DRRR-PLIIT!
THERE FOLLOWS THE KLUNK OF A SMALLER METAL OBJECT BUMPING A SOMEWHAT LARGER ONE...
NOO-OOOOO!
THEN...LEIA'S DECK GUN FIRES AS LUKE ORDERED WITH SPECTACULAR RESULTS!

AND DESPITE THE EXPLOSIVE THUNDER THAT FOLLOWS, THE YOUNG WARRIOR BATTLES HIS WAY THROUGH THE REMNANTS OF JABBA'S CREW...
... MOVING WITH UNBEATABLE DETERMINATION TO JOIN THE REBEL PRINCESS!

BUT THE STRUGGLE ABOVE THE SARLACC'S MAW CONTINUES...
YOU GOT ME... BUT YOU CAN'T OUTPULL THIS THING!
CHEWIE'S PASSING DOWN A BLASTER TO ME... IT'S TOO TRICKY A SHOT FOR HIM TO TRY FROM WHERE HE IS.
WAIT A SECOND! I THOUGHT YOU WERE BLIND!
LANDO... I'M BETTER. TRUST ME.
DO I HAVE ANY CHOICE? HEY! AIM A LITTLE HIGHER...
JUST HOLD STILL... HOLD... STILL...
THERE IS THE VIOLENT EXPLOSION OF LASER FIRE! AND...
YOU GOT IT! HAUL ME UP... HAUL ME UP!
AND BACK ON THE NOW FIERY SAIL BARGE...
HANG ON, PRINCESS, THIS RESCUE IS ALMOST OVER...

...AFTER THIS!
WITH FAR MORE AGILITY THAN ANOTHER SWING HE MADE ON THE FIRST DEATH STAR...
...LUKE DROPS THEM BOTH TO THE DECK OF THE RIGHTED SAND SKIFF.
SORRY THINGS GOT A LITTLE MESSY, GUYS!
THANKS FOR COMING AFTER ME, LUKE.
I HAD A LOT OF HELP, HAN. THINK NOTHING OF IT.
NO, I'M THINKIN' A LOT. THAT CARBON FREEZE WAS PRETTY CLOSE TO BEIN' DEAD. NOW COMIN' BACK... WELL, MY EYES AREN'T THE ONLY THINGS SEEING DIFFERENT, BUDDY.
AS THE ENGINES OF JABBA'S BARGE ERUPT IN A FIERY PAROXYSM FROM THE DAMAGE INFLICTED BY LEIA... THE LIMPING SKIFF MOVES TO PICK UP THE TWO REMAINING HELPERS FROM THE SAND WHERE THEY LEAPED.
SOMETIME LATER, TWO SHIPS LIFT OFF FROM TATOOINE'S TWIN-SUN BLEACHED SURFACE...HEADED IN DIFFERENT DIRECTIONS.
YOU COULD STILL COME WITH US TO THE FLEET, LUKE.
ARTOO AND I WILL JOIN YOU SOON. FOR NOW, I'VE A PROMISE TO KEEP... TO AN OLD FRIEND.

MEANWHILE, ABOVE THE GREEN MOON OF ENDOR, AN IMPERIAL SHUTTLE PASSES SWIFTLY THROUGH THE SECURITY SHIELD OF THE BATTLE STATION UNDER CONSTRUCTION...

IT BRINGS THE MOST IMPORTANT VISITOR THAT THOSE WHO SERVE THERE HAD EVER BEHELD. IMPORTANT. AND FEARFUL. THE EMPEROR!

RISE, LORD VADER. I WOULD SPEAK WITH YOU.

HE DEATH TAR WILL BE OMPLETED ON SCHEDULE, MY MASTER.
YES. YOU HAVE DONE WELL. NOW I SENSE YOU WISH TO CONTINUE YOUR SEARCH FOR YOUNG SKYWALKER. PATIENCE, MY FRIEND. IN TIME HE WILL SEEK YOU OUT.

...AND WHEN HE DOES, YOU MUST BRING HIM BEFORE ME. HE HAS GROWN STRONG. ONLY TOGETHER CAN WE TURN HIM TO THE DARK SIDE OF THE FORCE.

EVERYTHING IS PROCEEDING AS I HAVE FORESEEN.
THE EMPEROR CHUCKLES... AND AT THE SOUND, FROM THE VAST ARRAY OF TROOPS IN THE DOCKING BAY, EVEN HIS OWN SCARLET-CLAD PRIVATE GUARDS, THERE IS AN IMPERCEPTIBLE SHIVER...
...AND VERY DEFINITE RELIEF WHEN THE PAIR ADJOURN TO THE CONTROL STATION CHAMBER SPECIALLY CONVERTED INTO A TEMPORARY THRONE ROOM.

WHAT IS THY BIDDING, MY MASTER?
SEND OUR FLEET TO THE FAR SIDE OF ENDOR. THERE IT WILL STAY UNTIL CALLED FOR.

WHAT OF THE REPORTS OF THE REBEL FLEET MASSING NEAR SULLUST?
IT IS OF NO CONCERN. SOON THE REBELLION WILL BE CRUSHED...

...AND LUKE SKYWALKER WILL BE ONE OF US. YOUR WORK HERE IS FINISHED, MY FRIEND. GO OUT TO THE COMMAND SHIP AND AWAIT MY ORDERS.
YES, MY MASTER!

WORLDS AWAY ON THE GLOOMY, FOG-SHROUDED PLANET CALLED DAGOBAH, LIGHT GLEAMS FROM A TINY HUT. HERE, THE OBJECT OF DARTH VADER AND THE EMPEROR'S CONVERSATION MEETS WITH THE BEING HE CALLS MASTER.
THE FACE YOU MAKE! LOOK I SO BAD TO YOUR YOUNG EYES?
N-NO... OF COURSE NOT.
I DO, YES, I DO! SICK I'VE BECOME... OLD AND WEAK. YES! WHEN 900 YEARS OLD YOU REACH, LOOK AS GOOD YOU WILL NOT... SOON WILL I REST. YES, FOREVER SLEEP. EARNED IT, I HAVE.
YOU CAN'T DIE, MASTER YODA... I WON'T LET YOU. I NEED YOUR HELP. I WANT TO COMPLETE MY TRAINING.
TWILIGHT IS UPON ME. SOON NIGHT MUST FALL. THAT IS THE WAY OF THINGS... THE WAY OF THE FORCE.
STRONG WITH IT ARE YOU... BUT NOT THAT STRONG. STILL, TRAINED WELL YOU HAVE. NO MORE DO YOU REQUIRE. ALREADY YOU KNOW THAT WHICH YOU NEED.
THEN... I AM A JEDI?

NOT YET. ONE THING REMAINS. VADER...VADER YOU MUST CONFRONT. THEN, ONLY THEN, A JEDI YOU'LL BE.
MASTER YODA...I MUST KNOW...IS... IS DARTH VADER MY FATHER?

SILENCE FOLLOWS. THE LITTLE JEDI MASTER SEEMS MORE STOOPED AND EXHAUSTED THAN EVER. YET HE FEELS LUKE'S INSISTENCE, AND AT LONG LAST... ANSWERS.

TOLD YOU DID HE? YOUR FATHER HE IS. UNEXPECTED THIS IS ...AND UNFORTUNATE.
THAT I KNOW THE TRUTH...?

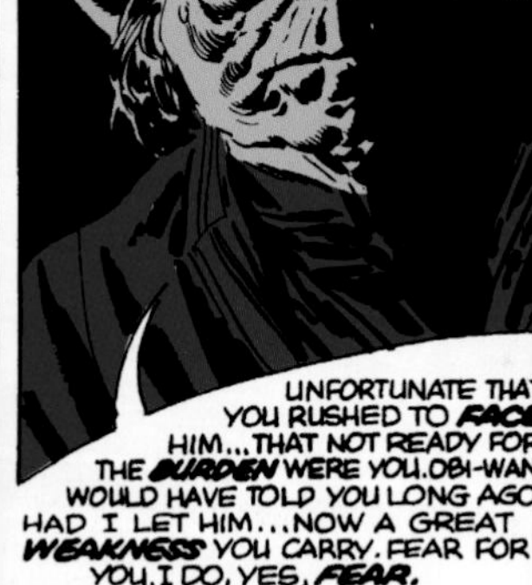

UNFORTUNATE THAT YOU RUSHED TO FACE HIM...THAT NOT READY FOR THE BURDEN WERE YOU. OBI-WAN WOULD HAVE TOLD YOU LONG AGO, HAD I LET HIM...NOW A GREAT WEAKNESS YOU CARRY. FEAR FOR YOU, I DO. YES, FEAR.

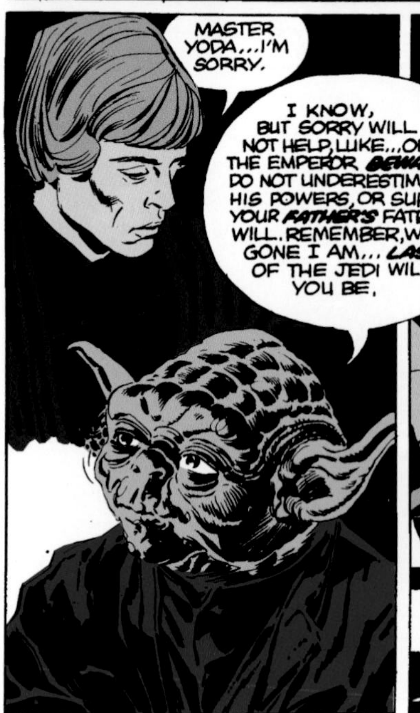

MASTER YODA...I'M SORRY.
I KNOW, BUT SORRY WILL NOT HELP, LUKE...OF THE EMPEROR BEWARE. DO NOT UNDERESTIMATE HIS POWERS, OR SUFFER YOUR FATHER'S FATE YOU WILL. REMEMBER, WHEN GONE I AM... LAST OF THE JEDI WILL YOU BE.

LUKE LEAVES YODA TO MUCH-NEEDED REST. BUT AS HE REJOINS A NERVOUSLY WAITING ARTOO-DETOO...HIS TEACHER'S WORDS CONTINUE TO HAUNT HIM.
I CAN'T DO IT. I CAN'T GO ON ALONE.
YODA AND I WILL BE WITH YOU ALWAYS.

BEN! BEN...WHY DIDN'T YOU TELL ME?
I WAS GOING TO TELL YOU WHEN YOU COMPLETED YOUR TRAINING. BUT YOU FOUND IT NECESSARY TO RUSH OFF UNPREPARED. WE WARNED YOU ABOUT IMPATIENCE.

YOU TOLD ME DARTH VADER BETRAYED AND MURDERED MY FATHER.
YOUR FATHER, ANAKIN, WAS SEDUCED BY THE DARK SIDE OF THE FORCE AND BECAME DARTH VADER. WHEN THAT HAPPENED, HE BETRAYED EVERYTHING THAT ANAKIN SKYWALKER BELIEVED IN AND DESTROYED THAT GOOD MAN FOREVER. WHAT I TOLD YOU WAS TRUE...FROM A CERTAIN POINT OF VIEW.

A CERTAIN POINT OF VIEW!
LUKE, YOU'RE GOING TO FIND THAT MANY OF THE TRUTHS WE CLING TO DEPEND GREATLY ON OUR POINT OF VIEW. BUT I DON'T BLAME YOU FOR BEING ANGRY. IF I WAS WRONG, IT CERTAINLY WASN'T THE FIRST TIME. YOU SEE, WHAT HAPPENED TO YOUR FATHER WAS MY FAULT...

...FROM A CERTAIN POINT OF VIEW...
WHEN I FIRST MET YOUR FATHER, DURING THE CLONE WARS, HE WAS ALREADY A GREAT PILOT. BUT WHAT AMAZED ME WAS HOW STRONGLY THE FORCE WAS WITH HIM. WITH FOOLISH PRIDE, I TOOK IT UPON MYSELF TO TRAIN ANAKIN IN THE WAYS OF THE JEDI.
MY MISTAKE WAS THINKING I COULD BE AS GOOD A TEACHER AS YODA. I WAS NOT. AND SO, WHEN THE EMPEROR SENSED ANAKIN'S POWER... HE WAS ABLE TO LURE HIM TO THE DARK SIDE.
MY MISTAKE HAS HAD DIRE CONSEQUENCES FOR THE GALAXY.

IF I HAD BEEN MORE PATIENT... IF I HAD TRAINED HIM BETTER...
THERE'S STILL GOOD IN HIM.
ONCE, I TOO THOUGHT VADER COULD BE SAVED, THAT HE COULD BE TURNED BACK TO THE GOOD SIDE... BUT HE COULD NOT... NOW HE IS MORE MACHINE THAN MAN, EVIL AND TWISTED...
I... CAN'T KILL MY OWN FATHER.

THEN THE EMPEROR HAS ALREADY DEFEATED YOU, DARKNESS WILL PREVAIL. HE KNEW, AS I DID, THAT THE FORCE RUNS STRONG IN THE SKYWALKER LINE AND THAT ONE DAY YOU WOULD BE A THREAT! YOU'VE BEEN REVEALED TO HIM AS OUR ONLY HOPE, LUKE...
...YET THERE IS ANOTHER. YOU HAVE A SISTER... A TWIN SEPARATED FROM YOU AT BIRTH AND BROUGHT SECRETLY BY ME TO FOSTER PARENTS... ON ALDERAAN! LEIA IS THAT OTHER HOPE...! BUT SHE IS UNTRAINED... UNREADY LUKE... YOU ARE THE LAST JEDI.
LEIA...! MY S-SISTER...! THEN YOU CAN'T LET HER GET INVOLVED NOW, BEN... SHE'LL BE DESTROYED! IT... IT'S I WHO MUST KILL LORD VADER!
YOUR FEELINGS SERVE YOU WELL... BURY THEM DEEP OR THEY MAY SERVE THE EMPEROR AS WELL.
LUKE STARES AT THE SHIMMERING MANIFESTATION OF HIS DEPARTED MENTOR... SHAKEN BY WHAT HE HAS LEARNED...
YOU CANNOT ESCAPE YOUR DESTINY, LUKE. YOU WILL HAVE TO FACE DARTH VADER AGAIN.

BOBA FETT
GALACTIC BOUNTY
HUNTER.

THE EMPEROR'S ROYAL GUARD.

THE *MILLENNIUM FALCON* DEPARTS TATOOINE.

Becton&Sev.

#3 IN A FOUR-ISSUE LIMITED SERIES

STAR WARS

RETURN OF THE JEDI

60¢
U.K. 25p
CAN. 75¢

3
DEC

THE OFFICIAL COMICS ADAPTATION!

STAN LEE PRESENTS: THE OFFICIAL COMICS ADAPTATION OF

STAR WARS

RETURN OF THE JEDI™

Adapted by ARCHIE GOODWIN Art by AL WILLIAMSON & CARLOS GARZON
Lettered by ED KING Colored by CHRISTIE SCHEELE & BOB SHAREN
Edited by MICHAEL HIGGINS & JO DUFFY Editor in Chief JIM SHOOTER

Based on the Story by GEORGE LUCAS
Screenplay by LAWRENCE KASDAN & GEORGE LUCAS.

CHAPTER THREE:
MISSION TO ENDOR!
SULLUST! HERE FIGHTERS AND BATTLE CRUISERS GATHER IN VAST NUMBER, GATHER TO SERVE THE REBEL CAUSE, GATHER TO MAKE THEIR BOLDEST AND GREATEST STRIKE AGAINST THE TYRANNICAL FORCES THEY HAVE OPPOSED SO LONG.
AND ON ONE OF THE LARGEST OF THESE VESSELS, SERVING AS REBEL COMMAND SHIP... A FINAL MEETING HAS BEEN CALLED.
DATA BROUGHT BY TRUSTED BOTHAN SPIES HAS BEEN CONFIRMED: THE EMPEROR HAS MADE A CRITICAL ERROR AND THE TIME FOR ATTACK IS AT HAND.

OOK AT HIM, CHEWIE... A GENERAL! YOU KNOW, I TOLD EM YOU WERE A 'FAIR' PILOT, LANDO... HAD NO IDEA THEY VANTED SOMEONE TO LEAD THIS CRAZY ATTACK.
FUNNY, SOMEBODY TOLD THEM ABOUT MY LITTLE MANEUVER AT THE BATTLE OF TAANAB, NOT THAT I WOULDN'T ASK FOR THE CHANCE ANYWAY.
I'M SURPRISED THEY DIDN'T ASK YOU TO DO IT!
HEY, HAVE YOU EVER SEEN A DEATH STAR? YOU'RE IN FOR A VERY SHORT GENERALSHIP, OL' BUDDY!

MAYBE THEY DID, BUT I'M NOT CRAZY. YOU'RE THE RESPECTABLE ONE, REMEMBER?

HAN'S STAYING ON THE COMMAND SHIP WITH ME. WE'RE BOTH GRATEFUL FOR WHAT YOU'RE DOING, LANDO... AND PROUD.

THEN, THE CHAMBER GROWS DARK AND HUSHED, AS A HOLOGRAPHIC IMAGE OF AN IMPERIAL CONSTRUCTION APPEARS... AND MON MOTHMA, SUPREME LEADER OF THE REBEL ALLIANCE, BEGINS TO SPEAK.

THIS IS THE EMPEROR'S NEW BATTLE STATION... ITS WEAPONS SYSTEMS ARE NOT YET OPERATIONAL. WITH THE IMPERIAL FLEET SPREAD THROUGHOUT THE GALAXY, VAINLY ATTEMPTING TO ENGAGE US...

IT IS RELATIVELY UNPROTECTED. MOST IMPORTANT, OUR SPY NETWORK HAS LEARNED THE EMPEROR IS PERSONALLY OVERSEEING THE CONSTRUCTION.

WHEN THE EXCITEMENT OF THIS INFORMATION DIES DOWN, ADMIRAL ACKBAR OF THE ALLIANCE'S MON CALAMARI ALLIES TAKES THE PODIUM.

THIS DEATH STAR IS NOT ENTIRELY WITHOUT DEFENSES. IT IS PROTECTED BY AN ENERGY SHIELD GENERATED FROM THE NEARBY MOON OF ENDOR.

NO SHIP CAN FLY THROUGH...NO WEAPON CAN PENETRATE IT. THE SHIELD MUST BE DEACTIVATED BEFORE ANY ATTACK CAN BE MADE.
BUT ONCE IT'S DOWN, OUR FIGHTERS WILL FLY INTO THE STATION'S UNCOMPLETED SUPERSTRUCTURE AND ATTEMPT TO HIT ITS MAIN REACTOR, SOMEWHERE INSIDE. THIS IS THE ATTACK GENERAL CALRISSIAN HAS VOLUNTEERED TO LEAD!
GOOD LUCK OL' BUDDY... YOU'RE GONNA NEED IT!
BUT LANDO SENSES NEW RESPECT BEHIND HAN'S JIBES, EVEN AS HE TURNS HIS ATTENTION TO THE NEXT SPEAKER... GENERAL MADINE.
WE'VE ACQUIRED A SMALL IMPERIAL SHUTTLE. UNDER THIS GUISE, A STRIKE TEAM WILL LAND ON ENDOR, OVERCOME THE SMALL CONTROL BUNKER SQUAD, AND DEACTIVATE THE SHIELD GENERATOR.
HAN, I WONDER WHO THEY'VE FOUND TO PULL THAT OFF?
GENERAL SOLO, IS YOUR STRIKE TEAM ASSEMBLED?
AFTER SUFFERING SEVERAL INCREDULOUS LOOKS WHICH MELT INTO ADMIRATION, THE NEW LEADER ADMITS...
UH...MY SQUAD IS READY BUT I NEED A COMMAND CREW FOR THE SHUTTLE.
WARRRRRRGH!
DON'T GET ANNOYED, CHEWIE. THIS IS GONNA BE ROUGH. I DIDN'T WANT TO SPEAK FOR YOU, OL' PAL. THAT'S ONE.
MAKE IT TWO. I'M NOT LETTING YOU OUT OF MY SIGHT AGAIN, YOUR GENERALSHIP.
AND I'M WITH YOU, TOO!

EVERY HEAD TURNS... AND THERE ARE CHEERS FOR THE NEW ARRIVAL IN THE BRIEFING CHAMBER.
THAT'S THREE!
AND AMID A HAPPY REUNION... ONLY ONE SENSES SOMETHING CHANGED AND TROUBLED IN LUKE SKYWALKER.
WHAT... IS IT?
NOTHING, LEIA. I'LL TELL YOU SOMEDAY.
IT IS A MATTER THERE IS NO TIME TO PURSUE. ALL URGENCY, ALL CONCERN IS FOR THE GREAT CONFLICT TO COME.
I MEAN IT, LANDO. TAKE THE FALCON. SHE'LL BRING YOU LUCK. BESIDES, SHE'S THE FASTEST SHIP IN THE FLEET.
I KNOW WHAT SHE MEANS TO YOU, HAN... PARTICULARLY AFTER SO MUCH TIME AWAY FROM HER IN JABBA'S HANDS. I'LL TAKE CARE... SHE WON'T GET A SCRATCH.
I'VE GOT YOUR WORD. NOT A SCRATCH.
GET OUT OF HERE, YOU PIRATE! I'LL SEE YOU SOON!
FRIENDS PART...
...AND A MISSION BEGINS.
I DON'T KNOW, LEIA. LOOKING AT THE MILLENNIUM FALCON BACK THERE, I GOT A FUNNY FEELING. LIKE... LIKE I'M NOT GOING TO SEE HER AGAIN.
COME ON, CAPTAIN... LET'S JUST FLY.

HAN SOLO DOES THAT... DESPITE COMPLAINTS FROM CHEWBACCA THAT THE EMPIRE DOESN'T DESIGN ITS SHUTTLES WITH WOOKIE IN MIND, DESPITE MECHANIZED BICKERING BETWEEN SEE-THREEPIO AND ARTOO-DETOO, AND DESPITE HIS OWN EARLY UNEASINES SOON, PERHAPS TOO SOON, THEY ARE APPROACHING THEIR DESTINATION...
...AND THE IMPERIAL SECURITY SYSTEM SURROUNDING IT.
TRANSMIT YOUR CLEARANCE CODE, SHUTTLE, PRIOR TO PASSAGE THROUGH THE DEFLECTOR SHIELD.
NOW WE FIND OUT IF THAT CODE WAS WORTH THE PRICE THE ALLIANCE PAID FOR IT AND THE LIVES OF THE SPIES WHO DIED OBTAINING IT.
DARTH VADER IS ON THAT COMMAND SHIP.
C'MON, LUKE... YOU'RE JUST JITTERY. BUT LET'S KEEP OUR DISTANCE, CHEWIE... WITHOUT LOOKING LIKE WE'RE KEEPING OUR DISTANCE.
YOU KNOW...FLY CASUAL.
BUT ABOARD THE HUGE IMPERIAL VESSEL AS THE SHUTTLE'S CLEARANCE IS PROCESSED...
I HAVE A STRANGE FEELING ABOUT THAT SHIP.
THEY'RE USING AN OLDER CODE, LORD VADER, BUT IT CHECKS OUT. SHOULD I HOLD THEM?
NO. LET THEM PASS. I WILL DEAL WITH THIS MATTER MYSELF.

ENDOR! AMID TOWERING TREES AND LUSH FOLIAGE, THE SHUTTLE IS HIDDEN AND THE REBEL STRIKE TEAM MOVES TOWARD ITS TARGET.
NOT ALL MOVE WITH EQUAL DEGREES OF ENTHUSIASM.
NO, I DON'T THINK IT'S PRETTY HERE, ARTOO. WITH OUR LUCK, IT'S INHABITED SOLELY BY DROID-EATING MONSTERS.
THREEPIO IS HUSHED. AHEAD... THE FIRST OBSTACLE.
TWO IMPERIAL SCOUTS! IT'LL TAKE TIME TO SNEAK AROUND THEIR CAMPSITE, AND IF THEY SPOT US AND REPORT... THIS WHOLE PARTY IS ALL FOR NOTHING. STAY PUT... CHEWIE AN' I WILL HANDLE 'EM.
QUIETLY, THERE MIGHT BE--
"--MORE OF THEM," COMPLETES LUKE'S THOUGHT, BUT IT GOES UNHEARD BY HAN AND CHEWBACCA AS THEY SUDDENLY CHARGE THE ENEMY...
...AND A BRAWL IS UNDER WAY!
THE CORELLIAN AND HIS WOOKIEE FIRST MATE ARE MATCH ENOUGH FOR THEIR OPPONENTS, BUT AS LUKE AND LEIA RUSH FORWARD... LASER FIRE ERUPTS!
TWO OTHERS ACROSS THE CLEARING!
SO MUCH FOR QUIET! THEY'RE GETTING TO THEIR BIKES... WE'VE GOT TO STOP THEM!

THE PAIR MOVE... RUNNING PAST THE BRAWL AT THE IMPERIAL CAMPSITE!
HEY! WAIT! WHAT ARE YOU TWO--
BLAST IT!

PURSUIT! LUKE AND THE PRINCESS LEAP TO THE MACHINES OF THE SCOUTS HAN AND CHEWBACCA ARE DISPATCHING...
QUICK! HIT THE CENTER SWITCH! IT'LL JAM THEIR COMLINKS!
BUT AS THEY NARROW THE GAP IN A HIGH-SPEED CHASE WEAVING IN AND OUT AMONG ENDOR'S TOWERING TREES...
LUKE! WE JUST PASSED TWO MORE SCOUTS! THEY'RE COMING AFTER US!
AND THEIR BLAZING LASER CANNONS CATCH LUKE WITH A GLANCING HIT!
KEEP AFTER THE LEAD MAN! I'LL TAKE CARE OF THE OTHER TWO... AFTER THIS ONE!
A KICK MAKES THE NEW ROCKET BIKE LUKE'S! HE SLAMS IT INTO THE BRAKING MODE...
...AND HIS TWO SURPRISED PURSUERS WHIP PAST HIM INTO HIS LINE OF FIRE.
ONE FALLS...

...BUT THE OTHER'S TWISTING FLIGHT LEADS LUKE TO NEAR DISASTER!
THE CRASH CANNOT BE AVOIDED...
...DEATH IS, ONLY BY A WELL-TIMED LEAP...

AND LUKE SCRAMBLES TO HIS FEET TO FIND HIS FOE CIRCLING BACK FOR THE KILL.

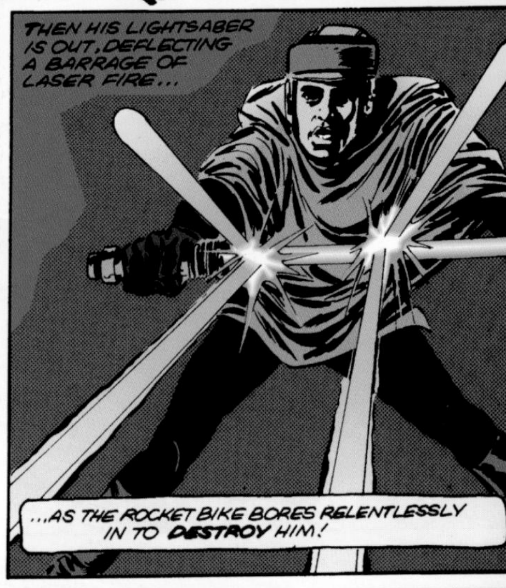
THEN HIS LIGHTSABER IS OUT, DEFLECTING A BARRAGE OF LASER FIRE...
...AS THE ROCKET BIKE BORES RELENTLESSLY IN TO DESTROY HIM!

IMPOSSIBLY, THE YOUNG JEDI SIDESTEPS AT THE LAST POSSIBLE INSTANT! HIS LIGHT BLADE FLASHES...
...SEVERING THE ROARING IMPERIAL VEHICLE'S CONTROL VANES!
IT IS OVER. UNTIL, CHILLINGLY, LUKE REALIZES THERE IS NO SIGN OF LEIA OR THE ENEMY SHE PURSUED.

UKE RUSHES TO REJOIN THE REBEL PARTY, PRAYING
HAT LEIA WILL HAVE FOUND HER WAY BACK TO THEM
LSO, AS ABOVE THE FORESTED MOON...
...THE NEW DEATH STAR CIRCLES AND THE EMPEROR HOLDS AUDIENCE.
ARE YOU SURE MY FRIEND? I KNOW A SMALL REBEL FORCE HAS PENETRATED THE SHIELD AND LANDED ON ENDOR, BUT--
MY SON IS WITH THEM. I FELT HIM, MY MASTER.
STRANGE THAT I HAVE NOT. I WONDER IF YOUR FEELINGS ON THE MATTER ARE CLEAR, LORD VADER.
THEY ARE CLEAR, MY MASTER.
THEN YOU MUST GO TO THE SANCTUARY MOON AND WAIT FOR HIM. HE WILL COME TO YOU... OF HIS OWN FREE WILL. I HAVE FORESEEN IT.
HIS COMPASSION FOR YOU WILL BE HIS UNDOING. HE WILL COME TO YOU... AND YOU WILL BRING HIM TO ME.
ENDOR. WITH THE MAIN PARTY PROCEEDING AHEAD, A SEARCH IS ON. A SEARCH FOR A COMPANION WHO HAS FAILED TO APPEAR. A SEARCH WHICH HAS LED TO THE AFTERMATH OF BATTLE.
I KNOW THAT'S HER HELMET, CAPTAIN SOLO, BUT ARTOO'S SENSORS FIND NO TRACE OF THE PRINCESS.
YEAH. WELL... I HOPE SHE'S NOWHERE NEAR HERE.

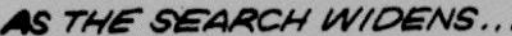
AS THE SEARCH WIDENS...

LEIA DEFINITELY SURVIVED THE WRECK... HERE ARE TWO MORE IMPERIALS SHE RAN INTO...
FROM THE LOOKS OF THEM, SHE SEEMS TO HAVE DONE ALL RIGHT. BUT WHERE IS SHE NOW?

THEN... SOMETHING IN THE AIR SENDS HAN'S WOOKIEE PARTNER CHARGING THROUGH THE HEAVY FOLIAGE! THE OTHERS FOLLOW TO FIND...
FOOD? I DON'T GET IT. DID SOMEBODY HANG IT OUT TO CURE, OR--
CHEWBACCA! WAIT! DON'T TOUCH--

NICE WORK, FUZZBALL! THINKIN' WITH YOUR STOMACH...! OLDEST TRAP IN THE GALAXY...AND WE'RE IN IT!
EASY, HAN. LET'S SEE...CAN ANYBODY REACH MY LIGHTSABER? THREEPIO...?
I FEAR NOT, MASTER LUKE. BUT PERHAPS ARTOO CAN CUT WITH--

AIEEEE! YOU WRETCHED LITTLE RUSTPOT! YOU COULD HAVE WARNED US YOU WERE ALREADY CUTTING!

BUT AS EFFECTS OF THE FALL WEAR OFF... A NEW REALIZATION DAWNS
OH, DEAR... I THINK WE'VE FOUND THE ONES WHO SET THE TRAP... OR THEY'VE FOUND US!
AND THE SIGHT OF THE GOLDEN DROID BRINGS EXCITEMENT TO THE SMALL SPEAR-WIELDING CREATURES...

...WHO PROVE LESS IMPRESSED WITH THEIR OTHER CAPTIVES.
POINT THOSE THINGS SOMEWHERE ELSE OR I'LL--
DON'T, HAN. IT'LL BE ALL RIGHT. THREEPIO, CAN YOU UNDERSTAND WHAT THEY'RE SAYING?
I COULD BE MISTAKEN, SIR... THEY USE QUITE A PRIMITIVE DIALECT. BUT... THEY APPEAR TO THINK I'M SOME MANNER OF DEITY.
THEN HOW ABOUT USING SOME OF YOUR DIVINE INFLUENCE TO GET US OUT OF THIS, GOLDENROD?!
THAT WOULDN'T BE PROPER, CAPTAIN SOLO! IT'S AGAINST MY PROGRAMMING TO IMPERSONATE A DEITY.
PROPER...?! LISTEN, YOU PILE OF BOLTS! IF YOU DON'T --
THRUSTING SPEARS MAKE HAN RECONSIDER INFLICTING PHYSICAL DAMAGE UPON THE NEW IDOL...
...AND SOON A PROCESSION MOVES THROUGH HIDDEN FOREST BYWAYS. THREEPIO IS BORNE BY SEDAN CHAIR AS BEFITS HIS NEW STATUS.
THE OTHERS ARE TRUSSED AND CARRIED MORE OMINOUSLY... LIKE FRESHLY CAUGHT GAME.
FINALLY, BY NARROW WOODEN WALKWAYS AND OCCASIONAL CRUDE VINE SWINGS, THEY ARE DELIVERED TO A VILLAGE HIDDEN HIGH IN THE GREAT TREES OF ENDOR, WHERE THE LOCALS, LED BY THEIR MEDICINE MAN, SWARM TO INSPECT THEM.
THREEPIO, IT'S TIME YOU SPOKE ON OUR BEHALF.

THE RESULTS ARE NOT ENCOURAGING. FIREWOOD IS STACKED UNDER HAN SOLO.
WELL? WHAT DID THEY SAY?

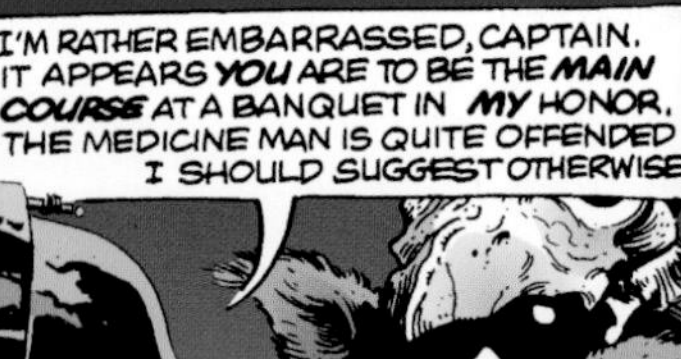
I'M RATHER EMBARRASSED, CAPTAIN. IT APPEARS YOU ARE TO BE THE MAIN COURSE AT A BANQUET IN MY HONOR. THE MEDICINE MAN IS QUITE OFFENDED I SHOULD SUGGEST OTHERWISE
LOOK, BRIGHT EYES, YOU'D BETTER TELL THAT SAWED-OFF LITTLE--

TELL THEM YOU ARE ALL MY FRIENDS, THREEPIO... AND MUST BE SET FREE!
LEIA! H-HOW...?

ONE OF THESE LITTLE FOLK-- THE EWOKS--FOUND ME AFTER MY RUN-IN WITH THE IMPERIALS. I GUESS HE WAS IMPRESSED SINCE THE EWOKS DON'T LIKE THEM EITHER!

BUT SHARING MUTUAL ENEMIES IS NOT ENOUGH TO DISSUADE THE MEDICINE MAN FROM HONORING TRIBE'S NEW DEITY.
THREEPIO, TELL THEM IF THEY DON'T DO AS YOU WISH, YOU'LL BECOME ANGRY AND USE YOUR MAGIC.
SIR...? WHAT MAGIC? I COULDN'T--

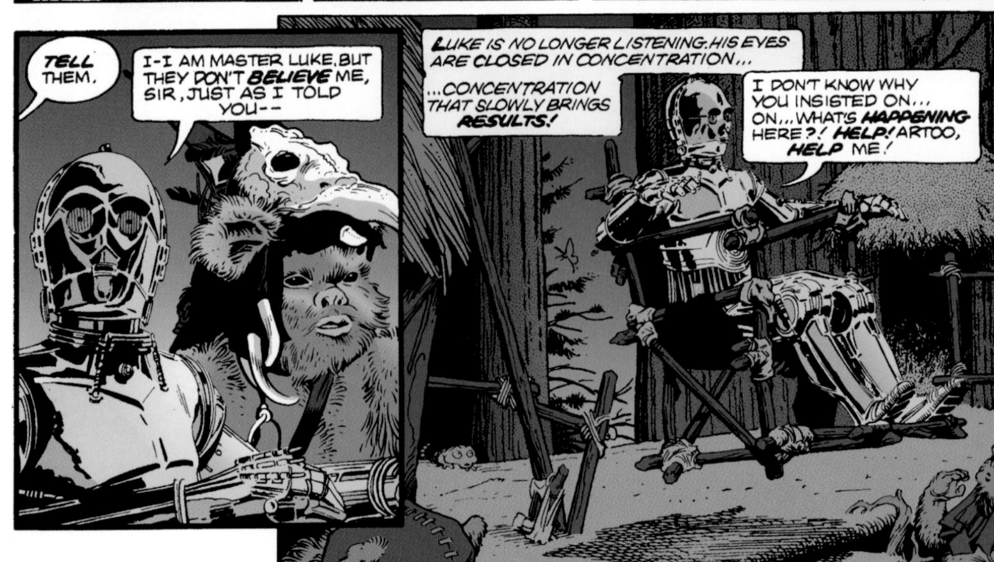
TELL THEM.
I-I AM MASTER LUKE, BUT THEY DON'T BELIEVE ME, SIR, JUST AS I TOLD YOU--
LUKE IS NO LONGER LISTENING. HIS EYES ARE CLOSED IN CONCENTRATION...
...CONCENTRATION THAT SLOWLY BRINGS RESULTS!
I DON'T KNOW WHY YOU INSISTED ON... ON... WHAT'S HAPPENING HERE?! HELP! ARTOO, HELP ME!

ENTLY, THE EWOK DEITY IS LOWERED BACK TO THE
ROUND. SUDDENLY, THERE IS A RUSH TO FREE HIS FRIENDS.
THANKS, THREEPIO!
WHY... WHY, I DIDN'T KNOW I HAD IT *IN* ME, MASTER LUKE!

A MEETING FOLLOWS IN THE TRIBAL CHIEFTAIN'S HUT WHERE THE PURPOSE OF THE REBEL MISSION AGAINST THE EMPIRE IS MADE CLEAR BY THREEPIO...
...OR AT LEAST AS CLEAR AS THE DROID'S IMITATION OF THE SQUEAKY EWOK DIALECT, WITH OCCASIONAL SOUND EFFECTS THROWN IN, CAN MAKE A SHORT HISTORY OF THE GALACTIC CIVIL WAR.

ND MANY ARGUMENTS, DISCUSSIONS, AND SPEECHES LATER...
NE ARE NOW PART OF THE *TRIBE*, CAPTAIN. THE CHIEF HAS
OWED TO HELP US IN ANY WAY TO RID THEIR LAND OF THE EVIL ONES.
JUST WHAT I'VE ALWAYS WANTED! WELL... *SHORT* HELP IS BETTER THAN *NO* HELP!

BUT NOT EVERYONE IS QUITE SO FORGIVING OVER THE INDIGNITIES SUFFERED.
BRAAAAP!

STILL, THE MEETING IN THE HUT IN TIME BECOMES A CELEBRATION. AS THE REVELRY GROWS, LUKE SKYWALKER MOVES QUIETLY AWAY INTO THE STILLNESS OUTSIDE, BUT HIS DEPARTURE DOES NOT GO UNNOTICED.
LUKE...? LUKE, WHAT'S WRONG?

EVERYTHING, I'M AFRAID. OR NOTHING. MAYBE THINGS ARE FINALLY GOING TO BE THE WAY THEY WERE *MEANT* TO BE.

LEIA... DO YOU REMEMBER YOUR MOTHER? YOUR REAL MOTHER? TELL ME WHAT YOU REMEMBER...TELL ME.
S-SHE DIED WHEN I WAS VERY YOUNG. I ONLY RECALL A LITTLE... FEELINGS, REALLY... IMAGES, SHE WAS VERY BEAUTIFUL. GENTLE, AND KIND... BUT SAD. WHY ARE YOU ASKING ME THIS?
I HAVE NO MEMORY OF MY MOTHER. I NEVER KNEW HER.
LUKE, WHAT IS IT? WHAT TROUBLING YOU?
DARTH VADER IS HERE ON THIS MOON, LEIA... I CAN FEEL HIS PRESENCE. BUT HE CAN ALSO FEEL MINE. AS LONG AS I'M WITH YOU... I ENDANGER THE WHOLE GROUP AND OUR MISSION.
HE'S COME FOR ME AND I HAVE TO FACE HIM.
IT'S NOT GOING TO BE EASY FOR YOU TO HEAR THIS... BUT YOU MUST. I MIGHT NOT BE BACK. AND IF I DON'T MAKE IT... YOU'RE THE ONLY ONE I TRUST.
HE'S MY FATHER, LEIA. DARTH VADER IS MY FATHER.
DON'T TALK THAT WAY, LUKE! YOU MUST SURVIVE. I DO WHAT I CAN, BUT I'M OF NO IMPORTANCE. WITHOUT YOU... I'M NOTHING. IT'S YOU... I'VE SEEN IT. YOU HAVE A POWER I DON'T UNDERSTAND... AND COULD NEVER HAVE!
YOU'RE WRONG, LEIA. THE LIFE FORCE RUNS THROUGH ALL LIVING THINGS. THE REBELLION WILL GO ON LONG AFTER I'M GONE.
LUKE, WHAT'S COME OVER YOU?

E FORCE IS STRONG IN MY FAMILY, LEIA. FATHER HAS IT. I HAVE IT. AND MY STER HAS IT... YOU, LEIA! BELIEVE ME... AND BELIEVE I MUST GO TO DARTH VADER. I'M THE ONLY ONE WHO CAN SAVE HIM.

ADING LUKE'S UNWAVERING EYES, A KNOWS SHE HAS HEARD THE TRUTH.

RUN AWAY, LUKE... FAR AWAY! IF HE CAN FEEL YOUR PRESENCE, GO AWAY FROM THIS PLACE! I WISH I COULD GO WITH YOU!
NO, YOU DON'T. YOU'VE NEVER FALTERED, LEIA. WHEN HAN AND I AND OTHERS DOUBTED, YOU'VE ALWAYS BEEN STRONG... NEVER TURNED AWAY FROM YOUR RESPONSIBILITY. I CAN'T SAY THE SAME.
WELL, NOW WE'RE BOTH GOING TO FULFILL OUR DESTINY.

KE, WHY? WHY ST YOU CONFRONT HIM?
THERE'S GOOD IN HIM. I'VE FELT IT. HE WON'T TURN ME OVER TO THE EMPEROR. I CAN TURN HIM BACK TO THE GOOD SIDE. I MUST TRY, LEIA. HE'S OUR FATHER.

TEARS GLISTEN IN THE EYES OF THE PRINCESS, BUT SHE SENSES THERE IS NOTHING MORE TO BE SAID. GENTLY, LUKE SKYWALKER EMBRACES HER...
GOOD BYE, SWEET, SWEET LEIA.
THEN HE MOVES AWAY, DISAPPEARING INTO THE MIST AND THE NIGHT.

MORNING! AN IMPERIAL WALKER HALTS AT THE EMPIRE'S ENDOR LANDING PLATFORM, WHERE ON ITS LOWER DECK, A TALL FIGURE WAITS PATIENTLY, OMINOUSLY...
LORD VADER! WE HAVE THE REBEL WHO SURRENDERED! HE DENIES IT, BUT I BELIEVE THERE MAY BE MORE OF THEM!

HE WAS ARMED ONLY WITH THIS, SIR... A **LIGHTSABER** ISN'T IT?
LEAVE US. CONDUCT A WIDE SEARCH OF THE AREA. IF YOU FIND ANY OF HIS COMPANIONS... BRING THEM TO ME.

AT LAST, THEY STAND ALONE... FATHER AND SON.
SO, YOU HAVE FINALLY ACCEPTED THE **TRUTH**.

TRUE SELF... YOU HAV
ONLY FORGOTTEN. THE
IS GOOD IN YOU. THE

DRIVEN IT FULLY FRO
YOU. THAT'S WHY YO
COULDN'T DESTROY M
THAT'S WHY YOU WON
TAKE ME TO HIM

YOU HAVE CONSTRUCTED **A SABER** TO REPLACE THE ONE LOST WHEN WE **LAST** MET. YOUR SKILLS ARE COMPLETE. INDEED, YOU ARE POWERFUL AS THE EMPEROR HAS FORESEEN.

COME WITH ME FATHER. I WILL NOT TURN AND YOU WILL BE FORCED TO DESTROY ME.

IF THAT IS YOUR DESTINY.

SEARCH YOUR **FEELINGS**, FATHER! Y
CAN'T DO THIS! I FEEL THE **CONFLICT** WITHIN YOU. LET GO OF YOUR HATE.
SOMEONE HAS FILLED YOUR MIND WITH FOOLISH IDEAS, YOUNG ONE. BEN ONCE THOUGHT AS YOU DO...

YOU DO NOT KNOW THE POWER OF THE **DARK SIDE**. I MUST OBEY MY MASTER. THE EMPEROR WILL SHOW YOU THE **TRUE NATURE** OF THE FORCE... **HE** IS NOW **YOUR** MASTER AS WELL.
IT IS TOO LATE FOR ME, MY SON.
THEN... THEN MY FATHER IS **TRULY** DEAD.

IMPERIAL SCOUT
ON SPEEDER BIKE
(ENDOR)

GENERAL LANDO CALRISSIAN

ADMIRAL ACKBAR'S
MON CALAMARI
COMMAND SHIP

THE EMPEROR
(DEATH STAR
THRONE ROOM)

IMPERIAL TIE
INTERCEPTORS
(TWIN ION
ENGINES)

#4 IN A FOUR-ISSUE LIMITED SERIES

STAR WARS™

RETURN OF THE JEDI

60¢
U.K. 25p
CAN. 75¢

4
JAN

THE OFFICIAL COMICS ADAPTATION!

STAN LEE PRESENTS: THE OFFICIAL COMICS ADAPTATION OF

STAR WARS

RETURN OF THE JEDI™

Adapted by ARCHIE GOODWIN

Art by AL WILLIAMSON, CARLOS GARZON, RON FRENZ & TOM PALMER

Lettered by ED KING Colored by CHRISTIE SCHEELE & BOB SHAREN

Edited by MICHAEL HIGGINS & JO DUFFY Editor in Chief JIM SHOOTER

Based on the Story by GEORGE LUCAS

Screenplay by LAWRENCE KASDAN & GEORGE LUCAS.

CHAPTER FOUR:
THE FINAL DUEL!
THE REBEL FLEET! THE FULL STRENGTH OF THE ALLIANCE COMMITTED TO ONE BOLD GAMBLE. AT ITS POINT, LEADING THE FIGHTER SQUADRONS... THE MILLENNIUM FALCON. AT ITS CONTROLS, WITH AN ENTIRE NEW CREW... LANDO CALRISSIAN.
AND, AS LANDO SIGNALS HIS SHIP'S READINESS, THE VOICE OF ADMIRAL ACKBAR RINGS OUT FROM HIS MON CALAMARI FLAG SHIP OVER ALL COMLINKS...
ALL CRAFT WILL BEGIN TO JUMP TO HYPERSPACE ON MY MARK! MAY THE FORCE BE WITH US!
NEXT STOP... THE DEATH STAR! BUT DON'T WORRY, MY OL' BUDDY HAN'S ALREADY AT WORK... HE'LL HAVE THAT DEFENSE SHIELD DOWN AS SCHEDULED!
OR THIS WILL BE THE SHORTEST OFFENSIVE OF ALL TIME!

THE EWOK'S NAME IS WICKET. HE IS THE ONE WHO FIRST BEFRIENDED PRINCESS LEIA. HE HAS REUNITED HIS NEW ALLIES WITH THEIR MAIN STRIKE FORCE AND LED THEM TO THE IMPERIAL SHIELD GENERATOR BUNKER.
HEY!
...AND IS NOW ABOUT TO DRAW OFF THE GUARDS AT ITS ENTRANCE!
HREE OF THE FOUR SCOUTS TAKE FF AFTER THE STOLEN SPEEDER IKE! AS FOR THE FOURTH...
OT BAD FOR A LITTLE BALL F FUZZ! JUST WISH HE'D HECKED WITH US FIRST! UESS HE KNOWS ENOUGH O GRAB THE NEAREST VINE ND LEAVE THE IMPERIALS HASING AN MPTY BIKE!
BUT CONCERN FOR WICKET HAS TO COME SECOND TO MOVING INSIDE; QUICKLY, QUIETLY.
WE'RE RUNNING OUT OF TIME, HAN. THE FLEET WILL BE OUT OF HYPERSPACE SOON.
NO PROBLEM YOUR ROYALNESS. SO FAR THIS IS EASIER THAN FALLING OFF A BANTHA!
AND WITH A BURST OF CONCENTRATED FIRE, SEALED DOORS FLY APART... BRINGING THEIR GOAL IN SIGHT.
FREEZE! INSIDE, EVERYBODY... LET'S GET THOSE CHARGES PLANTED!
BUT IF ALL GOES WELL FOR THE REBEL CAUSE ON ENDOR, EVENTS ARE PROCEEDING FAR DIFFERENTLY ABOARD THE NEW DEATH STAR...
WELCOME, YOUNG SKYWALKER! I HAVE BEEN EXPECTING YOU. I LOOK FORWARD TO COMPLETING YOUR TRAINING.
SOMEWHERE WITHIN THE GREAT BATTLE STATION, A GNARLED FINGER GESTURES...

...AND THE BINDERS ON LUKE SKYWALKER'S WRISTS CLATTER TO THE FLOOR, ALLOWING HIM TO STAND FREE BEFORE THE ONE BEING IN THE GALAXY HE WOULD MOST LIKE TO SEE DESTROYED.
LUKE REMAINS STILL.
IF YOU BELIEVE THE TIME WILL COME WHEN I CALL YOU MASTER... YOU'RE GRAVELY MISTAKEN. YOU WILL NOT CONVERT ME AS YOU DID MY FATHER.

YOU WILL FIND, MY YOUNG JEDI, IT IS YOU WHO ARE MISTAKEN.. ABOUT A GREAT MANY THINGS

AH... YOUR LIGHTSABER. A JEDI'S WEAPON, MUCH LIKE YOUR FATHER'S. BY NOW YOU MUST KNOW HE CAN NEVER BE TURNED FROM THE DARK SIDE. SO IT WILL BE WITH YOU.
NEVER. SOON, I WILL DIE, AND YOU WITH ME.

YOU REFER TO THE IMMINENT ATTACK OF YOUR REBEL FLEET? I ASSURE YOU WE ARE QUITE SAFE HERE
YOUR OVERCONFIDENCE IS YOUR WEAKNESS.
YOUR FAITH IN YOUR FRIENDS IS YOURS.

EVERYTHING PROCEEDS ACCORDING TO MY DESIGN. YOUR FRIENDS ON ENDOR... YOUR REBEL FLEET... ALL MOVE INTO A TRAP. IT WAS I WHO ALLOWED THE ALLIANCE TO KNOW ABOUT THIS STATION AND THE SHIELD GENERATOR.
FROM HERE, YOU WILL WITNESS THE FINAL END OF YOUR INSIGNIFICANT REBELLION. DOES THAT MAKE YOUR HATE SWELL? TAKE YOUR JEDI WEAPON... USE IT! I AM UNARMED.
NO... N-NEVER!

GIVE IN TO YOUR RAGE... IT IS UNAVOIDABLE. WITH EACH PASSING MOMENT, YOU MAKE YOURSELF MORE MY SERVANT. GIVE IN! IT'S YOUR DESTINY.
YOU, LIKE YOUR FATHER... ARE NOW MINE!

SOME DISTANCE FROM THE DEATH STAR, THE REBEL FLEET ROARS OUT OF HYPERSPACE! AT ITS HEAD, IN THE MILLENNIUM FALCON, LANDO CALRISSIAN IMMEDIATELY SENSES SOMETHING IS WRONG.
NO READING ON THE SHIELD BECAUSE WE'RE BEING JAMMED? HOW COULD THEY BE JAMMING US IF THEY DIDN'T... KNOW WE WERE COMING...?!
BREAK OFF THE ATTACK! FOLLOW MY LEAD... THAT SHIELD'S STILL UP!
BUT AS THE FLEET RESPONDS TO LANDO'S MOVE...
ADMIRAL ACKBAR! ENEMY SHIPS MOVING OUT FROM BEHIND THE SANCTUARY MOON! CUTTING US OFF! SENDING IN FIGHTERS!
A TRAP! LAUNCH ALL INTERCEPTORS! DOUBLE POWER ON THE MAIN BATTERY!
ONLY THEIR FIGHTERS ARE ATTACKING? WHAT ARE THOSE STAR DESTROYERS WAITING FOR?!
THE ANSWER TO THE QUESTION...
...COMES FROM THE DEATH STAR! COMES IN THE FORM OF A CRACKLING POWER BEAM THAT SLICES THROUGH THE REBEL FLEET, TURNING A MASSIVE BATTLE CRUISER INTO VAPOR!
OUR INTELLIGENCE WAS WRONG! THAT STATION IS FULLY OPERATIONAL! ALL CRAFT PREPARE TO RETREAT!
ADMIRAL, WE CAN'T GIVE UP AND RUN! WE WON'T GET A SECOND CHANCE! HAN WILL HAVE THE SHIELD DOWN... WE'VE JUST GOT TO GIVE HIM MORE TIME!

THE REVERSAL HAS COME WITH STUNNING SWIFTNESS. ONE MOMENT HAN, LEIA, AND THEIR PARTY WERE READYING CHARGE
THE NEXT, THEIR LOOKOUT WAS GONE AND THE SHIELD CONTROL BUNKER WAS FLOODED WITH IMPERIAL TROOPS, PART OF A LEGIO
PLACED ON ENDOR BY THE EMPEROR.
STEP LIVELY, REBEL SCUM! YOU SAW THE SCREENS INSIDE... THE REBELLION IS OVER FOR YOUR FLEET AS WELL AS YOU!
THE WORDS RING DEPRESSINGLY TRUE TO THE SMALL BAND OF CAPTIVES ON ENDOR. EVEN AS ON THE DEATH STAR, SIMILAR WORDS CHILL LUKE SKYWALKER...
THERE IS NO ESCAPE. SHOULD A MIRACLE OCCUR AND THE GENERATOR STILL BE DESTROYED, I'VE GIVEN ORDERS FOR THIS STATION TO BE TURNED ON THE ENDOR MOON AND DESTROY IT.
THE ALLIANCE WILL DIE... AS WILL YOUR FRIENDS.
THE LASER SWORD BEGINS TO SHAKE WHERE IT RESTS BY THE EMPEROR'S HAND...
...LUKE CAN RESIST NO LONGER! THE SABER LEAPS THROUGH THE AIR TO HIS BLACK-GLOVED HAND!
YES! IGNITE IT! STRIKE WITH ALL YOUR HATRED! MAKE YOUR JOURNEY TO THE DARK SIDE COMPLETE!
BEYOND THOUGHT, THE YOUNG JEDI ACTS...
...ONLY TO FIND ANOTHER LIGHT BLADE BLOCKS THE DEATH STROKE! AND AS THE EMPEROR'S PLEASED LAUGHTER ECHOES THROUGH THE THRONE ROOM... LUKE BEGINS THE DUEL HE HOPED NEVER TO FIGHT!

BUT IF THE SON HOLDS ANY RELUCTANCE AT THE CLASH... THE FATHER SEEMINGLY DOES NOT. DARTH VADER PRESSES FORWARD...
...STRONG, SKILLFUL, SURE! EXHIBITING MORE DEADLY INVINCIBILITY THAN EVER!

MEANWHILE, AS THE ENDOR CAPTIVES ARE HERDED TOGETHER UNDER THE GUNS OF AN IMPERIAL SCOUT WALKER...
HELLO! OVER HERE! DID YOU FORGET ABOUT US?

BUT THE STORMTROOPERS WHO CHARGE INTO THE BRUSH AFTER TWO AUDACIOUS DROIDS INSTEAD FIN
...EWOKS! THEY DROP FROM EVERYWHERE, DOWNING IMPERIALS, STEALING WEAPONS...

...AND THE SUDDEN DIVERSION IS ALL THE PRISONERS NEED.
ROWRRRRK!
LEIA! GRAB A BLASTER!
HEAD FOR THE BUNKER! THE CHARGES ARE STILL IN THERE! WE MIGHT MAKE IT YET!
AND WITH THE FUGITIVES IN CLOSE COMBAT WITH THEIR CAPTORS, THE SCOUT WALKER IS UNABLE TO BRING ITS GUNS TO BEAR!

BEYOND ENDOR, IN THE DEPTHS OF SPACE, LANDO AND ADMIRAL ACKBAR MAKE THE SAME TACTIC WORK ON A LARGER SCALE.
AT POINT-BLANK RANGE, WE WON'T LAST LONG AGAINST THESE STAR DESTROYERS, CALRISSIAN!
WE'LL LAST LONGER THAN AGAINST THAT DEATH STAR, SIR... AND NOW IT CAN'T FIRE AT US WITHOUT HITTING ITS OWN SHIPS!

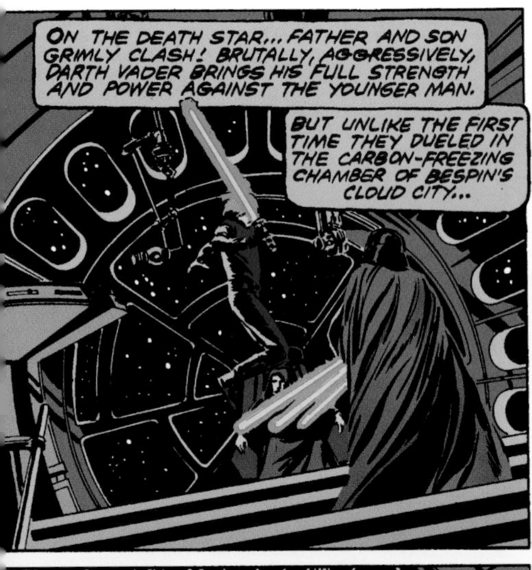
ON THE DEATH STAR... FATHER AND SON GRIMLY CLASH! BRUTALLY, AGGRESSIVELY, DARTH VADER BRINGS HIS FULL STRENGTH AND POWER AGAINST THE YOUNGER MAN.
BUT UNLIKE THE FIRST TIME THEY DUELED IN THE CARBON-FREEZING CHAMBER OF BESPIN'S CLOUD CITY...

...THIS IS A BATTLE OF EQUALS.
THE YOUNG JEDI HAS GROWN IN THE INTERIM...

...AND IF THERE IS ANY TRUE ADVANTAGE, IT SEEMS TO HAVE SHIFTED TO HIM.

THAT'S IT! USE YOUR AGGRESSIVE FEELINGS BOY! ATTACK! ATTACK! LET THE HATE FLOW THROUGH YOU!
BUT THE EMPEROR'S WORDS AWAKEN LUKE TO SOMETHING TERRIBLE RISING WITHIN HIM. HE STOPS... AND LOWERS HIS LIGHT-SABER.
I...I WILL NOT FIGHT YOU, FATHER. HERE... TAKE MY WEAPON.

THE DARK LORD, RISING FROM WHERE HE STUMBLED, CATCHES THE SWORD AS IT ROLLS TO HIM, ATTACHING IT TO HIS B

DON'T UNDERESTIMATE THE POWER OF THE **DARK SIDE**, LUKE... IT IS THE **ONLY** WAY YOU CAN SAVE YOUR FRIENDS! YES, YOUR THOUGHTS **BETRAY** YOU. YOUR FEELINGS FOR THEM ARE **STRONG**. ESPECIALLY FOR...

NO!

...**LEIA!** YES...! I SENSE IT... **FEEL** IT...! A SISTER...A **TWIN!** OBI-WAN WAS WISE TO HIDE HER... BUT YOUR FEELINGS HAVE NOW BETRAYED **HER** TOO! HIS FAILURE IS COMPLETE. IF YOU WILL NOT TURN TO THE DARK SIDE...PERHAPS **SHE** WILL!

THE DISCARDED WEAPON **FLIES** BACK TO ITS YOUNG OWNER.

NEVER!

AND THE DUEL BETWEEN FATHER AND SON RAGES AGAIN, MORE VIOLENTLY THAN EVER...

...WITH **LUKE** AS ITS DRIVING FORCE, SEIZED BY A FRENZY THAT SEEMS TO **CONSUME** HIM!

ANWHILE, WAR HAS COME TO THE SANCTUARY MOON OF ENDOR, AND THOUGH THE WAGING OF WAR IS WHAT
E EMPIRE DOES BEST, THIS FIGHTING IS NOT WHAT IMPERIAL TROOPS ARE PREPARED FOR...

THEIR FOES ARE SMALL, QUICK, AND ELUSIVE. THEY HIT AND RUN WITH CRUDE, UNORTHODOX WEAPONS AND TACTICS WHICH SHOULDN'T WORK...
...BUT WITHIN THE CRAMPED FOREST TERRAIN PROVE REMARKABLY EFFECTIVE! AIDED BY REBEL COMMAN-DOS AND ONE PARTICULARLY FEARSOME WOOKIEE...
...THE EWOKS SEEM TO BE HOLDING THEIR OWN! BUT AT THE SHIELD GENERATOR BUNKER, WHERE THE DROIDS JOIN HAN AND LEIA...
WHA-DEEEET!
OH, NO! CAPTAIN SOLO...ARTOO'S HIT!
BY THE TIME THE LITTLE GUY RECOVERS, IT'LL BE TOO LATE FOR HIM TO OVERRIDE THE LOCKING MECHANISM!
GIMME A HAND, LEIA! MAYBE I CAN HOT-WIRE THIS THING. LEIA...? DID YOU HEAR? I SAID--
THERE IS AN UGLY BURST OF LASER FIRE! THE PRINCESS DOES MOST OF THE SHOOTING...
...BUT NOT ALL!
LEIA! YOU KNOW I LOVE YOU. DON'T--
THANKS FOR CARING, GENERAL... BUT IT'S ONLY MY ARM. AND I'M AFRAID...

...WE HAVE BIGGER PROBLEMS!
THE SCOUT WALKER LOOMS OUT OF THE SMOKE OF COMBAT, GUNS TRAINED DIRECTLY AT THE BUNKER DOORWAY... AND THOSE IN IT!

WHILE IN SPACE, LANDO CALRISSIAN BATTLES TO KEEP HIS FIGHTERS WITHIN STRIKING DISTANCE OF THE DEATH STAR.

THIS IS ADMIRAL ACKBAR, GENERAL! THE JAMMING HAS STOPPED. WE HAVE A READING ON THE SHIELD. IT'S STILL UP!

I FEAR PRINCESS LEIA'S UNIT DIDN'T MAKE IT!

UNTIL THEY'VE DESTROYED OUR LAST SHIP... THERE'S STILL HOPE!

WITHIN THE CONVERTED CONTROL CHAMBER ABOARD THE DEATH STAR SERVING AS THE EMPEROR'S THRONE ROOM... THE TWO COMBATANTS FIGHT AS NEVER BEFORE.

DARTH VADER'S DEFENSE IS POWERFUL AND RELENTLESS...

...BUT IT IS ONLY A DEFENSE.

STEP BY STEP, LUKE DRIVES THE DARK LOR ONTO THE WALKWAY OVER THE BATTLE STATION'S MAIN ELEVATOR SHAFT...

...EACH STROKE OF HIS SWORD FORCING HIS FATHER...

... FURTHER TOWARD DEFEAT!

UNTIL...
SHRRAAAAK!
VADER'S LIGHTSABER SAILS INTO THE NEARLY BOTTOMLESS SHAFT AND SPARKS FLY FROM THE MECHANIZED STUMP THAT ONCE HELD HIS RIGHT HAND! THE EMPEROR'S LAUGHTER FILLS THE GREAT CHAMBER...
GOOD! KILL HIM! YOUR HATE HAS MADE YOU POWERFUL! NOW, FULFILL YOUR DESTINY AND TAKE YOUR FATHER'S PLACE AT MY SIDE!
LUKE'S LIGHT BLADE DANCES AT THE THROAT OF THE FIGURE FALLEN BEFORE HIM. HE STARES AT THE GREAT BODY, MORE MECHANICAL THAN FLESH... THEN CONSIDERS HIS OWN BLACK-GLOVED HAND AND FEARS FOR WHAT HE'S BECOMING.
NEVER! NEVER WILL I TURN TO THE DARK SIDE! YOU'VE FAILED, YOUR HIGHNESS! I AM A JEDI, AS MY FATHER WAS BEFORE ME!
YOUNG FOOL! ONLY NOW AT THE END DO YOU UNDERSTAND. YOUR FEEBLE SKILLS ARE NO MATCH FOR THE POWER OF THE DARK SIDE! NOW YOU PAY THE PRICE FOR YOUR LACK OF VISION.
FOR A MOMENT... HE IS SUCCESSFUL. THEN THERE IS ONLY PAIN! PAIN AND LASHING POWER THAT MAKES HIM SHRIVEL! AND WHEN IT SEEMS HE CAN ENDURE NO MORE... ITS MIGHT INCREASES!
EVEN IN HIS SURPRISE, LUKE TRIES TO USE THE FORCE TO DEFLECT THE BLINDING BOLTS OF ENERGY, THE EVIL LIGHTNING THAT SUDDENLY BOMBARDS HIM!
SO BE IT, JEDI! IF YOU WILL NOT BE TURNED... YOU WILL BE DESTROYED!
NOW, YOUNG SKYWALKER... YOU DIE!
AND THE FINAL HORROR FOR LUKE IS THE SIGHT OF HIS FATHER CRAWLING BACK TO THE EMPEROR... LIKE A DYING ANIMAL RETURNING TO THE FEET OF ITS MASTER...

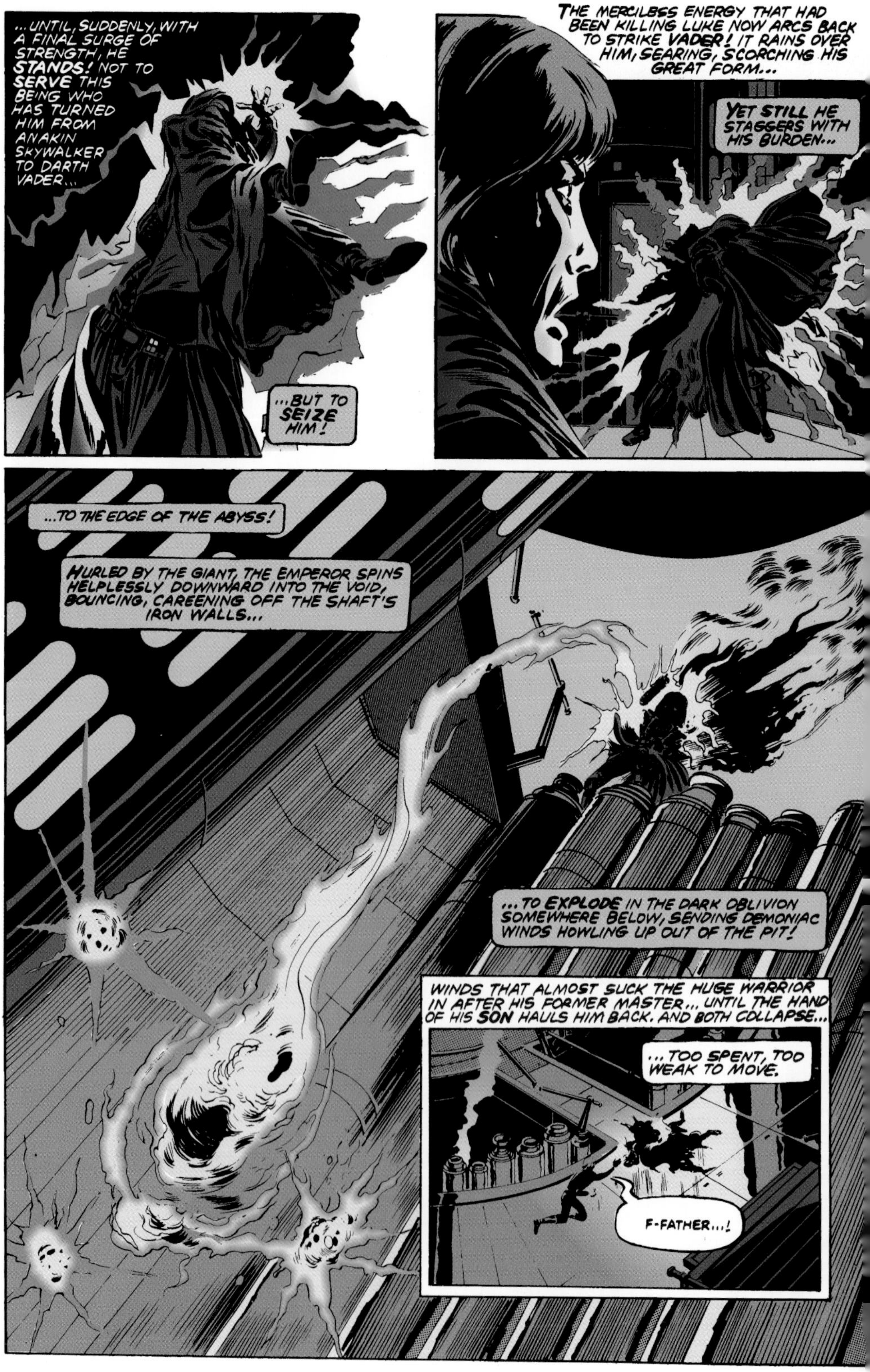

...UNTIL, SUDDENLY, WITH A FINAL SURGE OF STRENGTH, HE **STANDS!** NOT TO **SERVE** THIS BEING WHO HAS TURNED HIM FROM ANAKIN SKYWALKER TO DARTH VADER...
...BUT TO **SEIZE** HIM!

THE MERCILESS ENERGY THAT HAD BEEN KILLING LUKE NOW ARCS BACK TO STRIKE **VADER!** IT RAINS OVER HIM, SEARING, SCORCHING HIS GREAT FORM...
YET **STILL** HE STAGGERS WITH HIS BURDEN...

...TO THE EDGE OF THE ABYSS!

HURLED BY THE GIANT, THE EMPEROR SPINS HELPLESSLY DOWNWARD INTO THE VOID, BOUNCING, CAREENING OFF THE SHAFT'S IRON WALLS...

...TO **EXPLODE** IN THE DARK OBLIVION SOMEWHERE BELOW, SENDING DEMONIAC WINDS HOWLING UP OUT OF THE PIT!

WINDS THAT ALMOST SUCK THE HUGE WARRIOR IN AFTER HIS FORMER MASTER... UNTIL THE HAND OF HIS **SON** HAULS HIM BACK. AND BOTH COLLAPSE...

...TOO SPENT, TOO WEAK TO MOVE.

F-FATHER...!

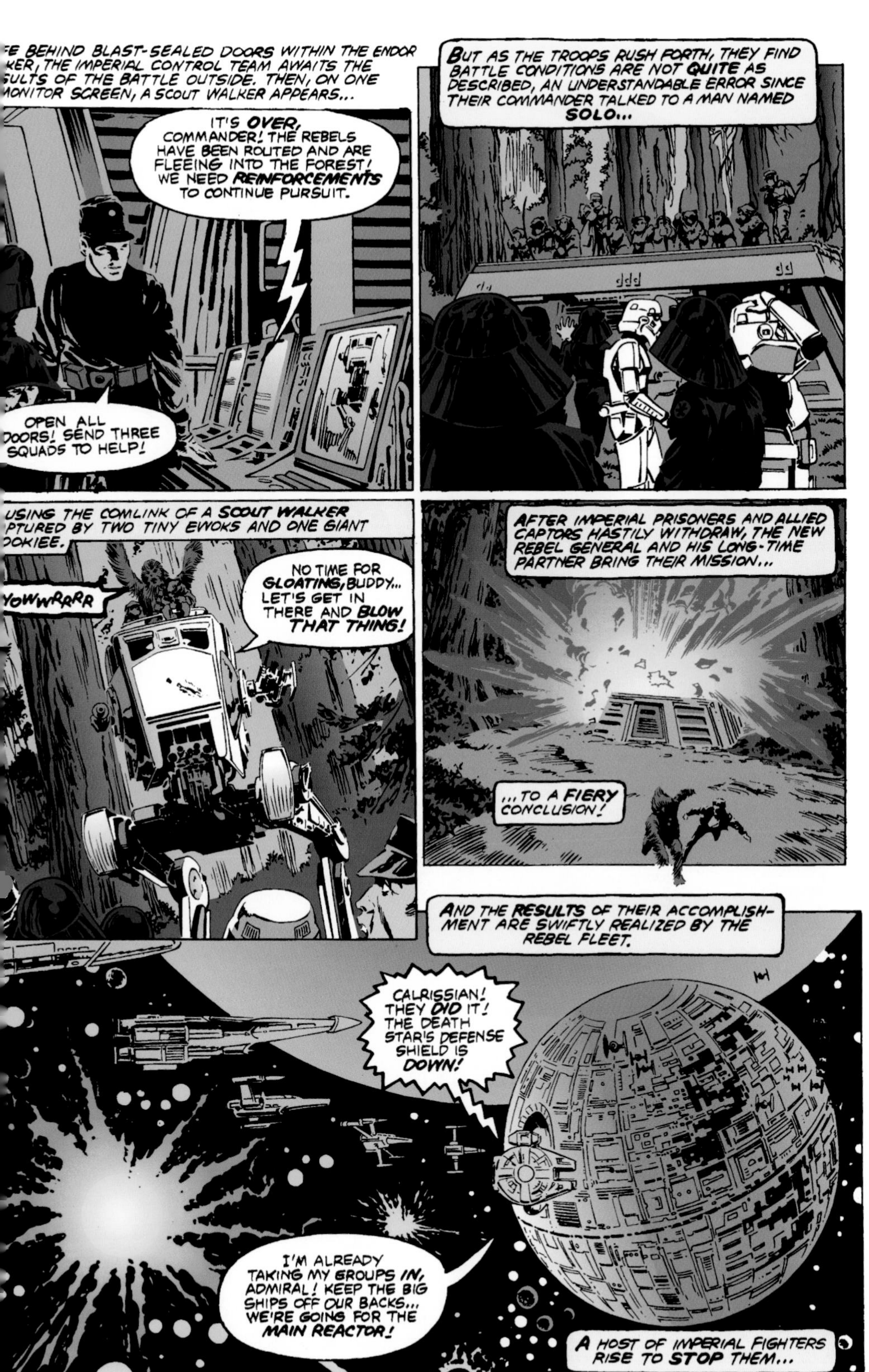
FE BEHIND BLAST-SEALED DOORS WITHIN THE ENDOR
KER, THE IMPERIAL CONTROL TEAM AWAITS THE
SULTS OF THE BATTLE OUTSIDE. THEN, ON ONE
MONITOR SCREEN, A SCOUT WALKER APPEARS...
IT'S OVER, COMMANDER! THE REBELS HAVE BEEN ROUTED AND ARE FLEEING INTO THE FOREST! WE NEED REINFORCEMENTS TO CONTINUE PURSUIT.
OPEN ALL DOORS! SEND THREE SQUADS TO HELP!
BUT AS THE TROOPS RUSH FORTH, THEY FIND BATTLE CONDITIONS ARE NOT QUITE AS DESCRIBED, AN UNDERSTANDABLE ERROR SINCE THEIR COMMANDER TALKED TO A MAN NAMED SOLO...
USING THE COMLINK OF A SCOUT WALKER
PTURED BY TWO TINY EWOKS AND ONE GIANT
OOKIEE.
YOWWRRRR
NO TIME FOR GLOATING, BUDDY... LET'S GET IN THERE AND BLOW THAT THING!
AFTER IMPERIAL PRISONERS AND ALLIED CAPTORS HASTILY WITHDRAW, THE NEW REBEL GENERAL AND HIS LONG-TIME PARTNER BRING THEIR MISSION...
...TO A FIERY CONCLUSION!
AND THE RESULTS OF THEIR ACCOMPLISHMENT ARE SWIFTLY REALIZED BY THE REBEL FLEET.
CALRISSIAN! THEY DID IT! THE DEATH STAR'S DEFENSE SHIELD IS DOWN!
I'M ALREADY TAKING MY GROUPS IN, ADMIRAL! KEEP THE BIG SHIPS OFF OUR BACKS... WE'RE GOING FOR THE MAIN REACTOR!
A HOST OF IMPERIAL FIGHTERS RISE TO STOP THEM...

...AND THE UNCOMPLETED SIDE OF THE BATTLE STATION IS A DEATH MAZE TO BE THREADED. YET, IN THE END, TWO OF THE REBEL CRAFT MAKE IT... AND THE MAIN REACTOR CHAMBER LOOMS JUST AHEAD!
T-TARGET'S TOO BIG, LANDO... MY PROTON TORPEDOES WON'T EVEN DENT THAT!
GO FOR THE POWER REGULATOR ON ITS NORTH TOWER, WEDGE... I'LL TAKE THE MAIN REACTOR! WE'RE CARRYING CONCUSSION MISSILES. THEY SHOULD PENETRATE AND START A CHAIN REACTION!
HUSTLE! ONCE I LET THEM GO, WE WON'T HAVE MUCH TIME, WEDGE! YOU SURVIVED THE FIRST DEATH STAR... DON'T WANT TO LOSE YOU HERE!
THE FALCON SWOOPS DANGEROUSLY CLOSE... CLOSER... TO ITS MASSIVE TARGET. THE FORMER GAMBLER AT HER CONTROLS TAKES NO CHANCES ON MISSING! THEN...
DIRECT HIT! NOW FOR THE HARD PART... GETTING OUT OF THIS PLACE!
FOR NOW THERE IS NOT ONLY THE SUPER-STRUCTURE MAZE TO WEAVE THROUGH... THERE IS THE EXPLOSIVE, EVER-MOUNTING CHAIN REACTION TO OUTRUN!
AND THE EFFECTS OF THE CHAIN REACTION ARE ALREADY BEING FELT THROUGHOUT THE DEATH STAR, INCLUDING ITS DOCKING BAY... WHERE TWO FIGURES IN BLACK PAINFULLY MOVE.
GO, MY SON... LEAVE ME.
NO! YOU'RE COMING WITH ME, FATHER! I'VE GOT TO SAVE YOU.
YOU ALREADY HAVE, LUKE...! NOW... HELP ME TAKE THIS MASK OFF... JUST ONCE... LET ME FACE YOU WITHOUT IT...
YOU'LL DIE...
NOTHING CAN STOP THAT NOW. LET ME LOOK ON YOU... WITH MY OWN EYES...!

SLOWLY, HESITANTLY, LUKE OBEYS... AND LOOKS DOWN ON A FACE WHICH THOUGH LIVID WITH SCARS, HAS REGAINED ITS HUMANITY. MONSTROUS EVIL HAS FADED... BUT THE COST IS HIGH.
I-IT'S TOO LATE, LUKE... IT'S... TOO... LATE...!
AND DARTH VADER, ANAKIN SKYWALKER... LUKE'S FATHER... DIES.
NUMBLY, THE LAST JEDI TURNS... DISAPPEARING INTO THE FIRE AND SMOKE BETWEEN HIM AND AN IMPERIAL SHUTTLE LOOMING BEYOND.
MOMENTS LATER... THE DEATH STAR ERUPTS! MOST OF THE IMPERIAL FLEET--INDEED, THE EMPIRE ITSELF--PERISHES WITH IT. THE DESTRUCTION IS TOTAL...
...EXCEPT, PERHAPS, FOR A FEW TINY VESSELS FORTUNATE ENOUGH TO SOAR FROM THE DREAD-NOUGHT BEFORE IT NOVAS INTO OBLIVION.

NIGHT ON ENDOR! A HUGE BONFIRE BURNS IN THE EWOK VILLAGE, THE CENTERPIECE OF A WILD CELEBRATION, AS REBELS AND THEIR ALLIES REJOICE IN ITS WARMTH.

MUSIC AND LAUGHTER SWELL.

PAST ANTAGONISMS AND MISUNDERSTANDINGS ARE FORGOTTEN.

OLD FRIENDS ARE REUNITED, AS ONE BY ONE THE WARRIORS RETURN...

...EVEN THOSE MOST FEARED FOREVER LOST.

AND IF LATER, WHILE THE REVELRY AROUND THE CAMPFIRE SWELLS, ONE AMONG THEM STANDS APART, HAUNTED, PERHAPS, BY KNOWLEDGE FEW OTHERS CAN EVER SHARE...
...HE IS STILL NOT ALONE.

THERE IS SOMEONE WAITING TO TAKE HIS ARM, TO DRAW HIM TO HER AND THE OTHERS...
...BAC INTO THE CIRCLE OF WARMT AND LOVE.

ADMIRAL ACKBAR ON THE BRIDGE OF HIS MON CALAMARI BATTLE CRUISER

EWOK WARRIOR
(ENDOR)

REBEL B-WING FIGHTER

LUKE SKYWALKER,
THE LAST JEDI

STAR WARS

RETURN OF THE JEDI™

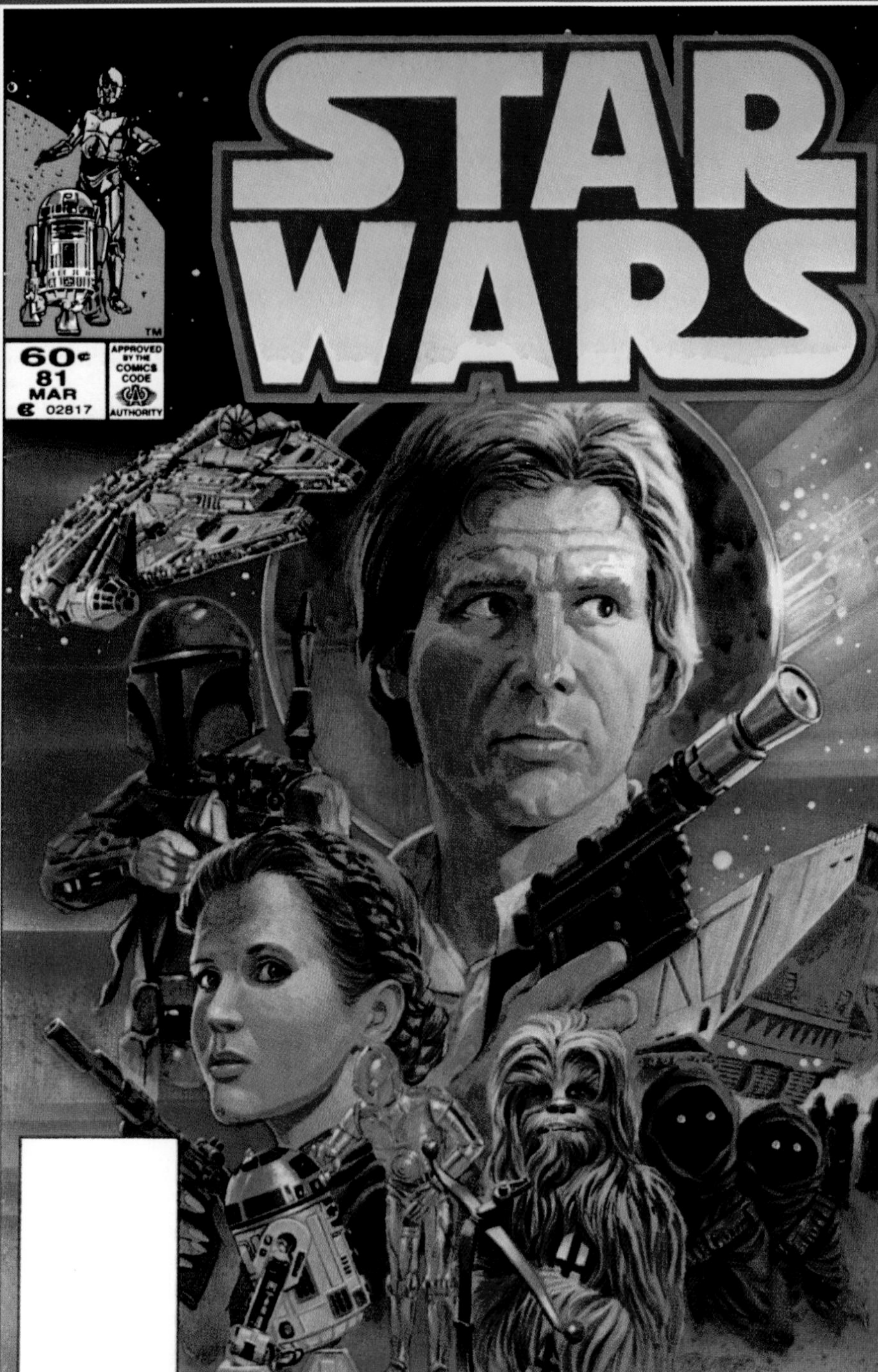
STAR WARS
TM
60¢
81
MAR
02817
APPROVED BY THE COMICS CODE AUTHORITY

JO DUFFY SCRIPT/PLOT RON FRENZ BREAKDOWNS PALMER/MANDRAKE FINISHES JOE ROSEN LETTERER GLYNIS WEIN COLORIST LOUISE JONES EDITOR JIM SHOOTER EDITOR IN CHIEF

YEAH, SOLO, I KNOW IT'S YOU, AND THAT'S EXACTLY WHY THE ANSWER IS NO, AND IT'S GONNA STAY NO. I'VE NEVER MUCH LIKED PIRATES...OR SMUGGLERS...
...OR CORELLIANS ...OR PEOPLE WHO DON'T PAY THEIR DEBTS... AND YOU FILL ALL THOSE CATEGORIES, SO I'M NOT LIKELY TO LEND YOU ANY MORE MONEY.
IN CASE YOU'VE FORGOTTEN, WHICH I HAVEN'T, YOU STILL OWE ME WHAT I LOANED YOU BACK ON HOTH...
IT'S NOT MY FAULT.

YOU MUST HAVE HEARD WHAT HAPPENED AFTER THE EMPIRE ATTACKED OUR BASE ON HOTH. I WAS TAKING ONE OF THE REBEL LEADERS--PRINCESS LEIA ORGANA--TO SAFETY AND THE IMPERIALS CAUGHT UP WITH ME.
I WAS FROZEN IN CARBONITE BY ONE OF THEIR BOUNTY HUNTERS--BOBA FETT. I ONLY JUST GOT FREE...

YEAH...WELL, I HEARD FETT WASN'T WORKING FOR THE EMPIRE. HE WAS WORKIN' FOR AN OLD ENEMY OF YOURS, JABBA THE HUTT, ANOTHER GUY YOU OWED MONEY TO.
AND JABBA WAS NO IMPERIAL. HE WAS JUST A GANGSTER.

BUT HAVEN'T YOU HEARD ABOUT ALL THE GREAT THINGS I'VE DONE SINCE I ESCAPED? I'M A GENERAL NOW...

HEY, IF THE PRINCESS AND OUR FRIENDS AND I HADN'T KNOCKED OUT THE SHIELDING DEVICE HERE ON ENDOR, THEN THE REBEL FLEET WOULD HAVE BEEN BLOWN AWAY BY THE NEW DEATH STAR...
I EVEN LOANED LANDO CALRISSIAN MY SHIP TO FLY WHEN HE DESTROYED THE DEATH STAR...THAT OUGHT TO BE WORTH SOMETHING.
WELL, HOORAY FOR YOU. NO DEAL, SOLO.

IT'S TOO BAD THAT SARLAAC MONSTER ATE FETT AND THE REST OF THEM BACK ON TATOOINE ...OTHERWISE I MIGHT HIRE HIM MYSELF.
THAT'S DECENT OF YOU, PAL ...REALLY CHARITABLE
I PROBABLY COULDN'T SPEND YOUR MONEY ANYWAY. NO ONE WOULD TAKE IT.

GOOD MORNING, HOTSHOT! HOW DOES IT FEEL TO BE ONE OF THE WINNERS FOR A CHANGE?
HUNH? OH, GOOD MORNING, LEIA.
"OH, GOOD MORNING, LEIA!"? CAN'T YOU DO A LITTLE BETTER THAN THAT?

MAYBE LIKE THIS...?
I'M SORRY ...I'VE GOT SOMETHING ON MY MIND, THAT'S ALL.
LIKE WHAT?

LIKE THE FACT THAT GETTING FREED FROM JABBA'S HEAD-QUARTERS, AND HELPING TO OVERTHROW THE EMPIRE ONCE AND FOR ALL HASN'T SOLVED THE REST OF MY PROBLEMS.
WHAT PROBLEMS?
WELL...CASH, TO NAME JUST ONE. A GUY'S GOTTA EAT SOMEHOW, AND I CAN'T SPEND MY REPUTATION AS A WAR HERO.
IF ANYBODY'D EVER TOLD ME THE DAY'D COME WHEN I'D SEE CHEWBACCA THE WOOKIEE CATCHING A NAP WITH A COUPLE OF LITTLE EWOKS, I'D NEVER HAVE BELIEVED HIM!

HAN...MY FAMILY WAS VERY WEALTHY BEFORE OUR WORLD WAS DESTROYED...I COULD LEND YOU SOME CREDITS...
OR THE REBELLION... YOU BELONG TO THE ALLIANCE NOW. THEY COULD ADVANCE YOU SOME...
THAT'S NOT THE POINT!

I ALWAYS MADE IT ON MY OWN BEFORE, AND I INTEND TO NOW.
I DON'T BELONG TO ANYTHING!
EEERRRUF?

HEY, LUKE...WEDGE...DO THESE EWOKS KNOW HOW TO THROW A PARTY OR DO THEY?
THEY DO, LANDO... AND WHY NOT? WE'RE WORTH IT.
DIDN'T YOU AND I SAVE THEM--AND THE REBELLION --BY BLOWING UP THE DEATH STAR?
WITH A LITTLE HELP FROM LUKE, COURSE...
AND A LOT OF HELP FROM CHEWBACCA, HAN AND LEIA, WEDGE.
LEIA, WHERE WAS HAN GOING? IS SOMETHING WRONG?
NO...NOTHING'S WRONG. AND EVERYTHING IS.
THINGS HAVE HAPPENED SO QUICKLY FOR HAN SINCE WE FREED HIM FROM THAT CARBONITE BLOCK...
ALMOST GETTING KILLED BACK ON TATOOINE, AND THEN JABBA AND BOBA FETT AND EVERY-ONE DYING INSTEAD.
AND THE THE LAST BATTLE HERE ON ENDOR, AND THE OVER-THROW OF THE EMPIRE AT LONG LAST...
I DON'T BELONG TO ANYTHING, OR ANYONE.
THAT'S A LOT, IN A SHORT PERIOD OF TIME, RIGHT ON THE HEELS OF FINDING OUT HE'S LOST A BIG CHUNK OF HIS LIFE IN HIBERNATION.
HAN NEEDS A LITTLE WHILE TO ADJUST, THAT'S ALL...
EXCEPT, MAYBE TO HER-- THE *MILLENNIUM FALCON*.
HELLO, BABY.
LANDO SWEARS HE AND CHEWBACCA TOOK GOOD CARE OF HER FOR ME WHILE I WAS FROZEN...
BUT A MAN LIKES TO CHECK OUT SOME THINGS FOR HIMSELF
I REALLY HAVEN'T HAD A CHANCE TO GET REACQUAINTED WITH HER...SINCE I GOT BACK.

DOESN'T SEEM ANY DIFFERENT... I GUESS THEY DID OKAY...
AFTER ALL... LANDO KNOWS WHAT SHE MEANS TO ME... SHE WAS HIS SHIP BEFORE I WON HER FROM HIM IN THAT GAME...
AND CHEWIE'S MY PARTNER... BEEN MY COPILOT FOR YEARS. I CAN COUNT ON HIM...
BUT A MAN STILL LIKES TO SEE FOR HIMSELF...
WELL, I'LL BE--! THEY'RE STILL HANGING HERE... JUST THE WAY I LEFT 'EM. THE DICE I WON HER WITH...
GOOD OL' CHEWIE...
RORF
WHO'S THERE?
GROWR?
CHEWIE? NO, NOTHING'S WRONG, PAL.
I WAS JUST CHECKIN' A FEW THINGS OUT ...MAKIN' SURE THAT EVERYTHING'S...
I'M JUST...
WHAT COULD POSSIBLY BE WRONG...?

I SHOULD HAVE THOUGHT OF THIS SOONER. ENDOR'S NOT THE ONLY PLANET IN THIS GALAXY, Y'KNOW...
THERE'S OTHER MONEY WAITING FOR ME, ON OTHER WORLDS...
WHICH WORLDS, HAN?
TATOOINE, TO NAME JUST ONE. I HAD SOME MONEY THERE, STASHED UNTIL I COULD GET ENOUGH TO PAY OFF JABBA.
AND SINCE HE SENT BOBA FETT AFTER ME BEFORE I COULD PAY 'IM, AND THEN JABBA DIED IN THAT BATTLE, THE SAME TIME FETT FELL INTO THE SARLAAC'S MAW OUT IN THE DESERT...
WELL, IT'S NOT LIKELY ANY OF THEM IS GOING TO COME BY AND TRY AND COLLECT NOW. I FIGURE I'VE EARNED THAT MONEY.
MAYBE YOU HAVE. WHY'D YOU AS ARTOO-DETOO AND ME ALONG?
WELL, MAN NEVER KNOWS WHEN HE MIGHT NEED A DROID--OR A GOOD COPILOT--AND SINCE CHEWIE WANTS TO STAY AROUND AND LEARN ABOUT THE EWOKS' HUNTING TECHNIQUES--
BLIP
BOOP
--AND SEE-THREEPIO HAD TO STAY BEHIND, SINCE HE'S THE ONLY ONE WHO SPEAKS THE LITTLE FURBALLS' LANGUAGE--
YOU TWO WERE ELECTED.
I SEE... AND YOU MAYBE BEING LONELY... OR WANTING OUR COMPANY. MAYBE EVEN LIKING US A LITTLE... HAD NOTHING TO WITH IT?
NOT A THING...
SWEETHEART.

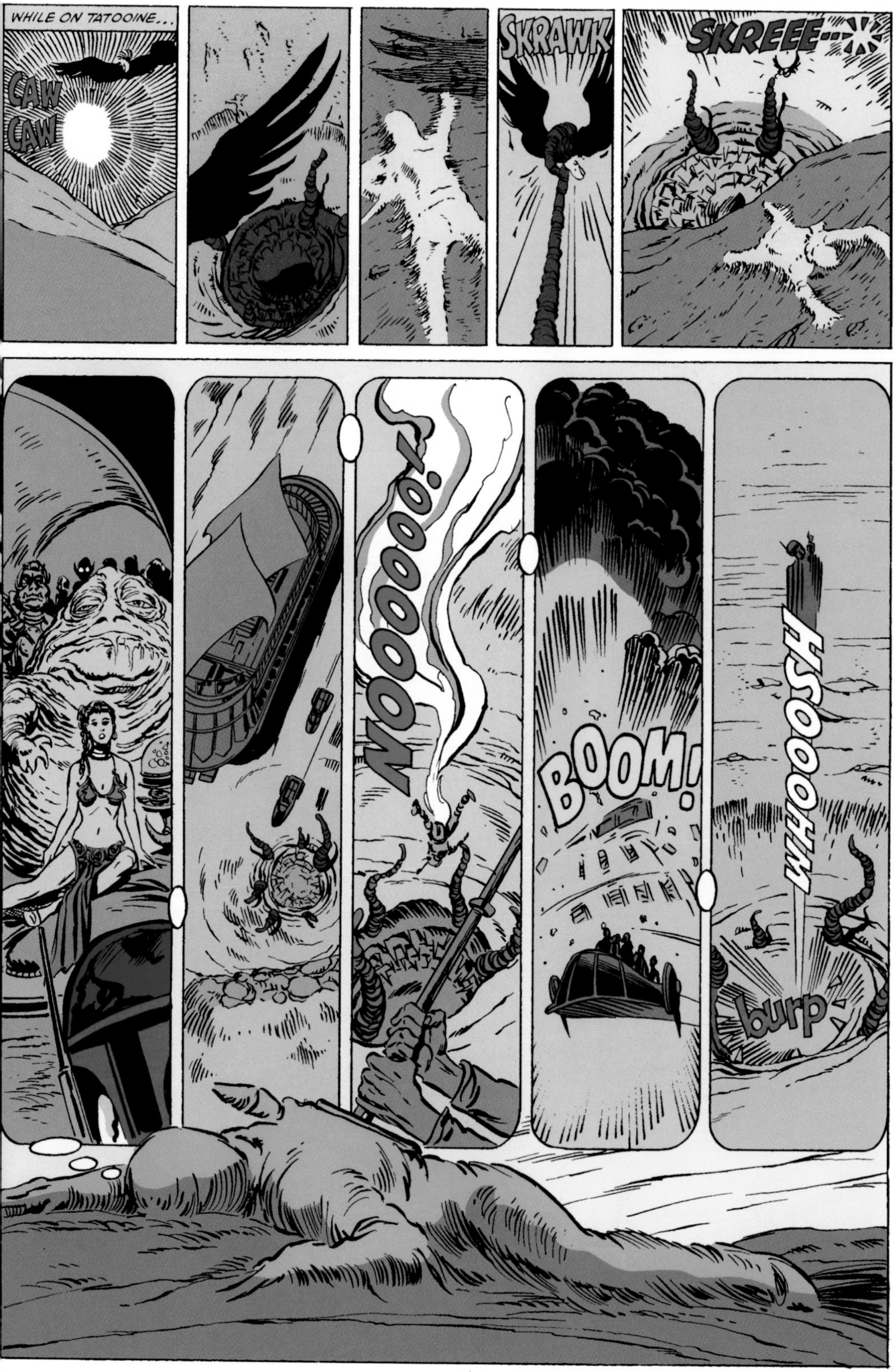

NOOOOOO!

BOOM!

WHOOOSH

burp

YES. I THINK THAT IS A DROID OF SOME SORT... OR A CYBORG ... ALTHOUGH I DOUBT THAT IT IS INTELLIGENT...

I WILL BE ABLE TO JUDGE FOR YOU BETTER, AFTER WE HAVE BROUGHT IT INTO THE SANDCRAWLER AND CLEANED IT.

IT DOES NOT MATTER. JABBA IS DEAD. THE SPOILS OF HIS LAST BATTLE BELONG TO YOU, MY MASTERS. HE WILL NOT COME TO CLAIM THEM.
WE WILL FIT THIS NEW DROID--OR CYBORG--WITH A RESTRAINING BOLT. THEN, IT IS YOURS, TO SELL, OR BREAK DOWN FOR PARTS, OR USE AS YOU WILL.

RRRRR
AAROOO!
UT-UT-UT-UT!
YES, THIS IS MOS EISLEY SPACEPTOR SPEAKING. CLEARANCE TO LAND DENIED, MILLENNIUM FALCON. YOUR PILOT'S NOT WELCOME HERE.
GIVE ME A BREAK, MOS EISLEY! WHO'M I TALKIN' TO, ANYWAY?
GARRICK. WHO'S THAT?
I THOUGHT IT WAS YOU, GARRICK. IT'S SOLO.
AREN'T YOU A PIECE OF SCULPTURE OR SOME-THING?
FUNNY, GARRICK. HA-HA. CAN WE LAND, OR CAN'T WE?
LAST TIME YOU LEFT THIS PLANET UNDER YOUR OWN STEAM, YOU AND CHEWBACCA TOOK OFF WITHOUT PAYING YOUR DOCKING FEES.
WE WERE IN A BIT OF A HURRY. I'LL PAY YOU LATER.
YOU ALWAYS SAY THAT.
HAN... I STILL HAVE A PRIORITY DIPLOMATIC CLEARANCE IN THIS SECTOR. LET'S GIVE HIM MY CODE. YOU CAN STRAIGHTEN THIS OUT LATER.
WELL...
SEE? SOMETIMES DOING THINGS THE NICE WAY GETS RESULTS.
MAYBE... BUT FEEDING GARRICK HIS OWN TEETH WOULD HAVE BEEN MORE SATISFYING.
NOT IF YOU EVER WANTED TO PARK HERE AGAIN. WHAT NOW?
NOW, WE GO SEE THE MONEY MEN...
BABEEP BEEP BEEP?
IF THAT'S A REQUEST TO RECHARGE YOURSELF, ARTOO, THERE'S A POWER SOCKET OVER THERE YOU CAN USE. WE'LL BE BACK SOON.

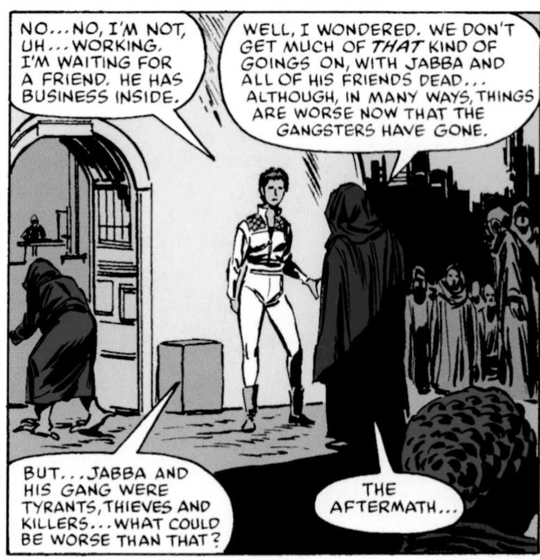
NO...NO, I'M NOT, UH...WORKING. I'M WAITING FOR A FRIEND. HE HAS BUSINESS INSIDE.
WELL, I WONDERED. WE DON'T GET MUCH OF THAT KIND OF GOINGS ON, WITH JABBA AND ALL OF HIS FRIENDS DEAD... ALTHOUGH, IN MANY WAYS, THINGS ARE WORSE NOW THAT THE GANGSTERS HAVE GONE.
BUT...JABBA AND HIS GANG WERE TYRANTS, THIEVES AND KILLERS...WHAT COULD BE WORSE THAN THAT?
THE AFTERMATH...

TAKE THE JAWAS, FOR INSTANCE. THOSE LITTLE SCAVENGERS WERE CLOSE TO STARVING. JABBA HAD RECENTLY PUT THEM OUT OF THE SCRAP METAL BUSINESS...PRETTY FORCIBLY!
THEY LEARNED A FEW OF HIS TRICKS. NOW THAT HE'S GONE, THEY'RE MEAN, AND GREEDY...THEY'VE GOTTEN SO THEY'RE ALMOST AS DANGEROUS AS SANDPEOPLE, IF THEY'RE CROSSED...

AND YOU KNOW WHAT SANDPEOPLE ARE LIKE...
I'M JUST GLAD WE LEFT ARTOO IN THE HANGAR, WHERE IT'S SAFE.
UH, NO...I REALLY DON'T.
WOOT?
WHILE...
WHADDAYA MEAN I CAN'T HAVE MY CREDITS?

THEY'RE NOT YOUR CREDITS. NO ONE CAN HAVE THEM. THAT ACCOUNT IS FROZEN.
WHY?!
BECAUSE, IF YOU MUST KNOW, WE WERE NOTIFIED THAT THAT CUSTOMER HAS BEEN FROZEN.

I AM NOT FROZEN!
I KNOW YOU AREN'T, BUT IT DOESN'T MATTER. YOU ARE NOT MY CUSTOMER.
WHY NOT?!

BECAUSE IF YOU WERE, YOU WOULD BE FROZEN IN CARBONITE.
I WAS. I GOT THAWED OUT!
I'M SORRY. I'M NOT AUTHORIZED TO DEAL WITH CUSTOMERS WHO'VE DONE THAT. YOU'LL HAVE TO TAKE THE MATTER UP WITH THE COMPUTER.

HAN?
HAN, WHERE ARE YOU GOING?
HAN?!
DID YOU GET THE MONEY?
NO, I DIDN'T!

WHY NOT?
HAN, WAIT FOR ME!
WHY BOTHER? WHAT GOOD WOULD IT DO YOU? HAVEN'T YOU HEARD? I DON'T EXIST...
AND I NEED A DRINK!

HEY, JUST WHERE DO YOU THINK YOU'RE GOING?
WITH YOU.

BUT YOU CAN'T GO IN THERE!
WHY NOT? AREN'T WOMEN ALLOWED?
YES... WOMEN ARE,..BUT NOT...
...LADIES.
LOOK, YOU CAN JUST DO WHATEVER YOU'D DO IF I WEREN'T HERE. I'LL DO THE SAME.

SO...THEY REALLY WOULDN'T LET YOU WITHDRAW YOUR CREDITS?
THAT'S RIGHT.
WHY NOT?
'CAUSE SOMEONE TOLD THE COMPUTER I WAS OUT OF CIRCULATION. AND I DON'T KNOW HOW TO ARGUE WITH COMPUTERS...AT LEAST NOT WITHOUT BREAKIN' 'EM...

HAN...
I'M GLAD YOU'RE BACK IN CIRCULATION. REALLY GLAD.

THANKS, LEIA...
I AM, TOO...

MMM... ME, TOO...
ARTOO!
HUNH? WHAT'S HE GOT TO DO WITH THIS?
ARTOO KNOWS HOW TO TALK TO COMPUTERS!
THERE'S NO SIGN OF HIM IN THE SHIP EITHER, LEIA.
BUT... WE TOLD HIM TO WAIT RIGHT HERE.
AND WHAT ARE ALL THESE STRANGE LITTLE FOOTPRINTS ON THE FLOOR?
YOU NOTICED 'EM, TOO, HUNH? I'M HOPING I'M WRONG...
BUT I SUSPECT WE MAY HAVE HAD A VISIT FROM SOME JAWAS.
HEY, GARRICK... YOU BEEN IN HERE WORKING ON THESE LAND-SPEEDERS ALL AFTERNOON?
YEP... ALL THE WORK BUT THE FINE TUNING'S DONE. WHY? WHAT'S IT TO YOU, SOLO?
DID YOU HAPPEN TO NOTICE ANYTHING SUSPICIOUS? MAYBE A SANDCRAWLER? SOME PROWLERS? A HORDE OF JAWAS MAKIN' OFF WITH OUR ARTOO UNIT?
HEY, WHAT DO I LOOK LIKE? AN IMPERIAL *STORM TROOPER?* I MIND MY OWN BUSINESS, AND I DON'T CARE WHAT ANYONE ELSE DOES.

HEY, BUDDY-BOY, HAVEN'T YOU HEARD? THE EMPIRE'S BEEN OVERTHROWN. THE EMPEROR AND HIS TOP GUYS ARE DEAD. IT'S A WHOLE BRAND NEW GALAXY OUT THERE...
PEACE AND LOVE... LAW AND ORDER.
GIVE ME A BREAK! THIS IS TATOOINE.
THE EMPIRE'S NEVER MEANT MUCH TO US HERE, EXCEPT FOR A FEW INCIDENTS THAT NEVER AFFECTED MOST PEOPLE.

MOS EISLEY'S MOS EISLEY. IT'S EVERY MAN FOR HIMSELF HERE, AN' LET THE STRONG SMART ONES HELP THEMSELVES!
THANKS FOR REMINDING ME.. I'D FORGOTTEN WHAT THE REAL WORLD'S ALL ABOUT...

COME ON, YOUR HIGHNESS! LET'S HELP OURSELVES TO THIS GOOD CITIZEN'S PROPERTY--
--TEMPORARILY, OF COURSE!
RIGHT.
HEY!

COME BACK HERE, YOU CREEPS!

NO.

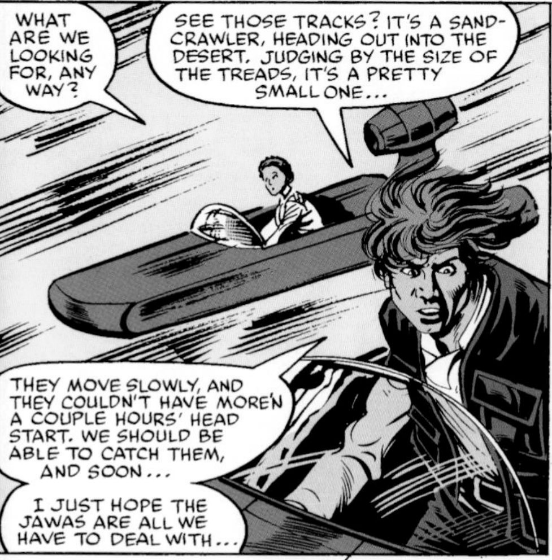
WHAT ARE WE LOOKING FOR, ANY WAY?
SEE THOSE TRACKS? IT'S A SAND-CRAWLER, HEADING OUT INTO THE DESERT. JUDGING BY THE SIZE OF THE TREADS, IT'S A PRETTY SMALL ONE...
THEY MOVE SLOWLY, AND THEY COULDN'T HAVE MORE'N A COUPLE HOURS' HEAD START. WE SHOULD BE ABLE TO CATCH THEM, AND SOON...
I JUST HOPE THE JAWAS ARE ALL WE HAVE TO DEAL WITH...

WHILE INSIDE...
PUHWHEET?
THAT IS CORRECT. YOU ARE WITHIN THE JAWAS' SANDCRAWLER. YOU HAVE BEEN FITTED WITH A RESTRAINING BOLT WHICH MAKES ALL ATTEMPTS AT ESCAPE FUTILE.

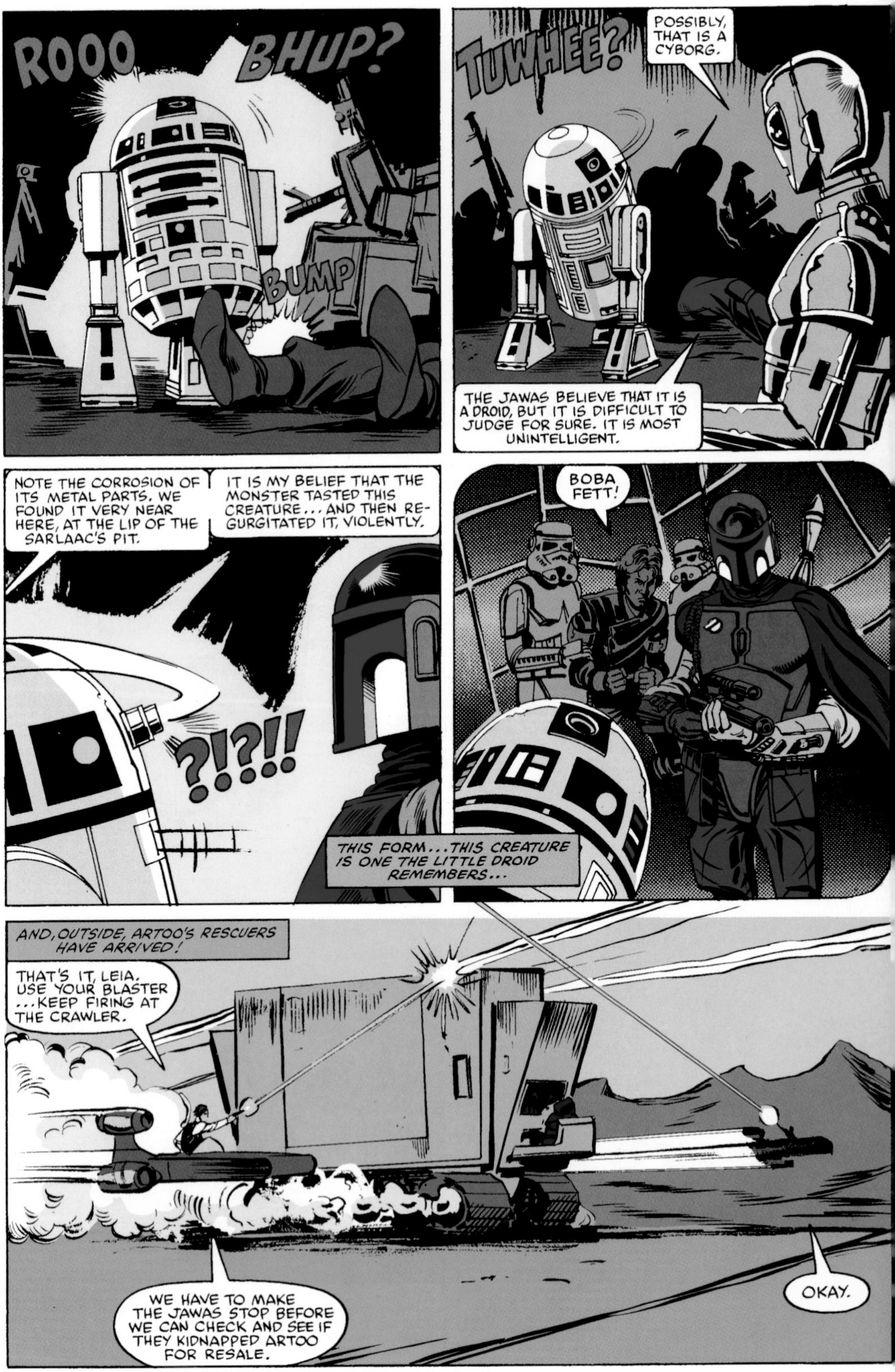

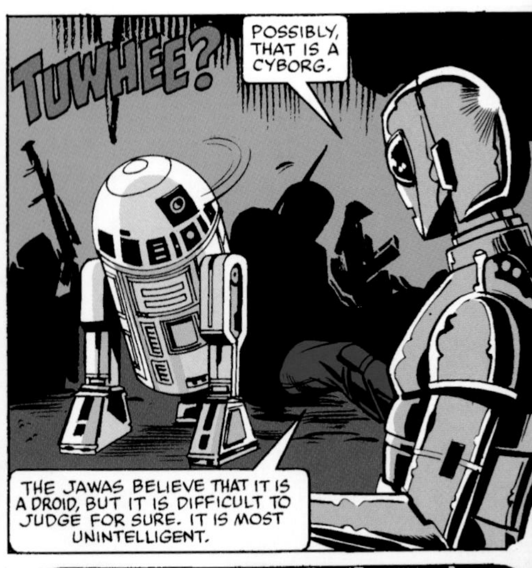

NOTE THE CORROSION OF ITS METAL PARTS. WE FOUND IT VERY NEAR HERE, AT THE LIP OF THE SARLAAC'S PIT.

IT IS MY BELIEF THAT THE MONSTER TASTED THIS CREATURE... AND THEN REGURGITATED IT, VIOLENTLY.

?!?!!

BOBA FETT!

THIS FORM...THIS CREATURE IS ONE THE LITTLE DROID REMEMBERS...

AND, OUTSIDE, ARTOO'S RESCUERS HAVE ARRIVED!

THAT'S IT, LEIA. USE YOUR BLASTER ...KEEP FIRING AT THE CRAWLER.

WE HAVE TO MAKE THE JAWAS STOP BEFORE WE CAN CHECK AND SEE IF THEY KIDNAPPED ARTOO FOR RESALE.

OKAY.

I THINK IT'S WORKING! THEY'RE SLOWING DOWN--OR MAYBE THEY'RE JUST UP TO SOMETHING...
ARTOO-DETOO, CAN YOU HEAR ME?

ARTOO, ARE YOU IN THERE?

WHY, THOSE DIRTY LITTLE...
LOOK OUT, LEIA. THE JAWAS HAVE GOT BLASTERS!
I KNOW! I KNOW!

VROOT!
WHOOP! WHOOP! WHOOP!

HALT. LIKE ALL OF US IN THIS CRAWLER, YOU BELONG TO THE JAWAS NOW.
NO MATTER WHO IS OUT THERE, NO MATTER WHAT THE OUTCOME OF THE FIGHT, YOU ARE GOING NOWHERE.
YYYYA
ZAP

IF YOU DISPLAY TOO MUCH INITIATIVE, THE JAWAS WILL BREAK YOU DOWN INTO PARTS, AND SELL YOU AS SCRAP...
AS THEY DO TO ALL DAMAGED OR DIFFICULT UNITS.

....

?

THIS IS GETTING US NOWHERE.

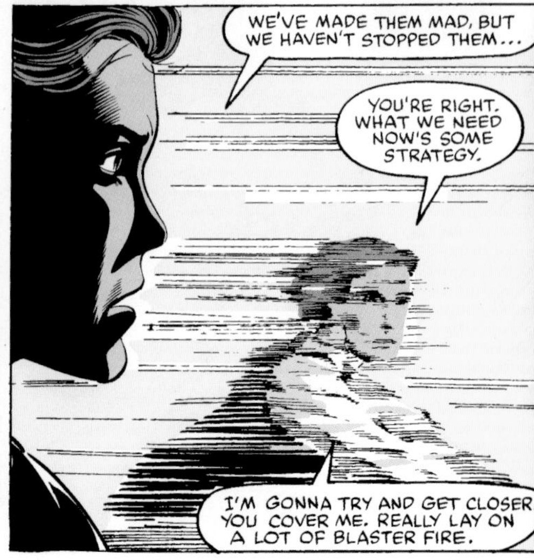
WE'VE MADE THEM MAD, BUT WE HAVEN'T STOPPED THEM...
YOU'RE RIGHT. WHAT WE NEED NOW'S SOME STRATEGY.
I'M GONNA TRY AND GET CLOSER. YOU COVER ME. REALLY LAY ON A LOT OF BLASTER FIRE.

PERFECT. THAT'S JUST WHAT I NEEDED.
BUT, HAN--!
I'M MAKING MY MOVE FOR THAT CRAWLER, NOW!
BUT, HAN...THAT SHOOTING WASN'T ME...IT CAME FROM SOMEWHERE BEHIND US!
VASHT
BOOM
OOOH-OH

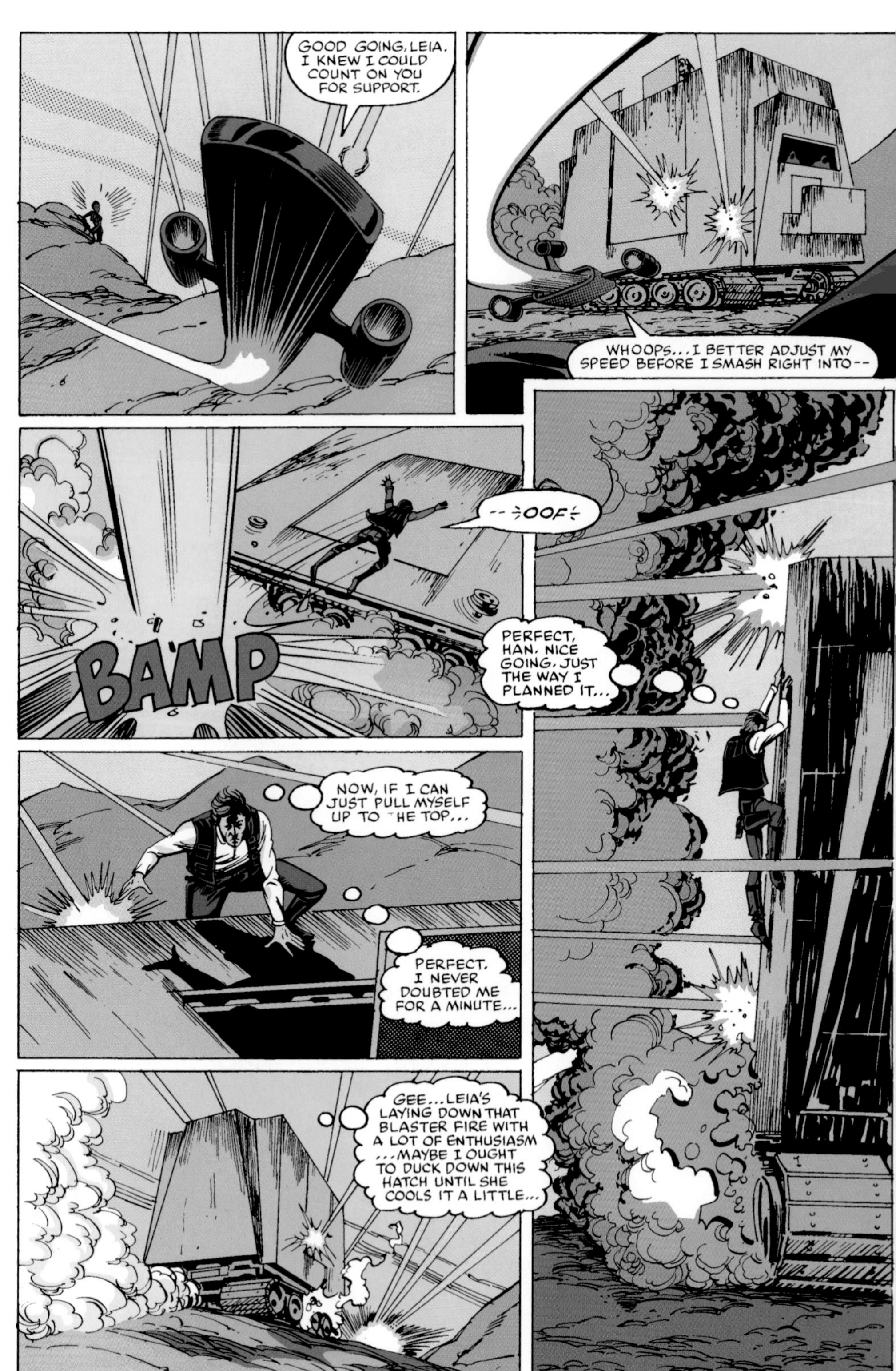
GOOD GOING, LEIA. I KNEW I COULD COUNT ON YOU FOR SUPPORT.
WHOOPS... I BETTER ADJUST MY SPEED BEFORE I SMASH RIGHT INTO--
--OOF--
BAMP
PERFECT, HAN. NICE GOING. JUST THE WAY I PLANNED IT...
NOW, IF I CAN JUST PULL MYSELF UP TO THE TOP...
PERFECT. I NEVER DOUBTED ME FOR A MINUTE...
GEE... LEIA'S LAYING DOWN THAT BLASTER FIRE WITH A LOT OF ENTHUSIASM ...MAYBE I OUGHT TO DUCK DOWN THIS HATCH UNTIL SHE COOLS IT A LITTLE...

ACK
HAN!
DID HE FALL DOWN THAT HATCH, OR JUMP IN? IS HE ALL RIGHT?
WHAT ARE THOSE THINGS?
AND WHAT ARE THEY RIDING?
HAN! HAN SOLO, CAN YOU HEAR ME?
YOU'VE GOT TROUBLE IN THERE. BIG TROUBLE.
YOUR SPEEDER DAMAGED THE SANDCRAWLER'S TREADS... THEY'VE JAMMED--AND IT'S CURVING... RIGHT TOWARD THE SARLAAC'S PIT!
HAN?!
UUUHN WHAT IN...?
BOBA FETT!
KEEP THE ORGANIC INTRUDER COVERED. HE WANTS TO ROB OUR MASTERS.

I... DON'T GET THIS. HOW'D HE SURVIVE THE SARLAAC? AND WHY DOESN'T HE JUST KILL ME. HE'S ARMED!
YOU IN THE SAND-CRAWLER--CAN YOU HEAR ME? YOU'RE IN REAL DANGER!
THAT SAND-CRAWLER IS HEADING INTO THE SARLAAC...
AND THE JAWAS ARE TOO BUSY TO STEER. THEY'RE IN THE MIDDLE OF A PRIVATE WAR WITH SOME ENEMIES...
...WHO RIDE ON GIANT BOVINE QUADRUPEDS...
SANDPEOPLE.

THOSE JAWAS ARE NO FOOLS... THEY'RE ABANDONING THE SAND-CRAWLER...
...NOW THAT THEIR ENEMIES HAVE BEEN ROUTED!

LOOK... I KNOW HOW YOU FEEL ABOUT ME, BUT THE ONLY WAY WE'RE GONNA GET OUT OF HERE IS TEAMWORK. SO I PROPOSE--!
DO I... DID I... KNOW YOU?
HUNH?!?
TELL ME.. PLEASE.
HALLELUJAH!

SURE... LATER. RIGHT NOW, JUST HOLD STILL WHILE I CLIMB BACK UP TO THE HATCH...

NOW, HAND ME THAT ARTOO UNIT... I'LL HAUL YOU UP NEXT...
MAYBE.
ROOP

HAN?!
BE RIGHT WITH YOU!

HAN! HURRY! YOU'RE ALMOST AT THE EDGE! YOU'RE RUNNING OUT OF TIME!
THE JAWAS HAVE ALL DESERTED YOU!
HAN! HAN?!
BLAST IT... I CAN'T LEAVE HIM... NOT WHEN HE'S LIKE THIS, AND HELPLESS... NOT EVEN BOBA FETT DESERVES THAT!
THAT'S GREAT, BUDDY. YOU'VE DONE A REAL GOOD JOB SO FAR. NOW, JUST GIVE ME YOUR HAND AND LET ME PULL YOU UP.
HURRY, OR WE'LL BOTH BE DEAD.
COME ON! WHAT ARE YOU WAITING FOR?
?
HAN, JUMP! HAN!!
H... HAN...?
HAN... SOLO...
HAN, THE CRAWLER IS STARTING TO FALL!
SOLO!!
OH, NO. NOT NOW...

HAN SOLO!
WOULD YOU GET OUT OF THERE BEFORE IT'S TOO LATE?
HEY--!!
BLAST--!
SOLO--!
SOLOOOOOO
SLUUHP
I WOULD HAVE SAVED HIM... I REALLY WOULD HAVE... I TRIED...
I KNOW...
HE JUST WOULDN'T LET ME...
SO MUCH FOR THE BRAND NEW GALAXY.
COME ON. IT'S A LONG WALK BACK TO MOS EISLEY.
BIP!

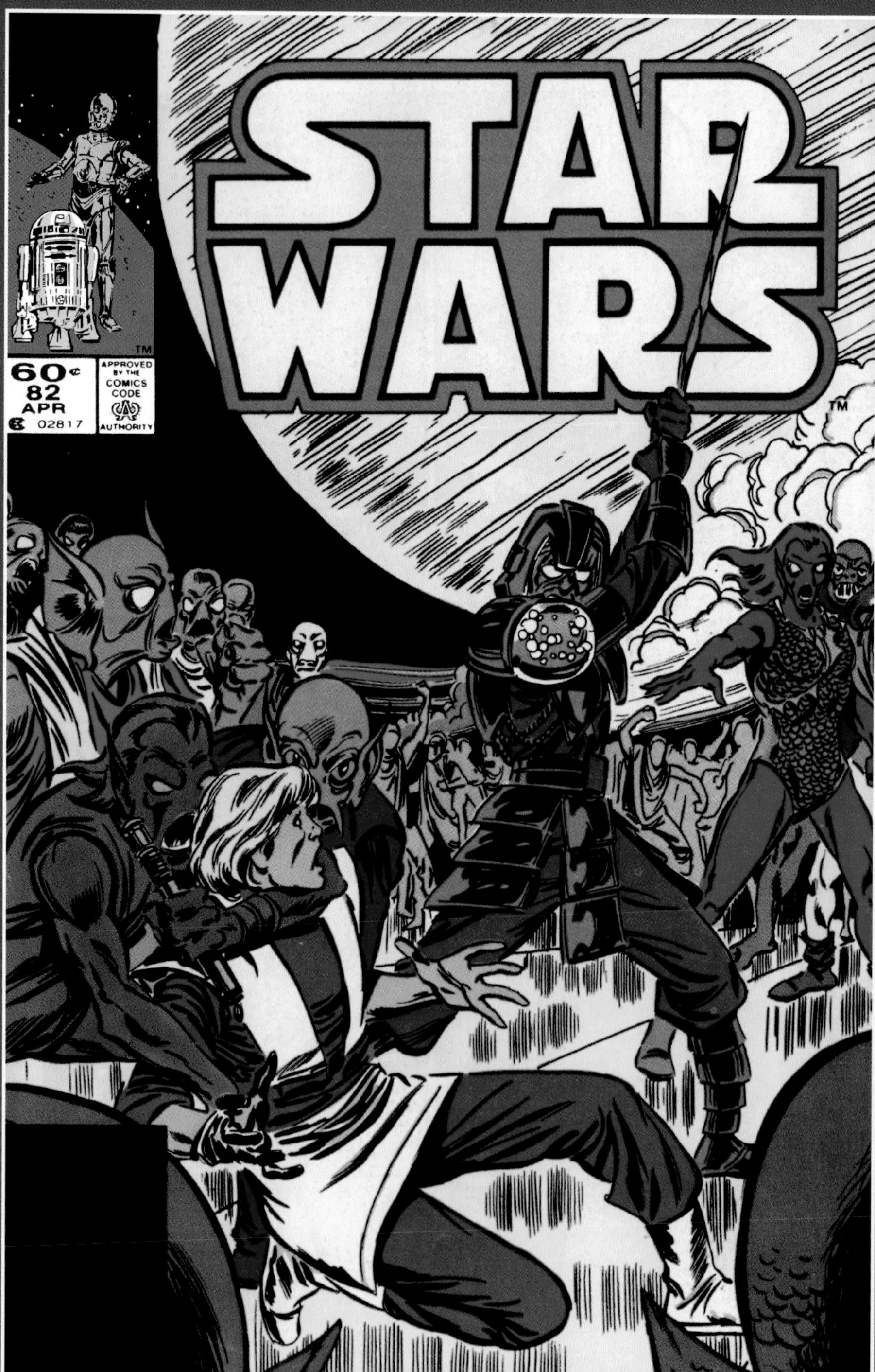
STAR WARS
TM
TM
60¢
82
APR
02817
APPROVED BY THE COMICS CODE AUTHORITY

Lucasfilm PRESENTS: STAR WARS THE GREATEST SPACE FANTASY OF ALL!
JO DUFFY SCRIPT AND PLOT
RON FRENZ BREAKDOWNS
M. HANDS FINISHES
JOE ROSEN LETTERS
GLYNIS WEIN COLORIST
LOUISE JONES EDITOR
JIM SHOOTER EDITOR-IN-CHIEF
GO AHEAD...IF YOU REALLY THINK YOU CAN BEAT ME, GIVE IT YOUR BEST SHOT, AND YOU'D BETTER NOT HOLD BACK...
I'M READY WHENEVER YOU ARE.
DIPLOMACY

I KNOW THEY'RE OUT THERE, SOMEWHERE, GETTING SET TO ATTACK ME...AND THEY HAVE THE ADVANTAGE OF NUMBERS.
I HAVE AN ADVANTAGE, TOO. THEY WON'T BE ABLE TO SURPRISE ME, IF I CONCENTRATE, AND TRY TO...

NO...*TRYING'S* WRONG... IF I JUST FEEL...DO... LET *THE FORCE* GUIDE ME...
NOT ANTICIPATE THE MOMENT, UNTIL IT COMES...

SPROINGG

VASH
RURF!
EYAAH!
RRUFF!

SINCE I CAN'T TAKE OUT THAT ENTIRE ARSENAL IN TIME...
...THE BEST THING TO DO IS TAKE MYSELF OUT OF ITS WAY.
YARP!
HHAH!
VIP
VORP
YAA!
YURF!

OOOOH...?

GRAAF!!
IT'S ALL RIGHT. I'M NOT HURTING WICKET... JUST KEEPING HIM LEVITATED... USING THE POWER OF THE FORCE...

OH... WELL DONE, LUKE... VERY IMPRESSIVE. THERE'S NOTHING LIKE SEEING A GUY BEAT UP A BUNCH OF CUTE LITTLE CREATURES A THIRD HIS SIZE TO GIVE YOU A GOOD IMPRESSION OF HIS FIGHTING SKILLS...
OH... HI, LANDO...

GROONK!
YEAH... CHEWBACCA HAS A GOOD POINT THERE... IS THAT HOW YOU JEDI KNIGHTS ORIGINALLY GOT YOUR REPUTATIONS AS FIERCE WARRIORS...
BY TAKING ON CREATURES LIKE THE EWOKS?
NOW, REALLY, MASTER LANDO, YOU'RE HARDLY DOING MASTER LUKE OR THE EWOKS JUSTICE... WHY, IF YOU'D BEEN HERE ON ENDOR...
DURING THE GREAT BATTLE WHEN WE FINALLY DEFEATED THE EMPIRE, YOU'D KNOW HOW FEROCIOUS EWOKS CAN BE, DESPITE THEIR SIZE...
AFTER ALL... WICKET AND HIS PEOPLE DID HAVE THE GOOD TASTE TO RECOGNIZE ME, A MERE DROID, AS THEIR GOD, UPON OUR ARRIVAL...
I THINK LANDO'S JUST KIDDING US, SEE-THREEPIO...

WELL, I REALLY APPRECIATE THEIR HELPING ME WITH MY LIGHTSABER PRACTICE.
WITH ALL OF THE FIGHTING OVER, AND ALL OF THE JEDI EXCEPT ME GONE, IT WOULD BE EASY TO GET RUSTY WITHOUT CONSTANT TRAINING.

FORGIVE US FOR INTERRUPTING YOU BEFORE YOU WERE THROUGH.
THAT'S ALL RIGHT, ADMIRAL ACKBAR... I'M STILL PART OF THE ALLIANCE, LIKE EVERYONE ELSE, EVEN IF THE REBELLION PART OF IT'S OVER...
WHATEVER YOU NEED ME FOR...

YES... THE END OF THE REBELLION IS WHAT WE ARE CONCERNED WITH NOW... WITH THE EMPEROR'S DEATH... AND THE DEATH OF HIS CHIEF AIDE, DARTH VADER...
AND THE DESTRUCTION OF THEIR GREATEST WEAPON AND MUCH OF THEIR FLEET IN THE BATTLE HERE, THE POWER OF THE EMPIRE IS SERIOUSLY BROKEN.
BUT WHAT REMAINS IN THEIR PLACES POSES A SERIOUS QUESTION...
LUKE... BEFORE THE EMPIRE, THERE WAS THE REPUBLIC. AND HOWEVER DECAYED OR IMPERFECT THE REPUBLIC MAY HAVE BEEN...
HOWEVER TYRANNICAL AND DESTRUCTIVE THE EMPIRE WAS, BOTH SERVED TO UNITE THIS GALAXY.
NOW... THERE IS NOTHING BUT THE REMNANTS ...AND WE WOULD BE AS EVIL AS OUR PREDECESSORS, IF WE SET UP A NEW SYSTEM OF GOVERNMENT, WITHOUT GIVING ALL PEOPLE THEIR SAY.
YOU ARE TO GO FORTH TO MEET WITH THE RULERS OF CERTAIN PLANETS, AND OFFER THEM THEIR CHANCE TO PARTICIPATE IN OUR COUNCILS...

GREAT. WHO'S GOING WITH ME?
WELL, MASTER LUKE... CHEWBACCA FEELS HE STILL HAS MORE TO LEARN FROM THE HOOJIBS AND MORE TO TEACH THEM... AND I'M NEEDED HERE TO TRANSLATE THEIR TONGUE...
AND I THINK THAT WITH PRINCESS LEIA AND HAN AWAY ON TATOOINE, SOMEONE OUGHT TO STAY AND KEEP AN EYE ON HOW THE ALLIANCE IS HANDLING THE AFTERMATH OF THE EMPIRE'S DEFEAT...
SO I'M ALONE?
NOT QUITE.
PLIF!
IT WOULD BE MY VERY GREAT PLEASURE TO ACCOMPANY YOU...

AS SPOKESMIND OF MY PEOPLE, THE HOOJIBS OF ABRA, I FEEL IT'S MY DUTY TO DO WHATEVER I CAN TO HELP YOU IN YOUR DIPLOMATIC EFFORTS.
AFTER ALL, I CAN GO ANYWHERE WHERE THERE'S PURE ENERGY FOR ME TO EAT, AND INTELLIGENT BEINGS TO COMMUNICATE WITH AND LEARN FROM.
THANKS, PLIF.
GOOD LUCK, LUKE... THERE'S AN X-WING SHIP FUELED FOR YOU, AND A FLIGHT PLAN OF THE WORLDS YOU'RE TO VISIT.
THANKS, ADMIRAL... MAY THE FORCE BE WITH YOU HERE UNTIL I GET BACK.
SHALL WE BE OFF?
MIGHT AS WELL...

...THEN, YOU'VE VISITED THIS WORLD--ISKALON--BEFORE?
THAT'S RIGHT, PLIF...NOT TOO LONG AGO, EITHER. WE WERE HERE ON A MISSION, BEFORE WE RESCUED HAN SOLO FROM THE BOUNTY HUNTERS...
IT WAS A BEAUTIFUL, PEACEFUL PLANET, AND I MADE SOME GOOD FRIENDS HERE, BUT...

I...FEEL SOMETHING DREADFUL AND SAD IN YOUR THOUGHTS, LUKE... PLEASE DON'T BOTHER ABOUT ME... IF IT HURTS YOU THAT MUCH, DON'T THINK ABOUT IT...
NO...IT'S ALL RIGHT. YOU'LL SEE FOR YOURSELF AFTER WE LAND, ANYWAY...

WHILE WE WERE HERE, THE EMPIRE BOMBED PAVILLION--ISKALON'S MAIN CITY...
SINCE THE ENTIRE NATIVE POPULACE IS AQUATIC, THAT AMOUNTED TO GENOCIDE...THE FEW SURVIVORS COMPLETELY TURNED AGAINST ALL AIR-BREATHERS, IN SELF-DEFENSE, AS A RESULT...
BARBARIC!
YEAH...

I...DON'T BELIEVE MY EYES!
WHAT'S WRONG...?

SOMETHING I NEVER THOUGHT I'D SEE...
AN OFFWORLD SHIP--AN AIR-BREATHER'S SHIP, BY THE LOOK OF IT--PARKED ON WHAT USED TO BE THE MAIN SECTION OF PAVILLION...

LET'S CHECK IT OUT.
MY DEAR FELLOW, ARE YOU ABSOLUTELY CERTAIN THAT'S WISE?
TRY TO HAVE A LITTLE FAITH, PLIF. WE'RE HERE AS GOOD-WILL AMBASSADORS, AFTER ALL...

I HAVE MY LIGHTSABER WITH ME...
SO, IF YOU THINK ANYONE'S TRYING TO HURT YOU, JUST LET ME KNOW, JUMP FOR THE SAFEST PLACE HANDY AND I'LL HANDLE IT...
VERY WELL...

WELL, IT'S A CORELLIAN SHIP--FROM HAN SOLO'S HOME PLANET--BUT IT LOOKS LIKE THE REGISTRATION MAY BE FORGED...COULD BE A PIRATE OR SMUGGLER, LIKE HAN WAS... THAT'S NORMAL FOR CORELLIANS...
I WONDER WHERE THE CREW GOT TO...

MY... GOOODNESS!
WHAT IS IT, PLIF? WHAT'S WRONG?
SO MUCH... WATER...!

PRETTY AMAZING AFTER THE FORESTS OF ARBRA, ISN'T IT? I KNOW HOW YOU FEEL...
I CAME FROM A DESERT PLANET MYSELF... AND EVERY OCEAN I SEE STILL SEEMS NEW TO ME, AND DIFFERENT AND STRANGE.

YOU!! AT LAST!

A ZELTRON...
YOU CERTAINLY SEEM TO HAVE SOME POWER OVER MEMBERS OF THAT SPECIES
OOF
MMM... ESPECIALLY THIS ZELTRON... SHE'S WHAT YOU MIGHT CALL AN OLD FRIEND.
HELLO, DANI.
LUKE, DARLING!
AVE YOU MISSED E? YOU MUST HAVE! I'VE MISSED YOU...
'M SO SORRY I EFT YOU WITHOUT ANY WARNING!
I LOVE YOU.
I KNOW.
THIS IS PLIF... HE'S A HOOJIB. AND BEHAVE YOURSELF AROUND HIM. HOOJIBS ARE TELEPATHIC.
I'M NOT ASHAMED OF MY FEELINGS FOR YOU...
OR ANY OTHER HUMANOID MALE WHO COMES YOUR WAY...
ALONE OR IN A GROUP, SO LONG AS HE'S STILL BREATHING.
PLIF... THESE ARE DANI'S PARTNERS. THE CORRELLIAN IS RIK DUEL, AND CHIHDO'S THE GREEN ONE WITH THE ANTENNAE...

GOOD TO SEE YOU AGAIN, KID. NO HARD FEELINGS ABOUT YOU TAKIN' OFF WITH DANI, EITHER, SINCE SHE CAME BACK RICHER THAN SHE LEFT.
THAT'S A CUTE LITTLE TOY YOU'VE GOT YOURSELF, THERE.
INDEED? WHAT'S A TOY?

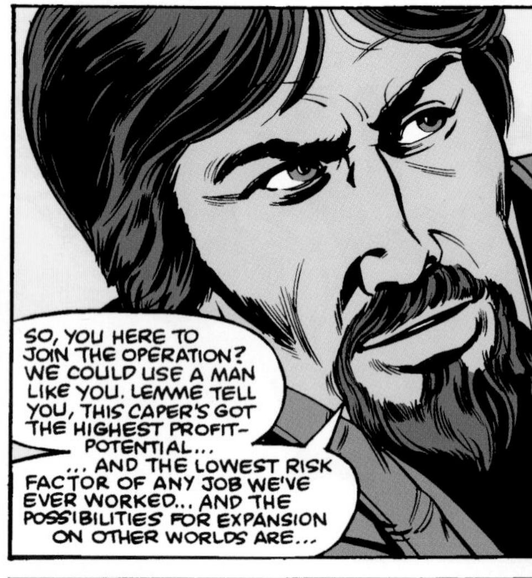
SO, YOU HERE TO JOIN THE OPERATION? WE COULD USE A MAN LIKE YOU. LEMME TELL YOU, THIS CAPER'S GOT THE HIGHEST PROFIT-POTENTIAL...
... AND THE LOWEST RISK FACTOR OF ANY JOB WE'VE EVER WORKED... AND THE POSSIBILITIES FOR EXPANSION ON OTHER WORLDS ARE...

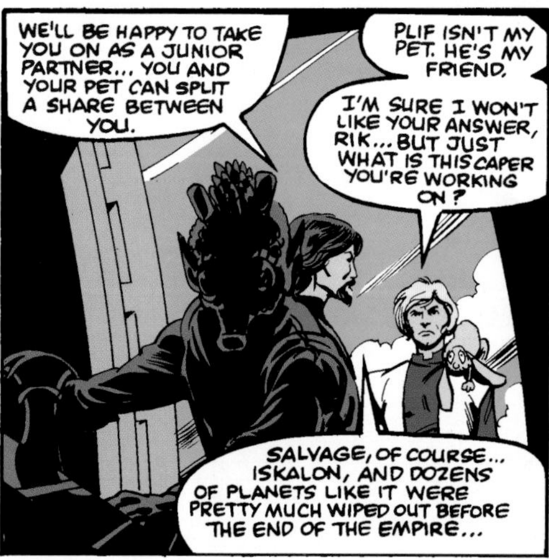
WE'LL BE HAPPY TO TAKE YOU ON AS A JUNIOR PARTNER... YOU AND YOUR PET CAN SPLIT A SHARE BETWEEN YOU.
PLIF ISN'T MY PET. HE'S MY FRIEND.
I'M SURE I WON'T LIKE YOUR ANSWER, RIK... BUT JUST WHAT IS THIS CAPER YOU'RE WORKING ON?
SALVAGE, OF COURSE... ISKALON, AND DOZENS OF PLANETS LIKE IT WERE PRETTY MUCH WIPED OUT BEFORE THE END OF THE EMPIRE...

THAT LEAVES A LOT OF GOODIES, TECH EQUIPMENT AND VALUABLES, JUST LYING AROUND WAITING TO BE CLAIMED...
WE'RE HEADING FOR ISKALON'S TWIN WORLD, GAMANDAR, JUST AS SOON AS WE'VE FINISHED HERE...

THAT'S THE MOST CALLOUS, IMMORAL THING I'VE EVER HEARD OF...
THESE PEOPLE AREN'T IMMORAL, PLIF... THEY'RE JUST SHALLOW, UNIMAGINATIVE, AND OPPORTUNISTIC. OTHER PEOPLE'S TRAGEDIES AREN'T REAL TO THEM...
SO KID, YOU IN, OR WHAT?

RIK... THIS MAY BE HARD FOR YOU TO UNDERSTAND... BUT I'M HERE ON A DIPLOMATIC MISSION. WHAT'S MORE, I WAS HERE ON PAVILLION THE DAY THE EMPIRE DROPPED THEIR BOMB.
HEY, GREAT! THEN THE WAY I FIGURE IT, YOU'RE ENTITLED TO SOME RESTITUTION, HUH?

BELOW...
DO YOU THINK THIS WILL WORK?
IT COSTS US NOTHING BUT A LITTLE EFFORT, IF OUR LEADER'S PLAN FAILS...

THE FOOD IS RICH...AND THE TRAIL WE'VE LAID LEADS RIGHT TO THE SURFACE...
LET'S BE AWAY... BEFORE THE TRAP WE'VE SET CATCHES US...

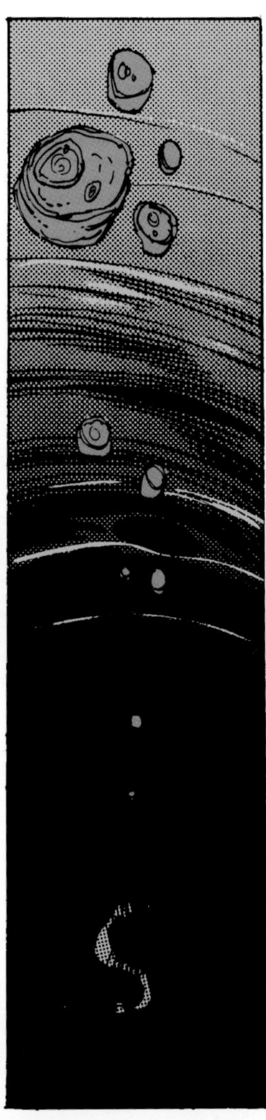

RIK...DANI, CHIHDO...HAVE YOU REALLY THOUGHT ABOUT WHAT IT IS YOU'RE DOING?
AS MUCH AS WE EVER DO, DARLING. I'D THINK YOU'D BE PLEASED.
UNTIL WE GET TO THE RESALE PART OF THE OPERATION, THIS CAPER IS TOTALLY OPEN AND ABOVE-BOARD.
YEAH... SO WHO'S IT HURTING?
THE ISKALONIANS.
AAAAHHHH... FROM WHAT I HEAR, THEY CUT OFF RELATIONS WITH THE SURFACE AFTER THE BIG BLOWUP...

SO THEY AIN'T LIKELY TO NEED THEIR OLD REBREATHING GEAR... AND WHAT DO A BUNCH OF FISH CARE ABOUT ARTWORK?
BUT THIS IS STILL *THEIR* WORLD. WHY CAN'T YOU RESPECT THEIR WISHES, AND STAY AWAY?

DON'T GIVE ME THAT RESPECT JAZZ, YOU LITTLE CROOK... YOU'RE HERE, TOO, AREN'T YOU? YOU AND THAT TOY!
AND DON'T GO TELLING ME YOU'RE HERE ON SOME MISSION FOR THE REBELLION, 'CAUSE I KNOW AS WELL AS YOU DO THAT THE REBELLION'S OVER NOW THAT THE EMPIRE'S FALLEN!
YEAH, IT'S A WHOLE NEW WORLD OUT THERE... YOU GOTTA BE SMART, STRONG, LOOK OUT FOR YOURSELF...
AN' IF A FEW OF A THE LITTLE GUYS WHO CAN'T HACK IT GET EATEN ALIVE...WELL, THEY SHOULDN'T WHINE...
...SHOULD THEY?
THAT'S ALWAYS BEEN THE WAY THINGS ARE, HASN'T IT?
LUKE... THAT MONSTER... IT'S--
I KNOW...

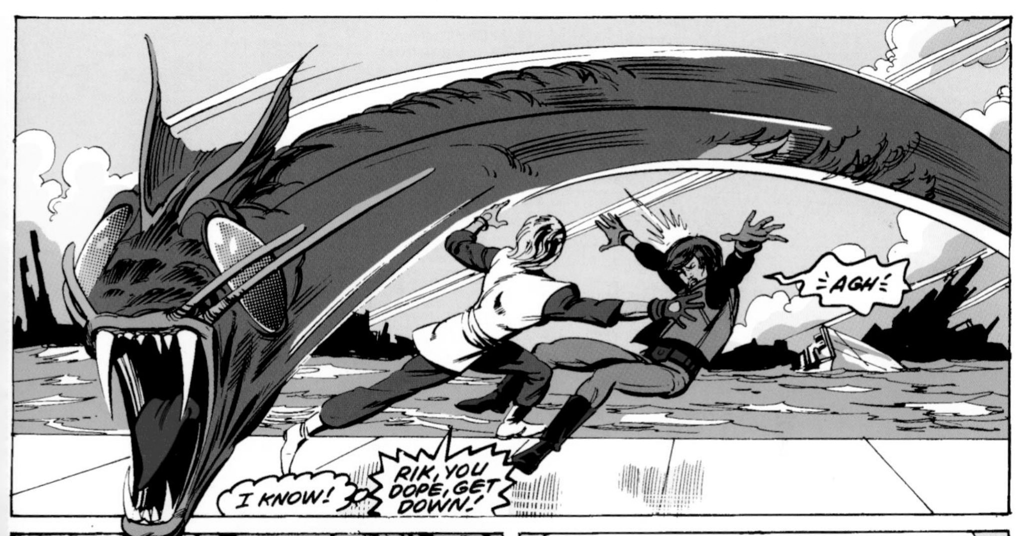

AGH
RIK, YOU DOPE, GET DOWN!
I KNOW!

IT'S CALLED A CHIAKI... IT SHARES YOUR VIEWS ON THE STRONG DEVOURING THE WEAK.
HA HA.

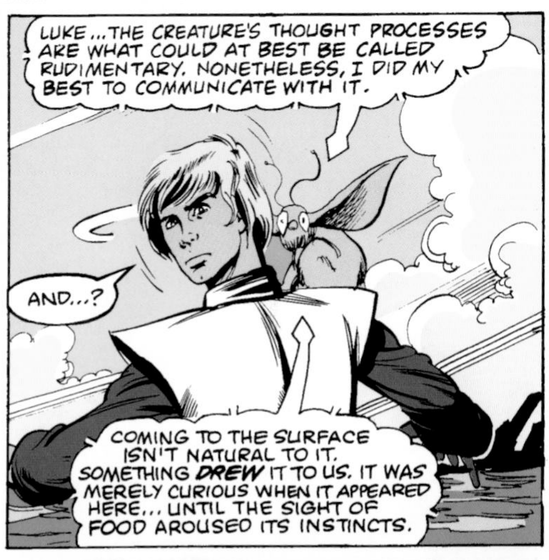

LUKE... THE CREATURE'S THOUGHT PROCESSES ARE WHAT COULD AT BEST BE CALLED RUDIMENTARY. NONETHELESS, I DID MY BEST TO COMMUNICATE WITH IT.
AND...?
COMING TO THE SURFACE ISN'T NATURAL TO IT. SOMETHING DREW IT TO US. IT WAS MERELY CURIOUS WHEN IT APPEARED HERE... UNTIL THE SIGHT OF FOOD AROUSED ITS INSTINCTS.

I SEE.
AND I--!
EH?

DANI! CHIHDO! GET OUT OF HERE!

HOW DID YOU KNOW?!
I DIDN'T KNOW... I FELT, WITH THE FORCE!
EEK!
BUT...WHO ARE THEY?
ISKALONIANS!
SORRY, CHIHDO, BUT I'LL HANDLE THIS BETTER IF I'M NOT DISTRACTED WORRYING ABOUT YOUR SAFETY!
OOOF
DANI, YOU NEVER TOLD US THE KID WAS THAT GOOD.
I NEVER KNEW HE WAS.
LUKE SKYWALKER HAS GROWN A GREAT DEAL, IN MANY WAYS, RECENTLY...
I'M SORRY, YOU GUYS...

I SYMPATHIZE WITH YOU MORE THAN YOU COULD GUESS...
BUT THAT DOESN'T MEAN I'M GOING TO STAND BY AND LET YOU HURT THESE PEOPLE, NO MATTER HOW MUCH THEY DESERVE IT...
OR HURT ME, FOR THAT MATTER.

UH-OH...TWO OF THEM, BEHIND ME, ARE PREPARING TO USE--!

STINGERS!
LET'S SEE HOW THE AIR-BREATHER STANDS UP TO THEIR POWER...

BLAST! THOSE GUNS, MODIFIED FOR UNDER-WATER USE, ARE SHORT-RANGE, BUT TERRIBLY POWERFUL...

STILL MY LIGHTSABER HAS THE POWER TO DEFLECT THEIR FIRE...

LISTEN, ALL OF YOU, I DIDN'T COME HERE TO ROB YOU OR TO FIGHT YOU...
PLEASE, LET'S TALK BEFORE SOMEONE IS HURT UNNECESSARILY.
COWARD! LET'S RUSH HIM!

DO SO, AND YOU PROVE YOURSELVES FOOLS! THE OFF-WORLDER ISN'T CONCERNED ABOUT HIS OWN SAFETY. HE'S WORRIED ABOUT YOURS.

ARE YOU ALL AS MINDLESS AS THE CHIAKI? IF YOU DON'T KNOW OUR ENEMY BY HIS EXCELLENCE... AT LEAST YOU SHOULD HAVE RECOGNIZED THE WEAPON OF LUKE SKYWALKER!
KIRO!

IT'S GOOD TO SEE YOU AGAIN, MY FRIEND. I HADN'T LOOKED FOR YOUR RETURN SO SOON!
WELL, I'VE RETURNED WITH GOOD NEWS. THE EMPIRE IS OVERTHROWN, ITS POWER BROKEN.

YOU THINK THAT IS NEWS TO US? THE ENTIRE SCHOOL HAS KNOWN IT, SINCE THE DAY THESE SCAVENGERS CAME!
US?
LUKE, HOW CAN YOU A WARRIOR AND OUR FRIEND, GO THE WAY OF THEIR KIND? HAVE YOU JEDI KNIGHTS NO HONOR?!
HEY, I'M JUST AN HONEST BUSINESSMAN TRYING TO GET BY.

BELIEVE ME, KIRO, I HAD NO IDEA THEY WERE HERE...THEY HAVE NO RIGHT TO BE HERE, AND NO STATUS IN THE EYES OF OUR PEOPLE...
THEN WHAT BROUGHT THEM HERE?
!
WELL...TO PUT IT IN TERMS OF THE BIOSYSTEMS... AFTER THE PREDATORS COME THE PARASITES AND THE SCAVENGERS.
I RESENT THAT!

I SEE. AND WHY HAVE YOU COME?
MY COMPANION, PLIF THE HOOJIB, AND I ARE REPRESENTING THE ALLIANCE OF FREE PLANETS...
WE'RE HERE TO SEE IF YOUR PEOPLE NEED ANY AID... AND TO INVITE THEM TO SEND A REPRESENTATIVE TO OUR CONGRESS.
EVERYONE IS TO HAVE THEIR SAY IN THE SETUP OF THE NEW INTERPLANETARY GOVERNMENTS AND TRADE SYSTEMS.
AND IF THEY WANT NO SAY?

MONE!
I AM VERY GLAD TO SEE YOU AGAIN, LUKE, BUT YOU MUST NOT REMAIN.
I SEE. I GATHER YOU'VE INHERITED YOUR FATHER PRIMOR'S POSITION AS LEADER OF YOUR PEOPLE.

YES! I SPEAK FOR THE SCHOOL NOW, AND AS THEIR LEADER, I TELL YOU...
YOU MUST GO, NOW. AND TAKE THE OTHER ALIENS WITH YOU.

MONE, I AGREE WITH YOU. THESE THREE SHOULD GO, AND I'LL SEE TO IT THAT THEY DO...
BUT, NOW THAT THE EMPIRE HAS BEEN OVER-THROWN, IT'S NO LONGER NECESSARY FOR YOU TO SHUT YOURSELVES AWAY.
THAT'S WHAT PLIF AND I CAME TO TELL YOU.

THE SCHOOL WILL DECIDE WHAT IS NECESSARY FOR ITSELF. WE NEED NO OUTSIDERS TO TELL US ANYTHING.
LUKE, PLEASE UNDER-STAND... AS THE LEADER, I MUST ALWAYS EXPRESS, AS BEST I CAN, THE WILL OF MY PEOPLE.

MY OWN WISHES AND FEELINGS DO NOT ENTER INTO IT...

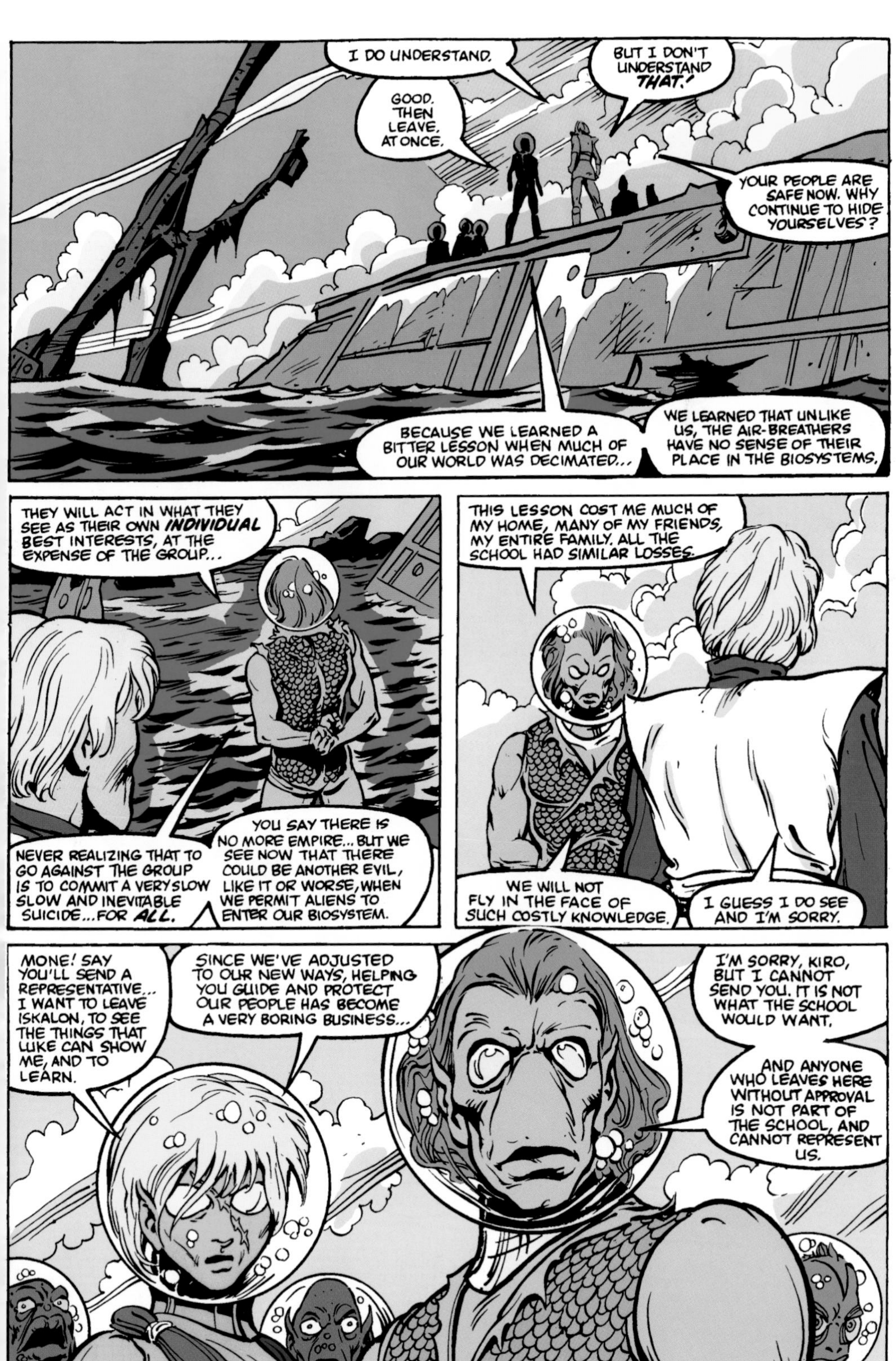
I DO UNDERSTAND.
GOOD. THEN LEAVE, AT ONCE.
BUT I DON'T UNDERSTAND THAT!
YOUR PEOPLE ARE SAFE NOW. WHY CONTINUE TO HIDE YOURSELVES?
BECAUSE WE LEARNED A BITTER LESSON WHEN MUCH OF OUR WORLD WAS DECIMATED...
WE LEARNED THAT UNLIKE US, THE AIR-BREATHERS HAVE NO SENSE OF THEIR PLACE IN THE BIOSYSTEMS.
THEY WILL ACT IN WHAT THEY SEE AS THEIR OWN INDIVIDUAL BEST INTERESTS, AT THE EXPENSE OF THE GROUP...
NEVER REALIZING THAT TO GO AGAINST THE GROUP IS TO COMMIT A VERY SLOW SLOW AND INEVITABLE SUICIDE...FOR ALL.
YOU SAY THERE IS NO MORE EMPIRE... BUT WE SEE NOW THAT THERE COULD BE ANOTHER EVIL, LIKE IT OR WORSE, WHEN WE PERMIT ALIENS TO ENTER OUR BIOSYSTEM.
THIS LESSON COST ME MUCH OF MY HOME, MANY OF MY FRIENDS, MY ENTIRE FAMILY. ALL THE SCHOOL HAD SIMILAR LOSSES.
WE WILL NOT FLY IN THE FACE OF SUCH COSTLY KNOWLEDGE.
I GUESS I DO SEE AND I'M SORRY.
MONE! SAY YOU'LL SEND A REPRESENTATIVE... I WANT TO LEAVE ISKALON, TO SEE THE THINGS THAT LUKE CAN SHOW ME, AND TO LEARN.
SINCE WE'VE ADJUSTED TO OUR NEW WAYS, HELPING YOU GUIDE AND PROTECT OUR PEOPLE HAS BECOME A VERY BORING BUSINESS...
I'M SORRY, KIRO, BUT I CANNOT SEND YOU. IT IS NOT WHAT THE SCHOOL WOULD WANT.
AND ANYONE WHO LEAVES HERE WITHOUT APPROVAL IS NOT PART OF THE SCHOOL, AND CANNOT REPRESENT US.

MONE, I...I--!
GOOD-BYE, LUKE!
PLEASE, GIVE MY REGARDS TO ALL OF THE OTHERS. TELL LANDO... THAT THE MEMORY OF MORE INNOCENT DAYS HELPS ME SOMETIMES.

BUT TELL HIM NEVER TO COME HERE.
RIGHT. SO LONG. TAKE CARE OF YOURSELF.
NICE CHAP. WAS HE ALWAYS SO SAD?

ALL RIGHT, YOU THERE. WE'RE LEAVING. NOW. AND I WANT NO ARGUMENTS.
YOU'RE RIGHT THEY'LL BE NO ARGUMENTS. JUST WHAT MAKES YOU THINK, THAT JUST ON YOUR SAY-SO, WE'LL...
BECAUSE I PERSONALLY DON'T INTEND...
IT'S A FREE GALAXY, AND...

...WE'LL BE READY WHENEVER YOU ARE.
GOOD.

LATER...

LUKE?

HMMM?

ISKALON HAS NO SPACE TRAVEL. WILL THERE BE ROOM FOR ME IN YOUR SHIP?

WHAT IS THAT STRANGE CLOTHING?

IT'S THE TRADITIONAL REBREATHER GARB OF ISKALONIANS TRAVELLERS. THE PLASTICS ARE HIGH-IMPACT, AND KEEP THE WATER CIRCULATING...

THE MORE MODERN SUITS WERE DESTROYED IN THE BLAST--OR CANNIBALIZED BY YOUR FRIENDS...

THEN, THE LEAST THEY CAN DO IS GIVE YOU A LIFT... MY SHIP ONLY SEATS ME AND PLIF, BUT WE'RE ALL HEADING THE SAME WAY ANYWAY...

NEXT ISSUE: STILL ACTIVE AFTER ALL THESE YEARS!

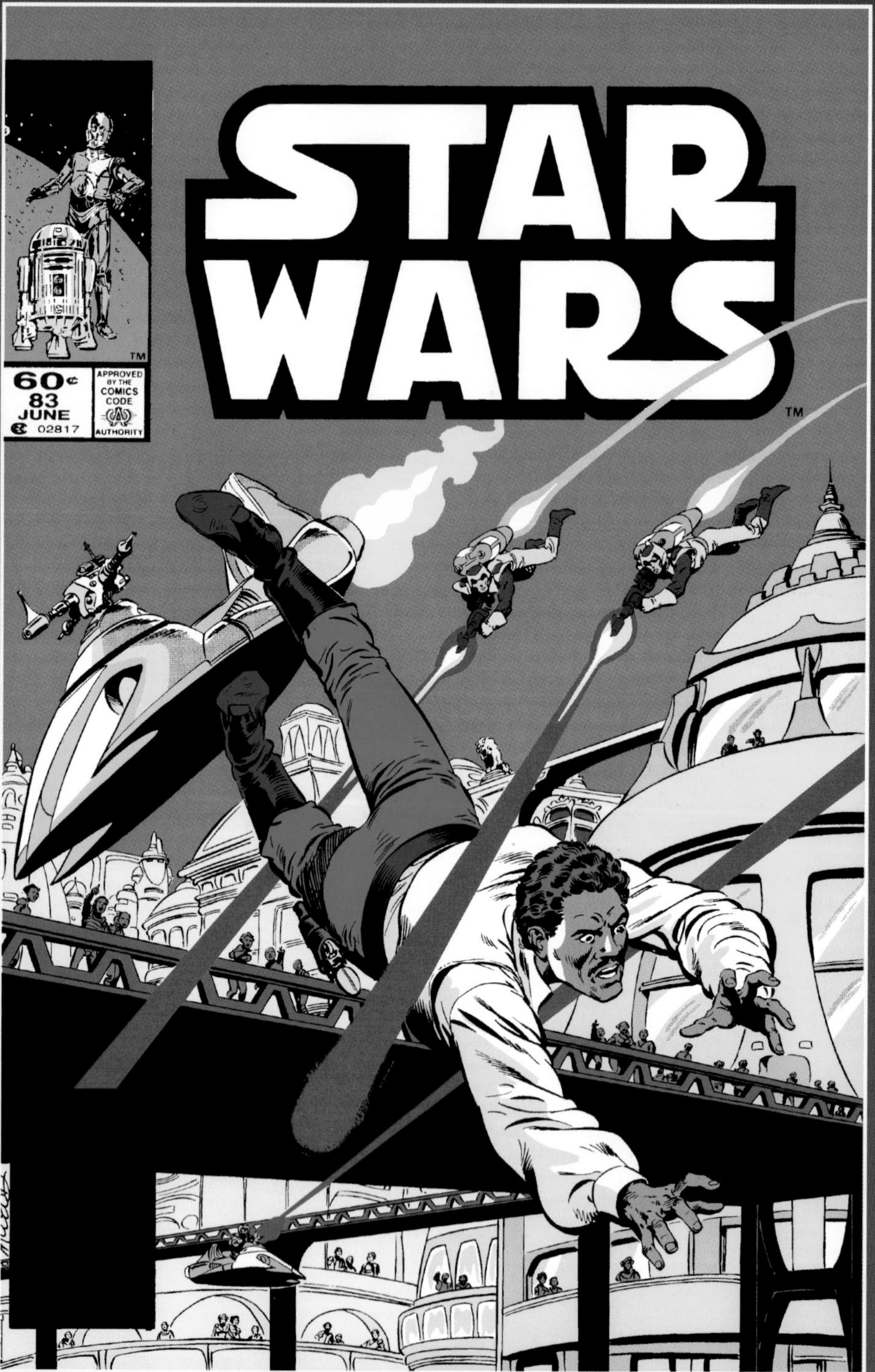

STAR WARS™

LINDA GRANT STORY · BOB McLEOD ART & LETTERING · GLYNIS WEIN COLORING · LOUISE JONES EDITOR · JIM SHOOTER EDITOR-IN-CHIEF

LOOK OUT!
THAT LAST BLAST DISABLED THE SLED!
JUMP BEFORE IT DRAGS US DOWN!
GRAB HOLD OF ME!
A LOT OF GOOD THIS WILL DO US--
--EXCEPT MAKE SURE WE CRASH TOGETHER ON THE ROCKS BELOW!
JUST HANG ON.
SATISFIED? REMINDS ME OF A TIME ON CALTINIA--
HOW CAN YOU REMINISCE WHEN WE'RE DANGLING HERE LIKE A COUPLE OF SITTING DUCKS!?
YOU SHOULD TALK. SO FAR YOU'VE BEEN NOTHING BUT A LIABILITY!
WELL, PARDON ME.
MIND IF I BORROW YOUR BLASTER?
HELP YOURSELF... AND MAKE IT GOOD!
NO PROBLEM.
I'M ALWAYS GOOD.

THAT'S STRANGE. ONE LUCKY SHOT SCARED THEM OFF.
"LUCKY?!"

I TAKE IT BACK.
DID YOU PUT THAT BLASTER AWAY YET?

ALLOW ME TO ASSIST YOU.
YOU OR PRINCESS DANU MIGHT SLIP AND HAVE A NASTY ACCIDENT.

FRIEND OF YOURS, DANU?
HE'S THE COMMANDER OF THE ROYAL GUARD.
WHAT ARE YOU DOING HERE, HARLECH?
PROTECTING YOU. QUEEN SARNA'S SPIES WARNED HER THAT REVOLUTIONARIES PLANNED TO AMBUSH YOU.
REVOLUTIONARIES? ATTACKED US?
THAT SURPRISES YOU? THOSE RUTHLESS INSURGENTS WANT TO OVERTHROW YOUR SISTER'S GOVERNMENT. WHY WOULDN'T THEY WANT TO ASSASSINATE YOU--A MEMBER OF THE ROYAL FAMILY?
LET'S NOT DELAY. THE QUEEN ANXIOUSLY AWAITS OUR VISITOR.

THE CITADEL TOWERS MAJESTICALLY OVER DROGHEDA'S RUGGED LANDSCAPE. REACHABLE ONLY BY SKY-SLED, THIS FORTRESS IS VIRTUALLY IMPREGNABLE.
WATCH YOUR STEP WITH HARLECH--HE MAY BE MY SISTER'S CLOSEST CONFIDANT--BUT I DON'T TRUST HIM.
I'M HERE AT YOUR SISTER'S REQUEST--NOT TO GET INVOLVED IN YOUR PETTY INTRIGUES.
BUT THANKS FOR THE WARNING. I'LL KEEP IT IN MIND.

SORRY ABOUT RETURNING HERE?
NOT AT ALL. I'VE OFTEN WONDERED ABOUT SEEING YOUR SISTER AGAIN. SHE'S NOT EASY TO FORGET.
BESIDES, I NEEDED AN EXCUSE TO LEAVE ARBRA AND DO SOME TRAVELLING.
MUST BE NICE. I'VE NEVER BEEN ANYWHERE BUT DROGHEDA.

SHORTLY, IN THE QUEEN'S THRONE ROOM...
WELCOME, LANDO. PLEASE RISE.
THE REST OF YOU MAY LEAVE. I'D LIKE TO ADDRESS OUR GUEST IN PRIVATE.

YOU TOO, DANU. THIS DOESN'T CONCERN YOU.

IT'S WONDERFUL SEEING YOU AGAIN. I WAS HEARTBROKEN WHEN MY FATHER FORCED YOU TO LEAVE DROGHEDA. OF COURSE, I COULDN'T BLAME HIM--NOT AFTER HE LEARNED THAT YOU INTENDED TO WORM YOUR WAY INTO THE FAMILY MINING BUSINESS-- AND OUR FORTUNE--BY MARRYING ME!
BE FAIR. YOU KNOW THE MINING BUSINESS WASN'T THE ONLY ATTRACTION FOR ME.

NOW, SARNA, WHY DID YOU SEND FOR ME?
NOT JUST TO TALK OVER OLD TIMES.
YOU'RE RIGHT. LET'S TAKE CARE OF BUSINESS FIRST. WE'LL HAVE PLENTY OF TIME LATER TO GET REACQUAINTED.

SINCE MY FATHER'S DEATH, I'VE RULED DROGHEDA THE BEST I CAN.
I'VE ALWAYS PUT THE WELFARE OF MY PEOPLE ABOVE EVERYTHING ELSE.

NOW A BAND OF REVOLUTIONARIES IS TURNING THE PEOPLE AGAINST ME. THEY ACCUSE ME OF BEING CORRUPT AND WANT TO DEPOSE ME!
MY SPIES HAVE LEARNED THAT THESE REVOLUTIONARIES HAVE TIES WITH THE EMPIRE. I WOULDN'T WANT TO SEE DROGHEDA'S RESOURCES USED TO RESURRECT THE EMPIRE.

YOU'VE GOT TO QUELL THIS REVOLUTION, LANDO.
WHY ME? HARLECH SEEMS CAPABLE ENOUGH.
BUT YOU'RE A REBELLION HERO.

AND THE REWARDS WILL BE... AMPLE...

HMMM...
SOUNDS LIKE A GOOD CAUSE. LADY, YOU'VE GOT YOURSELF A DEAL.

I KNEW YOU WOULDN'T LET ME DOWN!

MMM. I'D LIKE TO TRY THAT AGAIN.
DON'T TELL ME YOU NEED PRACTICE!
WE'LL TALK MORE LATER AFTER YOU'VE RESTED.

LADRA, SHOW OUR GUEST TO HIS QUARTERS.

THAT'S THAT.

NICE PERFORMANCE.
YOU LITTLE SNEAK! HOW DARE YOU EAVESDROP!

I'M JUST INTERESTED.
THAT'S A SWITCH! YOU'VE NEVER SHOWN ANY INTEREST IN THE FAMILY BUSINESS OR MY PROBLEMS.
OH, NOT THAT! LANDO! HE'S MORE ATTRACTIVE THAN I REMEMBERED.
HAVING HIM AROUND WILL BE FUN.

YOU'RE INFURIATING, DANU! DON'T YOU REALIZE I'VE GOT A CRISIS ON MY HANDS?
REALLY? WHAT?
WHILE THE REVOLUTIONARIES CONTROL THE MOUNT MERU MINE WE'RE LOSING MONEY DAILY--AND I'M BEING MADE TO LOOK LIKE A FOOL!
OH, THAT IS SERIOUS!

WATCH YOUR STEP, DANU!
AND ANOTHER THING--LANDO S HERE TO QUELL HE REVOLUTION--VOT TO HAVE A GOOD TIME. DON'T DISTRACT HIM!

ALL RIGHT, I GET THE MESSAGE.
ANYTHING I CAN DO TO HELP YOU?

THAT'S BETTER.
TOMORROW LANDO WILL LEAD AN ATTACK TO DRIVE THE REVOLUTIONARIES FROM MOUNT MERU. STAY WITH HIM. I'LL EXPECT A COMPLETE REPORT WHEN YOU RETURN.

AND DANU--DON'T GO NEAR LANDO UNTIL TOMORROW.
DON'T WORRY, SARNA, I'LL BEHAVE MYSELF. AT LEAST UNTIL THE CRISIS IS OVER. THEN I'M REALLY GOING TO PARTY!

BUT, I DOUBT THAT YOU, DEAR SISTER, WILL HAVE REASON TO CELEBRATE.

THE NEXT DAY AT MOUNT MERU MINE...
THIS IS FOLLY! THE REVOLUTIONARIES WILL CUT US DOWN BEFORE WE CAN REACH THE ENTRANCE!
YOU'D BE RIGHT, HARLECH--IF WE WERE GOING THROUGH THE FRONT DOOR.
GUARDS, TAKE COVER AND STAY OUT OF SIGHT. WHEN THE REVOLUTIONARIES LEAVE THE MINE, ROUND THEM UP. BUT DON'T HARM THEM. I WANT THEM CAPTURED--NOT MASSACRED.
HARLECH, FOLLOW ME.
I LOVE WATCHING A MASTER STRATEGIST AT WORK. WHERE ARE WE GOING?
I'M BETTING THE REVOLUTIONARIES WERE CLEVER ENOUGH TO PROVIDE THEMSELVES WITH AN EMERGENCY EXIT.
I STUDIED MAPS OF THIS AREA LAST NIGHT AND MADE SOME CALCULATIONS. I FIGURE IF THIS MINE HAS A BACK DOOR, IT SHOULD BE RIGHT ABOUT...
...HERE!
HMPH! LUCKY GUESS.
UH-UH. THAT'S AN EDUCATED GUESS.
THANKS FOR THE VOTE OF CONFIDENCE--I THINK.
STAY HERE. I CAN SNEAK IN EASIER WITHOUT AN ENTOURAGE
I HOPE. TOO BAD HARLECH GIVES ME THE CREEPS. I MIGHT NEED HIM

A SHORT DISTANCE WITHIN THE MINE...
DIDN'T EXPECT TO GET THIS FAR WITHOUT SOME OPPOSITION. THE REVOLUTIONARIES OBVIOUSLY AREN'T EXPECTING TROUBLE FROM THIS DIRECTION.
WATER TANKS! WHAT EVERY GOOD MINE NEEDS-- AND JUST WHAT I EXPECTED. BLOWING THOSE TANKS'LL TRIGGER ONE HECK OF A FLOOD!
WITH ONLY ONE TUNNEL DUG IN THIS NEW MINE, IT OUGHT TO WASH THE REVOLUTIONARIES RIGHT INTO THE GUARD'S ARMS!

WHAT'S THAT? OH BOY.

STEP AWAY, CALRISSIAN. AND HANDS OFF YOUR BLASTER.
WE DON'T WANT TO WASTE YOU--OR YOUR TALENTS--UNLESS WE HAVE TO.

NO DEAL. STEP BACK, PAL.
OR I BLOW THE TANKS...WITH MY HANDY REMOTE DETONATOR.

I'LL TAKE HIM!
A HERO IN EVERY CROWD!
LOOK OUT! THE DETONATOR!

THE DETONATOR? THEY ACCIDENTALLY TRIGGERED--

HIT THE DIRT!!

SO MUCH FOR THOSE FILTHY INSURGENTS! CALRISSIAN DID KNOW WHAT HE WAS DOING!
WHAT ABOUT HIM?
BWOOMM
HE CAN TAKE CARE OF HIMSELF. IF NOT, TOO BAD.
LET'S RETURN TO THE FRONT OF THE MINE-- AND DEAL WITH ANY SURVIVORS.

SOMEBODY, HELP ME! GASP
KEEP YOUR HEAD UP, LUGUS. I'M TRYING TO REACH YOU.
GRAB THIS ROCK IF YOU CAN.

THEY EMERGE BADLY SHAKEN, BUT STILL ALIVE.

THEN...
WATCH OUT!
GET BACK INSI--!

WHAT ARE YOU DOING? I SAID NO KILLING!

YOU'LL DIE WITH THE REST OF THEM!
:GULP: UH, I'M ON YOUR SIDE, REMEMBER?

HOLD ON! IT'S ME-- LANDO!
OH. I NEVER DID GET A GOOD LOOK AT YOU.

NO DISRESPECT, SIR--BUT MAYBE YOU SHOULD WEAR A UNIFORM FROM NOW ON.

HOLD YOUR FIRE! NO MORE KILLING!
LANDO! YOU'RE ALIVE?!
BARELY.
HARLECH, YOUR MEN DISOBEYED MY ORDERS.
WHY?
OVERZEALOUSNESS, CALRISSIAN--BROUGHT ON BY GRIEF FROM LOSING THEIR COMMANDER IN THE EXPLOSION, NO DOUBT...
NO DOUBT.
AT LEAST YOU'RE OKAY. THAT'S THE IMPORTANT THING.
I WON'T BE OKAY UNTIL I GET SOME ANSWERS.
HARLECH, GIVE THE DEAD DECENT BURIALS
OH, YES... SIR.
I'LL GET TO THE BOTTOM OF THIS...

"...BACK AT THE CITADEL."
WHERE ARE YOU TAKING THAT PRISONER? I INSIST THAT HE BE GIVEN TO MY INTERROGATORS.
NO THANKS. I REMEMBER YOUR FAMILY'S METHOD OF INTERROGATING. I'LL HANDLE THIS MY WAY.

I WON'T HURT YOU. I JUST WANT SOME INFORMATION.
YOU WON'T GET IT.
STRAIGHTEN ME OUT ABOUT THE POLITICAL SITUATION ON DROGHEDA. WHAT'S THE PICTURE?

WHAT DOES IT TAKE TO GET YOUR TRUST? THIS?
WHO TIPPED YOU OFF THAT THE MINE WOULD BE ATTACKED TODAY? YOU WERE EXPECTING ME, RIGHT?

HA! REALLY THINK YOU CAN PRY ANSWERS OUT OF A MAN WITH A LOADED BLASTER IN HIS HAND?

LISTEN! AM I ON THE WRONG SIDE IN THIS WAR? SARNA GIVES YOU REVOLUTIONARIES A BLOODTHIRSTY REP.-- BUT HER BOYS SHOW A REAL FLAIR FOR SLAUGHTER. OR IS EVERYONE ON THIS PLANET HOMICIDAL?
FILL ME IN ON THE REVOLUTION.
NOW THAT THE EMPIRE'S BEEN DEFEATED, ALL THE PEOPLE WANT IS--
AAH!
TCHOW

YOU... IDIOT...!
HE HAD A BLASTER ON YOU. I ASSUMED YOU NEEDED HELP!
THE BLASTER WAS EMPTY!
DEAD. BLAST IT! YOU HAD NO RIGHT TO INTERFERE.
OH, NO. DAR--
CLEAN UP YOUR DIRTY WORK, HARLECH. I'LL DEAL WITH YOU LATER.
LANDO! WAIT!
LEAVE ME ALONE, DANU. I'M FED UP WITH ALL OF YOU.
DON'T TAKE THIS OUT ON ME. I'M UPSET ABOUT WHAT JUST HAPPENED, TOO.
DID YOU KNOW HIM?
N-NO, WHY?
I THOUGHT YOU STARTED TO SAY HIS NAME...
WHERE ARE YOU GOING?
SOMEWHERE... ANYWHERE BUT HERE.

LATER...
LET'S ADD THINGS UP.
ONE--SOMEONE ARRANGED AN ATTACK ON MY ARRIVAL.
TWO-- THE REVOLUTIONARIES IN THE MINE WERE WAITING FOR ME. SOMEONE TIPPED THEM OFF.
THREE--IT'D HAVE TO BE SOMEONE CLOSE TO THE THRONE...SOMEONE WILLING TO TOPPLE THE ROYALTY.

HARLECH! THAT WOULD EXPLAIN WHY HE'D KILL A PRISONER WHO'S STARTING TO TALK.

YOU MISSED THE ACTION TODAY. WE WIPED OUT ANOTHER BATCH OF REVOLUTIONARIES.
GOOD! IF WE DON'T NIP THIS DEMOCRACY NONSENSE IN THE BUD, WE'LL ALL BE OUT OF WORK!

DEMOCRACY!?

SARNA, I'M FIGHTING A DEMOCRACY?
YOU CAN'T BARGE IN HERE UNANNOUNCED! WHO DO YOU THINK YOU ARE?
DON'T PULL ROYALTY ON ME!

YOU'VE BEEN LYING TO ME EVER SINCE I GOT HERE.
WHY DIDN'T YOU TELL ME THE PEOPLE WANT SELF-RULE?
OH.

THAT SHOULDN'T MATTER. BESIDES, YOU'LL STILL BE IN ON THE PROFITS-- I'LL EVEN INCREASE YOUR SHARE!
I MAY BE MERCENARY, BUT SINCE I JOINED THE REBELLION, I'VE EARNED A LOT OF PEOPLE'S RESPECT-- I'M NOT THROWING ALL THAT AWAY ON YOU!
FIND YOURSELF ANOTHER SUCKER. I'M LEAVING.
CONGRATULATIONS!
YOU JUST BECAME DANGEROUS.
SNAP
BUT I'M NOT ALONE! HARLECH-- WE'RE ON THE SAME SIDE NOW!
HAVE YOU LOST YOUR MIND, CALRISSIAN? ANY ENEMY OF THE QUEEN'S IS AN ENEMY OF MINE!
CUT THE PRETENSE, HARLECH! I FIGURED OUT THAT YOU'VE BEEN SPYING FOR THE REVOLUTIONARIES!
YOU... ACCUSE ME?! I'VE DONE NOTHING BUT EXECUTE QUEEN SARNA'S ORDERS.
I GUESS I OWE YOU AN APOLOGY, BUT THIS WILL HAVE TO DO!
STOP HIM!
DON'T WORRY! HE WON'T GET FAR!
SEEMS I'M ALWAYS LEAVING DROGHEDA IN A HURRY!

HAVE TO LOSE THEM AND REACH THE SKY-SLEDS...
...THEN FLY BACK TO MY SHIP AND--

--WHA--WHO'S--?

COULDN'T TRUST YOU BEFORE, LANDO-- BUT YOU'RE ON OUR SIDE NOW WHETHER YOU LIKE IT OR NOT.
"OUR SIDE?"

I'M THE REVOLUTIONARIES' CONTACT IN THE PALACE.
THEY CAN HEAR EVERYTHING SAID IN MY PRESENCE VIA THIS CRYSTAL TRANSMITTER.

I WARNED THEM YOU'D BE GOING IN THE BACK OF THE MINE. THAT'S WHY THEY WERE READY FOR YOU.
THE ATTACK WHEN I ARRIVED-- DID YOU ARRANGE THAT, TOO?
UH-UH. SARNA DID. THOSE WERE HER MEN-- A PLOY TO DISCREDIT THE REVOLUTIONARIES IN YOUR EYES.
WE HAVE TO GET OUT OF HERE-- THIS MUNITIONS ROOM IS WIRED TO BLOW UP!
WHY?

DON'T ASK QUESTIONS!
GO!
THANKS...BUT I WISH JUST ONCE SOMEONE WOULD TELL ME WHAT'S GOING ON HERE!

MEANWHILE, IN THE THRONE ROOM...
FIND LANDO!
IF HE ESCAPES, HE MIGHT BRING THE REBELLION DOWN ON US!
OUTSIDE THE PALACE...
HURRY--CLOSE THE GATES... SOMEONE'S ATTACKING US!
WHO WOULD DARE--?
PRINCESS DANU HAS SIGNALLED US--REVOLUTIONARIES ATTACK!
KNOCK OUT THE GATES!
STORM THE CITADEL!
THE REVOLUTIONARIES BLAST THE CITY WALLS, HITTING THE GUARDS' SMALL MUNITIONS SHED.
THE WAY IS CLEAR FOR THE REVOLUTIONARIES TO ENTER THE CITADEL...
HURRY UP! THIS IS OUR CHANCE!
EVERYBODY INSIDE WHILE THE GUARDS ARE BUSY WITH CALRISSIAN!

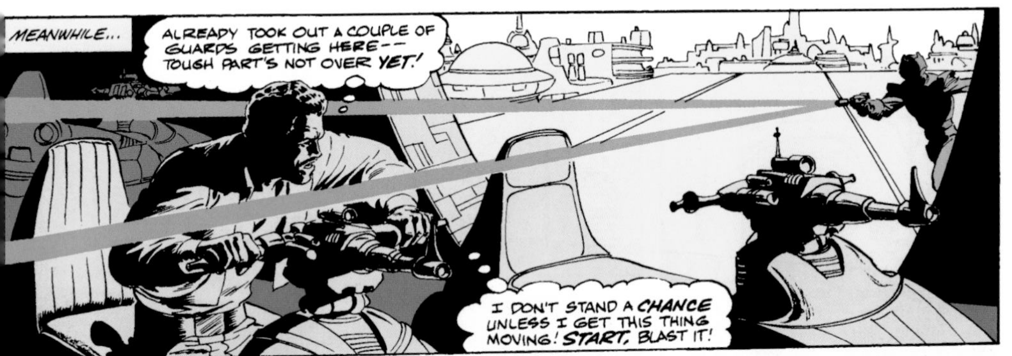

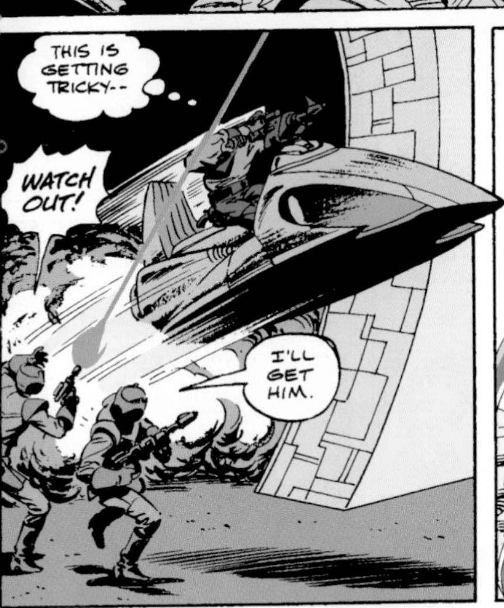

HAVE TO GO BACK TO THE PALACE!

THERE SHE IS--IN THE THRONE ROOM...

I HOPE THE GLASS DOME SHATTERS MORE EASILY THAN *I* DO!

AT THAT MOMENT...
WE'VE SEARCHED EVERYWHERE. CALRISSIAN'S GONE!
TOO BAD. YOU SLIPPING, HARLECH?
THAT'S ENOUGH!

CRASH
LANDO!
STILL HERE? I DON'T UNDERSTAND!

I'M GETTING SENTIMENTAL, SARNA-- I JUST COULDN'T LEAVE WITHOUT YOU!
WHAT--?
I NEED A HOSTAGE IF I'M GOING TO GET OUT OF HERE ALIVE.

THIS ISN'T USUALLY MY STYLE--BUT ANY PORT IN A STORM.
NO! YOU WOULDN'T!
DON'T BET ON IT, LADY! THESE ARE DESPERATE TIMES!

ANYONE TRIES TO STOP US-- DROGHEDA WILL BE SHORT ONE QUEEN.

WE CAN MAKE DO WITH A KING, CALRISSIAN.
GUARD, KILL THEM.
THERE'LL BE NEITHER KING NOR QUEEN ON THIS WORLD!

REVOLUTIONARIES? HOW--?!
WE NO LONGER ANSWER TO YOUR KIND, CAPTAIN-- AND WE HAVE MANY SCORES TO SETTLE!
OH, BOY...

YOUR MEN HAVE ALREADY SURRENDERED, HARLECH. THEY HAVE BETTER SENSE THAN YOU!
FACE IT-- THE MONARCHY IS FINISHED.
FOOLS! COWARDS!
I'M MORE THAN A MATCH FOR THE WHOLE LOT OF--
--ARRGH!
ZAP

HOW CAN ANYONE BE SO WRONG ALL THE TIME?
MAYBE HE'LL BE SMARTER WHEN HE COMES TO-- BUT I DOUBT IT!
OH, LANDO-- WE'LL HAVE A DEMOCRACY AT LAST!
DANU! YOU TREACHEROUS LITTLE...

WE OWE IT ALL TO YOU. YOU WERE THE PERFECT DECOY--DISTRACTING THE GUARDS WHILE THE REVOLUTIONARIES INVADED THE PALACE.
MY PLEASURE. I CAN THINK OF A SUITABLE REWARD...

ME, TOO. YOU GET TEN MINUTES TO GET TO YOUR SHIP AND TAKE OFF.
BUT--
YOUR DEAL WAS WITH SARNA-- NOT US.
TELL YOU WHAT... THERE'S SOME MONEY IN IT FOR YOU--IF YOU TAKE HER WITH YOU.

WHAT?! ME--IN EXILE?!
WHAT?! ME TAKE THAT BACKSTABBING SHREW?
FORGET IT! YOU COULDN'T PAY ME ENOUGH--

HMMMMM MONEY...

OKAY. DEAL. EVEN A LITTLE PROFIT BEATS GOING HOME EMPTY-HANDED.

SOON, ON LANDO'S SHIP...
DON'T BE MEAN. LET'S FORGIVE AND FORGET... PICK UP WHERE WE LEFT OFF.
NO WAY. I'M DROPPING YOU AT THE NEAREST INHABITED SYSTEM.
AFTER THAT, YOU'RE ON YOUR OWN.

YOU'RE NOT THINKING STRAIGHT. IMAGINE HOW MUCH MONEY WE COULD MAKE--WITH MY BRAIN AND YOUR SKILLS...
HAH! I'D BE THE BRAINS OF THE OPERATION--IF WE HAD ONE!

YOU... BRAINS! DON'T MAKE ME LAUGH.
NOW, HERE'S MY PLAN...
NOW, HERE'S MY PLAN...
End.

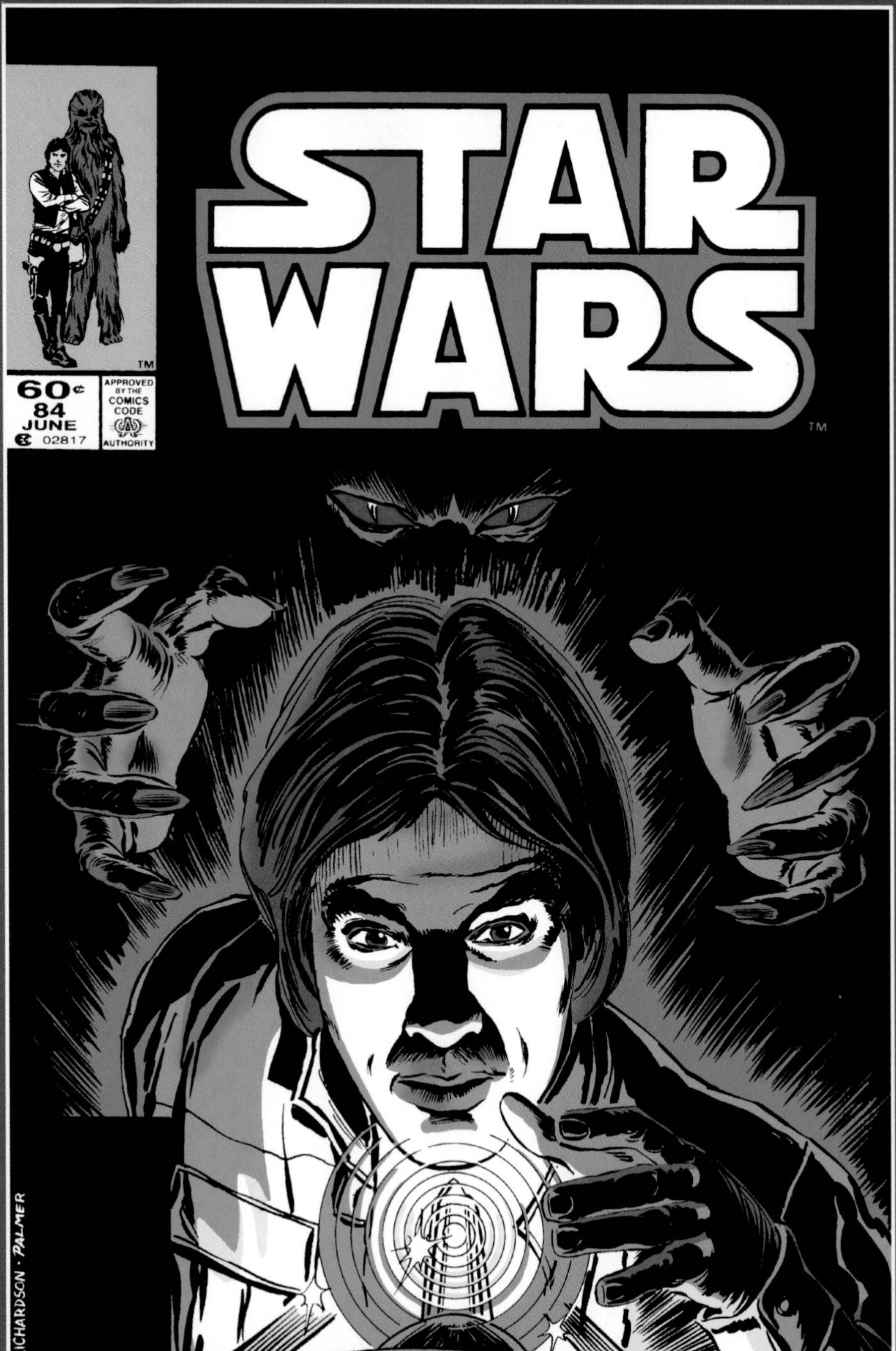

STAR WARS

TM

60¢
84
JUNE
02817

APPROVED BY THE COMICS CODE AUTHORITY

RICHARDSON · PALMER

REBEL LEADER HAN SOLO AND HIS WOOKIEE PARTNER CHEWBACCA HAVE JUST COMPLETED AN IMPORTANT DIPLOMATIC MISSION, INVITING LEADERS OF THE NEARBY PLANET ZHOTTA 3 TO THE GALACTIC CONGRESS WHICH WILL DECIDE HOW THE GALAXY, NOW FREED FROM IMPERIAL RULE, SHALL BE GOVERNED.
THE DULL STUFF TAKEN CARE OF, HAN AND CHEWIE HAVE MOVED ON TO MORE IMPORTANT BUSINESS...
SEOUL SEARCHING
IN A LOW-LIFE DIVE ON AN OUTLAW PLANET IN A BACK-WATER SECTOR OF THE GALAXY, HAN SOLO, CAPTAIN OF THE MILLENNIUM FALCON AND INTERSTELLAR CARD SHARK, HAS JUST CLEANED OUT EVERYONE WHO HAD ANYTHING TO LOSE.
OR ALMOST EVERYONE.
PAL, YOU'RE GONNA HAVE TO DO SOME FAST TALKIN' BEFORE YOU CONVINCE ME TO WAGER ANY OF MY BUCKS AGAINST THAT CHUNK A' GLASS.
AH, BUT CAPTAIN SOLO, IT'S NOT YOUR CREDITS THAT I WANT TO GAMBLE MY CRYSTAL AGAINST!
Lucasfilm PRESENTS: STAR WARS™ THE GREATEST SPACE FANTASY OF ALL!
ROY RICHARDSON WRITER * DAVID MAZZUCCHELLI PENCILER * TOM PALMER INKER * RICK PARKER LETTERER * GLYNIS WEIN COLORIST * JONES & NOCENTI EDITORS * JIM SHOOTER ED.-IN-CHIEF

I'M INTERESTED IN MUCH HIGHER STAKES-- IF YOU'VE GOT THE STOMACH FOR IT!
OLD MAN, I'VE GOT MORE THAN ENOUGH GUTS TO HANDLE ANY STAKES THAT YOU CAN COME UP WITH. MAKE YOUR BET.

ALL RIGHT, SOLO, IN ADDITION TO THE CRYSTAL, I OFFER THIS HOLO-MAP, WHICH CONTAINS THE STAR CO-ORDINATES...
...FOR THE SEOUL 5 SYSTEM.

SEOUL FIVE?!
SO YOU'VE HEARD OF IT, EH? WELL, THIS "CHUNK OF GLASS" IS A KEEPSAKE FROM SEOUL 5. YOU SEE...

...I BROUGHT IT FROM THERE MYSELF!

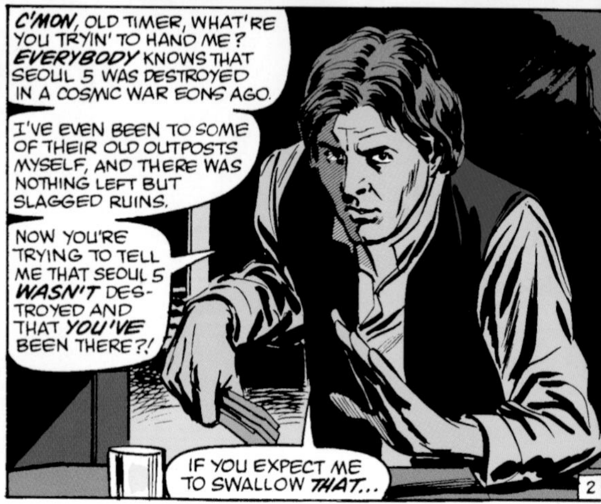
C'MON, OLD TIMER, WHAT'RE YOU TRYIN' TO HAND ME? EVERYBODY KNOWS THAT SEOUL 5 WAS DESTROYED IN A COSMIC WAR EONS AGO.
I'VE EVEN BEEN TO SOME OF THEIR OLD OUTPOSTS MYSELF, AND THERE WAS NOTHING LEFT BUT SLAGGED RUINS.
NOW YOU'RE TRYING TO TELL ME THAT SEOUL 5 WASN'T DES-TROYED AND THAT YOU'VE BEEN THERE?!
IF YOU EXPECT ME TO SWALLOW THAT...
2

I SAID I'VE BEEN THERE, AND I DON'T LIKE BEING CALLED A LIAR! NOW SHUT UP AND LISTEN!
BACK BEFORE THE WAR, I SERVED AS A FORWARD SCOUT FOR THE EMPIRE'S EXPLORATORY DIVISION.
I WAS RETURNING FROM A MISSION WHEN A METEOR KNOCKED MY SHIP OUT OF CONTROL JUST AS IT WAS ENTERING HYPER-SPACE.
"I WARPED BACK INTO NORMAL SPACE IN AN UNCHARTED SECTOR, NEAR AN UNKNOWN SOLAR SYSTEM...
"...AND SET DOWN FOR REPAIRS ON THE FIFTH PLANET, WHICH MY INSTRUMENTS SHOWED TO BE HABITABLE.
"I LANDED ON THE EDGE OF A RUINED CITY AND DECIDED TO EXPLORE WHILE MY SERVICE DROID FINISHED THE REPAIRS.
"I RECOGNIZED THE STRUCTURES AS SEOULIAN BECAUSE I'D ONCE BEEN GARRISONED ON ONE OF THE OUTPOST PLANETS YOU DESCRIBED.
" AFTER SOME EXTENSIVE EXPLORING, I DISCOVERED A TRAIL OF GLOWING RODS THAT LED ME DEEP INTO ONE OF THE STRUCTURES...
...AND INTO A CHAMBER THAT CONTAINED A CACHE OF THESE RADIANT CRYSTALS."
I ONLY TOOK ONE, INTENDING TO RETURN WITH A LARGER SHIP TO MAKE A COMPLETE HAUL OF ARTIFACTS.
BUT THE WAR BROKE OUT, AND I NEVER HAD THE RESOURCES FOR A RETURN TRIP. UNTIL NOW, THAT IS.
YOU SEE, SOLO, I WANT TO WAGER MY CRYSTAL AGAINST YOUR SHIP.
3

WHAT?! YOU EXPECT ME TO WAGER THE MILLENNIUM FALCON AGAINST A PHONY MAP AND A PIECE A' BROKEN GLASS? YOU'RE--
WATCH.

AS THE OLD PILOT BOWS HIS HEAD IN CONCENTRATION, A LOW HUM RADIATES FROM THE CRYSTAL AND A FEELING OF BUILDING POWER PULSES THROUGH THE AIR...

HMMMMMMM

GRO-ONK!
CHEWIE, DON'T TELL ME YOU BELIEVE ALL THIS BANTHA--

YOW!
GRONK?!

HA-HA-HA! BESIDES BEING WORTH A FORTUNE AS AN ARTIFACT, THE CRYSTAL IS ALSO CAPABLE OF BOOSTING ANY SORT OF ENERGY SOURCE, EVEN MENTAL ENERGY!
FOOMP!

O.K., OLD MAN, PLAY YOUR HAND.
4

A FULL SYSTEM! THERE'S ONLY ONE HAND THAT CAN BEAT THAT, AND THE ODDS AGAINST YOU HOLDING IT ARE ASTRONOMICAL.

OH, YEAH?

WHY, YOU CHEATING PIECE OF INTER-GALACTIC--! I'LL BLAST YOUR--

WHUMP!

DID YOU HEAR THAT?! THOSE GRUBBERS CHEATED US OUT OF OUR MONEY!

GWOOF!
BLAST 'EM!!
YEAH, TALK ABOUT YOUR SORE LOSERS!

GRONK!
YEAH, YEAH, WE LOST THE MONEY, BUT I'VE GOT THE MAP AND THIS! LET'S GO!
5

MOMENTS LATER, THE MILLENNIUM FALCON SOARS INTO SPACE!
SHEESH, CHEWIE! WHAT A TIGHTWAD PLANET!
YOU ALMOST HAD TO BE RUDE TO THAT ATTENDANT BEFORE HE'D TAKE AN I.O.U. FOR OUR DOCKING FEES!

NOW, LET'S SEE IF THAT OLD FOSSIL KNEW WHAT HE WAS TALKIN' ABOUT. THE CO-ORDINATES ARE IN, SO...

...HIT IT! SEOUL 5, HERE WE COME!

I HOPE!

HOURS LATER, THE FALCON EMERGES INTO AN UNKNOWN SYSTEM, NEAR AN UNCHARTED PLANET.
SO FAR, SO GOOD! THIS SYSTEM FITS THE OLD MAN'S DESCRIPTION. LET'S TAKE HER DOWN TO THE LANDING SITE HE SHOWS ON THE MAP!
6

CHEWIE, LOOK AT THOSE RUINS! THIS HAS GOTTA BE IT!
RRRARG! HRRRG!
WHAT?! HUMANOID LIFE-FORMS? BUT THE OLD GUY DIDN'T SAY ANYTHING ABOUT NATIVES! ARE YOU SURE?
GRUMPH
OKAY, OKAY! I'LL TAKE YOUR WORD FOR IT! THAT CLEARING MUST BE THE LANDING SITE. SET HER DOWN QUICK!

BRZOOOOOOOOSSSSHHH!!

CHEWIE, I'VE GOT A BAD FEELING ABOUT THIS...
... I THINK YOU SHOULD STAY HERE AND GUARD THE FALCON.
GRONNK!

DON'T WORRY, I KNOW WHAT I'M DOING! JUST STAY HERE AND BE READY FOR A QUICK TAKE-OFF!
I'M SURE THIS IS NOTHING I CAN'T HANDLE ALONE!

HRMPH!
WHATTA YOU MEAN, YOU'VE "HEARD THAT BEFORE"? NEVER MIND! I'LL BE BACK BEFORE YOU KNOW IT!
HRMPH!
7

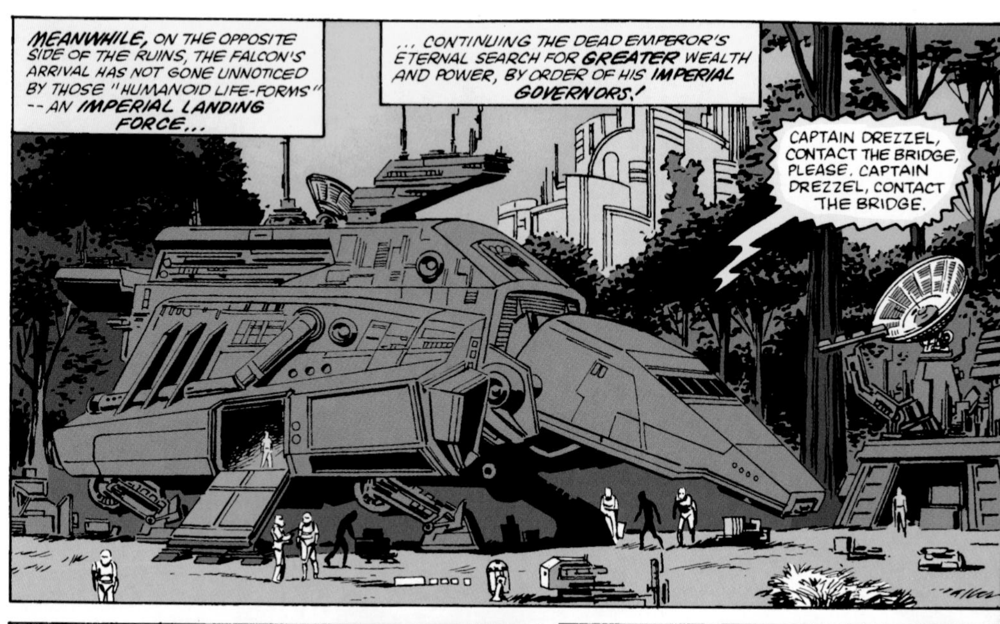
MEANWHILE, ON THE OPPOSITE SIDE OF THE RUINS, THE FALCON'S ARRIVAL HAS NOT GONE UNNOTICED BY THOSE "HUMANOID LIFE-FORMS" -- AN IMPERIAL LANDING FORCE...
... CONTINUING THE DEAD EMPEROR'S ETERNAL SEARCH FOR GREATER WEALTH AND POWER, BY ORDER OF HIS IMPERIAL GOVERNORS!
CAPTAIN DREZZEL, CONTACT THE BRIDGE, PLEASE. CAPTAIN DREZZEL, CONTACT THE BRIDGE.

DREZZEL HERE. WHAT IS IT?
SIR, WE'VE TRACKED THE DESCENT OF AN UNAUTHORIZED SHIP. IT LANDED SOMEWHERE ON THE FAR SIDE OF THE CITY.
VERY WELL, CREWMAN. I'LL SEE TO IT. OUT!

SQUAD THREE! REPORT FOR PATROL DUTY AT ONCE! REPEAT! SQUAD THREE! REPORT TO ME, ON THE DOUBLE!

ALSO, ADJUTANT SSSSK!, REPORT TO THE CAPTAIN IMMEDIATELY. REPEAT, SSSSK!, REPORT TO ME IMMEDIATELY!
SOUNDS LIKE THE CAPTAIN'S CALLIN' HIS PET FURBALL AGAIN. THAT FLEABAG GIVES ME THE CREEPS!
YEAH, ME TOO. WONDER WHAT DREZZEL WANTS HIM TO SNIFF OUT THIS TIME?
8

I DUNNO, DO YOU THINK HE CAN REALLY READ MINDS, LIKE THEY SAY?
I HOPE THAT THE OVERGROWN SCRUFF-BALL CAN'T, OR HE MIGHT--

YEEAAAA!
AAARRRGGG!!

UHHH!
BE THANKFUL, SCUM...

...THAT THIS "SCRUFF-BALL" LIMITED HIS TELEPATHIC ASSAULT, OR YOU WOULD HAVE BEEN REDUCED TO THE VERY LUMPS OF UNSENTIENT PROTO-PLASMIC SLIME THAT YOU SO RESEMBLE!

NOW, BACK TO YOUR POSTS! I'VE BUSINESS WITH THE CAPTAIN!
UHH...
STINKIN' FURBALL!
9

ELSEWHERE, IN THE HEART OF THE ANCIENT CITY...
WONDER WHY THIS PLACE ISN'T SLAGGED, LIKE THE OTHERS THAT THEY'VE FOUND? MAYBE THEY WERE WIPED OUT BY SOME KINDA GERM WARFARE ATTACK?
AND WHAT ABOUT THOSE LIFE READINGS, HMM? ACCORDING TO THE MAP, I SHOULD BE COMING UP ON MY NEXT LAND-MARK, SOME KINDA...
...STATUE?
SHE STANDS ALONE IN THE HUGE SQUARE, DWARFED, BUT NOT DAUNTED BY THE TOWERING STRUCTURES SURROUNDING HER.
SOLO KNOWS, SOME-HOW, THAT THE CLOAKED STATUE IS A "SHE," EVEN THOUGH HE CAN'T SEE THE FACE OR FIGURE.
THERE IS A STRANGE SORT OF MATERNAL FAMILIARITY ABOUT THE STATUE THAT CAUSES HIM TO PAUSE, FOR A MOMENT, IN HIS SEARCH FOR WEALTH.
10

BUT ONLY FOR A MOMENT.
C'MON, SOLO, SNAP OUT OF IT. YOU'RE HERE FOR THE BUCKS, NOT TO ADMIRE THE SCENERY.
NOW, ACCORDING TO THE MAP, THERE'S A SWITCH HIDDEN SOMEPLACE IN THE INSCRIPTION THAT OPENS A SECRET DOOR.

I'M SURPRISED THE OLD GUY SAT AROUND AND LEARNED ENOUGH SEOULIAN TO FIGURE THIS STUFF OUT. LIFE SURE MUST HAVE BEEN AWFUL DULL BACK ON THAT OUTPOST...
LET'S SEE, THE SWITCH IS SOMEWHERE IN THIS PASSAGE... "THIS IS THE MOTHER GODDESS ONRAI, SHE WHO GIVES AND NEVER RECEIVES, MISTRESS OF THE PLANET NOTRON, CRADLE OF ALL HUMANS IN THE GALAXY. IF YOU WOULD LEARN MORE, TOUCH ONRAI, AND DOORS WILL OPEN."

WELL, SISTER, I HATE TO DISAGREE WITH YOU ON THAT...
...BUT I CAN THINK OF AT LEAST A HALF-DOZEN OTHER PLANETS THAT MAKE THAT SAME CLAIM. BUT, SINCE THAT LAST LINE OBVIOUSLY MEANS THAT IF I TOUCH THE SYMBOL FOR ONRAI, YOU'LL OPEN THE SECRET DOOR FOR ME I WON'T ARGUE THE POINT. THEOLOGY ALWAYS GAVE ME A HEADACHE, ANYWAY.

ARG!

SOME KINDA... ALIEN MIND PROBE... PAWIN' AT MY BRAIN! BUT... WHERE'S IT COMING FROM?

UHH... I HAD TO ASK!
THEY MUST BE THE HUMANOIDS CHEWIE PICKED UP!
11

YESSSS, SSSSK! HAS HIM NOW, CAPTAIN! HE IS A SLIMY TREASURE-HUNTING PIRATE, AND HE'S HIDING... HIDING...

...BEHIND THAT STATUE!

HO-KAY, FUN-TIME'S OVER. LET'S SEE IF I CAN DISCOURAGE THESE GUYS A LITTLE.
ZARK
ZARK
ZARK

GUESS THEY'RE NOT THE DISCOURAGIN' KIND!
THE BLASTED MAP BROKE WHEN I DROPPED IT, AND I CAN'T REMEMBER WHICH SYMBOL I WAS SUPPOSED TO PRESS! I'D BETTER-

STOP FIRING, YOU FOOLS!
I CAN'T CONCENTRATE! HE'S GOING TO--

--START PRESSIN' AN' HOPE FOR THE--

--BEST?
12

WHAT?! I'M FLOATING DOWN! THIS IS SOME KINDA ANTI-GRAVITY CHUTE! BUT THIS WASN'T IN THE MAP!
I GUESS THE OLD GUY ONLY PUT DOWN THE THINGS THAT HE KNEW HE'D HAVE TROUBLE REMEMBERING. TOO CHEAP TO BUY A LONG HOLO-TAPE, I BET.!
HE'S PROBABLY GETTIN' A REAL KICK OUTTA THE THOUGHT OF ME FALLIN' THROUGH THAT TRAP DOOR, WHEREVER HE IS.
HAHAHA! WELL, THE JOKE'S ON HIM! HIS LITTLE SURPRISE SAVED MY HIDE!
I JUST WONDER WHAT OTHER LITTLE SURPRISES ARE WAITING FOR ME?
UMF! I SURE HOPE THAT TUBE NEXT DOOR IS THE "UP" CHUTE. AH, GOOD...
...MAYBE I WON'T NEED THE MAP ANYWAY. IF THE OLD GUY WAS TELLING IT STRAIGHT, THESE GLOWING RODS SHOULD LEAD ME RIGHT TO THE CRYSTALS.
THE TRAP DOOR SNAPPED SHUT BEHIND ME, SO I DOUBT THOSE TROOPERS WILL BE FOLLOWING ME DOWN...
...BUT I'D BETTER GET A MOVE ON, JUST IN CASE.
HMMMMMMmmmmmmmmmmmm
LOST IN THOUGHT, SOLO FAILS TO NOTICE THE LOW, OMINOUS WHINE COMING FROM THE CRYSTAL AT HIS SIDE.
13

...BEAT ME TO IT.

WELL, LOOKS LIKE NO ONE'S AROUND NOW, BUT SINCE THEY OBVIOUSLY KNOW ABOUT THIS TUNNEL, I'M SURE THEY'LL BE HERE ANY MINUTE, SO...

BLAST IT, THIS IS WHAT I GET FOR PUSSYFOOTIN' AROUND!
I'D BETTER DUCK OUT OF SIGHT!

OH, WONDERFUL! NOW I HAVE TO DEAL WITH THESE GUYS.
I'VE GOT TO GET THE CRYSTALS BEFORE THEIR BRAIN-BLASTING BUDDY SHOWS UP!
GOOD THING THEY STOPPED CATERWAULING WHEN I STEPPED AWAY FROM 'EM. THAT'S ANOTHER THING THE OLD GUY--
WONDER WHY DREZZEL RADIOED FOR US TO GUARD THESE ROCKS?
AREN'T YOU A LITTLE SCRUFFY FOR A STORM-TROOPER, MY BOY?

WHA?!

QUIETLY, LAD. AS YOU CAN SEE, WE ARE QUITE INCAPABLE OF DOING YOU ANY HARM. I AM DR. XATHAN, ARCHEOLOGIST, AND THIS IS MY AID, FEM NU-AR. AND YOU ARE--?
A PIRATE, FROM THE LOOKS OF IT. BUT PERHAPS YOU HAVE A SHIP...?
THE NAME'S SOLO, AND YEAH, I'VE GOT A SHIP. WHAT'S IT TO YOU?

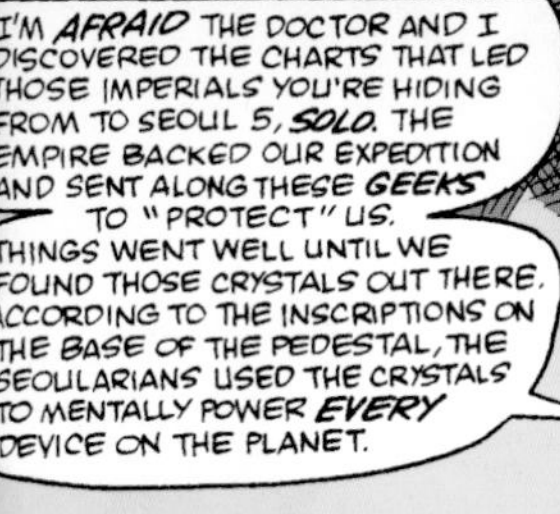

I'M AFRAID THE DOCTOR AND I DISCOVERED THE CHARTS THAT LED THOSE IMPERIALS YOU'RE HIDING FROM TO SEOUL 5, SOLO. THE EMPIRE BACKED OUR EXPEDITION AND SENT ALONG THESE GEEKS TO "PROTECT" US.
THINGS WENT WELL UNTIL WE FOUND THOSE CRYSTALS OUT THERE. ACCORDING TO THE INSCRIPTIONS ON THE BASE OF THE PEDESTAL, THE SEOULARIANS USED THE CRYSTALS TO MENTALLY POWER EVERY DEVICE ON THE PLANET.
BUT, UNKNOWN TO US, SSSSK.!, THE CAPTAIN'S PET TELEPATH, WAS CONSTANTLY MONITORING OUR THOUGHTS, AND REPORTED OUR DISCOVERY THE MOMENT WE TRANSLATED IT.
THE BARBARIANS CONFINED US AND CONFISCATED THE CRYSTALS FOR WEAPONS DEVELOPMENT. WE DON'T INTEND TO SEE THE CRYSTALS' POTENTIAL WASTED THAT WAY. YOU MUST HELP US ESCAPE WITH THEM! WE DON'T HAVE MONEY, BUT--
OKAY, OKAY, SISTER, GIVE YOUR TONGUE A BREAK! I'LL HELP YOU!
15

THAT WAS SOME SPEECH, BABE. YOU REMIND ME OF SOMEONE--
SAVE IT, SOLO. JUST UNTIE ME!

HOW'S THAT FOR GRATITUDE?
WELL, THE REBELLION WILL BE PLENTY GRATEFUL IF I PULL THIS OFF!..

...NOT TO MENTION THE FACT THAT I'LL BE RICH!
I'LL JUST STUN THESE GUYS--

PEEOW!
ZANG

LET'S GO!
UH-OH!

MY EARS! WHY ARE THE CRYSTALS REACTING LIKE THAT?
IF I EVER SEE THAT OLD GEEZER AGAIN, I'M GONNA MURDER 'IM!
MMMMMNNNN
EEEEEE
NNNNG
HHHMMMMMM
I THOUGHT I HEARD SOMETHING EARLIER! BUT I CAN THINK OF ONLY ONE THING THAT WOULD CAUSE THIS SORT OF REACTION!

YOUNG MAN, I DEMAND TO SEE WHAT YOU HAVE IN THAT BAG!
HMMMMMMM

WELL, UM, I MEANT TO SHOW YOU THIS...

...BUT, IN ALL THE EXCITEMENT, I JUST PLAIN FORGOT!
I KNEW IT! THE KEY CRYSTAL!
DO YOU REALIZE--?

STORM TROOPERS!
GET DOWN!
BUT YOU'VE GOT TO LISTEN!

SOLO, THE EMPIRE MUST NOT GET ITS HANDS ON THAT CRYSTAL! IT'S THE KEY TO CONTROLLING THE OTHERS--!
YES, BUT--
DOC, I DON'T INTEND FOR THEM TO GET US OR THE CRYSTALS! SEE THAT DOORWAY BEHIND US?

THEN RUN FOR IT! I'LL COVER YOU!
STUBBORN FOOL!
17

THEY'RE GETTIN' AWAY! RUSH 'EM!
GAAK!
HOLD YOUR FIRE, FOOLS!

CAP'N DREZZEL!
I TOLD YOU TO GUARD THE CRYSTALS, DOLTS, NOT BLAST THEM TO BITS!
LET SSSSK! HANDLE HIM, CAPTAIN. THE SLIME WON'T ESCAPE AGAIN!

IT GOT KINDA QUIET, ALL THE SUDDEN. WONDER WHAT'S GOIN' ON?

UH-OH.
HMMMMM
I HAVE YOU PIRATE! NOW, WRITHE!
MMMMM MM
YAA-A-RGH
18

THIS FREAK IS HITTIN' ME WITH EVERYTHING HE'S GOT... BUT I'M HOLDIN' HIM OFF! IT'S THE CRYSTAL! THE OLD MAN SAID IT COULD BOOST MENTAL ENERGY...
...BUT HAS IT GOT THE POWER TO BEAT THIS CREEP AT HIS OWN GAME?
YES!
YYOOOWWLL
UNN...EXHAUSTED... BUT CAN'T PASS OUT NOW... GOTTA ESCAPE...
AS SOLO BATTLES TO STAY ON HIS FEET, HE SLUMPS ACROSS THE ALIEN PEDESTAL...
...AND THE ACTIVATED CENTER CRYSTAL LOCKS INTO PLACE!
HMMMM
THE CHAMBER IS FLOODED WITH A SENSES-NUMBING RUSH OF LIGHT AND SOUND AS THE OTHER FOUR COME TO FULL POWER!
OOOOOOOEEEEEEEEEEE
19

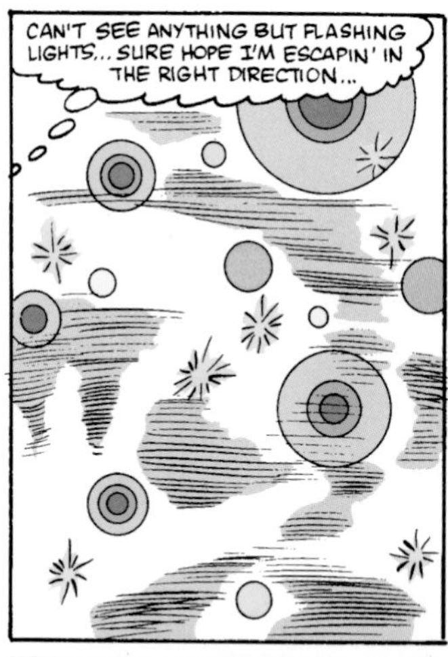
CAN'T SEE ANYTHING BUT FLASHING LIGHTS... SURE HOPE I'M ESCAPIN' IN THE RIGHT DIRECTION...

...WAIT... I SEE SOMETHING AHEAD... ARE THEY STORM TROOPERS, OR...

SOLO!
ARE YOU ALL RIGHT, M'BOY?

WHAT HAPPENED? WHERE ARE THE CRYSTALS?
JUST GET IN THE TUBE, DOC! I'LL EXPLAIN ON THE WAY UP!
EEEEEEEE

...AFTER THAT, THE CRYSTALS WERE TOO HOT TO PRY LOOSE, SO I RAN FOR IT. THE WAY THEY WERE BUILDIN' UP ENERGY, I'M AFRAID THEY'RE GONNA BLOW!
BLOW?! SOLO, THOSE CRYSTALS ONCE RAN THIS WHOLE PLANET! DO YOU HAVE ANY IDEA WHAT KIND OF POWER YOU'VE UNLEASHED?
JUDGING FROM THE HASTE WITH WHICH WE DEPARTED THE GROUND BELOW, MY DEAR, I WOULD SAY THAT HE PROBABLY HAS A PRETTY FAIR IDEA!
WE'RE COMIN' UP ON THE EXIT. HIT THE GROUND RUNNIN'!

IT SOUNDS AS IF YOUR FEARS ARE ABOUT TO BE REALIZED, M'LAD.
I WOULDN'T HAVE MINDED BEIN' WRONG JUST THIS ONCE!
"JUST THIS ONCE." HAH!
RRRUMMMMMMMBBLE!
AT LEAST YOU'RE NOT COMPLAINING, M'LADY. YOU DID RECEIVE A LITTLE SOMETHING, AFTER ALL.

THINK YOU LANDED FAR ENOUGH AWAY, SOLO?
NU-AR, NOW IS HARDLY THE TIME TO COMPLAIN!
DOC, I'M STARTIN' TO THINK THAT ANYTIME IS THE RIGHT TIME FOR HER!

GRONK!
CHEWIE! REMEMBER THAT QUICK TAKE-OFF WE WERE TALKING ABOUT?

HRRRGGG!
I SEE 'EM! I SEE 'EM!
IGNORE 'EM! JUST ACTIVATE OUR REAR SHIELDS AND GET US OUT OF HERE! EVEN THE AIR'S SHAKIN' NOW!

WING LEADER TARGET IS COMING INTO RANGE.
LASER'S ENERGIZED AND READY TO FIRE.
ON MY COMMAND, FIRE!
21

RIDING THE CREST OF THE TREMENDOUS BLAST, THE **MILLENNIUM FALCON** ZOOMS TO SAFETY!

ZZZZSSHH

HAVEN'T SEEN A BLAST LIKE THAT SINCE WE **BLEW AWAY** THE **DEATH STAR**, EH, CHEWIE?

WHAT A TERRIBLE LOSS OF ARCHAEOLOGICAL KNOWLEDGE!

BUT AT LEAST THE EMPIRE WON'T BE ABLE TO USE THE CRYSTALS TO BUILD **MORE** HORRIBLE WEAPONS!

AND, BEFORE YOU GET THE IDEA THAT WE ARE UNGRATEFUL, MY THANKS FOR A RESCUE WELL DONE!
BELIEVE IT OR NOT, SOLO, THAT GOES DOUBLE FOR ME!
WELL, SISTER, SOMETIMES I DO AMAZE EVEN MYSELF!

SO DO I, SOLO, SO DO I.
'BOUT TIME I GOT A PLEASANT SURPRISE OUT OF THIS TRIP!
22

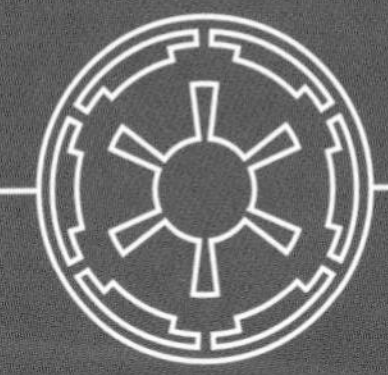

STAR WARS
60¢
85
JULY
02817
APPROVED BY THE COMICS CODE AUTHORITY
THE WRONG PLACE FOR HUNTED HEROES IS...
HUNTER'S WORLD!

Long ago in a galaxy far, far away. . .there exists a state of cosmic *civil war*. A brave alliance of *underground freedom fighters* has challenged the tyranny and oppression of the awesome *Galactic Empire*. This is their story!
Lucasfilm PRESENTS: STAR WARS THE GREATEST SPACE FANTASY OF ALL!
JO DUFFY SCRIPT & PLOT * BOB McLEOD BREAKDOWNS * TOM PALMER FINISHES * RICK PARKER LETTERS * GLYNIS WEIN COLORS * ANN NOCENTI EDITOR * JIM SHOOTER EDITOR-IN-CHIEF
THE HERO
LANDO CALRISSIAN!!!

WHEREVER YOU ARE, I'M WARNING YOU... IF IT TAKES ME THE REST OF MY LIFE -- IF I HAVE TO SEARCH EVERY MISERABLE PLANET IN THIS ENTIRE GALAXY, SOME DAY, I'M GOING TO FIND YOU, AND WHEN I DO...
... I'M GOING TO GET MY REVENGE, SURE AS MY NAME IS DREBBLE!
LISTEN, DREBBLE... IG-88 AND ME ARE MORE THAN HAPPY TO GO AFTER CALRISSIAN FOR YOU -- WE'RE BOUNTY HUNTERS AN' WE'LL GO AFTER ANY ONE, IF THE PRICE IS GOOD ENOUGH.
AN' WE GOT SORT OF A GRUDGE AGAINST CALRISSIAN OURSELVES AFTER THE WAY HE AND HIS BUDDIES MESSED UP OUR OPERATION ON STENOS, AT THE SAME TIME AS WE PICKED UP OUR WINGED FRIENDS HERE...
BUT THERE'S ONE THING WE BEEN WONDERIN' ABOUT.
AND JUST WHAT IS THAT, BOSSK?
HHHHSSSSS!
EVEN I, A DROID CONFESS TO FEELING A CERTAIN CURIOSITY ABOUT IT.
WHATEVER YOUR QUESTION IS, SPIT IT OUT!! DON'T ACT SHY JUST BECAUSE YOU'RE IN MY TAVERN.
WHAT'S LANDO CALRISSIAN EVER DONE TO YOU? WHY YOU GOT IT IN FOR 'IM?
WHY?! I'LL TELL YOU WHY. BECAUSE THAT SO-CALLED BUSINESSMAN IS NOTHING BUT A ROTTEN CONFIDENCE ARTIST.
BECAUSE HE DOUBLE-CROSSED ME! BECAUSE THAT SMIRKING, POSTURING CLOWN IS--
2

-- A CHEAT?! ME?
GRONK!
CHEWBACCA... CHEWIE, LISTEN TO THE MAN. LANDO WOULDN'T CHEAT YOU. HE JUST GOT LUCKY, THAT'S ALL.
LISTEN TO HAN. HE'S YOUR FRIEND. HE WOULDN'T LIE.
OOOOoHHH...
RRUF!
HEY... IF IT MEANS ALL THAT MUCH TO YOU, WE'LL SAY THE EWOKS MIS-DEALT THAT HAND. WE CAN PLAY IT AGAIN.
GRUF
AWROO
I KNEW WOOKIEES HATE TO LOSE, BUT...
S'OKAY, LANDO. LET 'EM COOL OFF FOR A WHILE.
YEAH, BUT THERE GOES OUR GAME.
SO WHAT?
IT'S NOT LIKE THE LITTLE FUZZBALL'S SHOWED ANY SIGNS OF LEARNING THE RULES... OR EVEN TAKING THE WHOLE THING SERIOUSLY.
3

YEAH. HOW THE EWOKS CAN BE SUCH TERRIFIC FIGHTERS AND STILL BE SUCH ROTTEN GAMBLERS IS BEYOND ME.
UH... HAN... I KNOW CHEWIE'S GOT A TEMPER AND ALL, BUT GOING OFF LIKE THAT JUST ISN'T LIKE HIM. WHAT'S REALLY WRONG?
AN OVERDOSE OF RESPONSIBILITY.
OL' CHEWIE'S A FAMILY MAN. HE HASN'T BEEN TO HIS HOMEWORLD IN A LONG TIME, AN' NOW THAT THE EMPIRE'S BEEN OVER-THROWN, HE'S REALLY ITCHING TO GO.
BUT HE DOESN'T WANT TO... NOT UNTIL HE'S SURE THE FIGHTING'S REALLY OVER. HE AIN'T ABOUT TO RUN OUT ON US, EVEN FOR A VISIT, WHEN WE MAY STILL NEED HIM.
HEY, HAN! LANDO!
WHAT IS IT, WEDGE?
MON MOTHMA AND ADMIRAL ACKBAR HAVE CALLED A BRIEFING SESSION. THEY WANT EVERYONE IN THE BIG CLEARING, ON THE DOUBLE.
RIGHT WITH YOU, WEDGE.
HEY, CHEWIE, COME ON. THE BRASS WANT US!
WHAT KIND OF BUSINESS WILL WE BE GOING OVER?
OH, FROM WHAT I HEAR, THEY'LL BE DISCUSSING INTELLIGENCE REPORTS, MAKING NEW ASSIGNMENTS, GIVING US A RUNDOWN ON HOW OUR ALLIANCE HAS DONE SINCE THE REBEL-LION SUCCEEDED... THINGS LIKE THAT.
BY THE WAY... EITHER OF YOU GUYS EVER HEAR OF A CHARACTER CALLED CAPTAIN DREBBLE?
DON'T THINK SO. WHY?
OH, I HEAR SOME OF THE BUSINESS CONCERNS HIM.
HAN, THIS IS TERRIFIC.
WHAT IS?
DREBBLE... IT'S THE NAME OF AN OLD ENEMY OF MINE, A GUY WHO MADE THINGS PRETTY HOT FOR ME WHILE YOU WERE IN HIBERNATION, FROZEN BY THOSE BOUNTY HUNTERS WHO CAUGHT YOU.
TO GET EVEN, WHENEVER I'VE HAD TO USE AN ALIAS IN A SITUATION THAT WAS LIKELY TO GET ME INTO TROUBLE--LIKE GOING UNDERCOVER AGAINST THE EMPIRE--I'VE USED DREBBLE'S NAME.
LOOKS LIKE *MY* LUCK HAS FINALL CAUGHT UP WITH *HIM*!
4

... BECAUSE WE HAVE NO MORE RIGHT TO RULE THAN OUR PREDECESSORS, THE EMPEROR AND HIS FOLLOWERS, HAD, WE ARE MERELY ACTING AS A STABILIZING FORCE FOR THE GALAXY...
...UNTIL SUCH TIME AS ALL THE PEOPLE WHO HAVE BEEN FREED FROM THE EMPIRE'S TYRANNY CAN AGREE AMONG THEMSELVES UPON A MUTUALLY SATISFACTORY SYSTEM OF INTER-PLANETARY GOVERNMENT AND TRADE.
TO THAT END, WE HAVE BEEN SENDING OUT EMBASSIES, INVITING THOSE WORLDS WHICH ARE SOUND TO SEND THEIR REPRESENTATIVES TO US AND HAVE THEIR VOICE, AND OFFERING AID TO THOSE IN NEED.
COMMANDER LUKE SKYWALKER AND PRINCESS LEIA ORGANA ARE BOTH OFF ON SUCH MISSIONS AT PRESENT.
WE SHALL BE NEEDING ADDITIONAL VOLUNTEERS FROM AMONG YOU TO VISIT THE WORLDS OUTLINED EARLIER IN THIS SESSION.
THANK YOU, MON MOTHMA... AND NOW, TO OUR FINAL ORDER OF BUSINESS, BEFORE WE CALL FOR THE VOLUNTEERS... IN THE FINAL DAYS BEFORE THE END OF THE EMPIRE, THE NAME DREBBLE BEGAN TO TURN UP IN OUR REPORTS WITH A CERTAIN REGULARITY...
ALTHOUGH WE KNEW NOTHING OF THIS MAN, IN LIGHT OF WHAT WE HAVE HEARD OF HIS RECENT ACTIVITIES, WE HAVE NO ALTERNATIVE.
HERE IT COMES.
... BUT TO DECLARE DREBBLE A HERO OF THE GALAXY. HIS NAME IS BEING OFFICIALLY ADDED TO THE LIST OF THOSE WHO'LL BE DECORATED AS SOON AS WE CAN LOCATE THEM.
WHAT?! A HERO?
OH, YES. FROM WHAT I HEAR, THIS DREBBLE IS QUITE SOMETHING. WHY, HE HELPED TO TOPPLE THE IMPERIAL FORTRESS ON THE PLANET GAMANDAR... ...AND THEN HE BROUGHT AN ENTIRE GANG OF CUTTHROAT THIEVES TO THEIR KNEES. I WISH I COULD MEET HIM!
BUT...BUT I...BUT HE...BUT DREBBLE...
"TERRIFIC," HUNH, LANDO? I GUESS YOU FIXED HIM!
5

UH, ADMIRAL...?
YES, GENERAL SOLO?
I'D LIKE TO VOLUNTEER FOR ONE OF THE DIPLOMATIC MISSIONS. CHEWIE AND I-- AN' OF COURSE OUR SHIP, THE MILLENNIUM FALCON, WOULD LIKE THE RUN THAT STARTS WITH THE PLANET KEYORIN.

?

ADMIRAL ACKBAR? IT'S POSSIBLE THAT A JOB LIKE THAT MIGHT NEED THREE AMBASSADORS, NOT TWO. I'D LIKE TO TAG ALONG IN MY SHIP, THE COBRA, IF THAT'S OKAY.
VERY GOOD, GENERAL CALRISSIAN.

JUST WHAT DO YOU THINK YOU'RE DOING, GENERAL?
THE SAME AS YOU, GENERAL-- ARRANGING A LITTLE VACATION FOR YOUR CO-PILOT. IT WASN'T HARD TO FIGURE WHAT YOU WERE UP TO.
HROON?
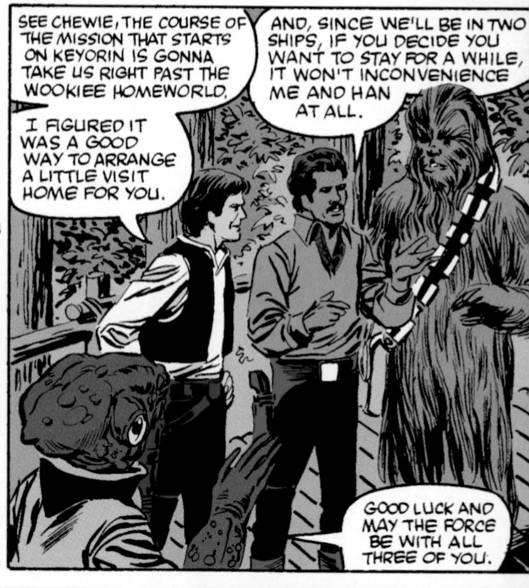
SEE CHEWIE, THE COURSE OF THE MISSION THAT STARTS ON KEYORIN IS GONNA TAKE US RIGHT PAST THE WOOKIEE HOMEWORLD.
I FIGURED IT WAS A GOOD WAY TO ARRANGE A LITTLE VISIT HOME FOR YOU.
AND, SINCE WE'LL BE IN TWO SHIPS, IF YOU DECIDE YOU WANT TO STAY FOR A WHILE, IT WON'T INCONVENIENCE ME AND HAN AT ALL.
GOOD LUCK AND MAY THE FORCE BE WITH ALL THREE OF YOU.

HROWR!!

WELL, LANDO, HERE IT IS--KEYORIN, THE HUNTER'S WORLD.
HUNTER'S WORLD?
YEAH. WE CAN LAND AS SOON AS OUR CLEARANCES COME THROUGH.

EITHER OF YOU EVER BEEN HERE BEFORE?

WURF
ME, NEITHER, BUT IT SEEMS... AH, REALLY CHARMING. JUST LOVELY.
GREAT. THEN WHEN WE GET TO THE BOSS'S PLACE, BETTER LET ME DO ALL THE TALKING. I KNOW THE LOCAL APPROACH.
FINE.

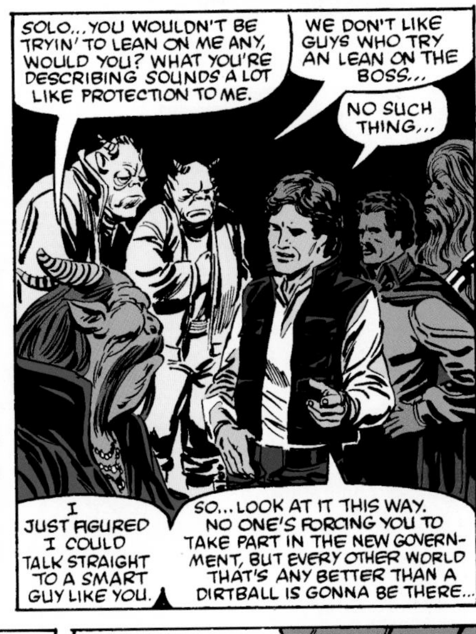
SOLO... YOU WOULDN'T BE TRYIN' TO LEAN ON ME ANY, WOULD YOU? WHAT YOU'RE DESCRIBING SOUNDS A LOT LIKE PROTECTION TO ME.
WE DON'T LIKE GUYS WHO TRY AN LEAN ON THE BOSS...
NO SUCH THING...
I JUST FIGURED I COULD TALK STRAIGHT TO A SMART GUY LIKE YOU.
SO... LOOK AT IT THIS WAY. NO ONE'S FORCING YOU TO TAKE PART IN THE NEW GOVERNMENT, BUT EVERY OTHER WORLD THAT'S ANY BETTER THAN A DIRTBALL IS GONNA BE THERE...

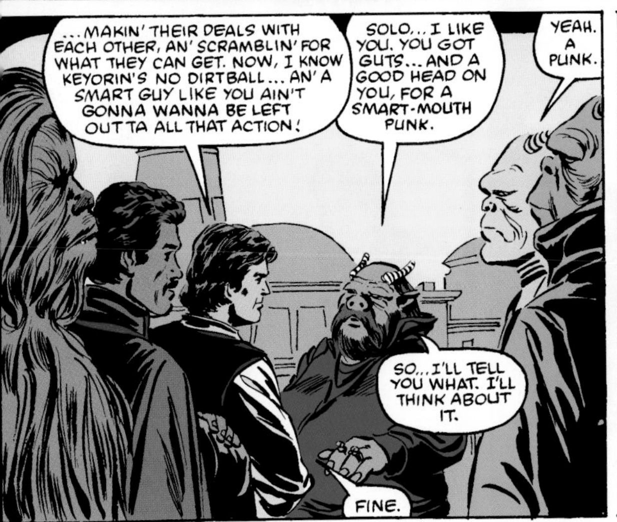
...MAKIN' THEIR DEALS WITH EACH OTHER, AN' SCRAMBLIN' FOR WHAT THEY CAN GET. NOW, I KNOW KEYORIN'S NO DIRTBALL... AN' A SMART GUY LIKE YOU AIN'T GONNA WANNA BE LEFT OUTTA ALL THAT ACTION!
SOLO... I LIKE YOU. YOU GOT GUTS... AND A GOOD HEAD ON YOU, FOR A SMART-MOUTH PUNK.
YEAH. A PUNK.
SO... I'LL TELL YOU WHAT. I'LL THINK ABOUT IT.
FINE.

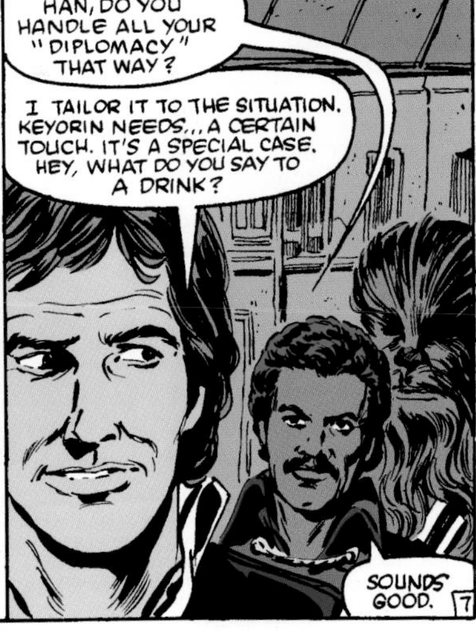
HAN, DO YOU HANDLE ALL YOUR "DIPLOMACY" THAT WAY?
I TAILOR IT TO THE SITUATION. KEYORIN NEEDS... A CERTAIN TOUCH. IT'S A SPECIAL CASE. HEY, WHAT DO YOU SAY TO A DRINK?
SOUNDS GOOD.
7

SEE... THAT'S ANOTHER LITTLE FRINGE BENEFIT OF COMING TO THIS PLACE. KEYORIN HAS THE BEST-STOCKED BARS IN THE ENTIRE SYSTEM.
IT ALSO SEEMS TO ATTRACT A LARGE GROUP OF... COLORFUL CHARACTERS. WHAT'S THE STORY ON THIS PLACE?
EVENING, EVERYONE
HI, BOSSK.

OOUUHR?!
SPUT!
B-B-B-BOSSK?

WHAT'S THE MATTER WITH YOU TWO?
HAN, WOULD YOU FINISH TELLING ME ABOUT KEYORIN?
AND, PLEASE, KEEP YOUR VOICE DOWN.

WHY?! AN' WHY ARE YOU GUYS HIDIN' YOUR FACES?!
SOMEONE CAME IN WE DON'T WANT TO SEE... HAN, WHY DO THEY CALL THIS PLACE THE HUNTER'S WORLD?
BECAUSE AS LONG AS YOU DON'T MESS WITH THE BOSS OR ANY OF HIS BOYS, AND YOU GIVE 'EM THEIR CUT OKAY, ANYTHING YOU WANT TO DO HERE'S LEGAL. A LOT OF BOUNTY HUNTERS COME HERE.
OH, GREAT.

WOULD YOU TWO STOP WHISPERING AND TELL ME WHAT'S WRONG?!
SSSSHHH!

HAN... TRY TO KEEP AN OPEN MIND ABOUT WHAT I'M GOING TO TELL YOU... SEE, WHILE YOU WERE A PRISONER, THE TRAIL WE WERE FOLLOWING TO YOU GOT PRETTY COLD AT ONE POINT.
AND, I FIGURED THERE'S NOBODY FOR FINDING MISSING PEOPLE OR THINGS LIKE CRIMINALS WHO FIGURE THERE'S SOMETHING IN IT FOR THEM.
SO...TO KIND OF GET THINGS GOING... KNOWING YOU WERE OUT OF ACTION, CHEWIE AND I SET YOU UP WITH A COUPLE OF GANGS, PLANNING TO FOLLOW THEM TO YOU...

AND... ONE OF THE BOUNTY HUNTERS I TRICKED INTO GOING AFTER YOU--A GUY WHO'S STILL PRETTY MAD AT ME--JUST WALKED IN HERE.

YOU GUYS GOT MORE BOUNTY HUNTERS AFTER ME...AND YOU WERE DOING IT TO HELP ME?
ARE YOU BOTH CRAZY?!!
QUIET!
THE LAST THING WE NEED NOW IS TO START ATTRACTING ATTENTION.

I SEE WHAT YOU MEAN.

LET'S JUST PAY OUR BILL QUIETLY AND LEAVE.
THE OWNER'S IN THE BACK.
DING!
BARKEEP! WE'D LIKE TO SETTLE OUR TAB!
DING!

YES, YES, BE RIGHT WITH--

--YOU!
YOU!
9

GET THEM!
LET'S GET OUT OF HERE!

WE'RE LUCKY THESE ALLEYWAYS ARE TOO NARROW FOR A STENAX TO FLY IN... IF THOSE TWO WERE AIRBORNE, WE'D BE SUNK RIGHT NOW!

LOOK! DO YOU SEE WHAT I SEE?
HAN SOLO!
UH-OH!
GET HIM!

NICE GOING, LANDO. WHO ARE *THOSE* GUYS?
I'M NOT SURE...
10

ULP
HAH! GOTCHA! NICE OF IG-88 TO RADIO AHEAD TO US THAT YOU WERE COMING, WASN'T IT?
YOU AIN'T GOT US YET, PAL!

THAT GUY BEHIND US IS--!
I KNOW! BOSSK. I RECOGNIZE HIM NOW. HE'S THE ONE WHO'S WORKIN' WITH THE DROID, IG-88, AND THE PAIR OF STENAXES.
WHO WERE THOSE OTHERS?

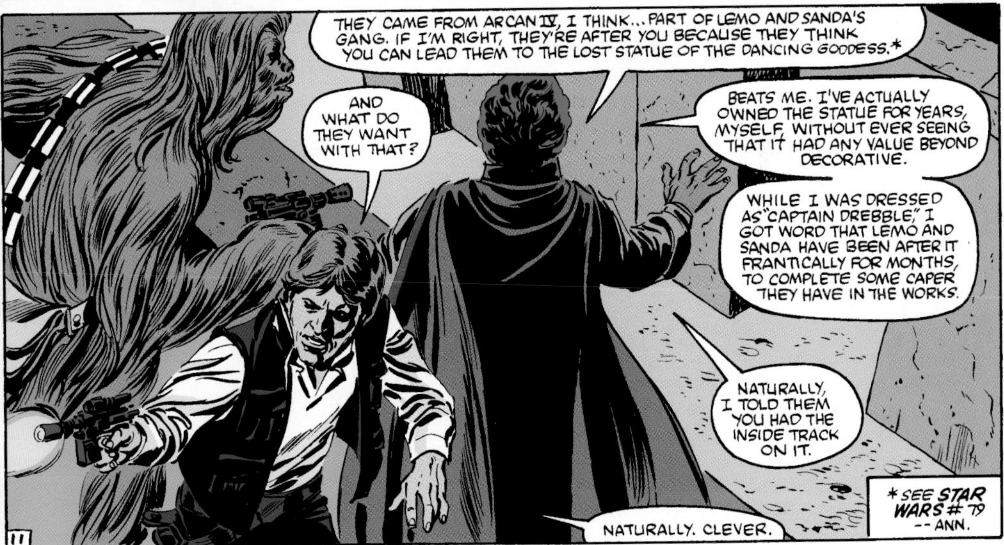
THEY CAME FROM ARCAN IV, I THINK... PART OF LEMO AND SANDA'S GANG. IF I'M RIGHT, THEY'RE AFTER YOU BECAUSE THEY THINK YOU CAN LEAD THEM TO THE LOST STATUE OF THE DANCING GODDESS.*
AND WHAT DO THEY WANT WITH THAT?
BEATS ME. I'VE ACTUALLY OWNED THE STATUE FOR YEARS, MYSELF, WITHOUT EVER SEEING THAT IT HAD ANY VALUE BEYOND DECORATIVE.
WHILE I WAS DRESSED AS "CAPTAIN DREBBLE," I GOT WORD THAT LEMO AND SANDA HAVE BEEN AFTER IT FRANTICALLY FOR MONTHS, TO COMPLETE SOME CAPER THEY HAVE IN THE WORKS.
NATURALLY, I TOLD THEM YOU HAD THE INSIDE TRACK ON IT.
NATURALLY. CLEVER.
*SEE STAR WARS #79 --ANN.
11

THERE THEY ARE!! GET THEM, OR WE DON'T GET PAID!
TIME WE WERE MOVING ON, FELLAS...
JUMP FOR IT!
WE'VE GOT TO MAKE IT BACK TO THE HANGAR WHERE WE LEFT THE SHIP.

I DOUBT WE COULD BE THIS LUCKY TWICE.

SURPRISE.

JUST HOW DIFFICULT DID YOU THINK IT WOULD BE TO FIGURE OUT YOU WERE HEADING BACK TOWARD YOUR SHIPS ?

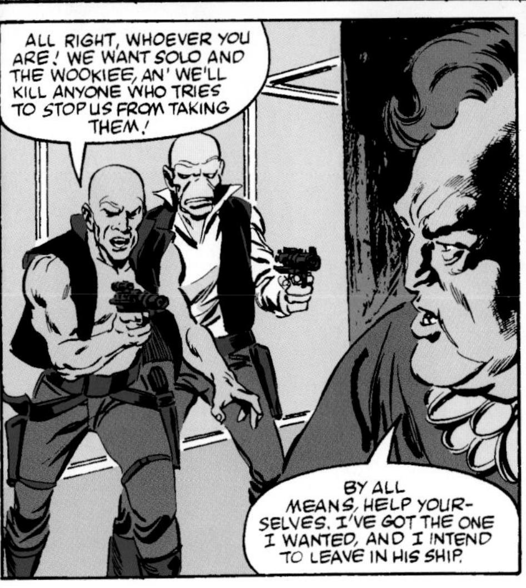
ALL RIGHT, WHOEVER YOU ARE! WE WANT SOLO AND THE WOOKIEE, AN' WE'LL KILL ANYONE WHO TRIES TO STOP US FROM TAKING THEM!
BY ALL MEANS, HELP YOUR-SELVES. I'VE GOT THE ONE I WANTED, AND I INTEND TO LEAVE IN HIS SHIP.

HUNH?!
YOU'VE JUST SAVED ME THE TROUBLE OF KILLING HIS FRIENDS TO FORE-STALL ANY DRAMATIC RESCUES. 'BYE, NOW!
13

...GONNA ASK YOU AGAIN, SOLO! WHERE IS THE DANCING GODDESS?
AND I'M GONNA TELL YOU AGAIN-- I HAVE NO IDEA, AN' I DON'T REALLY CARE!
STOP LYING TO US, HAN! LEVEL WITH ME, FOR OLD TIMES' SAKE BEFORE I HAVE TO MAKE THINGS... UNPLEASANT FOR YOU.
I AM LEVELING WITH YOU, SANDA. AND I DON'T WANT TO HEAR ABOUT "UNPLEASANT."
YOU THINK IT'S ANY PICNIC HANGING BY YOUR WRISTS IN A COLD WAREHOUSE, FOR HOURS AT A TIME, FROM A PAIR OF ENERGY BINDERS?
RIGHT. NOW I'M GONNA LET THE BOYS LOOSE ON YOU. YOU'RE A TOUGH GUY, HAN. I GIVE YOU AN HOUR, MAYBE TWO, BEFORE YOU START BEGGING ME AND SANDA TO LISTEN TO YOU.

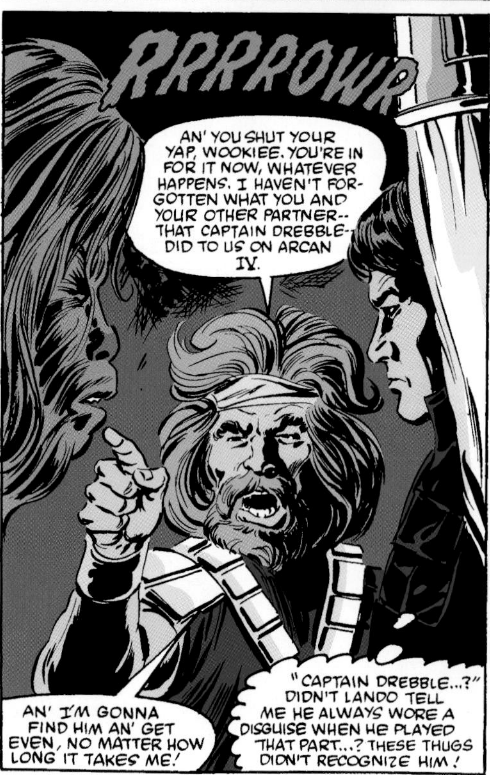

RRRROWR
AN' YOU SHUT YOUR YAP, WOOKIEE. YOU'RE IN FOR IT NOW, WHATEVER HAPPENS. I HAVEN'T FORGOTTEN WHAT YOU AND YOUR OTHER PARTNER--THAT CAPTAIN DREBBLE--DID TO US ON ARCAN IV.
AN' I'M GONNA FIND HIM AN' GET EVEN, NO MATTER HOW LONG IT TAKES ME!
"CAPTAIN DREBBLE...?" DIDN'T LANDO TELL ME HE ALWAYS WORE A DISGUISE WHEN HE PLAYED THAT PART...? THESE THUGS DIDN'T RECOGNIZE HIM!

LEMO... I GOT NOTHING LEFT TO LOSE. SO, I MIGHT AS WELL TELL YOU. THAT DREBBLE CHARACTER PLAYED US BOTH FOR SAPS. HE LIED TO YOU.
IT'S NOT ME WHO KNOWS WHERE THE GODDESS IS... HE HAS IT.
WHAT--?!
OF COURSE, IF YOU'D RECONSIDER ON THAT TORTURE STUFF...I MIGHT TELL YOU WHERE YOU CAN FIND HIM...
14

WELL, WELL, WELL. LOOK WHO'S AWAKE AT LAST!
UUNGH! DREBBLE...
I HAD CONTEMPLATED JUST TAKING YOU BACK TO THE BAR AND WORKING ON YOU THERE... BUT BOSSK TELLS ME YOU VISITED WITH THE BOSS THIS AFTERNOON... AND I WOULDN'T WANT TO TAKE A CHANCE ON HIS ACTUALLY LIKING YOU OR CARING WHAT HAPPENS TO YOU.
SO, WE'RE GOING BACK TO MY HOMEWORLD--A PLACE WHERE YOU FIRST CHEATED ME--TO ENJOY OURSELVES.
NICE OF YOU TO COME PREPACKAGED FOR EASY HANDLING, WITH YOUR OWN SHIP. I ONLY WISH I KNEW WHAT HAPPY CHANCE HAD BROUGHT YOU HERE...

QUIT GLOATING, DREBBLE. WHERE ARE MY FRIENDS? TELL ME WHAT YOU'VE DONE WITH THEM!

I DIDN'T HAVE TO DO A THING. THAT OTHER GROUP WANTED THEM SO BADLY, I DIDN'T SEE ANY REASON NOT TO HAND THEM OVER.
YOU DIDN'T--!

WHAT ARE YOU WORRYING ABOUT THEM FOR, CALRIS-SIAN? WORRY ABOUT YOURSELF. WHY DO YOU THINK DREBBLE HIRED STENAXES?
YOU KNOW WHAT THEY'RE CAPABLE OF.

RIGHT NOW I WISH THEY WERE CAPABLE OF FLYING THIS SHIP. WHAT DO ALL THESE STUPID BUTTONS DO, ANYWAY?
CLICK

HUH?
IT'S NOTHING BUT A HOLOGRAM.
...SO, ALL ALLIANCE PERSONNEL, PLEASE RECALL, AS A MATTER OF SIMPLE JUSTICE...

...THAT AS SOON AS WE CAN LOCATE HIM, WE WILL BE GIVING COMMEN-DATIONS AND A DECORATION FOR BRAVERY...
...TO CAPTAIN DREBBLE.
15

DID YOU HEAR THAT? DID YOU HEAR THAT?!
CAN YOU BELIEVE IT? ME, DECORATED FOR BRAVERY?
AND BY THE ALLIANCE, TOO! THEY'RE A BIG ORGANIZATION, YOU KNOW. POWERFUL. AND THEY'VE GIVEN ME A TITLE. MADE ME AN OFFICER.
CONGRATULATIONS, SIR!
OF COURSE I HEARD IT. I JUST DON'T BELIEVE IT.
"CAPTAIN DREBBLE." I LIKE THE SOUND OF THAT. HAS A NICE RING TO IT, DON'T YOU THINK?

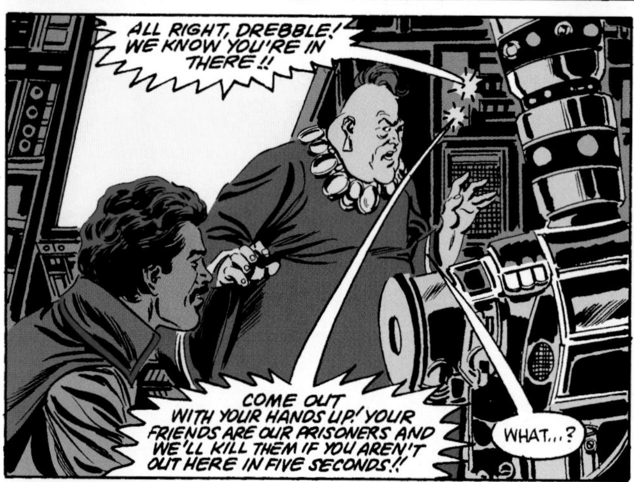
ALL RIGHT, DREBBLE! WE KNOW YOU'RE IN THERE!!
COME OUT WITH YOUR HANDS UP! YOUR FRIENDS ARE OUR PRISONERS AND WE'LL KILL THEM IF YOU AREN'T OUT HERE IN FIVE SECONDS!!
WHAT...?

FRIENDS? WHAT FRIE--

--EEK!

THOSE COWARDS! THOSE DOUBLE-CROSSERS! WHOEVER THEY ARE, THEY WON'T GET AWAY WITH THIS!
NO ONE TAKES FRIENDS OF CAPTAIN DREBBLE HOSTAGE AND LIVES TO TELL THE TALE!
16

C'MON, SOLO... I KNOW YOU BETTER THAN LEMO DOES... AND I SAY YOU WERE HOLDING OUT ON HIM. TELL ME WHAT YOU REALLY KNOW, AND WE CAN BE GONE BEFORE THEY GET BACK, AND SPLIT THE HAUL.
NO WAY.
OR... I CAN MAKE IT TOUGH ON YOU... AN' WHEN LEMO AN' SANDRA GET BACK, IT'LL BE YOUR WORD AGAINST MINE WHY I DID IT!

CHEWIE... I'M COUNTING ON YOU, I JUST HOPE YOU'VE FIGURED OUT WHAT IT IS I NEED YOU TO DO...

HUNH? HEY?! WHAT'S THE MATTER WITH HIM?

HE'S PROBABLY DEAD. WOOKIEES CAN'T TAKE PROLONGED STRESS.
NOW, JUST A--

--AAAAH!
GROWR!!
17

NICE WORK, PAL. THE SADISTIC LITTLE CREEP WAS SO STARTLED, HE BACKED RIGHT INTO ME.

NOW... YOU GONNA ACTIVATE THE RELEASE ON THESE BINDERS...
URK!
...OR AM I GONNA RELEASE YOUR HEAD FROM YOUR NECK?

I THOUGHT YOU'D SEE IT MY WAY.

AND DON'T WORRY TOO MUCH ABOUT YOUR WRISTS. AFTER THE FIRST COUPLE OF HOURS, THE BLOOD STOPS CIRCULATING TO YOUR HANDS...
...AND THEY GET TOO NUMB TO HURT MUCH.

COME ON CHEWIE. WE GOTTA FIND LANDO...
...AND SAVE HIM FROM LEMO AND SANDA, IF THERE'S STILL TIME!
18

REMEMBER, TROOPS. IT'S NOT WHETHER A MAN LIVES OR DIES THAT'S IMPORTANT. IT'S HOW HE DIES. AND WITH WHOM.
I DO APPRECIATE THIS, YOU KNOW.
WHY NOT, DREBBLE? YOU'VE BEEN A GOOD BOSS.
BESIDES, THEY HAVE US ALL SURROUNDED.
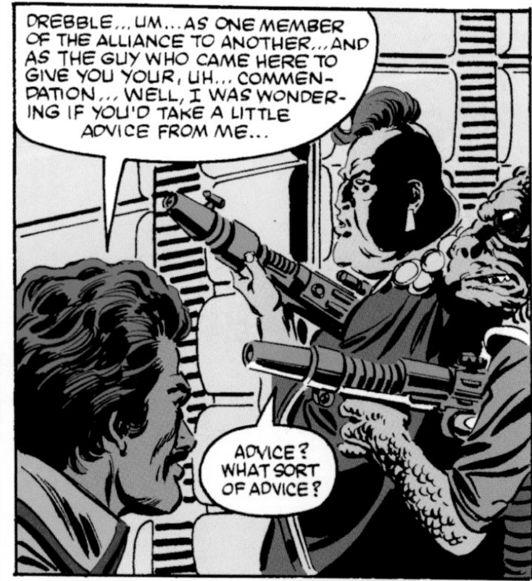
DREBBLE... UM... AS ONE MEMBER OF THE ALLIANCE TO ANOTHER... AND AS THE GUY WHO CAME HERE TO GIVE YOU YOUR, UH... COMMENDATION... WELL, I WAS WONDERING IF YOU'D TAKE A LITTLE ADVICE FROM ME...
ADVICE? WHAT SORT OF ADVICE?
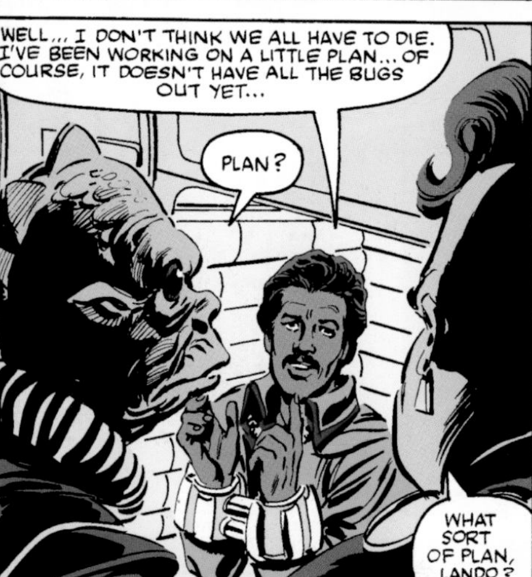
WELL... I DON'T THINK WE ALL HAVE TO DIE. I'VE BEEN WORKING ON A LITTLE PLAN... OF COURSE, IT DOESN'T HAVE ALL THE BUGS OUT YET...
PLAN?
WHAT SORT OF PLAN, LANDO?

OH... I DON'T KNOW IF IT'S WORTH BOTHERING YOU WITH, CAPTAIN. IT PROBABLY ISN'T ALL THAT GOOD ANYWAY... AND IT WOULD TAKE AT LEAST SIX OF US TO PULL IT OFF... AND I'M IN THESE BINDERS...

DREBBLE, I'LL ONLY TELL YOU ONCE MORE...
VERY WELL. HERE I COME...
THIS BETTER WORK.
19

I JUST HOPE NO ONE SHOOTS TILL EVERYONE'S IN POSITION.
NOW WE'VE GOT YOU!

AND WE'VE GOT YOU! DROP YOUR BLASTERS, LEMO!

I'D RATHER DROP YOU, SOLO! EVERYONE, KILL!

NOW! DO YOU HEAR ME? NOW!
HAN, CHEWIE, NO! YOU DON'T HAVE TO DO THIS!
WE CAN'T STOP NOW, PAL!
20

HHISSS!

SSSHREE!

EGAD! OUTFLANKED BY STENAXES. WHERE DID THEY COME FROM?

WHO CARES? WE SURRENDER.

GOOD. BECAUSE IF ANY OF YOU THREE, OR THAT WOOKIEE, MAKES A MOVE, YOU'RE AS GOOD AS DEAD.

"AS GOOD AS DEAD?" AS GOOD AS DEAD?! THAT'S GRATITUDE! WE CAME HERE TO SAVE YOU! IS THIS ANOTHER ONE OF YOUR CLEVER PLANS, PAL?

YOU'VE REALLY OUTDONE YOURSELF THIS TIME, "CAPTAIN DREBBLE."

21

IT WAS NOTHING. ALL IN A DAY'S WORK FOR A HERO AND HIS LOYAL BAND, OF COURSE.
WHAT--?
YOU AND THE WOOKIEE ARE FREE TO GO, OF COURSE. TAKING YOU TWO PRISONER WAS THE MEREST OVERSIGHT, OF COURSE.
OF COURSE.

OH... LANDO. AREN'T YOU FORGETTING SOMETHING?
AM I?
MY... AHEM... MY COMMENDATION.
OH. OH... OF COURSE.

GET OUT OF THIS ONE, PAL.
OF COURSE! WAIT RIGHT HERE... IT'S IN MY SHIP... WON'T BE A SECOND...

HERE YOU ARE, DREBBLE... A RARE MAN DESERVES A RARE GIFT. ENJOY IT IN GOOD HEALTH, AND ALWAYS REMEMBER, YOU'VE EARNED WHATEVER FORTUNE IT BRINGS YOU.
THE DANCING GODDESS!
HOW PRETTY!

NEXT THE ALDERAAN FACTOR!

STAR WARS GRAPHIC NOVEL TIMELINE (IN YEARS)

Omnibus: Tales of the Jedi—5,000–3,986 BSW4
Knights of the Old Republic—3,964–3,963 BSW4
The Old Republic—3653, 3678 BSW4
Knight Errant—1,032 BSW4
Jedi vs. Sith—1,000 BSW4
Omnibus: Rise of the Sith—33 BSW4
Episode I: The Phantom Menace—32 BSW4
Omnibus: Emissaries and Assassins—32 BSW4
Twilight—31 BSW4
Omnibus: Menace Revealed—31–22 BSW4
Darkness—30 BSW4
The Stark Hyperspace War—30 BSW4
Rite of Passage—28 BSW4
Honor and Duty—22 BSW4
Blood Ties—22 BSW4
Episode II: Attack of the Clones—22 BSW4
Clone Wars—22–19 BSW4
Clone Wars Adventures—22–19 BSW4
General Grievous—22–19 BSW4
Episode III: Revenge of the Sith—19 BSW4
Dark Times—19 BSW4
Omnibus: Droids—5.5 BSW4
Boba Fett: Enemy of the Empire—3 BSW4
Underworld—1 BSW4
Episode IV: A New Hope—SW4
Classic Star Wars—0–3 ASW4
A Long Time Ago . . . —0–4 ASW4
Empire—0 ASW4
Rebellion—0 ASW4
Boba Fett: Man with a Mission—0 ASW4
Omnibus: Early Victories—0–3 ASW4
Jabba the Hutt: The Art of the Deal—1 ASW4
Episode V: The Empire Strikes Back—3 ASW4
Omnibus: Shadows of the Empire—3.5–4.5 ASW4
Episode VI: Return of the Jedi—4 ASW4
Omnibus: X-Wing Rogue Squadron—4–5 ASW4
Heir to the Empire—9 ASW4
Dark Force Rising—9 ASW4
The Last Command—9 ASW4
Dark Empire—10 ASW4
Boba Fett: Death, Lies, and Treachery—10 ASW4
Crimson Empire—11 ASW4
Jedi Academy: Leviathan—12 ASW4
Union—19 ASW4
Chewbacca—25 ASW4
Invasion—25 ASW4
Legacy—130–137 ASW4

Old Republic Era
25,000 – 1000 years before
Star Wars: A New Hope

Rise of the Empire Era
1000 – 0 years before
Star Wars: A New Hope

Rebellion Era
0 – 5 years after
Star Wars: A New Hope

New Republic Era
5 – 25 years after
Star Wars: A New Hope

New Jedi Order Era
25+ years after
Star Wars: A New Hope

Legacy Era
130+ years after
Star Wars: A New Hope

Vector
Crosses four eras in the timeline

Volume 1
Knights of the Old Republic Volume 5
Dark Times Volume 3

Volume 2
Rebellion Volume 4
Legacy Volume 6

BSW4 = before *Episode IV: A New Hope*. ASW4 = after *Episode IV: A New Hope*.

STAR WARS OMNIBUS COLLECTIONS

STAR WARS: TALES OF THE JEDI

Including the *Tales of the Jedi* stories "The Golden Age of the Sith," "The Freedon Nadd Uprising," and "Knights of the Old Republic," these huge omnibus editions are the ultimate introduction to the ancient history of the *Star Wars* universe!

Volume 1 ISBN 978-1-59307-830-0 | $24.99 **Volume 2 ISBN 978-1-59307-911-6 | $24.99**

STAR WARS: X-WING ROGUE SQUADRON

The greatest starfighters of the Rebel Alliance become the defenders of a new Republic in this massive collection of stories featuring Wedge Antilles, hero of the Battle of Endor, and his team of ace pilots known throughout the galaxy as Rogue Squadron.

Volume 1 ISBN 978-1-59307-572-9 | $24.99 **Volume 2 ISBN 978-1-59307-619-1 | $24.99**

Volume 3 ISBN 978-1-59307-776-1 | $24.99

STAR WARS: BOBA FETT

Boba Fett, the most feared, most respected, and most loved bounty hunter in the galaxy, now has all of his comics stories collected into one massive volume!

ISBN 978-1-59582-418-9 | $24.99

STAR WARS: EARLY VICTORIES

Following the destruction of the first Death Star, Luke Skywalker is the new, unexpected hero of the Rebellion. But the galaxy hasn't been saved yet–Luke and Princess Leia find there are many more battles to be fought against the Empire and Darth Vader!

ISBN 978-1-59582-172-0 | $24.99

STAR WARS: RISE OF THE SITH

Before the name of Skywalker–or Vader–achieved fame across the galaxy, the Jedi Knights had long preserved peace and justice . . . as well as preventing the return of the Sith. These thrilling tales illustrate the events leading up to *The Phantom Menace*.

ISBN 978-1-59582-228-4 | $24.99

STAR WARS: EMISSARIES AND ASSASSINS

Discover more stories featuring Anakin Skywalker, Amidala, Obi-Wan, and Qui-Gon set during the time of Episode I: *The Phantom Menace* in this mega collection!

ISBN 978-1-59582-229-1 | $24.99

STAR WARS: MENACE REVEALED

This is our largest omnibus of never-before-collected and out-of-print *Star Wars* stories. Included here are one-shot adventures, short story arcs, specialty issues, and early Dark Horse Extra comic strips! All of these tales take place after Episode I: *The Phantom Menace*, and lead up to Episode II: *Attack of the Clones*.

ISBN 978-1-59582-273-4 | $24.99

STAR WARS: SHADOWS OF THE EMPIRE

Featuring all your favorite characters from the *Star Wars* trilogy—Luke Skywalker, Princess Leia, and Han Solo—this volume includes stories written by acclaimed novelists Timothy Zahn and Steve Perry!

ISBN 978-1-59582-434-9 | $24.99

STAR WARS: A LONG TIME AGO. . . .

Star Wars: A Long Time Ago. . . . omnibus volumes feature classic *Star Wars* stories not seen in over twenty years! Originally printed by Marvel Comics, these stories have been recolored and are sure to please *Star Wars* fans both new and old.

Volume 1: ISBN 978-1-59582-486-8 | $24.99 **Volume 2: ISBN 978-1-59582-554-4 | $24.99**

Volume 3: ISBN 978-1-59582-639-8 | $24.99 **Volume 4: ISBN 978-1-59582-640-4 | $24.99**

AVAILABLE AT YOUR LOCAL COMICS SHOP OR BOOKSTORE!

To find a comics shop in your area, call 1-888-266-4226

For more information or to order direct: • On the web: darkhorse.com • E-mail: mailorder@darkhorse.com

• Phone: 1-800-862-0052 Mon.–Fri. 9 AM to 5 PM Pacific Time

A Word about the Omnibus Collections

Dark Horse Comics' *Star Wars* omnibus collections were created as a way to showcase actual novel-length stories or series, and to provide homes for "orphaned" series, single-issue stories, and short stories that would otherwise never be collected or fall out of print.